10TH ANNIVERSARY — COLLECTOR'S EDITION

GATES OF THE NECRONOMICON

THE SECRET ANUNNAKI TRADITION OF BABYLON

by Joshua Free

*Originally published in four installments by the
Mardukite Chamberlains in 2009-2010
as the Complete Year 2 Research & Curriculum,
Revised & Expanded for this 2019 Edition.*

PUBLISHED BY THE **JOSHUA FREE** IMPRINT REPRESENTING

Mardukite Truth Seeker Press — **mardukite.com**

© 2009–2019, JOSHUA FREE

ISBN : 978-0-578-43283-0

— GATES OF THE NECRONOMICON —

Sumerian secrets and mysteries of Mesopotamia are finally revealed in the first complete modern guide to Babylonian tradition. An anthology of arcane history, theory and esoteric practices spanning thousands of years, by the author of the underground bestseller—*"Necronomicon: The Anunnaki Bible."*

———————

This amazing source book of esoteric archaeology reveals the secret Anunnaki tradition of Babylon, forbidden knowledge spanning thousands of years— from the Sumerian origins of civilized systems in ancient Mesopotamia to the underground occult traditions of Aleister Crowley, Kenneth Grant, and millions of people who have read Simon's Necronomicon.

———————

Joshua Free, world renown esoteric expert and Director of the modern "Mardukite Research Organization," invites the Seeker on an incredible progressive journey to illuminate the most ancient and inaccessible facets of human history, spirituality and religious tradition on the planet.

———————

For the first time ever, anyone can discover the secrets of the Sumerian Anunnaki and the origins of all physical and metaphysical systems born from the Mesopotamian Mystery Tradition that directly led to Babylonian religion— a unique combination of Sumerian, Akkadian, Assyrian and Chaldean lore revealed with perfect clarity for all modern readers: the academic, esoteric and even the "just curious."

———————

Originally published in four installments,
the *Gates of the Necronomicon* anthology
collects some of the most critical contributions
from the modern "Mardukite Research Organization."

MARDUKITE
10TH ANNIVERSARY

GATES OF THE NECRONOMICON

THE SECRET ANUNNAKI TRADITION OF BABYLON

by Joshua Free

**MARDUKITE
CHAMBERLAINS**

MARDUKITE

— TABLET OF CONTENTS —

INTRODUCTION—ANCIENT MESOPOTAMIA
(LIBER 51/52)

PART ONE—THE SUMERIAN ANUNNAKI
(LIBER 50)

PART TWO—NECRONOMICON REVELATIONS (LIBER R)

APPENDIX—CROSSING TO THE ABYSS & SIMON'S NECRONOMICON (LIBER 555)

10TH ANNIVERSARY — COLLECTOR'S EDITION

GATES OF THE

NECRONOMICON

THE SECRET ANUNNAKI TRADITION OF BABYLON

by Joshua Free

MARDUKITE

—INTRODUCTION—
ANCIENT MESOPOTAMIA
(LIBER 51/52)

— 0 —
ESOTERIC ASSYRIOLOGY OF THE 21ST CENTURY

*"When the sculptures and huge, dramatic bas-reliefs from Babylon and Nineveh,
uncovered by the excavations of Layard and Rawlinson in the mid-19th century,
began to arrive in Europe, the people were enthralled but they were also fickle. The
greater accessibility of Egypt, and the sheer quantity of the material excavated and
exported, pushed Babylon and Assyria into the background, and the civilizations of
the Tigris and the Euphrates began to be perceived as colorless and dull, even by
esotericists."*
~ R.A. Gilbert, *Foreword* of L.W. King's
Babylonian Magic & Sorcery

Mystics of every age go forth explaining an almost *quantum* vision of reality and
existence: entangled, interconnected—*All-as-One*. While this might seem a truly
obscure approach to crossing the current threshold of what is typically deemed an
"academic" topic; it is not. Consider for a moment that our *mythic past* is very
much rooted in *truth*—albeit misunderstood but a *truth* that has been conveniently,
or forcefully, forgotten among mass awareness.

Politics and the general *human condition* evolving outside of the *Ancient Mystery
School* have, throughout history, taken its toll on accounts of said *truth*, as becomes
quite evident concerning the history of the geographic region known as
Mesopotamia.

Humans, accepting a *mortal* paradigm, are unaware of one critical aspect of the
cosmos—one that they can not see based on limited perceptions and reality
experiences schematized by semantic labeling—that *Universal Truth* is actually
unchanging. Some have even put forth to call it "Cosmic Law." In spite of the best
(or worst) human efforts across time, the *Truth* has survived to remind us of our
origins, to instruct us on where we have to go and perhaps, most importantly, the
standards we should live by to get there. Mere survival of *Secret Doctrines* by
select cabals is not enough. For as the world was once plummeted into *Dark Ages*
only to be *reincarnated* in an *Age of Enlightenment*, the "esoteric" *truth* did not
resurface in public "exoteric" consciousness—in fact, it went the other direction:
underground and into *vaults* of obscure "occult" factions.

Original and intended meaning behind esoteric symbolism, used to preserve the
integrity of *mysteries*, became as confounded and obscure to mystical practitioners
and "magicians" as the nature of their own organizations. What's more: they
convinced themselves that they *did* have true comprehension of it—and so,
eventually, politics reflecting the surface world became no less existent in the
underground. As above; so below ...*apparently.*

Quests to satisfy an innate desire to pursue *truth*, particularly what has been known as the *Secret of the Ages*, are as obvious in realms of science and academia as they are in the world of the occultist. "Esotericists" are not the only ones interested in unearthing these matters, nor are they even the original ones. Only the methodologies and intentions differ. And yet again—all is connected.

Without intellectual and scholarly pursuits by historians and academicians, we might have far fewer clues to reconstruct our *mental image* of the past. Where then would the *truth seeker* turn to draw inspiration? From fanciful distortions of pantheism and anthropomorphic fairy-tales passed around by the uninitiated? Certainly, not.

Recovery of the *truth* of mankind's past is paramount to understanding humanity's destined future. It should come as no surprise then that the geographical region associated with its origins remains victim to unyielding war and suffering for thousands of years—further enshrouding our efforts to unveil with a patina of public hesitation and doubt painted by political opinions toward modern *Middle East* activity. For our current esoteric purposes, focus is restricted to what academicians call the *Ancient Near East*—or *Mesopotamia*.

For over a century, modern pursuit of the *Great Babylonian Mysteries* remained primarily restricted to two approaches: Firstly, the late 19th century archaeological excavations inspiring academic Exoteric Assyriology; and the Second, derived from the same, made crude esoteric attempts at reviving a working understanding. In the first, no attempt is made at philosophical or mystical pragmatism; the entire field of study left as dry as the desert sands it is drawn from. In the second, early works of these stoic academicians are used at face value to base a revival mystical tradition—often giving little regard for *specifics* of the *system* and effectively requiring many additional facets of knowledge directly appearing nowhere on the same fractured clay tablets and artifacts excavated from these ancient sites. Fortunately, the 21st century *truth seeker* has a *third* option to explore.

In 2008, a revolutionary esoteric underground organization known as the "Mardukites" appeared, publicly visible, and a completely new breed of *next generation* "Esoteric Assyriologists" emerged on the scene—one that would not blindly accept the given data from their predecessors—at least not at *face value*. For over a decade the diversely organized research group sought out the most ancient writings rendered on clay tablets from *Babylonia*—now available to the public as a complete collection in Joshua Free's "*Necronomicon: The Anunnaki Bible*." These writings demonstrate an integral link directly between our origins and the remaining evolution of human civilization. Our chosen method and the resulting clarity revealed concerning the identity, nature and progression of this *incredible* subject matter show undeniable superiority to what was previously available. But, that is what we call *progress* (much needed for this field).

The *Mardukite* approach to reconstructing the *Babylonian* vision begins with first revealing the incredible misnomer that the field of study has endured far too long, for essentially, the applicable term "Assyriology" is a lie. It is not even semantically correct for our current pursuits of *analysis* using the same physical *evidences* brought to light by late 19th and early 20th century archeology. The name questionably applies to the field at all! And although some early scholars acknowledge this grave misrepresentation of the science, it has as yet gone unchallenged in contemporary academics.

George G. Cameron explains in his foreword to Edward Chiera's "*They Wrote on Clay*" (1938): "Few there are indeed who know that the name of our science, 'Assyriology' is based on an accident—the fact that the first large group of texts ever discovered were written in Assyrian. Assyrian itself is but one dialect." Misapplication arises with use of the term to denote study of any and all ancient cuneiform-using cultures. Mardukites do not propagate this blatant disregard for the political and spiritual history of Mesopotamia. Although cuneiform-literate and sharing a similar "Anunnaki" tradition, the Assyrians were actually northwestern foreigners to Babylon. The two are not the same.

As previously mentioned, any true esoteric analysis or mystical application are absent from the earliest academic-archaeological pursuits. These efforts mainly emphasized the *recovery* and *accumulation* of translatable materials, much of which are not yet coherently transliterated into English language even a century after their discovery. Most materials readily available to *seekers* during the *pre-mardukite* era of research and development are severely fragmented, confounding itself in the information relay.

Earliest attempts at understanding ancient Mesopotamia made by "Assyriologists" of the late 19th and 20th century, included: E.A. Budge, Edward Chiera, L.W. King, S.L. Noah Kramer, Franqois Lenormant, R.C. Thompson and L.A. Waddell. Their renderings have already received long-standing public attention for those who sought it. The variegated cultural influences and often violent history of *Babylonia* has left a confusion of names, titles and images that have required over a century to flush out to any practical ends, by scholars and mystics alike.

Origins for the field-name of "*Assyriology*" are derived from French excavations at the city ruins of *Khorsabad, Nimrud, Nineveh, Sippar* and *Lagash* (*Telloh*) in the 1840's. However, a true scientific pursuit was ignited when the royal library archives of the Assyrian king *Assurbanipal* were discovered. Thousands of clues, in the form of cuneiform tablet writings, illuminated a prehistoric legacy formerly thought of as completely forgotten and never again salvageable.

Then, in the 1880's, German archaeologists unearthed *Babylon...*

— 1 —
: MESOPOTAMIAN MYSTERIES :
BEFORE BABYLON – THE LAND OF SUMER

"Here [in Babylon] is real death. Not a column or arch still stands to demonstrate the permanency of human work. Everything has crumbled to dust. The very temple tower, the most imposing of all these ancient constructions, has entirely lost its shape. Where are now its seven stages? We see nothing but a mound of earth – all that remains of the millions of its bricks. Here the ancient mysteries and their tombs have been sleeping quietly for millenniums. In a few months, perhaps in a few days, the ground will be broken by trenches as in a battlefield. And the repose of the poor dead will be disturbed by the frantic search for records and data. . ."
~ Edward Chiera
From a letter to his wife

Before Babylon—when history had not yet been written—the land now known to modern man as the "Middle East" was first occupied by "gods" of antiquity—the *Anunnaki*. These super-human figures molded and shaped human consciousness and the systematized civilization we so easily take for granted in the "Western World" today. The wheel of time forced the age of "gods" to become an era of "men" and *their* ways, but the ancient foundations built in Mesopotamia remain strong among us today.

Classical period Greeks may be credited with the term: *Mesopotamia*—meaning "A land between two rivers." More literal than poetic, the title accurately describes thre region known to the ancients as *Babylonia*—the "Land of the Gates of the Gods" and the "City of Star-Gates" established primarily between two rivers—the *Tigris* and the *Euphrates*. Today, the term *Babylonia* is used to distinguish post-Sumerian *empires* maintained by *Babylonian* kings, a lineage made famous by Hammurabi, the powerful "Mardukite" systematizer of Babylon.

Commonly compared to the fertile Nile region of Egypt, *Mesopotamia* is also a river-delta system—and, like the Nile to the Egyptians, this system of life-giving waters proved to be inseparable from prosperity of the people. The plain was cultivated successfully by use of the first "aqueduct-irrigation" systems. Accurate construction and upkeep of these canals were vital to keep *Babylonia* habitable in all seasons. Eventually, as they were abandoned under foreign control, dissolution of the aqueduct system resulted in complete collapse of *Babylon* as the "throne of the earth" and the lands returned to the indistinct sand they were born from.

Ancient Mesopotamia is famous for its original inhabitants—those who occupied the area before, and reestablished it after, a "Great Flood"—"Uruk" Sumerians and

"Akkadian" Babylonians (and then later Assyrians); indigenous folk calling their native land *kengir*—meaning "local." The proto-Sumerian "Ubaid" launched the first primary post-diluvian Mesopotamian cities: *Eridu, Ur, Isin, Larsa, Lagash, Nippur* and *Uruk* (also known as *Erech* and possibly the origins of the name *Iraq*), all situated on established foundations from a former age.

Charting exact political boundaries of *Babylonia* is difficult. They are not generally agreed upon—no more today among scholars and nationalists then by those who once physically fought for them in periods of antiquity. For as long as humans have been involved, the area has been plagued with constant conflict. Mesopotamian territory often included areas beyond the pathway of the two rivers, which even themselves changed positions and course over time with alteration (and then absence) by human intervention.

Ancient *Babylonia* essentially occupies present-day Iraq, in a region bordered by mountains separating it (on the east) from Iran; ancient Persia. To the south, the empire once extended to the Persian Gulf where the archetypal city of *Eridu* was founded. On the western front, Mesopotamia is separated from the Mediterranean and Magan-Egypt (Khem) by the vast expanse of Arabian desert, and just north of this: the land of Syria.

The full expanse of the "Ancient Near East" includes geographical locations now occupied as Iran, Iraq, Saudi Arabia, Yemen, Oman, Lebanon, Israel, Syria and the United Arab Emirates. Mesopotamian kingdoms also included (at some time or another) occupations in modern-day Turkey, Armenia, Afghanistan, Pakistan, Egypt and Sudan. The modern term "Middle East" is a Euro-centric political semantic replacing academic usage of the "Near East," as opposed to the "Far East" or "oriental." With few exceptions, the Ancient Near East and its *Anunnaki* legacy is the direct origin of most major world religions in history, including (but not limited to) Zoroastrianism (Mazdaism), Mithraism, Canaanite, Yezidism (Yazdanism), Baha'i Faith, Manichaeism (Mandaeism), Islam, Judaism and Christianity.

The legendary city of Babylon stood alongside the western-laying of the two rivers, the *Euphrates* (in the Greek language) called *burannon* or *perath* by the Sumerians (and *puratu* by the Assyrian Babylonians)—all meaning simply "river." It is considerably longer of the two rivers—at 1,800 miles—forming first in the heights of the mountains at 11,000 feet above sea level. It quickly drops off then falls approximately one foot per mile for the last 1,200 miles of its run. The pathway taken by the river has consistently moved westward with the absence of human intervention and canals—creating more area "between" the rivers. The water levels are indicative of the equinoxes, like the Egyptian Nile, with the *Euphrates* rising in the spring and lowering in the autumn – though unlike the Nile, which is altered by the summer monsoon season, the levels of the *Euphrates* river peaks in the springtime.

Opposite the *Euphrates*, the broad eastern river runs 1,150 miles and, like the other, the path has also shifted to what archeologists believe to be its more 'natural' flow with the abandonment of the irrigation canals. The Greeks pronounce the Assyrian name for the river as *Tigris*, essentially meaning *"serpent river"* (*i-di-ik-lat*) although the original Sumerian identification meant *"fast as an arrow"* (*idigna* or *id-dagal-la*). Babylonians found the *Tigris* to be too wild to cross easily or irrigate with. The water levels also rise and fall in direct opposition to the cycle of the *Euphrates*. Ancient cities founded alongside (and making use of) the *Tigris River* include *Nineveh, Calah (Nimrud)* and *Asshur.*

Before emptying into the Persian Gulf, the *Euphrates* and *Tigris* join together forming a marshy delta region called the "Great Swamp." The prehistoric city of *Eridu* was once a lavish capital there, at the coast of the Persian Gulf. Today, however, ruins and remains of *Eridu* now rest 130 miles away from the sea. This shift over time is attributed to a "shrinking" Persian Gulf, creating more land— approximately *72 feet* of it *per* year!

"E-RI-DU" [*House in the Distance, Built*] is the original Mesopotamian home of the Anunnaki god ENKI—a prototype-city of *Babylon* built prior to the "Great Flood," then later rebuilt, ever remaining the sacred precinct of ENKI in *Babylonia*. It is the oldest capital city of the Ubaid (proto-Uruk) Sumerians, dated to over seven-thousand years ago. Its remains are found at *Tell abu Shahrain* (Arabic name). The Anunnaki god MARDUK and his demigod son NABU both apprenticed there, learning the esoteric and intellectual sciences from ENKI. In *Eridu*, the modern practices of "ceremonial" and religious "magic" (or "magick" if you prefer) are also born.

The Ubaid-Sumerians or proto-Sumerians occupied Mesopotamia before the Uruk-Sumerians—origins of what we call the *historical* "Enlilite Sumerians" from a period of at least the Fifth Millennium B.C. The name designation (*"Ubaid"*) comes only from modern archaeological excavation of ruins at *Tell Ubaid*—a primitive city built near the area later established as the Uruk-Sumerian city of Ur. True urban systematization became present during Uruk occupation and was later perfected by the Babylonians, who inspired Empire-builders forever thereafter.

Distinct natural terrain separate Mesopotamia into northern and southern parts; a factor long exploited for political purposes to define boundaries. Originally, southern *Sumer* (Also called *Sumeria, Shinar, Babili, Babylonia* or *Chaldea* in varying texts) and northern *Akkad* each were ruled by their own governors, called a *patesi*. [Modern "Mardukites" retained usage of the title to indicate a priest/minister-bishop of a particular region or diocese.] A post-Sumerian unification of the two lands and rise of the *Babylonian Empire* led to replacing this role with the *lugal*—a title applied to the *"Mighty King of both Sumer & Akkad"*—Literally: *lu*—man; *gal*— great or lofty. The "Big Man"—*The King.*

The northern half of Mesopotamia was once forested and so it retains features of prairie and plains mixed with a mountainous supply of stones and crystals. The southern part is naturally more barren, primarily swamps and marshes mixed with arid desert. Without the aid of an incredible irrigation system, the *Babylonian Empire* would never have had the freedom and sustainability to survive and flourish as the spiritual and political epicenter of the ancient world.

The ever-changing shape of the land was once expertly engineered to meet the needs of an awe-inspiring unparalleled civilization. Proper cultivation of the land was the original key—making societal life possible among humans, and of this knowledge they attributed to the *gods*— great beings who taught the people how to shape the land and launch city-life to sustain their own livelihood on earth. With the 'land between the rivers' prepared and consecrated, *kingship* could now be *lowered* from *heaven*.

— 2 —
: SARGON & THE SUMERIANS :
DIVINE RIGHT IN THE LAND OF SUMER

An examination of the Sumerian and Babylonian King-Lists will reveal the belief that "kingship" was "sent down" from "heaven" as decreed by the gods. To this we might add that a similar tradition has been followed by many indigenous ancient cultures. These dynastic lists originate by Sumerian hands, but the were later recatalogued in Babylon by Nabu Priest-Scribes. Similar King-Lists have also been found in Egypt and they all suggest some very amazing notions for the contemporary mind to grasp.
~ Joshua Free
From the original Liber-51

"Divine Right" to reign on earth "lowered down" from the "heavens" to *Eridu*—but "kingship" moved. Prior to the establishment of *Mardukite Babylon*, most Uruk-Sumerian activity concentrated in southern parts of Mesopotamia. *Eridu*—the home of ENKI—becomes a secondary capital when Sumerian cultural and "religious" emphasis develops in the *Enlilite* city of *Uruk* (also called *Erech*).

To establish *Uruk* as a capital *holy city* in the consciousness of Sumerians, the national *ziggurat* temple-shrine of ANU, the E-ANNA, was built there to accommodate rare appearances made by the highest *Anunnaki* Divine Couple—ANU and ANTU—on earth. This *ziggurat* was later "gifted" to the Anunnaki goddess INANNA-ISHTAR, from which she based her own worldly rule.

Kingship is central to establishing "societal systems," forming the basis of Sumerian and Babylonian lore and all paradigms born from the Anunnaki (traditions). Examination of ancient *King-Lists* from Mesopotamia reveals an archaic premise that "kingship" was *brought down* or *sent down* from the "heavens" as decreed by the gods. Of course, the idea of *monarchy* or kingship was not always executed by humans to the highest regard; misuse of these systems leads to their inevitable breakdown.

The complete text of the cuneiform *King-Lists* is found as the Tablet-K Series in *"Necronomicon: The Anunnaki Bible."* The oldest example in Sumerian language is the *Weld-Blundell Prism*. These records were later adapted by Babylonian scribes and then by the classical Historian Berossus in the 3rd Century B.C. A similar chronicle was prepared around the same time for Egypt by the Historian Manetho.

Chronology of the *King-Lists* are separated by a critical event, one found within cosmological records of all ancient cultures—the *Deluge* or *Great Flood*. This means that Sumerian civilization actually began in *antediluvian* times, prior to the *Deluge*. The *King-Lists* are consistent with this time scale too, but the shifting sands of Mesopotamia provide us few direct clues. Ancient sites were often dismantled or found in ruins and later built over by cultural successors. What this signifies is that the pre-Babylonian, pre-Sumerian *Ubaid* periods are not the true absolute origins for this prehistoric civilization, but instead are origins for civilized efforts resumed after the earth was stable for societal habitation again, probably following the last Ice Age.

Ancient writings do not dispute that a pre-Sumerian "civilizations" and other Anunnaki "experiments" have come and gone on the planet. Archeologists can successfully confirm identities of the *King-Lists* until c. 3200 B.C., yet these records continue into the past for another 420,000+ years.

Sumerian and Egyptian records are very clear about the nature of the beings occupying seats of kingship at its inception—*gods*. Original *overseers* were considered *divine*, thought to have come from the stars/sky and bringing with them the knowledge and technologies that could cultivate humanity. Reign of these *divine* beings was eventually replaced by *hybrid demigods* (part-*Divine*; part-*human*) until finally passed to control of a specialized segment—*Royal Blood*—of mankind. Hybrid offspring of gods as kings were *demigods*, which required both parents to be 'divine', but the offspring could be born on earth. "Part-" or "half-" divine 'kings' later emerging in the population required only one 'divine' or 'demigod' parent.

ANCIENT LIFESPANS ON THE KING-LISTS

"Divine" = *10,000's* of years old
"Demigod" = *1,000's* of years old
"Deity/Hero" = *100's* of yeas old

god + god = demigod (*"divine"*)
demigod + god = demigod (*"lordly"*)
god + human = deity (*"half-divine"*)
demigod + human = deity (*"half-divine"*)
deity + human = hero/deity (*"quarter-breed"*)

At each stage of development, the concept of *dynastic succession* remains paramount—the idea that "Divine Blood" flows from the heart of *true* kings in the lineage, which in turn may be passed on to their offspring. The tradition of *Divine Right to Rule* is as ancient as human society altogether and may even have origins beyond only this planet. Cosmological tablets illuminate a similar tradition of *Divine Succession* practiced by the *Anunnaki* ("sky gods")—particularly ANU, ENLIL and ENKI—describing control of heavenly domains and celestial zones.

Origins of the word "ruler," "regent" and "realm" all reflect the perceived "god-like" nature of the original "King" role. After the unification of the two lands of Mesopotamia, one hero-man—one *lugal*—was elevated to the position of a blessed and lofty *demigod.* More than simply a title of power, this role required the person to be an active intermediary between the people and the *gods* and thus acted as a powerful *priest-king*.

Interconnectedness between the "realm" and the king was inseparable. The king and his land are one. The king and his people are one. The fate of one has proved to reflect in the other throughout history and populations couldn't deny observing it— a good and just king resulted in social expansion and a fruitful land, whereas rule of unjust ungodly tyrants weakened the integrity of the *Babylonian Empire* every time.

Properly guided kings realized they were essentially a *Divine Representation* on earth and with this came great responsibility. In fact, the freedoms, responsibilities and penalties of Mesopotamian society all *rose* relative with class—quite different even, than what we see often today. The 'true' kings understood that they existed *for* the people, representatives of the *gods* on earth, exercising a *divine power* reflecting the *gods* themselves during the cultivation of the "human condition."

Descent of kingship came from the *gods of heaven* themselves, but is carried in the hearts of men—passed on as genetic memory. Recognition of "Divine Blood" conjured a system known as *jure divino*—the episcopal law (from the Greek *episkopos*, meaning "overseer") upheld by an individual "anointed" or "chosen" by *God*.

> *"I am Sargon, the Mighty King of Akkad.*
> *MARDUK smiled upon me,*
> *And by his love, I was made a ruler of the kingdom."*

Sargon of Akkad (*Sharru-Kin*)—also called Sargon-the-Great—is sometimes confused by amateur researchers with another later Babylonian king sharing the same name, Sargon II, an Assyrian who appears on the scene nearly two-thousand years afterward during the *Neo-Babylonian Empire*. Sargon is the first "Babylonian" King to reign supreme over all of the lands in Mesopotamia. He is founder of the Akkadian dynasty and the archetypal World Emperor, but was also the first *Mardukite King*—a chosen chamberlain, blessed by the Anunnaki god MARDUK, patron deity of *Babylon*. A chaotic anti-Sumerian hold on the land by a pre-Babylonian tribe called the Umma was relinquished in c. 2600 B.C. by Sargon. [Although texts developed by scribes of Nabunidus—known as the "long chronology"—indicate this time as c. 3750 BC.]

Similar to the story of Moses, Sargon is the bastard son of a priestess. He is placed in a reed basket and floated down a river, found, then raised by the *King of Kish*. He grows up to overthrow the king and declares himself supreme in *Akkad* and then setting his sights on *Sumer*—the campaign for a southern Mesopotamian takeover ensues, beginning with the city of *Uruk*. His sophisticated military operations coupled with a weights and measures standardization allowed unified organization of the first "world empire."

Sargon's son Rimush (c. 2580 B.C.) reigned after his father's death, becoming the self-proclaimed *King of Kish*—a title which cost him his life. After his murder, his brother Manishtusu replaced him, during which another tribe, the Elamites, revolt. His son, Naram-Sin, named himself the *King of the Four Quarters* and successfully conquered the Magan lands located on the Arabian peninsula, separating Mesopotamia from Egypt. He wrongfully did so in the tradition of the Enlilite *Anunnaki gods*—rejecting his Mardukite heritage—and as punishment for supporting a neo-Sumerian Renaissance, the rapid expansion caused the heart of a once-Mardukite global empire to weaken...*for a time*.

— 3 —
: SIFTING SUMERIAN SANDS :
UNEARTHING THE ANUNNAKI LEGACY OF KINGS

*"Since Marduk created me to be king and Nabu has culled his people to my realm –
as the love I have for my own life, so do I feel toward the building and reign of
their cities."*
~ King Nebuchadnezzar II
The Mardukite Tablet-L Series
"Necronomicon: The Anunnaki Bible"

The Akkadian Dynasty of Sargon began in northern Mesopotamia—in the land of Akkad. Akkadian territory and influence was of only tribal significance during the early rise of Sumerians proper, but when Sargon used his military to unify the "two lands" of Mesopotamia, he established the first post-Sumerian empire in the world. Indeed, for the first time, the lands of *Akkad* and *Sumer* were governed from a single capital: Sargon's city of *Agade* (the city of *Akkad* in the land of *Akkad*, like *Babylon* in *Babylonia* or *New York*, *New York*), a city named after the word "unity" in Akkadian language.

As a culture and language, Akkadian evolved alongside, but separate, from the southern Sumerians. It is fortunate, however, that they were participants in the same Celestial *Anunnaki* tradition. Akkadians possessed their own distinct proto-Semitic culture and language, but shared the Sumerian dedication to an *Anunnaki* "pantheon" and also used a refined version of cuneiform 'wedge-styled' writing to represent their own language, which replaced the Sumerian *emegir* mother-tongue. Akkadian language also evolved separately as other Semitic languages, like Hebrew, Canaanite, Phoenician, Arabic and Aramaic.

Assimilation of many pre-Babylonian (Sumerian) "programs" and Enlilite "systems" permitted a social transition into post-Sumerian or "Mardukite" ideologies. This energetic change and paradigm-shift in human consciousness occurred simultaneously as humanity entered the astrological Age of Aries in 2160 B.C. Several Sumerian literary cycles (cuneiform tablet series) are retained almost verbatim—inscribed by a new order of scribes and magician-priests using Akkadian language. For example: *Inanna-Ishtar's Descent into the Underworld* and the *Epic of Gilgamesh* are both of purely Sumerian (pre-Babylonian) origin. Versions simply remained existent in Babylonian libraries.

This new (post-Sumerian) Babylonian-Akkadian literary and religious tradition shifted emphasis from an Enlilite "World Order" to a dedication of MARDUK. The "Mardukite Legacy" replaces the old paradigm altogether.

Although the actual identities of the Supernal Trinity (ANU, ENLIL and ENKI) and Anunnaki pantheon already established remain, the emphasis turns to the "younger generation" of Anunnaki, best represented in Babylonian Tradition.

THE ANUNNAKI "SUPERNAL TRINITY"

ANU—the *distant* "Father" in *heaven* who birthed and "commanded" the Anunnaki gods visiting earth.

ENLIL—the *local* "Father" in the *skies* who established the Sumerian "World Order" of Anunnaki gods of earth.

ENKI—the *patron* "Father" on *earth* who maintains all Anunnaki "systems" and cosmic "programs" of existence.

The new Babylonian vision heralded the new god MARDUK as a local patron deity of *Babylon*. This replaced the more primitive rural ideals of Sumerian life with systematized urbanization that humans continue to live in the shadows of. All these new traditions attributed to MARDUK and *Babylon* were inherited from his *Anunnaki* father, ENKI—magic and wisdom, sciences and religion; these become central to city community infrastructure.

In pre-Babylonian *Sumer*, ENKI assisted his brother ENLIL in the development of the *cosmos*—the organization of physical worldly systems (or 'world order'). ENKI is given domain of the physical sciences, mathematics and esoteric magic. Among the "Race of Marduk" (*Mardukite Babylonians*), ENKI is sometimes referred to as "Our Father." This arm of the Supernal Trinity is shared with his espoused consort NINKI, also known as DAMKINA.

By earlier Sumerian standards during the Age of Taurus (c.4200-2160 B.C.), ENLIL is the heir to *"Anuship"* in *"Heaven"*—the position of "God" for the local universe. Later duality observed in the Babylonian pantheon between lineages of ENKI and ENLIL occurred 'on earth as it is in heaven'. ANU, by name and title, is the "Father in Heaven," the All-Father to the *gods*—but particularly the biological parent to both ENKI and ENLIL.

Most of Sargon's immediate descendents did not possess his same integrity when he first conducted his world building campaign—even as militant as he was. His dynasty was soon replaced by the Enlilite Gutians in c. 2450 B.C. When their reign in Mesopotamia was rejected, confusion swept over the region until an acceptable dynasty was established. The new dynasty came again from Lagash. Of the *patesi* in that line the most influential include Urbau, who expanded the cult-power of the E.NINNU in Lagash as well as many other religious centers. Then, King Gudea cultivated further abundance and economic prosperity by opening and securing trade routes.

With the death of Gudea's son, Ur-Dingirsu, no proper heir was brought forth and the dynastic line ended (c. 2250 B.C.) allowing the "seat of power" to be passed back to the old Sumerian city (and "Third Dynasty") of *Ur*, led by Ur-Engur (Ur-Nammu) who focused on the fortification of the Babylonian infrastructure, but with a reinstatement of the former "glory" of ENLIL and the "Old Ways." His son, Dungi (better known as Shulgi), called himself the *High Priest* of ANU when he began to reinforce significance of the *Eridu* site and the legacy of ENKI. But there is much more to this part of the story.

The patron deity of the famous Sumerian city, *Ur*, is the *Anunnaki god* NANNA (called SIN by the Babylonians, meaning "moon"). A long-standing Enlilite patronage to NANNA-SIN in *Ur* was maintained as payment for a "life-debt owed," when the *god* personally arranged the marriage between Ur-Nammu and "a high priestess of the Temple of Ur." In the balance of this, the dynasty of Ur sought a truly 'Sumerian' Renaissance, which fought hard to thwart any advancement of the Mardukites. [This prestigious city is remembered in biblical accounts as "*Ur of the Chaldeans.*"]

Shulgi (Dungi) continued efforts toward an anti-Mardukite "Sumerian Renaissance" ushered in by his father's pact with NANNA-SIN. Economic and agricultural abundance was found under his reign, but uprisings and social rebellions sparked by this "new" Mardukite movement grew rather than diminished. Shulgi became a "lover" to the Enlilite *Anunnaki goddess queen* INANNA-ISHTAR, and under her blessing began fighting newly formed "Nabu-tribes" (ancient Mardukites) in 2095 B.C. This continuing even after the mathematical shift to the Age of Aries—a task he passed down to his son, Amar-Sin (*A.Mar-Su.en*—"Son of the Moon God"), a warlord king who unleashed vengeance on all (Mardukite) rebels. The "Great War" ensued between 2048 and 2024 B.C., resulting in unleashed nuclear weapons (born of *alien* knowledge) against these pro-Mardukite westerners, the *Amorites*.

Akkadians knew of this group evolving on the outskirts of their Semitic lineage—the *Amurru* (Sumerian – *A.Mar-Tu*). This unique culture and language developed independent of the Sumerians, centralized around the cult-city center of Mari, west of the Euphrates, often referred to in lore as the "*Land of Martu*" (*Amar* to the Egyptians). Much like other Mardukite efforts in Enlilite territory, the Judeo-Christian biblical accounts reflect a harsh bias towards these "Canaanites" stating in the *Book of Jubilees* (called the *Leptogenesis*) that: "The former giants, the *Rephaim*, gave way to the *Amorites*, an evil and sinful people whose wickedness surpasses that of any other, and whose life will be cut short on the earth."

Development of early Amorite ("Mardukite") culture contributed not only to the collapse of the *Ur III* Dynasty, but also to the founding of *Babylon* as a proper city-state and the division of Sumerian Mesopotamia into republic-styled Amorite Kingdoms, a system that remained primarily in effect for at least four centuries, from 2100 B.C. to 1700 B.C.

Amorite tribes first began forming in Mari (Syria) and Canaan around 2400 B.C. In biblical literature, "Amorite" and "Canaanite" appear synonymous. Three hundred years later (c. 2112 B.C.) the Amorites arrived onto the Mesopotamian scene during the confusion and chaos following the fall of the Akkadian Empire. These nomadic hunter-gatherers, once preferring temporary shanty towns and tents over Enlilite Sumerian city life, began to adopt agriculture, homesteading and assimilated native Mesopotamian cultural systems as they re-stabilized the post-Sumerian world of *Babylonia*. Various kingdoms were established throughout the lands. Multiple city-states observed their own Amorite Dynasties, but only one would be responsible for launching a true Mardukite Empire—Hammurabi, famous King of Babylon.

— 4 —
: CODES OF HAMMURABI :
BUILDING BABYLON AND BEYOND

"Whereas Sargon seems to have relied upon his power and his terror tactics to keep people under control, Hammurabi presents himself almost like a modern politician in that he wants to be loved; he wants the people to like him; he's going to set up laws that will protect them, not laws that will terrify them or force them into submission."
~ Amanda Podany
California State Polytech, Pomona

In the post-Sumerian "Mardukite" era of Mesopotamia, Anunnaki traditions and systems were sealed under MARDUK, heir-son of ENKI. During this shift to the Age of Aries—the sign of MARDUK, represented by the Ram—"divine politics" fueled religion, spirituality and the global reality experience. The famous "creation stories" and "esoteric symbolism," serving basis for all future traditions and societal reality systems, were forged onto cuneiform tablets of quasi-propaganda supporting a 'Babylonian' paradigm by the priest-scribes of ('led by' or 'dedicated to') NABU, heir of MARDUK. The "Younger Generation" of Anunnaki become figures central to the structure of Mardukite Babylonian systems. These traditions are a direct evolution of the previous Sumerian legacy. It charts progression of a particular Anunnaki "family" in Mesopotamia and is not simply an arbitrary assimilation or recreation, as evident in similar "Celestial" pantheons found elsewhere in "classical mythology."

Long after the vision put forth by Sargon, the next most famous and influential contributor to a "Mardukite Babylon" in Mesopotamia was King Hammurabi (1790 B.C. by the short chronology). In homage of MARDUK's own legacy put forth in the '*Enuma Elis*' (the "*Epic of Creation*" text given fully in "*Necronomicon: The Anunnaki Bible*"), King Hammurabi reconstructed the *ziggurat* temple-shrine and earth-home of the Anunnaki god MARDUK, the E.SAG-ILA. The structure was once built in even more remote times in an attempt to establish a Mardukite "World Order" prematurely during Mesopotamia's early evolution – an effort brought down by the Enlilite Sumerians in the archetypal fall of the "Tower of Babel."

The region around *Babylon* hosted human occupation since at least the Third Millennium B.C. (the period of Sargon of Akkad around 2300 B.C.). That being said, the independent *Babylonian* city-state of the "Mardukite" legacy we know today was invigorated primarily by efforts from the Amorite Dynasty; specifically Hammurabi, who goes on to replace the former Enlilite Sumerian tradition in total with a complete Mardukite Babylonian establishment.

Under the reign of Hammurabi, Sumerian language became denationalized and scribes began recording all literature in the "new" Akkadian (Old Babylonian) language. This literary tradition accounts many pre-Assyrian era tablets of Babylonia found and translated today. This Babylonian literary revolution allowed a means to evolve a firmly rooted Anunnaki tradition with an emphasis on MARDUK as the supreme "King of the Gods"—thus completely replacing the previously accepted Sumerian paradigm.

King Hammurabi is considered the greatest empire engineer since Sargon of Akkad, and in many ways was culturally and spiritually superior. Efforts conducted during his forty-two year reign allowed a centralized 'world government' of *Babylon* to form that not only served the people on an emotional, cultural and religio-spiritual level, but also reaching record-breaking energetic and monetary heights in global wealth, power and influence. Ruling in honor of MARDUK allowed Hammurabi to bring *Babylon* to fruition with cultural and spiritual heights that would not be visited again for at least a millennium—the Neo-Babylonian era of Nebuchadnezzar II.

Of the many conventions and systems first introduced to human civilization from *Babylon,* Hammurabi's legal code is one of the most significant to note—made popular in mass-consciousness as the "*eye for an eye*" methodology, but best known simply as the "Code of Hammurabi." While tyrannical and draconian penalties are the most frequently cited examples of the "Code," details of the 282 laws established, for the first time, a complete methodology of citizen rights, property rights, social rights and even feminine equality rights in addition to the creation of a "class" system.

The "Code of Hammurabi," by its own account, does not actually originate from Hammurabi's own mind. He considered himself merely a catalyst for the reign and power of something *greater* than himself—that of the patron deity, MARDUK. The "Code" or Law of Hammurabi, is what modern Mardukites call the "*Book of the Law of Marduk*."

The Mardukite source book anthology—"*Necronomicon: The Anunnaki Bible*"— relays *The Book of the Law of Marduk* as it was given to the race of Dragonblood Kings—those who ruled in the name of MARDUK on Earth. Priests and priest-kings of *Babylon* ruled by a covenant: the descent of kingship on Earth from Heaven in honor of MARDUK who granted freedom for men to rule in Mesopotamia as in Egypt. They did so in his name. And often took on his name and the name of his family members during their reign. But, after Khammurabi's death, invasion by the Hittites broke this Babylonian dynasty, followed by a series of mysterious "sea-kings" that eventually spawn a second Babylonian dynasty: the *Kassites.*

— 5 —
: THE KASSITE DYNASTY :
PRESERVING A LEGACY OF LEGENDS

"The Hittite Empire spread over all of Antolia and parts of Syria and north Mesopotamia, including regions of different background, culturally, ethically & linguistically, including Sumerian & Akkadian."
~ Hans G. Guterbock
The Art & Literature of the Hittites

When the *Old Babylonian* age ended, loose social organization and a broken political system left the empire open for a new dynastic power change. Fortunately for *Babylon*, a pro-Marduk force known as the Kassites (c. 1750 B.C.) came down from the Zagros Mountain region northeast of *Babylonia*. Kassite culture assimilated MARDUK with their own deity-name, *Shuqamuna* (possibly from *Shakyamuni*, meaning "Buddha"). They defended *Mardukite Babylon* against years of struggle with the Hittites who sought to claim *Babylonia* for themselves.

In 1595 B.C. (some sources suggest 1651 B.C. depending on chronology), the Hittites successfully enter Babylon and "steal" MARDUK. Historians usually interpret this to mean that they *"removed the image of Marduk"* from the temple—the main statue or *idol* representing the 'seat of power' in Babylon. Others might conclude that the Anunnaki god himself was actually captured while still residing on earth. In either case, the Kassites devoted over two decades in battle toward recovering and returning the *"idol"* to the temple. Overcoming tremendous struggles against the Hittites, by the grace of MARDUK, the Kassite Dynasty established its own reign of *Babylon*, with few minor exceptions, for nearly half a millennium.

Kassites were a diplomatic people, enjoying trade relations with most of the known world, including Egypt, which was undergoing a spiritual revolution under the rule of Amonhotep IV (1350 B.C.), better known as Akhenaton. This new pharaoh changed the face of Egypt by installing his "Mardukite" *Marduk-Aten-Ra Star-Religion*. Archaeological evidence shows significant diplomatic correspondence exchanged between Akhenaton and at least two Kassite Kings: Kadashman Kharloe I and Burnaburiash II. These clay tablets are referred to by scholars as the "Amarna Letters"—all of which are written in *cuneiform* and not *Egyptian* characters. Scholars named the collection for the site where they were discovered at in 1887—*Tell el Amarna*—a modern Arabic name for of the ancient city of *Akhenaton*. Cuneiform tablet versions of Mesopotamian epics were also unearthed from there, most likely kept by Egyptian scribes and magician-priests for academic purposes.

Toward the end of their rule, the Kassites primary issues were no longer with the Hittites, but instead with a new rising force from the east, *Elam*. These Elamites replaced Mesopotamian dynasties with their own and also succeed in stealing a relic from *Babylon* to their city of *Susa*—the *stele* of the *Code of Khammurabi*. Sovereignty in *Mardukite Babylonia* begins to pass to those *most able*. Salvation of the land often required the "Eye and Hand of Marduk" to pass to foreigners as stewards in wait of launching a *Neo-Babylonian* empire—the "Fourth Dynasty of Babylon."

An *Assyrian* dynastic *patesi*, Marduk-Shapik-Zeri laucnhed campaigns to reunite the lands in 1200 B.C. This new northern "Assyrian" dynasty included Nabuchadnezzar I ("Nabu-kudurri-usur" in Assyrian) who recovered the *stele* from the Elamites in 1125 B.C. But, real efforts toward a *Neo-Babylonian* empire were quickly thwarted by the Arameans and several small short-lived dynasties. A true *"Babylonian Renaissance"* would have to wait for the proper visionary to manifest.

— 6 —
: RISE OF THE ASSYRIANS :
FROM ASHURBANIPAL TO NEBUCHADNEZZAR II

"Even though the Assyrians were 'all powerful' they still had their sense of cultural inferiority – They saw Babylonia as the Source: the best tablets; the 'real' cuneiform culture, much as in the way 19th century Americans might have looked to England as the place where you would find 'real' English literature and such."

~ Jerrold Cooper
John Hopkins University

Most historians consider the *Assyrians* as simply an extension of ancient Enlilite Sumerians, but they are actually quite more than this. Most of their history and lore, as with the rest of Mesopotamia, has been academically misappropriated. Where the Kassites assisted in carrying over "Mardukite" culture to post-Akkadian Babylonia, the Assyrians were also custodians of the legacy until the greatest heights of "Neo-Babylonian Renaissance," witnessed under the rule of Nebuchad-nezzar II, the Chaldeo-Assyrian King of Babylon.

The "Assyrian" culture was named for a particular deity—ASSUR or ASHUR. This name applied to the people, the culture and the language, in addition to their native region of the name of their capital city. *Assur, Ashur, Assur, Asar, &tc.*—all of these are derived from an epithet for MARDUK, the god of *Babylon*, and the Assyrians recognized this. Academic "Assyriologists" ("Sumeriologists," *&tc.*) have often mistakenly attributed the chief Assyrian *Anunnaki god* ASHUR ("*The One Who Sees*") with the chief deity observed in the original Sumerian pantheon: ENLIL, or at the very least, his heir-son, NINURTA (NINIB). Mardukite records and deductive reasoning rooted in historical consistency would suggest this is not the case. Assyrians observed an Anunnaki tradition centered on MARDUK, but of course in their own language.

The homeland of the *Assyrians*—their kingdom and realm—is more accurately an extension of the *Akkadian* culture—the "Old Babylonians." By 1000 B.C. the *Assyrians* had *Akkadians* populations of *Akkad* and became the next race of ancient-originating Semitic people in Mesopotamia. As with the Akkadians and Kassites once blessed by MARDUK in times of need, arrival of *Assyrians* in *Babylon* eventually proved positive for its continuing legacy.

A Mardukite emphasis first returns to *Babylonia* with the reign of Nabu-mukin-apli (1000 B.C.) and the eighth dynasty of *Babylon*. This dynasty makes significant cultural efforts toward restoration of Mardukite temples and national statuary—all refinished in gold and *lapis lazuli*, the official "sacred" blue-hued stone of *Babylonia*. This period of peace, prosperity and cultural development began leading the population toward a true *Neo-Babylonian Renaissance*. But not everything was peaceful in Mesopotamia. Babylonians experienced frequent uprising from western Sutu tribes: nomadic Enlilite Aramaean desert dwellers. Suti even prevented national religio-political festival ceremonies from occurring—on several occasions barring ceremonial procession of the NABU statue from *Borsippa* (a site near *Babylon* sacred to the Babylonian scribe god) during the annual New Year Spring Equinox (A.KI.TI or *Zagmuk*) ceremony. [This national observance involving statuary idols was a symbolic reenactment of activities once observed of the Anunnaki themselves when they identifiably walked among the people of earth.]

During this struggle, Nabu-apla-iddina (in *Babylon*) worked to maintain the highest peace with his rivals as possible, including the Assyrian king, Ashurnasipal II. He even formed a peace treaty with Ashurnasipal's son, King Shalmanesar II. Nabu-appla-iddina also launched a "literary" *Renaissance* in *Babylon* (and *Borsippa*) by reviving the "Order of Nabu"—priest-scribes and magicians dedicated to salvaging and recopying older cuneiform tablets of esoteric, spiritual (religious), political, astronomical or scientific value. But, where *Sumerian* tablet-cycles were focused on antiquated establishments of world order, pantheistic hierarchies, divine politics and religion—we see something quite different in post-Sumerian paradigms of the *Assyrians*.

The Assyrian paradigm, foregoing religious and spiritual standards, emphasized battle, warfare and militant conquest, particularly what could be credited to a "Legacy of Kings." Where the previous Mesopotamian Kings were often respected for their role in establishing order by their working *with* the "gods" directly, the Assyrians spend their developmental years focused on territorial disputes and material conquests. To their credit, however, the Assyrian Empire revolved around the most formidable military force known to the ancient world, introducing standards for many military innovations: cavalry, archery, siege engines, war ships, chariots, and battering rams.

Starting in the Ninth Dynasty of Babylon, King Nabu-nasir (750 B.C.) installed the "*Babylonian Chronicle*," a new practice of event recording for scribe-priests using a new local standard annual dating system—"A.N." (*Anno Nabonassan*). Other Kings in the dynasty included Nabu-nadin-zeri (735 B.C.), killed during a riot; and Nabu-suma-ukin II (732 B.C.), replaced after only one month by an Aramaen chief, Nabu-mukin-zeri. He was killed in a siege on *Babylon* by the Assyrians King Tiglath-Pileser III, founder of the Tenth Dynasty of Babylon and the "*Neo-Assyrian Empire*." In 720 B.C., the throne was assumed by a Chaldean prince, Marduk-apla-iddina II (the biblical *Merodach-Baladan*). He struggled for control of *Babylon* against Sargon II, who succeeded in keeping him out of *Babylon* for over a decade. But after Sargon's death, Marduk-apla-iddina II resumed power of the throne and succeeded in sparking chaotic revolution in *Babylonia* before dying in exile (700 B.C.)—forcing Mesopotamia once again into political confusion for a time.

* * *

Eleven miles southwest of Babylon city, and many years before its modern redis-covery, archaeologist Henry Rawlinson began excavation (in the 1850's) of ruins of a different ancient city—*Borsippa*—the sacred precinct of *Nabu*, the Babylonian god of writing, cuneiform tablets and magic. At first, archaeologists thought they had discovered the ruins of Babylon, but they had found something else altogether —*Bad-Tibira* in the original Sumerian; or in Babylonian-Akkadian, the name reads *Til-Barsip*. Its present-day Arabic name is *Birs Nimrud*. Among these ancient re-mains—the E.ZIDA—Nabu's ziggurat *"Temple of the Seven Spheres,"* built on anti-quated remains by the first major public Mardukite King—*Hammurabi*—and later restored by the last major Mardukite King—*Nebuchadnezzar II*. [It is from this temple and others in Babylon that the "Seven-fold Order" significant to the "Mar-dukite Babylonian Anunnaki Tradition" are derived.]

An avid reader and collector of all tablets available in Mesopotamia, the "Royal Library" archives of the Assyrian King, *Ashurbanipal*, maintained a complete record of everything that could be recorded—but in the Assyrian language. This so vastly influenced early archaeologists that scholars named the entire academic field after the collection—"Assyriology." Such intellectual pursuits, however, were not always so prominent among leadership in Mesopotamia as many of the rulers spent most of their time and energies maintaining or expanding their physical realm through battle and conquest.

With the death of *Ashurbanipal* came the fall of Assyrian power in Babylon. The *Babylonians* elected a king from among their own revolutions—*Nabopolassar*. He then joined forces with the *Chaldeans* and the *Medes* in defeating the Assyrians at their capital of *Nineveh*, and then later the *Egyptians*. Aging and war-worn after several successful victories against two empires, he wisely passed power of the throne to his son, while still living. His son—the famous Mardukite King, *Nebuchadnezzar II*.

King Nebuchadnezzar II supported a prosperous pro-*Mardukite* era for nearly fifty years. He maintained peaceful unity of *Sumer* and *Akkad* (*Babylonia*) in the name of *Marduk* and *Nabu*. He restored many city centers and sacred ziggurat temples. Before his death, he predicted an impending end to the glory of his *Chaldean Em-pire in Babylon* – and the actions of the kings who were to be his successors invariably proved him right. [See also the "Sajaha" Tablet-S Series in *"Necronomi-con: The Anunnaki Bible."*]

The city of Babylon served as a geographic capital of the entire *"Babylonian Empire."* As a dynamic city-state, the conditions of Babylon constantly adjusted to change in accordance with the forces in play, but one ideal remained constant: the relentless determination to reach an apex of esteem and glory—and according to their tradition, reign by *Divine Right*. Installation of *"Mardukite World Order"* into human consciousness continued to radiate from the city of Babylon; its *Mardukite* designation being, literally—*"Babylon"*—from the Akkadian *bab.ilu*, meaning *"Gateway of the Gods"* or *"Star-Gate to Heaven."* [In original Sumerian, the name is written as the logograms: "KA.DINGIR.RA.KI."]

Walking in the shadows of a legacy born from ancient icons—*Sargon* and *Khammurabi*—the third and last legendary "Mardukite King" brought Babylon to unforeseen heights during reign of the *Neo-Babylonian (Chaldean) Dynasty—Nebuchadnezzar II*. Following the years of chaotic discord in *Babylonia* and irreverence in the *holy city*, all that had been built or could be restored proper to the national gods—MARDUK and NABU—*Nebuchadnezzar II* commissioned in Babylon during his lifetime.

Before Nabuchadnezzar's death, his heir-son, Awel-Marduk (560 B.C.), also written Amel-Marduk ("Evil Marduk"), reigned for only two years. He usurped the throne against the will of his father (who was still in power) and was murdered by his brother-in-law and successor Nergal-sharezer, in assistance to the true king. None again would be as great as Nabuchadnezzar II. Any short-lived reform efforts to maintain integrity of *Babylonia* were therefore quickly dissolved by one of the most unjust anti-Mardukite Kings of *Babylon* (555 B.C.) in the midst of an otherwise perfect *Mardukite Renaissance*.

Following the death of Nabuchadnezzar II and its chaos, the "Seat of Babylon" was usurped by an Assyrian rebel calling himself *Nabonidus*. His name meant *"Nabu is exalted,"* though his suppression of the Mardukites, desecration of holy sites and violation of countless traditions would indicate that he lived by another creed. *Nabonidus* fell prey to the old Sumerian "cult of the moon god"—the lunar-cult associated with the Anunnaki god NANNA-SIN. *Nabunidus* chose the pre-Babylonian Enlilite "lunar cult" in lieu of following the solar (and stellar traditions) of the Mardukite Babylonians. He even forbid the Mardukite *Akiti* (*Akitu*) "New Year" festival of the spring equinox from taking place. MARDUK was forced to take action, whether literally or in spirit. To prevent the utter annihilation of his people, the "Eye and Hand of Marduk" would again fall upon foreigners.

Cyrus the Great marched on Babylon and rightfully dethroned Nabonidus, igniting the Persian Dynasty of Babylon. His first action upon entering the city—to pray, make sacrifice and participate in nationalist ceremonies at the "Temple of Marduk." In fact, he attributed all of his success in taking control of *Babylon* to the power of the *Anunnaki god* MARDUK. [This is recorded on the Tablet-L Series of *Necronomicon: The Anunnaki Bible*.] His lineage is allowed to continue until the arrival of, and replacement by, the Greek Hellenistic Dynasty of Alexander the Great in 330 B.C.

And the rest, as they say: *Is history...*

— 7 —
: CUNEIFORM TABLETS :
THE BIRTH OF WORLD SYSTEMS

"The education of the Babylonians was entirely in the hands of the priests, who derived their knowledge from Nabu, the inventor of writing and letters, and every kind of learning — the Lord of "Houses of Tablets" (or books), i.e. the first libraries."
~ E.A. Wallis Budge
Babylonian Life & History

The overt observable evolution of Sumerian civilization into a *Babylonian Empire* —the facts—as described previously regarding history, may not altogether seem remarkable on the surface. However, the *seeker* should keep in perspective just how quickly all of this developed from seemingly nothing. It is true that societal living was originally organized around *state religion*, but prior to this it was culminated not by social relationships shared between people, but by their living relationship with the earth. Where first we have loosely organized nomadic hunter-gatherers forced to wander about or dwell in caves, essentially rolling the dice of chance for their survival, very little time passes before a sweeping urbanization of Mesopotamia, developed around structured agricultural farming and pasturing.

Mesopotamia may be credited with many *"firsts"* during the development of early human history. It is, however, the incorporation and evolution of "writing" that the Sumerians are most esteemed for—something undoubtedly developed by necessity for continuous civic growth, spiritual and scientific progression. In fact, it is *only* with *writing* that we have *any* concept at all of "history." Everything *prior* to this inception for our times, is rightfully considered "prehistoric"—those times accompanied by no written records.

According to ancient cuneiform tablets, the original decision to cultivate civilization in Mesopotamia was not born from men, but from a distinct group of beings known as the *Anunnaki*—those that appeared to "come down from the sky" and were later considered *deities* and *gods* of the original "pantheon"—those who "decree the fate on Earth." Cuneiform tablets also describe Anunnaki motives for "genetically upgrading" humanoids: to make them fit as material workers for these *"gods."* [Described on the "Creation & Disposal of Men" Mardukite Tablet-G Series in *"Necronomicon: The Anunnaki Bible."*] This started long before what we call the *"Deluge,"* under the direction of these "divine" *overseers*—not yet the mortal priest-kings found in popular historical chronicles—prior to what we know as *"human* civilization."

Anunnaki control of the "heavens" and "aero-space" rested with the god ANU and his son ENLIL, respectively. The material world, however—the realm most integrated with human life—became the domain of ANU's other son, E.A., called ENKI—whose name means "Lord (*En*) of the Earth (*Ki*)" in Babylon. While the majority of ancient Mesopotamia was classified "Enlilite" territory, origins for the esoteric "Arts of Civilization" emerge from ENKI's own southern city of *Eridu* on the ancient coasts of the Persian Gulf. Here we find systematic origins of "true" human civilization. Born of innate necessity and survival of material systems, use of esoteric "*Secret Doctrines*" allowed data to condition the human psyche through integration of "worldly systems." The means by which this has always been executed on earth: "*media*"—the *written word*.

It is evident that practically all ancient cultural "mythologies" share a unique anthropological belief: that indigenous humans were somehow "engineered" apart from their natural evolving timeline on the planet, and further given a knowledge of something "outside of themselves" that was directly responsible for this. *Cuneiform tablets* speak of this "outside" and "intervening" force as a group of beings called *Anunnaki*—though they are known by a myriad of other names as well, particularly among diverse cultures and languages around the globe.

According to the *cuneiform* texts, the *Anunnaki* sought to prepare the earth for habitation, but found the physical nature of the work on earth was not suited to them. They employed their "army"—known as the IGIGI ("Watchers")—to do manual labor. And after some years pass, even this group revolts. The *Anunnaki* hesitantly decide to upgrade existing hominids, fashioning a new class of "worker." Today, we now see a cliché concept emerging in the "New Age" that acknowledges humans as a slave-species built by and for "gods"—or at least these "Anunnaki" figureheads later interpreted as the mythological "gods" of antiquity. The *Sumerians* and *Babylonians* weren't "stupid." The "mythologies" reflected in their writing are not drawn from ignorance or people unaware of "natural phenomenon." Skeptical scholars minimize the true significance of history by putting forth fallacies. Cuneiform literature left behind suggests a highly intellectual and spiritual culture with a deep understanding of the *cosmos* from the beginning, even when expressed though a limited vocabulary.

Much like early Egyptians using hieroglyphics, the first Sumerian "cuneiform" writing (named in Classical times from the Latin "*cuneus*," meaning "wedge") was also a tradition of picture-writing etched with sticks and fingernails. Refinement of the writing style continued throughout the *Sumerian* age, but around 2100 B.C., the script-form changed dramatically with a gift from NABU for his Babylonian scribe-priests—the reed *stylus* pen. There are many who seem easily dismissive of the current subject matter in this book, or that simply find the topic of *cuneiform tablets* to be boring and without relevance. As a monumental cornerstone in human development, the perfection of writing in Babylon is the very reason we have such vast collections available today to glean lore of this extraordinary and forgotten empire. Without this specific esoteric literary tradition, we would be left clueless.

* * *

Early picture-writing proved sufficient for many things. The goals of its use were simple—primarily survival. Hunting grounds, natural dangers and even some elaborate stories could all be marked with a primitive pictorial language. Humans navigated obstacles of communication easily enough using speech and gesture—so, what then was the purpose of writing?——of the *words that stay?*

All of the civic systems on the planet, those that distinguish the "elevated" social network of the "human animal," depend on a communication relay of the written word to be effective. And with the creation of the stylus, this was accessibly possible—a methodology for "systems" was broadcast wide among the masses. Its successful implementation aided Anunnaki "control" of an exponentially growing human population. But it was a "Mardukite" inception—the result of two efforts: the birth of systems in *Eridu* by ENKI (with the aid of, not surprisingly, his heir-son MARDUK), and also the ratification of writing in *Babylon* by NABU (heir-son of MARDUK) much later. By combining these two facets, the "Arts of Civilization" were activated in Babylonia.

The human psyche became conditioned to societal living, now connecting two aspects internally: *pictures* and *words*. The two were already one in form—as picture writing—but only in the vaguest sense. Use of a *stylus* changed this by not only speeding up the flow and form of written images, but as a straight-edged tool, this pen eliminated *curvature* of any characters. No longer would someone have need to draw out an image of several animals to depict them. A series of quick hashed-wedge marks could be used to represent it instead—and in the conditioned human consciousness, the two would become inseparable in meaning.

Solidification of abstract concepts and ideas represented as "words" actually changes the way the brain thinks—changes the way in which one experiences these aspects of reality and what the words actually represent. Mentally adopting a label system for fixed nouns and names creates an internal database called a 'schema' which manipulates experiences and affects memory. An academic consensus is that these "perceptions" are evolutionary advantages, adapting one to the environment that an individual is reared to. This certainly was not evolutionarily necessary for the survival of the species, but for the survival of the *system*, by which matters of commerce and state, laws and government, roles and order, religion and trade could all be *fixed* to writing, securing an imprinted history and fate on the human consciousness to *words that stay.*

The cuneiform wedge-writing system is designed quite differently than more recently used classical alphabets, such as the "Roman" letters this book is printed in. In fact, cuneiform is not an alphabet at all, but a series of symbols used to represent phonetic sounds or "syllables"—typically combinations of a consonant and a vowel. Thus, we have no ancient cuneiform form of a letter "*B*," but there are signs for the sounds: *ab, ib, ub, ba, be, bi* and *bu.*

Babylonian refined *stylus*-based cuneiform, combined with the ease of clay tablet construction, resulted in a plethora of written records in the ancient world. Eventually, a "royal library" was established in *Babylonia* (often in *Borsippa*) as a Temple of NABU, maintained by the official librarian-priest sometimes known as a *Rab Girginakki* in Akkadian language. Efforts to create and preserve similar "archival libraries" later occurred throughout Mesopotamia—always under the direction of the current *authority* in power. By 2000 B.C., Babylonian law required all transactions be documented and duplicated by official *scribe-priests*.

While writing itself was prevalent, for an exceptionally long period of human history, only higher classes of citizen were required to learn reading and writing. Dependency on scribe-priests as "interpreters of writing" among the common masses became great. Any discovered indiscretion or falsehoods relayed in this process were severely punished, which strengthened the faith of the people in these "life-depending" (and "life defining") public records and deeds of ownership.

By necessity, the *cylinder-seal* was developed—a clay signature-seal uniquely fashioned for an individual and often worn or carried like a large bead long before signet rings. This small cylinder could be *rolled* across a tablet surface to create a rectangular stamp-mark. And just to be sure there was no tampering, the NABU scribe-priests developed a unique way of enclosing and preserving signed clay tablets within clay envelopes with a duplicate signed inscription on the outside. In special circumstances an additional copy would be retained by the archivist. These practices promoted the original form of banking and commerce—trading in kind, complete with a notarized receipt. If this were not enough, a new *system* of conceptual civic wealth was integrated: the possession of land property—or *real estate*—authorized and governed by the state, ownership of which was not represented by physical occupancy, but by *written deeds*.

The full implications of these *Anunnaki, Babylonian,* and *"Mardukite"* systems are not so obvious to the common man—and certainly not to early "Assyriologists" either. Seldom do we consider the covert governing body that originally dictated these systems and regulated their integration into social consciousness. Such might be easily overlooked or taken for granted by contemporary minds thinking of little than one-foot-in-front-of-the-other. And yet it is entirely connected to where humans are, were and will be. Definitions, semantics, knowledge boundaries and the ability to coherently and permanently record them into histories, calendars, maps, property deeds and even "secret esoteric knowledge"— completely and utterly changed human reality experience... *forever!*

— 8 —
: PRIEST-SCRIBES OF NABU :
THE SECRET SOCIETY OF BABYLON

"The Palace of Ashurbanipal, King of the World, King of Assyria, who in Assur and Belit puts his trust, on whom Nabu and Tasmitu have bestowed broad ears, who has acquired clear eyes. The valued products of the scribe's art, such as no one among the kings who has gone before me had acquired, the wisdom of Nabu, unequaled, as so much as can be found, I have had inscribed on tablets and arranged in groups. I have revised, and for the sign of my reading, have set in my Palace this library – I, the ruler, who knows the Light of Assur, the King of the Gods."
~ King Ashurbanipal
Dedication on the Royal Library

What academic scholars term *"Babylonian Mythology"* is actually an evolution of the former *Sumerian Anunnaki* legacy—the progression of an archetypal *Anunnaki* family in Mesopotamia and *not* simply a cultural assimilation or reapplication of a similar pantheon. This is what we see in later classical mythoi, such as the Greeks and Romans, which simply regurgitate the same ancient themes with new names. Likewise, the esoteric Babylonian religious and political pantheon should be viewed as an extension of the older Sumerian one. This gives rise to many misunderstandings and misconceptions when interpreting of tablets from varying origins and time periods. In this case, however, the Babylonian spiritual, religious, cultural and political focus is transferred to activities of a "younger generation" of *Anunnaki gods*, as "sealed" coherently in the Babylonian Tradition.

In the "Mardukite" Babylonian paradigm, ANU's position as "heavenly father" (turned "grandfather" by the "younger generation") remains unchallenged, and retains the numeric designation of 60, the perfect *whole* number (like our 100) in Mesopotamian mathematics. Controlling more worldly concerns—the position of "earthly father" for the local universe (numerically designated 50), is a title first bestowed to ENLIL, royal heir of ANU according to "Enlilite" Sumerian tradition. ENLIL's heir-son—NINURTA or NINIB—was next in succession to continue the "Enlilite" legacy. Although ENKI was given the role of "Lord of the Earth" (with a numeric designation of 40), the division between the domains of ENLIL and ENKI blur—both literally and figuratively.

In the Sumerian paradigm ENLIL and ENKI aid one another in the foundation of the material world, but by the time of the Babylonians, each had their own dedicated following—essentially splitting the global population into dualism.

According to early Babylonian tablets, this schism first occurred concerning the genetic upgrade of original humans themselves, and then over their "disposal" during the *Deluge*. ENLIL, an *Anunnaki* nationalist, high commander and heir to ANU, was understandably reserved about the creation and assistance of humans. ENKI, the chief scientist and esoteric magician of the *Anunnaki* (with a dynastic line that is not granted the same royal distinction as ENLIL), sees potential in the human race to preserve his own legacy on earth and that of his son, MARDUK.

As cuneiform writing evolved, the face of the religion changed and crystallized into more familiar versions of the Mesopotamian mysteries it is defined by today. Mystical and religious tablets were avidly created in Babylon to not only solidify and protect the traditions, but actually *manipulate* them. This primitive logic is a basis for many semantic *systems* still active today. In short—reality is based on the experience of the *realm*, the world of light that we see and acknowledge stimuli from. The world of light is separated into *forms*, which require *classification* as "things." These *classifications* must work together within a coherent *system* to carry any conceptual or functional meaning. [This is what enables the current author to write these *words* and have a reader comprehend them *later*.]

While basis of writing is to collect "data," it is the interpretation within conscious-ness that equates it to *facts*. "*Words that stay*" are "*facts*" collected about *reality*—the internal processing of cohesive *experience*. In ancient Mesopotamia, we find historical tablets detailing deeds of kings and cosmological tablets describing the deeds of gods—these are the *beliefs* about *reality* dictated for the population and presented as *facts*. Conclusively, as far as the human condition is concerned: the *written word dictates reality*. And to be fair, while men and kings go to their graves each believing in their own truth, these thousands of years later, it is the *written word* from their era that has survived them all.

* * *

Mardukite priests of Babylon were, by nature, *Priests of* ENKI, following a tradition from the ancient *systems* born in *Eridu*. Beyond simply *collecting data* to support a public belief system, the first pragmatic mystical and religious use of writing was the recording of ("esoteric") *Secret Doctrines* and ("exoteric") *incantations*—used later religiously as *appeals* to the *gods* for material worldly assistance. This developed more "*figuratively*" in time as the temple-shrine *ziggurat*-homes of the *Anunnaki gods* themselves became occupied instead by worldly representatives of the same roles.

In the beginning, people were instructed to petition their needs to the temple-priests, who would in turn make appropriate offerings and incantations to the deity involved. This *system* is still installed in society today—in both religion and politics—where ministers or authorities act as intermediaries between citizens and perceptibly "higher powers." Here we see a distinction between the exoteric "surface" *system*-religion of public opinion separate from esoteric practices and traditions of the scribe-priests, temple-priests and priest-kings themselves. The *scribes* research and write the tablets, the *temple-priests* enact the tablets and the *kings* enforce the tablets.

Mardukite Babylon could hardly be considered ruled by MARDUK's own lineage —but all of *Babylonia* was still maintained under his care by way of "chosen" priest-kings who were nearly all under the influence of a prestigious secret society —one that changed the shape of Mesopotamia, and the remaining world thereafter, with nearly two millennium of unbroken covert operation in *Babylonia*: the *Priest-Scribes of* NABU.

An unusually enigmatic figure in Mesopotamian history, NABU is listed only among the Babylonian "Mardukite" hierarchy of *Anunnaki gods*. His numeric designation is 12—indicative of cycles, time and esoteric knowledge or "magic." NABU is heir-son to the dynasty of MARDUK, born of SARPANIT, an earth-born wife taken by MARDUK. She was "human," but descended directly from *Adapa*, the first genetically upgraded human by the *Anunnaki god* ENKI (known in Egypt as PTAH). This makes NABU earth-born and little more than half-divine.

NABU shared the dynasty of MARDUK (the Egyptian RA, AMON and ATEN) with an estranged brother, named SUTU (also *Satu* or *Sati*, the Egyptian SETH), whose name means *mountain* or *life of the mountain*. Another "half-brother rival" is listed as ASAR (the Egyptian OSIRIS). Clearly this dynastic family also appears in Egypt under many names, but our current focus is *"Mardukite Babylon."*

The name 'NABU' (*"who speaks for"*) indicates a "herald" or "announcer." The word made its way into the Semitic-Hebrew language as *nabih*, meaning "prophet." By the time of "Old" *Mardukite Babylon*—around 2150 B.C., corresponding with the "Age of Aries," the end of the *Old Kingdom* in Egypt and the launch of the "royal" *Dragon Court* by Ankhfn-khonsu—the temple-city and cult center of NABU was localized near *Babylon* at *Borsippa*.

In Babylon, earthborn NABU is transferred the epithet TUTU, replacing a previous Sumerian agricultural goddess, NISABA, who is briefly given credit for pictorial *cuneiform* in Sumerian tradition. As NABU-TUTU he reflects a *"druidic"* role— the Babylonian "nature-deity" called upon at the New Year Festival of *Akiti* to bless the crops and provide fertile land. By that same paradigm, MARDUK would be a "sky-deity," representing a domain of the starry sun that shines down on the land.

In this ancient literary tradition, NABU represents the epitome of the *"pen is mightier than the sword."* Where previous *Anunnaki gods* had cultivated civilization with their contributions—the *cattle and grain* had already been brought, the *pickax* had already been given, *&tc.*—NABU offers the *reed stylus* and reformation of cuneiform writing. This sparked renewed interest in the arts of *Eridu*—the *Secret Doctrines* of esoteric "magic" and science from ENKI and MARDUK.

Writing allowed the *"Arts of Civilization"* to be systematized on records of an *Ancient Mystery School*, and NABU is the original guardian of these "Tablets of Destiny"—powerful "information" that "sealed" material creation to the *Divine Right* of the *Anunnaki*.

As the "Keeper of Secrets," NABU proved necessary in developing the literary tradition that allowed *Babylon* and the supremacy of MARDUK to be possible. NABU was a mastermind in the company of the most intelligent beings in this corner of the Universe. In the establishment of *Babylon*, NABU was successful in developing his own unique cult following that was often rivaling that of even MARDUK. This original "cult" of NABU still exists even to this day as an esoteric sect called the "Mardukite Chamberlains."

The magic and mysticism of *Babylonia*—born in *Eridu*, then extrapolated and reformed by Mardukite Priest-Magicians and the Order of NABU—was restricted to the priests and treated wholly religious in nature, but rooted in the ancient power and technologies of the *gods*. "Magical" texts from this age are primarily hymns and prayers. The later doctrines or scriptures made public, first originated as historical documents among Mesopotamians, cuneiform tablets chronicling creation and universal order, the genesis of man, the flood cycle and the eventual restoration of civilization. These were all later reinterpreted by other cultures as their own.

Responsibility for forging and preserving this Babylonian literary tradition on clay tablets rested with the Order of Nabu, a secret force that sought to shape the history and future legacy of Babylon in dedication to MARDUK. Seeing the popularity of the mystical traditions of ENKI to this present day, the familiarity with the "Marduk-versus-Tiamat" Typhonian archetype, the rising interest in the Babylonian systems and Anunnaki in addition to the Freemason and Illuminati attentions originating with this sect—it is the current author's opinion that the efforts of the ancient Order of Nabu proved quite successful.

— 9 —
: MARDUKITE MONOLATRY :
THE STAR-RELIGION OF BABYLON & EGYPT

"Marduk's rise to supremacy did not end polytheism— the religious belief in many gods. On the contrary, his supremacy required continued polytheism, for to be supreme to other gods, the existence of other gods was necessary. He was satisfied to let them be, as long as their prerogatives were subject to his control; but what Marduk expected was that they come and stay with him in his envisaged Babylon— prisoners in golden cages, one may say."
~ Zecharia Sitchin
Earth Chronicles: End of Days

The Babylonian *"Star Religion"* of MARDUK sought to "occult" and conceal the previously laden Sumerian religious designations of the *Elder Gods*. Early Sumerian traditions were not very systematic, or even a true "religion," making them easily overlapped by the first clearly defined *systemology*—one that served as an archetype for all later human civilization on the planet. Directly exported forms of this stellar cult included Hermetic Tradition, Atenism, Zoroastrianism, Mithraism, and of course the Semitic-Judeo system.

Original systems integrated into human consciousness were not at first the "mono-theism" defined by academic scholars. This appeared later when *Enlilite* standards transformed into *Jehovah* or the Christian "God" as a single personification. In Hebrew, *El* (ENLIL) and *Ia-Yahweh* (ENKI) are separate beings, a belief debated the early Christian Yahwist and Elohist sects.

Later Christian authorities likened the ancient myths to "One God" surrounded by *"lesser angels,"* but this still does not adequately explain the anthropomorphic manifestation of the One God on earth being the same as, one-to-one, The Absolute All-present All-knowing All-powerful "Divine Source." We mainly see remnants of this distinction in Gnostic Mysticism, Elohist Christianity and modern Mardukite interpretations.

Contemporary historians often simplify, likening the Mardukite stellar-cult to a religious "monotheistic" standard. But the tradition is more correctly termed: *monolatrism*. This was a confusing concept for some—and probably remains so today—as even the Assyrians were completely *pantheistic*, exalting *Assur* (MARDUK), but venerating and working with many other "personal deities" as representations of the "Divine."

Babylon became the "seat of the gods," but by Mardukite standards, this was intended differently than either *monotheism* or *polytheism* can provide. The basic program became as follows: There are many *gods* but the way is through *One*, idealized in Babylonian tradition as MARDUK and his consort SARPANIT via the holy receptionists, NABU ("Divine Secretary" or "Librarian of Babylon") and his consort TESHMET (or TASMIT), the "Listener of Prayers."

The work performed to usurp the ancient *Fifty Names* from the *Enuma Elis* ("*Epic of Creation*") for MARDUK also illuminates the idea of "many *gods* as *One*" or the "*One* manifest with many *faces*," but with the central figure on earth always returning to MARDUK as *divine representative*. Assuming the *Fifty Names* connected to an ancient "Divine Decree" of FIFTY—by Anunnaki numeric designation of World Order, equaling the rank of ENLIL, the "Lord of Command."

Babylonian myth and magic systems are dedicated to MARDUK's "Divine World Order." It is illustrated through the original mystical "kabbalah" system: *ten gates, two doors* and *seven levels*—just like the design for MARDUK's *ziggurat*— E.TEMEN.AN.KI—"*The Temple of Heaven and Earth*." These *Ziggurats*—artificial "mountain-home temple-shrines of the gods"—stood as giant stepped-pyramids in honor of the patron deity of a city-state, so named from the *Akkadian* word for them: "*Zi-kur-ra-tu*." And each ancient Mesopotamian city had one.

Of course, stepped pyramids are not only found in Mesopotamia—but many other prehistoric cultures, too. They are unique in function as "residences," seldom seen in more traditional Egyptian pyramids. However the oldest pyramids of Egypt are actually stepped-pyramids. But in Mesopotamia, extraordinarily large stepped pyramids elevated the actual temples, shrines and astronomical observatories—yet they once served as earthly homes for the star-raced "gods" to the most ancient religion on the planet.

THE EVOLUTION OF RELIGIO-MAGICAL SYSTEMS

Sumerian	*Unity, celestial-cosmic*
Babylonian	*Hierarchy, temple-religions*
Egyptian/Hermetic	*Names, magical-mysticism*
Sumerian	*Petition to the Most High*
Babylonian	*Petition to a pantheon*
Egyptian/Hermetic	*Petition to hierarchy of spirits*

Systemology of the "Mardukite" Babylonian Religion reflects many aspects of *animism* and *pantheism*—the belief that everything possesses an innate or inherent "spirit" or *Divine Spark* that entangles it to the "eternity of the cosmos" or the *All-as-One* (*Divine Source*). This "everything" includes fragmentation of distinct personalities or "Self." Cuneiform tablets distinguish these aspects as *utukku* (the *Divine Spark* or animating "spiritual essence") and *edimmu* (the "identity program" or soul of the body). In the related Egyptian tradition, these aspects are equated to the *ka* (life-force) and *ba* (personality) of an individual being.

NABU-scribes forged the *Enuma Elis*—a kind of cosmogenetic *"Epic of Creation"* central to the religion. But, the political purpose of this document was to bestow MARDUK with the *"Tablets of Destiny,"* enabling him world control or World Order. The covert cosmological beliefs were, however, actually *monistic*. This means that the *Divine Source* represents a single unifying principle, agent or "element" (referred to in some materials as the *All-as-One*) defining: One Existence - One Truth – One Cosmic Law. The later philosophy and practices of *Hermetic mysticism* are, therefore, not "invented" during the classical age, but are actually imported from a more antiquated *Ancient Mystery School* born in Babylon.

— 10 —
: MARDUK & THE ANUNNAKI :
MESOPOTAMIAN MYTHOLOGY IN BABYLON

"Like Napolean, who decided he did not need to be crowned according to the rules and crowned himself without further ado, so the Assyrian priests gave the honor to Ashur simply by taking the old Babylonian tablets and recopying them, substituting the name of their own god for that of Marduk. The work was not very carefully done, and in some places the name of Marduk still creeps in. . ."

~ Edward Chiera
They Wrote on Clay

Babylonian literary tradition, in addition to implementing a social system, focused primarily on one thing: *religious myths*. The Mesopotamian "mythos" is not called such to indicate any *fictions*. The real meaning of a *mythos* or *mythoi* in human history concerns the *systemology* of human consciousness—a paradigm of reality. Thus, a "mythology" was once little more than documentation of history—the deeds of gods, demigods and kings. Cultural emphasis on these characters is what, in essence, *creates* a mythology—a way of seeing the world as shared by a large group. It didn't take long for this methodology to be *covertly manipulated* to serve the political integrity of the *Babylonian Empire*.

Historically, "mythology" emphasizes activities that few relate to today—human interaction with the "*gods*." More often than not, descriptions of these encounters commonly involve a particular geographic feature—*mountains*. And where mountains were not accessible, the *gods* worked in conjunction with *humans* to construct "*zikkurat*"-*pyramids*, from the Akkadian description "*zaqaru*"—"artificially built mounds." In Sumerian language, the word for mountain is *kur*, the same as their name for the "primordial dragon" of the cosmos in pre-Babylonian mythology.

Surviving cuneiform tablet-sources intermittently make mention of "*dragons*." At some juncture; the "universe," the "planet earth" and the "blood of men" are all coined "dragon" in nature. The first legendary figures confronting "dragons" become *archetypes* for the "King of the Mountain." In the oldest Sumerian versions, these are ENLIL, NINURTA and even INANNA-ISHTAR. Given that "Enlilite" patina on these records, the name of MARDUK appears nowhere on these original epic tablet-cycles. During the early Sumerian age, MARDUK—called ASARLULI —was the first "magician-priest" of *Eridu*. This antediluvian cult center was later known in legend to the Greeks in their own language and mythic interpretation as the "*Temple of Poseidon*." Therefore, although there are many "lost civilizations" on the planet, scholars have confused semantics regarding the Greek renderings of "*Atlantis*"—information they recovered from the Egyptians long after the fact.

The Babylonian *"Epic of Creation"* (academically named *"Enuma Elis"* for its opening lines) was often observed in ancient traditions for its *"systemological"* value above its *"cosmogenetic"* qualities. However, it is *set* in a time before "earth" or "men" and describes the evolution of them both out of an unfolding "created universe"—progressive *"fragmentation"* of the *All-as-One* into parts. This has esoteric implications quite unique to ancient "Mardukite" lore—As already fragmented being the *"Anunna"* the "Secret Doctrines of the Cosmos," as used them to their advantage systematically when dealing with "humans."

In the *"Enuma Elis"* we are given a political account of MARDUK slaying the "cosmic serpent" or *dragon*, representing his "overcoming of chaos" in the cosmos to establish his own universal or "world order." This was actually an "old concept" revived from pre-Babylonian (Sumerian) use of the *kur* in earlier mythologies. By performing this feat or conquest, MARDUK became the *"King of the Anunnaki,"* a title was bestowed upon him (according to the *"Enuma Elis"*) as a reward from the *"Council of Anunnaki"* for his dragon-slaying feat. Performing this feat, even if only symbolically and in archetypal consciousness, the "Mardukite" forces are given *Divine Right* to exercise the powers of the *Anunnaki* on Earth.

The *Enuma Elis* forms the cornerstone of Mardukite usurpation of the Sumerian Anunnaki hierarchy. The work also illustrates a distinction between eras of older generations: a race of *"Ancient Ones"* led by the primordial dragon, TIAMAT; the "Elder Gods" or *Anunna* of prehistorical renown, such as ANU, ENLIL and ENKI; and a "Younger Generation" of *Anunnaki* in the Babylonian pantheon under MARDUK, which included many of his Enlilite peers: NANNA-SIN, INANNA-ISHTAR, SAMAS (SHAMMASH) and NERGAL.

While in *Eridu*, MARDUK is not actually attributed among early Sumerian *Anunnaki gods*—not listed among the pantheon. In fact, MARDUK is initially the primary high-ranked leader of the IGIGI ("Watchers") and during this role sets a new *status quo* in *Eridu*—and then in *Babylon*—concerning intermarriage between *Anunnaki* with humans, as described on ancient cuneiform tablets. For this "indiscretion," by Enlilite "World Order" standards, he was denied any future *Divine Right*. His argument remained that he was never going to be given his *"Right"* anyway, and furthermore, that his chosen consort, SARPANIT, was a seventh generation descendent of *Adapa*, the hybrid man born from direct genetics of ENKI, and therefore "Dragonblood." But the decree had been made. If it would not be *given* in order to reign on Earth in Babylon during his time—the *Age of Aries*—then "Divine Right" would have to be *taken*.

* * *

Contemporary archaeologists first became aware of the Babylonian *"Epic of Creation"* cycle in 1849, when cuneiform tablets were recovered during an expedition of the "Royal Library of Ashurbanipal" in *Nineveh*. Its contents were first published academically in 1876. They received significant attention from historians, mythographers and biblical scholars—not only because of their antiquity, but because of how significant the work turned out to be in deciphering the "methodology" of all ancient religions. In short—scholars discovered that the Babylonian *"Epic of Creation"* was the basis of the Judeo-Christian *"Book of Genesis."* But, after so many centuries of misinformation, *who would believe it?*

Multiple versions of the *"Enuma Elis"* and other Mesopotamian creation-cycles exist but there is one key element that many esoteric practitioners and academic historians miss when appropriating origins for the tablets within the "bigger picture." All tablet-cycles making reference to "MARDUK" at all, are purely *Babylonian*—not Sumerian. They reflect usurpation and transfer of "power" in Mesopotamia to *Babylon*, the control of the empire by priest-magicians and dragon-kings—authorities of religious and spiritual systems for the people and their relationship with the "Gods." The usurpation was covert. Publicly, "Divine Right" *could* be demonstrated to coincide with the "World Order" decreed by ANU, ENLIL and ENKI in prehistoric times, *using* the *Enuma Elis* to elevate MARDUK and develop *Babylon* as the earthly seat of godly power!

ENUMA-ELIS : THE SEVEN TABLETS OF CREATION

I.
a.)—ABSU (*the Abyss*) and TIAMAT (*the Cosmic Dragon*) are first forms form the One (*All*).
b.)—Generations of "gods" are born and begin to make too much noise.
c.)—TIAMAT entrusts her vizier KINGU the power to fight for her.
d.)—TIAMAT creates calamity and a horde of monsters as ammunition.

II.
a.)—ENKI reveals the plot against the gods to ANSAR.
b.)—A primary discourse from the first tablet is repeated.

III.
a.)—ANU, ENLIL and ENKI do not stand fit to battle against TIAMAT.
b.)—MARDUK is petitioned to champion the Anunnaki gods.
c.)—MARDUK asks for supreme divinity if successful; to be *Chief God*.

IV.
a.)—The Anunnaki agree to MARDUK's terms and prepare him for battle.
b.)—MARDUK receives a "cloak of invisibility."
c.)—MARDUK enchants his favored weapon: a bow.
d.)—MARDUK destroys KINGU with a thunderbolt.
e.)—TIAMAT is slain; her minions are scattered and sent to "secret places."
f.)—MARDUK fashions a *"Gate"* to seal these energies separate from the material universe.

V.

a.)—MARDUK seals the cosmic systems of "Lights," "Spheres" and "Degrees" under himself.

b.)—The material-matix *below* is fragmented by the "seven," while the *heights* remain divided into "twelve."

c.)—The *"Anunnaki Star-Gate"* system is sealed throughout the Universe.

d.)—MARDUK sets up a throne for himself next to ANU.

VI.

a.)—The Anunnaki praise MARDUK for his feats.

b.)—The "Key to the Gate" (of the *Abyss* and the *Dragon*) is "hidden" in genetic memory of the *"Race of Marduk,"* including humans upgraded by ENKI.

c.)—Babylonian systematization begins.

VII.

a.)—Having slayed TIAMAT and granted power over material creation, MARDUK takes the names and numbers of ENLIL.

b.)—MARDUK takes the "signs" and esoteric knowledge ("magic") of ENKI.

c.)—MARDUK fractures then seals all systems on Earth under his name.

Politically, the *Enuma Elis* allowed the *"Law of Marduk"* (for example, the *"Code of Hammurabi"*) to be upheld. In religious ceremonies—such as the Babylonian New Year Akiti Festival—the *Enuma Elis* was part of the preliminary "rites" conducted of any public or private working. Any significant rituals and even smaller operations of "magic" or "personal devotion" (within the tradition) were usually "opened" with a recitation of the *Epic*. The words cement the basis of all Mardukite *"magic"*—a term used by anthropologists and esoteric practitioners of the Mardukite movement, but which the ancients simply viewed as *"Life."*

The older public ("exoteric") Sumerian *Epics of Creation* are hardly true creation "epics." Their systematic or quasi-cosmological basis is often restricted to a few opening lines, such as:

> *AN carries off heaven;*
> *ENLIL carries off earth.*

To a purely pre-Babylonian *"Sumerian"* cosmology, this simplistic methodology simply *stood* by its own right unquestioned. Such simply *was* and had *always been*. To glean anything deeper, one would have had to become initiated to the "mystery tradition" observed by Babylonian magicians and scribes—the overseers of the "Realm" that supported the *"Dragon-Kings"* ruling by the "Divine Right" of their *"dragon blood"* that originally "descended from the heavens"—from the "gods."

A more physical representation of the *"dragon"* also appears in *Babylon*, though surviving records are obscure. MARDUK had two half-brothers (fathered by ENKI but not necessarily born of NINKI)—NINGISZIDA (*Ningishzidda* or *Ni-(n)rah*) and NINAZU or *Tis(h)pak*. The famous "Dragon of Babylon" first belonged to TISPAK, was later given to MARDUK (as shown in popular artistic depictions) and eventually it came to to the care of NABU. The best renderings are left left Nebuchadnezzar II in his construction of walls and gates of the Babylonian Renaissance.

The traditional name for the dragon name is *Sirius* or *Sirrus,* sometimes spelled phonetically as *"Sirush"* or *"Sirrush."* In Akkadian, the name for the species is *mushussu* or *mushhushshu*, meaning "furious serpent,"—from *mush-us,* or "monster." [This species should not be confused with the *usumgal,* or "Great Cosmic Serpent" used to represent the universe.] Far away in the African Congo, a description of the *mushussu* matches a species of *sauropod* (now believed to be extinct) called *mokele-mbembe* by the indigenous tribes who claimed to have killed one. This could effectively connect dragon-lore with the (*sa-ru-us/saurus*) dinosaurs. Yet, where dragon-lore is universal, contemporary knowledge of dinosaurs has only been in public evidence for the last 200 years.

"Mastery of Dragons" has long-standing associations with *godhood* ever since these earliest renderings. Evidence still remains in Judeo-Christian lore: the *One God* was eventually seen as 'too great' to be concerned with mortal battle and so the 'dragon-slaying' motif was passed on to "ambassadors" or "emissaries" of God— first *St. Michael* (the archangel most closely associated with MARDUK) and then among chosen mortals like *St. George*. Overt publicly visible possession of a live dragon as both a *royal pet* and *icon* of the holy city further led to securing a worldly "seat of god" for *Babylon* in the consciousness of the masses.

— 11 —

: BABYLONIAN MAGIC :
THE ART OF PRIESTS, MAGICIANS & KINGS

"Systematic traditions, 'hermetically sealed' within themselves, later rose from Semitic grimoire-styled ceremonial magic, not surprisingly influenced by 'Egypto-Babylonian' forms of ritual magic—first the domain of Enki and then Marduk and his scribe-son Nabu. Priest-magicians of Babylon would not actually have personally used 'grimoire-like' magic themselves. This was not their way. At best, They invoked the powers of the Anunnaki with incantations in the name of Marduk —but the manner of using 'secret names' as properties of Marduk, or any other demigod, is a much more recent addition to the Hermetic system. . ."

~ Joshua Free
–From the original Liber R

Under the banner of a *"New Age movement"* led by *"esotericists,"* we are witnessing a revival of pragmatic spiritual and ritualistic elements drawn from ancient pagan and occult methodologies. We should be seeing no shortage of authentic Mesopotamian lore—being the origin of these later *systems*. But this information is not readily accessible and esoteric success is not achieved via pouring through a *kabbalastic grimoire* written by some *medieval sorcerer*. For this, the *seeker* will have to dig a little harder in the desert sands – into the heart of the true and authentic, antiquated and originating arts of the priests, magicians and kings!

During the era of the first *ziggurat* temples—the *Anunnaki* age—all "magic" constituted "spiritual assistance" governed by the state, ruled by priest-kings and temple attendants. All official "mystics" of *Babylonia* were employed by the temples and scribe-houses. There were undoubtedly many others with access to esoteric knowledge who confined themselves to their arts in the *outlands*, beyond the awareness of the societal "realm." The "common" class in Mesopotamia, however, did not really practice "magic" in the way it is generally classified by anthropologists. Personal religious devotions were primarily composed of *hymns* and *prayers* learned from the temples.

Cuneiform tablets describing "magical" ceremonies list required religious artifacts and items that the average person would not have access to or the ability to afford. *"Magic"* from this period is restricted to the priests. Use of a temple, for one, appears key—a tradition continued among some modern *lodges* of "ceremonial magic." Access to tablets themselves—records and *"incantation-prayers"*—maintained directly by the priests—was not generally given to just anyone. And you had to be able to read them and memorize them. General collections of these tablets were seldom kept, except priest-kings maintaining their own personal libraries.

According to *Mardukite Tablet-B*, from *"Necronomicon: The Anunnaki Bible"*—

> *"The priest is to observe pious ways, and Rites of Offering at the Altar of Sacrifice. This is performed by intoning prayers [incantations] from tablets in conjunction with offering of incense, grain [bread], honey [with butter] and libations of buttermilk (or wine). Sacred "holy" oil [and water] make an appearance in virtually all ancient Babylonian rites—water and oil frequently placed in bowls before icons [of deities] in temples, in addition to offerings of alabaster, gold and lapis lazuli."*

At the temple-shrines, the Altar of Offering was set before the *"Boat of the Gods."* The same imagery appears in Egyptian Tradition—a "Boat of the Gods" carrying seven figures, *e.g.* the *Seven Anunnaki Gods* of the Babylonian "Younger Generation." Smaller personal altars could surely be constructed by a devotee appealing to their *god*, but became more prominent with the rise of *"figurative mysticism,"* because originally, these offerings would be physically received by a *god*, or via their "priestly secretaries." Common religious offerings included food and drink, incense and oil, even lavish jewelry and clothing, all of which were carried up the *ziggurat* steps—up the *"ladder to heaven"*—to be placed before the feet of the *god*. When the *gods*, themselves, were not present, it was customary to have an *official* piece of statuary left in their place. Thus, it is easy to see how these original activities evolved into later *magical* and *religious* practices.

White was the most common color worn by the priests, although black was also used and even favored by the temple-priestesses. Priestly attire included the infamous "conical hat," popularly associated today with classical "wizards," but which can be seen worn by *gods*, kings and priest-magicans in ancient Mesopotamia, Egypt and eventually elsewhere. Gold and *lapis lazuli* commonly appear as both "magical ritual aids" and prestigious offerings to the gods. Babylonian temples and sacred structures were often designed to radiate these hues. Wands, necklaces and carried bags of loose *lapis lazuli* are often mentioned on esoteric tablets, in addition to golden rings and "amulet-plates" marked with specific seals and cuneiform glyphs.

Modern implementation of a "practical magical system" based on the "Mardukite" Babylonian paradigm is different than what the contemporary mind—even an *"esoteric"* one—is fundamentally familiar with. As opposed to later magicians who appear to have had to connive and fool hierarchies of spirits into assisting them, threatening them and even in fear of some retroactive revenge, the original magical system used by priests of *Babylonia* was rooted in a deep personal relationship of "authority" with the cosmos. Scribes maintained the "sources" of not only their religious power, but a fundamental system of civilization promoting progression of the human species into today. All of this, according to tradition, rested in the power of the *Anunnaki gods*—and the priest-kings and scribes were installed to be sure this was never forgotten.

— 12 —
: STARGATES OF BABYLON :
THE ANUNNAKI POWER OF STARFIRE

"True indeed, there was a supreme name which possessed the power of commanding the gods and extracting from them a perfect obedience, but that name remained the inviolable secret of Enki. In exceptional cases the priest besought Enki, through the mediator Marduk, to pronounce the solemn word in order to reestablish order in the world and restrain the powers of the Abyss. But the priest did not know that name, and could not in consequence introduce it into his formulae... He could not obtain or make use of it, he only requested the god who knew it to employ it, without endeavoring to penetrate the terrible secret himself."
~ M. Lenormant
Chaldean Magic & Sorcery

Compared to a more recent world full of "magical" folk traditions—where love potions are in no short supply and acquisition of cosmic favor is as a matter of spinning around seven times while whistling or throwing feathers to the north winds—the original stoic and sacred rites of "divine magic" are rooted in a "mystical" tradition based on a direct relationship, and personal "authority" *earned*, with the *Anunnaki gods*. The mere existence of an ancient "Anunnaki hierarchy" produced the later mystical and religious concept of "*spiritual pantheons*"— pantheons cataloged by *kabbalistic magicians* in later attempts to uncover the "secret of the ages," or more specifically, the secret "*magic word*" that granted authority with the *forces* of the *cosmos*.

In regards to modern "Mardukite" revivals by any practitioner or group—since such cultural revisits are common in the "New Age" mystical paradigms—the *specific* ancient ideology put forth in this book should be kept in mind, particularly if performing "meditations" or metaphysical experiments. Connecting true esoteric knowledge—one-to-one—with physical symbolism or graphic representations, is another important key for effective mystical revival traditions. For example, in the absence of access to the shrines of Babylon and physical *ziggurat* temples, modern practitioners often use "creative visualization," advanced "meditation" techniques, or other mystical methods of "astral travel" to connect with the same "energetic forces." Contrary to some beliefs, the *Anunnaki* specifically, are not the "UFO-driving aliens" heard of today. However, the *Anunnaki* are very powerful beings who made such deep impressions on the "Akashic Field" that their identities still remain accessible today.

Modern psychology, quantum physics, and practical mysticism all suggest that the energetic self does not properly distinguish a reality barrier between what it encounters or experiences in the body as "day-to-day" from what is possible in properly executed ritual drama. In ancient times, the priests reinforced cultural beliefs in society through dramatic reenactments of ancient myths, thereby making them part of "day-to-day" social consciousness—allowing for this "*magic*" to become *reality*. All of it, of course, *really* being a matter of *perspective*. For whatever we may attribute to our "accomplishments of things," it is our belief that we can execute them that makes anything possible.

The Babylonian "Religio-Magic" System was developed by ancient *Mardukites* as a means of sealing power of an older generation of *gods* under MARDUK—with his holding a "*kingship*" over the "younger generation" of *Anunnaki* that served devotional needs of post-Sumerian *Babylonia*. Thus, cosmic power was accessed *through him* and worldly power was dispatched *by him*. And, so long as they could be honored within the confines of the prescribed system, "Enlilite" figures such as INANNA (ISHTAR), NERGAL (ERRA), NANNA (SIN) and SHAMMASH/ SAMAS (UTTU) and NINURTA (NINIB) all appear within the younger pantheon observed by the *Mardukites* even though they are *not* descendents of ENKI (as are MARDUK, SARPANIT and NABU). "*Sealing*" this *system* in Babylon is what caused the city-name to be interpreted literally as the "*Gate of the Gods*"— "*bab*" (as "gateway") and "*ilu*" (meaning, "god," "star" or "heaven").

The archetypal theme of "gateways" appears at the heart and soul of all esoteric "religion" and "spirituality" born in Mesopotamia. When we are confronted with matters of the "divine"—or that which is *otherworldly* (of the "*other*")—the symbolism of the "*gate*" is nearly always present. As the mind perceives it, "*gates*" are literally "thresholds," "portals," "doorways" and "windows" into what is deemed *Other*—what is *beyond* our preset daily awareness. The "*Secret Doctrines*" suggest there is only *one* reality—one existence in wholeness—but fragmented (from our point of view) into arbitrary parts via these "veils," "levels," "layers" and other "boundaries" of existence and awareness.

* * *

Since the 1970's practical efforts have been made toward modern revival of a "Mardukite" Babylonian "Gatekeeping" (or "Gatewalking") tradition. But most available lore is derived from ancient literature describing an era of history when priests and magicians worked alongside *Anunnaki gods* in establishing and preserving physical *gates* and *shrines*. These structures clearly served multiple purposes in the ancient paradigm, both those that were known to the population— and those unknown.

Following in the pious footsteps of *Babylonian priests*, whether a modern *seeker* or revivalist *practitioner* has been truly *self-honestly* dedicated to the *system* or not, the primordial power of these currents, to be useful or channeled directly—must be first respected. This path, if it is to be applied today, requires cumulatively developed "spiritual authority" developed from working with the archetypal currents of this pantheon with "techniques" dating back to a ancient time of kings, priests and magicians.

The "*magic*," then—if we are to call it that—comes directly from a *working* relationship between the individual (priest or magician) and the "powers" controlling the specified domains. In the ancient world, all facets of life were thought to be the domain or under the influence of some "unseen" force—but a force that could be understood and communicated with through magic and religion. This led to the solidification of civilized humans under a "world order"—but one that was transmutable and subject to additional programming and control.

For modern purposes, the term "*Gatekeeping*" or "*Gatewalking*" really applies to the "Mardukite" (*Babylonian*) specific method of *kabbalistic* "pathworking"—predating and serving as origins for the more commonly known Semitic "*Kabbalah*" (or "Cabala"). The methodology is used today by modern "*Mardukite Chamberlains*"—those who actively participate in a revival of the ancient *Mardukite* paradigm as it applies to the modern world. [*Mardukite Chamberlains* are an *active* branch of an otherwise *passive* research organization rooted in both scholarly and esoteric purposes.]

Where a temple is not accessible, "*magic carpets*" and "*statuary*" can be set out to consecrate an area for *priestly magic*. Some ritual texts refer to an "*image of your god and goddess,*" whereas others mention using a line of "*seven winged figures*" indicative of the "Younger Generation." As is common in modern traditions, personal sacred space (outside of the temple) is observed as a *mandala* or "sacred circle." Representing ceremony and agriculture, the boundary of the circle was originally marked by consecrated "*flour of Nisaba*"—or the "*flour of Nabu,*" as Babylonian tradition evolved. This is performed the same way a modern "*esotericist*" might draw theirs ritual circle in chalk, &tc.

As advice to the priest or magician, the *Tablet-Q Series* in "*Necronomicon: The Anunnaki Bible*" offers this step—

> "*Make your invocation to Marduk and Sarpanit. Then call in [invoke] the Supernal Trinity— Anu, Enlil and Enki, followed by a conjuration [consecration] of the Fire and Four Beacons [lamps] of the Watchtowers [cardinal directions]. Perform the 'Incantation of Eridu' and call forth the presence of your personal sedu [guardian watcher spirit].*"

As a very ancient belief, using mystical conjuration to summon a "personal watcher-spirit" is not unique only to Egypto-Babylonian or *Hermetic* systems. The *sedu* (meaning "spirit," "genius" or "intelligence," much like the Greek word "*daemon*") is also the origins of an Assyrian concept later relayed as the more commonly known "guardian angel" in later Semitic traditions. According to Babylonian beliefs, every person *had* one. This belief may not have been shared by all since lines from some of the original incantations are requests to initially "acquire" a *sedu* and a *lamassu*. In either case, we are again confronted with a "magic" that carries a strength dependent on one's own true understanding and personal relationship with the cosmos.

There are many types of "beings" in the universe, the *Anunnaki* are only one—perhaps the first—to engineer reality for humans on Earth. These "angelic" traditions become more mysterious as they evolved. Identities of IGIGI-"Watcher" spirits fade when contrasted to a host of other forces in existence—some of them seeming *malignant*. During the ancient Mesopotamian age, the "Demonic Spirits" that humans required protection from were often the resonance of pestilence and warfare. Most of the ancient *taboo*-sins or "*bans*" (listed in "*Necronomicon: The Anunnaki Bible*") were meant to keep the people clean and free of infections and disease. Laws were put forth to keep people civil, without them having to murder or eat one another.

A regiment of strict personal cleanliness was essential among the priest and magician class—not only in their conductance of ceremony, but in their everyday walking lives as well. Keeping hair trimmed, or even shaved, was a part of daily ritual—it aided in thwarting personal insect infestations. Use of eye makeup, once thought to be purely decorative, actually had some evolutionary advantages for desert living. Black eye-shadow, particularly beneath the eyes (as used by today's athletes) assists in reducing the sun-glare common to open sandy areas.

"Divine Names" play a key role in both ancient and modern magical or priestly (mystic) work. Sometimes several "names" or mythic "titles" for the same entity are invoked. Even the priest-magician must proposition the *gods* by properly introducing himself with recitation of his lineage. For example, "*I, so-and-so, the son of so-and-so and so-and-so, whose god and goddess is so-and-so and so-and-so. . .*" All of the spoken words involved are really, then, quite direct. *Who are you? Who are you calling? What is the message?*—Just as if you are dealing with a *Divine Secretary*, and yes, the Babylonians even installed NABU and TESHMET to this real position! The system is very "formal."

Keep in mind that the entire effectiveness of the priest's magical work was based on their personal relationship with the *gods*—not simply their ability to discern a *secret number* or precisely memorize an *incantation formula*. These later "magical" beliefs evolved more recently as the *gods* seemed to become more distant from our world. Original ritualized *petitions* for "divine" assistance seem more akin to requesting help from a *friend* or *authority*. There is a certain measure of *tact* involved, perhaps once common knowledge, that later developed as "occult correspondences." In this case—*This one is only home after 5. That one is more content around the smell of roses. Offer to take this one to lunch first. Mondays are NOT that one's day! &tc. &tc.* How often is this true of our own "Judicial System" even today? Those who made this work their everyday lives in the temples generally knew this type of information, particularly in regards to their own patron deities. Circulation of *"grimoires,"* *"prayerbooks"* or unauthorized *"spellbooks"* among the masses began as the system evolved from those "outside" the ranks of the national tradition—from those not even sworn to its sanctity. Secrets of the "Ancient Mystery School" are not dependent on widespread dispersion for them to exist—the Power is there for *any* that choose to take it.

— 13 —
: MARDUKITE MAGIC :
ANCIENT RITES & RITUALS OF ERIDU

"Through Marduk, the power of Eridu—incantation-prayer and "intention"—was taught to the scribes of Nabu and the Mardukite Priests, who were taught to attract and compel the 'gods' in the name of Marduk, always incanting the word-formula of the highest order: Nabu invoked by way of the name of Marduk; Marduk invoked by way of the name of Enki, Our Father, who in turn would invoke by the name of Anu—and so was born the concept of magical hierarchies, an ideal that was convoluted and obscured when employed later (during the Middle Ages and such), particularly distorted by the Judeo-Christian paradigm as evident in many popular grimoires"

~ Joshua Free
—Book of Marduk by Nabu
Necronomicon: The Anunnaki Bible

A modern seeker interested in esoteric philosophies has undoubtedly found countless "primers" of magic and sorcery or other ritual "grimoires." Many contemporary guides employ "creative visualization" and "New Thought" techniques—the same ones used by popular self-help gurus and motivational mentors—as well as other forms of meditation, conscious breathing, mental concentration or focus of will. These methods are actually quite effective in the right hands. The material world experienced by an individual is subject to that person's own "energies" and perspective (internal "set") in addition to their interactions with other "energies." Nonetheless, physical "ceremony" is often sought as a necessary step in crossing the thresholds of our own psyche.

Many versions of *"Erudite"* magic are found throughout Mesopotamian "religio-spiritual" (or "magical") cuneiform tablets. Incantations used in the "Mardukite Babylonian Anunnaki Tradition"—from those tablets forged by priest-scribes of the *Order of Nabu*—are actually invoked from the "perspective" (*"authority"*) of NABU. This reflects how the tradition was learned verbatim from MARDUK.

Both scholarly and esoteric texts concur that the "Opening Ritual" for *Mardukite magic* originates with a rite called—*"The Incantation of Eridu."* It is perhaps the most fundamental "formula" of the magical system in *Babylonia*. It returns one's focus to the heart of the *system* and the roles of its main figures—NABU as "Director," and the appropriation of his father, MARDUK as the "Chief." This is what is acknowledged in the *"Incantation of Eridu,"* also known as the *"Incantation of the Deep,"* alluding to another name for the far-away abode of ENKI near the *Persian Gulf.*

Ceremonial "affirmations" activate the *"covenant"* of Anunnaki power sealed in *Eridu*, and then in *Babylon*. This allows a practitioner to assume a representative *"god-form"* as the *"Priest of Eridu"*—a title first bestowed upon MARDUK by ENKI in the Sumerian age, then passed onto NABU during standardization of the *Babylonian* era. An esoteric key is in effect here. The priest conducts the "incantations" ("ceremony") as an embodiment of the intermediary "messenger" *deity*. This is the original meaning of the word *"invocation."* The priest is *not* "evoking" or "conjuring" some apparition—he is directing the flow of *Cosmic Order* by calling specific personality energies "into" *himself.*

The magician is *approaching* his deity as himself—*a servant priest*—and petitions to assume the *godform*, whereby he continues the ceremony as a *divine representation* of the invoked *god*. Similar principles appear within Semitic mysticism and the Judeo-Kabbalah. An an excellent ceremonial example is found in contemporary Catholicism, when the priest *"assumes the Christ-form"* to effectively perform "alchemical transmutation" on the sacramental bread and wine. He conducts this rite as a representative of Jesus on earth, an imitative ritual drama, reenacting the "Last Supper." In the "Mardukite" system observed in *Babylon*, the god invoked is typically MARDUK. This is affirmed with the priest's first utterance of—*"It is not I, but Marduk, who speaks the incantation"*—activating and sealing the system for "practical" use.

Consider the lines of this incantation, adapted for the Mardukite *"Conjuration of the Fire God"* from *Tablet-Y* series in *"Necronomicon: The Anunnaki Bible"*—

> *It is not I, but Marduk, Slayer of Serpents,*
> *Who summons thee.*
> *It is not I, but Enki, Father of the Magicians,*
> *Who calls thee here now.*

As previously introduced, the ritual operates from the perspective (*"authority"*) of NABU, speaking for MARDUK. Many variations of this rite exist, including several Assyrian "exorcisms." As an example, one of these cuneiform tablets, translated by R.C. Thompson, relates the opening lines—

> *The Priest of E.A. [Enki] am I.*
> *The priest of Damkina [Ninki] am I.*
> *The messenger [Nabu] of Marduk am I.*
> *My spell is the spell of E.A [Enki].*
> *My incantation is the incantation of Marduk.*
> *The 'magic circle' of EA [Enki] is in my hand.*
> *The 'tamarask' of ANU, in my hand, I hold.*

Opening lines from the modern *Mardukite* version in *Tablet-Y* read—

I am the Priest of Marduk,
Son of Our Father, Enki.
I am the Priest of Eridu,
And the Magician of Babylon.

The Assyrian version continues as follows—

EA [Enki], King of the Deep
See me favorably.
I, the magician, am thy slave.
March thou on my right hand,
Assist me on my left;
Add thy pure spell to mine.
Add thy pure voice to mine.
O god that blesses me, Marduk,
Let me be blessed, wherever my path rests.
Thy power, shall god and man proclaim.
And I too, the magician, thy slave.

E.A. Budge translated an older version for *"Babylonian Life & History,"* where we see another Mardukite method for petitioning the "younger pantheon" of Anunnaki to the side of the priest—

I am the Priest of EA [Enki].
I am the Magician of Eridu.
Samas [Shammash] is before me.
Nanna [Sin] is behind me.
Nergal is at my right hand.
Ninurta is at my left hand.

Adding to this, the modern *Mardukite* version appends—

Anu, above me, King of Heaven.
Enki, below me, King of the Deep.
The power [blood] of Marduk is within me.
It is not I, but Marduk, who performs the incantation.

The priest mystically sheds singular awareness of his "mortal spark," even if only for a moment—to experience *"transcendental magic"* clad in *godhood*. Direct parallels may be drawn from this rite to others found in "Hermetic" magic and the "Kabbalah." Rising on the planes of perception, awareness and knowing—as a *god*, speaking on behalf of the *Chief* of the pantheon—the magician-priest is now able to influence worldly affairs in the *original* and most powerfully direct "magical" means known—a direct interface with the *gods* as one of their own.

— 14 —
: "ON EARTH, LIFE" :
AKITU—THE BABYLONIAN NEW YEAR

"The Babylonian observation of the annual (solar) year starts with the 'Mardukite' observation of Zagmuk—meaning 'the beginning of the year' or 'new year'. This 12-day festival is fixed to arrange its height at the beginning of the month of Nissanu, the 'Spring Equinox' or March 21st, also coinciding with the beginning of the astrological wheel, when the sun enters Aries."

~ Joshua Free
The Book of Zagmuk by Nabu

In ancient *Babylon*, the New Year Festival was the central most religio-political "Mardukite" event marking the beginning of the annual cycle. At that time in "celestial history," the spring equinox observation of *Akitu* (or *Akiti*) coincided with the sun entering the *"Aries"* zone, the zodiacal sign of MARDUK. This spring festival symbolized not only agricultural fertility and renewal of the land on earth, but also a restatement or reinforcement of the national position of MARDUK and his role in the universe.

The Akkadian name for the final day of the festival—*Akiti* or *Akitu*—translates roughly to *"On Earth, Life."* Most scholars usually only recognize the "agricultural" significance and not necessarily the "political" and "mystical" functions of the observation. True, the *Akitu* festival took place twelve days before the annual crops were planted—but, this large public national "celebration" also reconfirmed supremacy of MARDUK and the *Babylonian* Pantheon, making it the single most important ancient "holiday" for the Mardukite tradition.

After a time of gods had come and gone, the priests and kings continued to observe these ceremonial customs using representative "images" or statuary to symbolized the "divine presence" of MARDUK and NABU as they made a procession each year through the streets of *Babylon*. [The applicable parallels to "Easter" (*&tc.*) are innumerable as we progress our understanding of the ritual text.]

Each of the twelve festival days begins at dawn. The *High Priest* of the *"Temple of Marduk"*—the E.SAG-ILA or *"House of Marduk"*—goes and prepares the temple and other ceremonial areas before dawn, then makes a "general invocation" to MARDUK, before the "image" (statue) of the *god* in his shrine.

On the first day of the festival, *after* the priests carried out morning services, the King accompanies a procession around the city of *Babylon*, showing the people that he carried the official "royal" regalia of his position—the *"Crown of Anu,"* the

Scepter of Dragonblood, &tc. This is to secure the symbolism of "worldly material reign" firmly in the consciousness of the population. Transfer of this power to the king by the gods demonstrates his *"Divine Right to Rule."* Then, portions of the *"Enuma Elis"* are read to prove that MARDUK is authorized to dispense this "divine right."

During the second day, the *High Priest* is charged to ritually cleanse the temple with consecrated waters from both rivers of *Babylon*—the *Tigris* and the *Euphrates*. Sweet *fragrances* of juniper and cypress fill the air. The official image (statue) of NABU is carried from the nearby city of *Borsippa* and left just outside of *Babylon* at the *Uras Gate*.

The sacred symbols of "worldly material reign" are removed from the King by the *High Priest* and taken by procession to the *Temple of Marduk*, where the symbols are placed before the (statue) feet of the *god*. These "sacred objects" are only "returned" to MARDUK briefly, so that the *Anunnaki King* may dispense them "officially" back to the *Earthly King* who rules the Babylonian nation in the name of MARDUK. This also demonstrates to all concerned that these symbols of reign are only "borrowed" by kings, who are really "stewards" for MARDUK on Earth. The statue of MARDUK is brought outside the *Esagila* and the King makes his appeal to rule before it. Then, the items of power are returned to the King by the *High Priest*, and a procession ensues back to the palace, showing the people that the King has been granted the "Divine Right" by MARDUK.

Day three involves a reenactment of the *"Enuma Elis,"* followed by a procession of the image/statue of NABU on a pathway of reeds. NABU is brought before the Sumerian *"Temple of Ninurta"* (sometimes called the *"Temple of Fifty"*) where he is to "defeat" two enemies (*"evil gods"*) in the name of MARDUK. A dramatization is performed—two statues are destroyed before his image. NABU is then left at the *"Temple of Ninurta"* until the sixth day of the festival.

On the fourth day, both statues are ritually "cleansed" by the *High Priest*. The image of MARDUK is returned to the *Esagila*, where MARDUK is symbolically "imprisoned within the mountain" (or "pyramid")—which had happened during the fall of the first "Tower of Babel" in prehistory. In one account, he is trapped is by "two evil gods," presumably the same ones that NABU defeats. A more accurate explanation according to tradition is that his imprisonment was a political punishment for the death of *Dumuzi* (or *Tammuz*)—consort of INANNA-ISHTAR. MARDUK remains "buried alive"—*dead but dreaming*—for three days. During this, on the fifth day, the epic cycle of INANNA-ISHTAR—known as the *"Descent to the Underworld"*—is recited (or dramatized) and NABU finally enters the city again on the sixth day.

Ceremonial applications of the seventh day are derived from a wisdom series, given as the *Book of Nabu-Tutu Tablet-T* series in *"Necronomicon: The Anunnaki Bible."* Here, the young prophet-son deity—NABU—approaches the *voice* of the *"unseen god,"* MARDUK as *Amon-Ra* entrapped in the "pyramid." During the festival, NABU—the statue/image of NABU—is brought before the image of the imprisoned "MARDUK" statue to receive the mysteries from the "unseen god."

A great victory procession of MARDUK and NABU commences on the ninth day. Their statues and those of their consorts—SARPANIT and TESHMET—are cleaned on the tenth day before they are receive a final grand celebratory procession on the eleventh day. Then after the priests conduct closing "consecration" rites at dawn on the twelfth day, the images/statues are retired to their appropriate places and Babylonian work-a-day life returns to normal.

— EPILOGUE —
: A BRAVE NEW BABYLON RISING :
by "Sortileges" David Zibert

Conflict. . . Unrest. . .
  On earth as it is in heaven. . .

At the precipice of a planetary evolution, the *world* ends.
  It always does.

Global tensions rise to unprecedented heights with the passing of each day. The *bright future* once wrought for mankind grows dark for the race as a whole. To it: arcane philosophy failed; ageless religion failed; humanistic ideals failed; and every magic spell and scientific formulae furthers sealing mortal man in his own self-made systematic prison, driving the coffin nail home—a single-track to travel upon furthering our journey into the *downward spiral* sending a world into inevitability. . .

  . . .apocalypse.

And this is my hope for the world, shared from the depth of my soul and joined in the voices of many self-honest truth seekers who have seen for themselves. . . renewal!

The mystics know; the children know; even the *birds* know – the world is *ending*. Of course, this does not imply the blatant physical, material and totalitarian destruction of humans (so let us not employ the same scare tactics of every evangelizing preacher under the sun), it is instead the ending of *a human world*.

Recorded legends on ancient tablets point toward an era of *renewal* that will give way to the fabled *Golden Age*, a *Brave New World*—a true *new age*. But this is no *new* idea at all, rather it is something predicted by the main tenets of every true spiritual path throughout history, differentiated solely by semantics and appearing as varied as opinions from the *Second Coming of Christ* to the the cosmic collapse of the material universe by some rift in space-time or even *dark matter* and *black holes*.

You can label and interpret, even sugarcoat, what is happening any way you like— the simple fact remains: There is an undeniable feeling shared throughout the collective human consciousness that *something* is about to happen—that something *is* happening—and yet it all seems to endlessly cycle back and forth in some determined fragile balance.

So *what* are we to do?

While the bungled confusion of the world plagues the mind with anxiety demons and victimization tendencies, the answer couldn't be simpler: *we must provoke the end of the world*, in this case, through a *massive paradigm shift*, meaning the necessary return of the *true spirituality*. By this, I mean the original *stuff*; untainted; undefiled through time by the analytical minds and personal truths of men corrupted into *systems*—fragmented from the whole; never the tween shall meet; *thank you, call back later*. It may seem like nothing new; but *no*, this time *it is different*.

In the wake of this self-honest planetary need for a *Great Awakening*, and on the cusp of a true *new age*, many "cults" have risen in recent past, loosely termed "pagan." Yet, in all of their once revolutionary efforts marked upon human consciousness, what they have to offer is often really only a "turn of the wheel," simply providing a different container for the *same content*, proving to us once again that humanity has not evolved much since the days of antiquity.

Understand we are not here to tell you what to think, raising our "*Mardukite literature*" to some new authoritarian heights, but we are offering critical information and data correction for your noggin so that you might *self-honestly* think for *yourself*. The emphasis here on *self* is not merely some glorification of individualism or newfangled ego-worship, but an affirmation that if we really want to change the *world*, we had better clean up and change our *self* first. When each human being takes the responsibility to grasp the *self-honest* realizations of who they are and where they come from, what the world is and how it was made, of the stuff dreams and stars are made of, the *universe* and *everything*—when the experience of all these things can be done *honestly* from *self*, then the race will see an end to the current melancholy, heinous nonsense that is happening and has been happening for quite some time—a condition that is actually *anathema* to the survival of the very creatures that keep these things the way they are!

The premises we use to chart a *new world* are simple enough:

- *Every* human being has the potential and responsibility to experience life in *self-honesty*.

- *Every* human being has the right and freedom to demand this of their existence.

- *Every* human being has to embrace *some universal oneness* in order to live in harmony with itself as a race of brethren; with the Earth as a base of homestead; and with the universe as a matrix of existence. Only then can humans experience true *unity with all life, the universe and everything!*

This is our *true* and *destined* existence.

But what has kept man from achieving these ends? Why is it that the shortcomings of humanity throughout history seem to keep repeating recursively? Why has *everything* failed? As with all else, we find that the answer is again quite simple: *because humans are forgetful*.

We forget easily; we are often sad; we suffer; we lose sight. To regain anything meaningful for the present and any hope for the future, we must remember what once was, and fortunately for us, an order of some of the earliest mystics thought of just that—so they created *cuneiform-writing*.

This book, as with the remaining "cycle" of literature produced by the "*Mardukites*," is sure to present to you ideas of "history" and "magic" in ways you have never seen, or maybe even imagined before. The tradition that it represents does not deal in rudimentary hierarchical *grimoires* or the application of general hermetic principles upon some historical ethnocentric tradition. The "Mardukite" work runs much deeper than even this. It presents *The System*—the *archetypal* system—that has formed the basis for every mystery tradition to later emerge.

In other words: if you can correctly understand the means and motives of the mysteries and religion of Babylon and Sumer, you will correctly be able to interpret "history" and "magic" as a whole—whatever these words may mean to you. You will become privy to the beauty of the original efforts that have mostly deteriorated with time, probably attaining its lowest evolutionary depths in Christian-controlled medieval Europe – or even in the practices of modern day Jews and Muslims who use religion to shroud political reasons for killing one another. Even more important perhaps, you will become aware of what *really* happened in ancient Babylon, and understand whether or not it really was the *right* way to execute *Divine Order*, and why.

Indeed—the focal point of the modern *Mardukite* movement has never been about bringing back the *verbatim* "Babylonian paradigm" one-to-one, because this would only be the "turn of the wheel" again, and we've already grown dizzy and tired by such ventures. *This time*, it's all about fixing what went wrong, actually fixing the problem of *systems*, the root of all problems really, at the core. When every individual takes up the *Sword of Truth* against the world, executing the *acid test* of *self-honesty* on reality, then no doubt a *new*, better, *upgraded* aeon will really begin for mankind. This, we call: *New Babylon!*

To those who *also* feel called to pursue this with us, we say:

WELCOME HOME!

—PART ONE—

THE SUMERIAN ANUNNAKI

(LIBER 50)

— 00 —
: ABZU :
THE PRIMORDIAL ABYSS

For some, it is far too esoteric to say—the true and actual nature of all existence is an "Infinity of Nothingness." Yet, the most ancient spiritual texts suggest this is so. One may even believe they understand the meaning of the very words "*infinity*" and "*nothingness*"—but there is no guarantee this has been properly relayed in the past. Mysterious lore of the *Abyss* is reflected in mystical accounts from around the globe, spanning the entire evolution of human civilization.

A true understanding of this critical state is paramount to real "mystical" work— what is hidden at the heart of most ancient esoteric spirituality. Secrets of the *Ancient Mystery School* affected all systematized living, including the Sumerians. These "secrets" evolved, giving way to later Chaldeo-Babylonian "systems"— forms of "mysticism" and, dare we call it, "magic." Today, we see renewed interest in these matters among both academic scholars and those in the contemporary New Age. But, since the philosophies of the "Classical" era, shamanic cultures of Europe, or even the Egyptians all seem more "accessible" to the modern "*seeker*," the deeper and more ancient mysteries of Mesopotamia seem to often fade into shadows. Outside of the original esoteric sects, imaginations of the uninitiated surged passed their historical understanding, and a plethora of traditions and systems diverted from the main well-springs, continuing to deflect consciousness further from truly understanding primordial origins.

On the "Arcane Tablets," the *Primordial Abyss* was originally nameless—an "Infinity of Nothingness." As the latent, unmanifest, potentiality of "*Everythingness*," the *Abyss* is the "All-Source" for any manifestation of *things* in material existence. This concept was not only abstract to the ancients, it remains in the realm of *esoterica* today. To compensate, "pantheist" philosophers arose to equate universal forces with more tangible concepts—physical places names for beings or "creatures." Originally used to philosophically illustrate examples, such beings and places were *so closely* identified with otherwise esoteric concepts in the minds of the general population, that they were blatantly assimilated in consciousness as direct embodiments of these cosmic forces or principles.

Cuneiform tablets from the priest-scribes of NABU also provide evidence for an ancient belief in an "All-Encompassing Being" *begotten* of "the Abyss and the Primordial Sea." This means the *true infinity* of "nothingness" or what we might call "zero" is actually an *a priori* unity of "infinite aspects of itself" as all possible aetheric space—the "nothingness" and the "spaces between" as "One," "All," or rather, "None." This "formula" is generally represented as "*zero times zero*" or "OO"—the *sign of Infinity*. To quote the English philosopher, George Henry Lewes

—If zero "0" is the sign of vanished quantity, then the Infinite "00" is the sign of continuity.

Fundamentally, the beauty and simplicity of the infinitude of space and pure potentiality of existence is enough for an "All-Encompassing Being," but this is an almost "static" existence with no forces in movement—quite simply All-is-One (*or none!*) in the universe. This background non-existence is not animated—not manifest—and so requires "motion" for any existence. This was born of duality, but of the highest spiritual intent and not to be confused with some mundane spiritual morality. For it was only by the opposition of the primordial currents of "chaos" and "order"—"No-Thing" and "All-Things"—that the cosmos were causally set in motion with a pendulum-like drive toward constant activity, progression and "unfoldment" that we call "existence." The "unrest" of forces is a necessary condition for "Cosmic Law," "The All" or "One" to exist; fragmented by its very first division—that of "existence" and "naught"—the *first dichotomy.*

The *pure potentiality* of "infinite shape, form and variety, in all time, space and quantity" was difficult to relay in primitive language. However, esoteric interpretation of the most ancient Sumerian semantics of an "All-Being" is best reflected by the original meaning of the word "ILU" in Chaldeo-Babylonian literature. The original concept appeared in Sumerian language as "DIN.GIR," meaning "All-God," but later cultural pantheistic interpretations applied this term to individual personified "gods." The "Babylon" city, nation and culture was actually named in honor of their own spiritual quest—a "re-connection" with this "*Source*" by "ascending" the "Ladder of Lights" or "BAB.ILU"—The Gateway to God, or original "Tower of Babel."

True esoteric meaning was lost in time as the word was equated with "gods." An evolving Mesopotamian language system also associated it to "stars," almost changing the function of *Babylon* in consciousness as the "Doorway to the Stars," or as fictional character Daniel Jackson would prefer, a "Star-Gate." Original symbolism and simplicity of the truth is immediately shattered when enters philosophers, scholars and religious scientists—for we have all-too-easily overlooked a stumbling block when interpreting the most ancient tablets concerning divinity. As Lenormant explains in *Chaldean Magic & Sorcery*—

> "[For] the idea of ILU was too comprehensive and too vast to receive a very definite exterior form, and consequently [too obscure for] the adoration of the people. The personality of ILU was not clearly defined for a long time; his office and title as "God One" were at first given to ANU, "the ancient god," and the first person of the supreme trinity, which was afterward held to emanate from ILU; the priests did not distinguish the primordial principle from the chief of this trinity."

It is here, from the start of our discourse of the *"Sumerian Anunnaki,"* that a *seeker* must first learn to differentiate the "pantheistic personalities" of cultural mythology from the raw esoteric representations. When we exclusively focus on outward expressions of relative stories and histories, any deeper esoteric truths are shroud in mystery and lost to interpretation. If we were to base our cosmogony on purely Chaldeo-Babylonian accounts, one might be led to assume that ANU is born from ILU directly, and then in many regards becomes one and the same as ILU. Mythological "Order" of the *cosmos* is entrusted to the Sumerian "All-Father" of the *Anunnaki gods* as an embodiment of the same. But, physically and literally, Sumerian tablets do not actually ascribe ANU the position of *a priori* "First Being."

Sumerian mythology is troublesome when concerning names, since many titles can be shared by a single being, and what's worse, these titles often get exchanged between various beings at different times and by different tablet authors. At least three sets of "Divine Union" are found to precede the existence of ANU on many of the Sumerian tablets. These names are transliterated by early Sumeriologists as: ABZU and TIAMAT; MUMMU and LAKMU (or LAHMU and LAHAMU); and, ANSAR and KISAR.

The first pair of names are the most applicable to our current chapter—titles with attributes traditionally associated with the *"Abyss"* (ABZU) and the *"Primordial Sea"* (TIAMAT), which as One, compose "nothingness" and "everythingness." Some interpretations confuse these two principles as the same, but they are not. Where the *Abyss* is an infinity of unmanifest potential, the *primordial sea* is an infinity or recursive continuum of form—the *First Cause*—or the "Law" put in motion as infinite manifestation. [The later "Divine Couples" are intended to represent this "2=0" creative principle of "Order" in the *cosmos*.]

Biblical scholars now have conceded to the idea that the Semitic books, like *Genesis*, are indeed the product of a far more ancient Mesopotamian literary influence. "God," the creator of existence, is found alone and everywhere at once, a *"primordial sea"* washing through an *"infinite abyss."* Samuel Kramer summarizes in his *Sumerian Mythology*—

> *"First was the primeval sea.* Nothing concerning the origin or creation of the primeval sea has as yet been discovered in the available Sumerian texts, and the indications are that the Sumerian sages looked upon the primeval sea as a kind of first cause and prime mover."

In the Babylonian *Enuma Elis* "Epic of Creation," ABZU (or APSU) is the first name given, and to it the trait of "primeval," or else the "one who was from the beginning." This persona is later passed on to the local sun by later philosophers and mythographers. In the rendering from our companion title, *"Necronomicon: The Anunnaki Bible,"* we read—

And the primeval APSU, who birthed them,
And CHAOS—TIAMAT, the Ancient One,
Mother to them all.

And from the bastardized version from the Simon "*Necronomicon*"—

And naught existed but the Seas of ABSU,
the Ancient One,
And MUMMU TIAMAT,
the Ancient One, who bore them all.

Where TIAMAT is listed with ABZU ("*and their waters were as one*"), MUMMU is introduced to us in some versions as a "counselor" or "vizier"—a messenger for the pair. The "Epic" continues, informing us that that the other "Divine Couples" were called into being and/or created. Yet, on some other tablets, the word MUMMU or NAMMU is attributed to an *Anunnaki goddess*, a "pantheistic personification" of a humanoid deity synonymous with abstract cosmic role of TIAMAT. Kramer goes on to illustrate this—

> "The goddess Nammu, written with the ideogram for 'sea' is described as 'the life-mother, who gave birth to heaven and earth' [*ti-ama-tu-an-ki*] (or *ama-palil-u-tu-dingir-sar-sar-ra-ke-ne*, 'the mother, the ancestress who have birth to all the gods'). Heaven and Earth were therefore conceived by the Sumerians as the created products of the primeval sea."

Opening lines of the "*Epic of Creation*" confirm these beings existed "*before the heavens and earth were named,*" meaning before material existence were divided into an ordered existence—for in the beginning was All-as-One, and even in the first creative expression, "*their waters were as one.*" The first progression or motion of the creative force was to manifest its "every-thing-ness" and "no-thing-ness"—the all-encompassing universe—distinguished on cuneiform tablets by uniting the most basic Sumerian words for "heaven" and "earth," or else, AN and KI. Literally: "heaven-earth," the Sumerians understood AN-KI to mean "universe"—the entirety of the *cosmos*, both "seen" and "unseen."

These powers are called forth to bare witness and offer aid to every charm and prayer of Mesopotamian magic and religion—

Spirit of the Heavens, Remember!
Spirit of the Earth, Remember!

— 0 —
: TIAMAT :
THE PRIMEVAL DRAGON

The first creature spawned from out of the abyss—the *Cosmic Dragon*—to whom the Sumerians would give no less a title than: "Mother of All Creation." In Hebrew, the word is "*tehom*," meaning "the deep" or "primordial sea," by which this force receives recognition in the Semitic *Genesis*. In an infinite universe not yet manifest, the "*primeval dragon*"—TIAMAT—is the "*first cause*" made by the Absolute, the first fragmentation from wholeness and oneness into existence—the "Law of ALL" put in motion.

In most ancient mythology, the *primeval dragon* is personified as the "Mother of All Creation." This force, identifiably female, is credited with creation of the other "*gods*," including all corporeal spirits visible on earth in ancient times as the "*Anunnaki*." This belief found its way into modern "New Age" theories explaining physical aspects of the *gods* as "reptilian" in nature, descended from a "Great Cosmic Dragon." By definition, all existences fall under this "*Cosmic Law*"—all existences are extensions of the same "*Universal Agent*."

The essence of wholeness (or duality in wholeness) is represented in the Mesopotamian pantheon as "divine unions" or couples. Both the male and female aspects are seen as reflections of as one—though like the physical sexes manifest of man, they are divided for our interpretation as being "god" and "goddess." Depending on the tablet sources, the deeds and attributes of one are often placed on the other, demonstrating that the full qualities are complete only when paired. For this reason, early scholars examining the Creation tablets mistook ABZU (*the Abyss*) as literal "consort" of TIAMAT. But after *his* "death," in the Babylonian account, her husband-partner is listed as KINGU.

Let us be clear, however, that more than ABZU, KINGU or any other primordial name listed on pre-Anunnaki lists of "rulership" in heaven, it is the *primeval dragon*—called "TIAMAT"—that is attributed all active ability of creation in the Universe. As the primal force or "prime mover" of a physical existence that came out of the *Abyss*, our first "deity" (if we are to call it such) is not only a dragon, but female, and her consort is given the more passive role for the act of creation. Under the epitaph of "*Nammu*," "*Mammu*," "*Mummu*," "*Mammi*" or "*Mami*" (of which was later assimilated into the Babylonian goddess ARURU, among others), she is the "Creator Goddess" and "Mother of All Mortal Life," offering up her blood (or "sand from her beaches") to be mixed with the "Breath of ENLIL" and "Waters of ENKI" for the creation of human life on earth.

The "name" of MUMMU is actually evoked in Babylonian magic—the "Grimoire of Marduk" or "Book of Fifty Names"—derived from the seventh tablet of the *Enuma Elis*. The thirty-fourth name listed is "MUMMU," who as we have said, is sometimes confused with TIAMAT, but is instead her "vizier" or "chief-minister"—the "active messenger principle." From the "Mardukite" perspective, all aspects of the Fifty Names are attributed to the power of MARDUK in *Babylon*—

> "...the power given to Marduk to fashion the universe from the flesh of TIAMAT offers wisdom concerning the condition of life before the creation, and the nature of the structures of the Four Pillars whereupon the Heavens rest."

This active principle—MUMMU—is described both as the "Creator of the Universe" and also the "Guardian to the Gate to the Outside," but is not originally a "power" of MARDUK, by Sumerian standards. Based on what we know concerning Babylonian adaptations of earlier Sumerian literature, the "Fifty Names" adopted by Marduk in their tradition were really names of the fifty preexisting "*Anunnaki gods*," some of which are actually mentioned in the *Enuma Elis*, playing active roles during the infamous "war in heaven." It is equally possible, on a cosmological level, that these names reflect some fifty "primary elements" composing the *cosmos* at its material inception. The Babylonian "*Epic*" describes the turbulent formation of earth and humans from "star-stuff" using symbolism of a violent battle between MARDUK and TIAMAT. Michanowsky queries in "*Once and Future Star*"—

> "The great riddle is why the primordial sea, which according to Sumerian belief, brought forth the world around us without conflict or confrontation, had suddenly been recast [in Chaldeo-Babylonian literature] in the image of a vicious demon mother who had to be denounced as a menace to law and order and then cruelly destroyed."

With the rise of later generations of gods, a theme of unseating or dethroning the positions of the original and most ancient pantheon took hold. This dualistic viewpoint is most obvious during the Babylonian era, including later Assyrian offshoots. We see the first militant acknowledgment of a generational gap between the "younger" and "elder" pantheons in the "*Enuma Elis*," where the "elders" are either demonized as "evil," removed from the system entirely, or given only passing mention. Compared to earlier Sumerian beliefs, this dualism would seem artificial, created for the sole purpose of elevating the position of the younger pantheon, observed in Babylon, as the supreme forces in the local universe and thereby usurping their ancestors. What could not be done physically was accomplished in a manner that ruling classes have used since the dawn of history: the very alteration of said *history*.

Lore of this rebellion is found in post-Sumerian religious and mystical doctrines that identify with a "good versus evil" motif. We see it in the foundations of nearly all later traditions. From Babylon it spread east to Persia and west to Egypt, where its oldest forms are drawn as antagonistic moral dogmas held by Chaldeo-Babylonians, Egyptians and Zoroastrians. The Semitic traditions also inherited this "dualism," as reflected today in contemporary forms of Islam, Judaism and Christianity—all of which are strongly rooted in opposition and polar worldviews. This is found nowhere in ancient Sumer and seems to attach itself later on to the *Primeval Dragon* icon. It is, perhaps, only loosely based on the "Destruction of KUR," understood by modern Sumeriologists only in relation to other known pantheons, as Kramer does—

> "...the monstrous creature which at least in a certain sense corresponds to the Babylonian goddess Tiamat, the Hebrew Leviathan and perhaps the Greek Typhon."

In the more widely known version of the Mesopotamian "Epic of Creation" [translated fully in "*Necronomicon: The Anunnaki Bible*"] we are given an amazing account of how the patron of Babylon—MARDUK—fights and destroys an "evil dragon," TIAMAT. We are spared no gruesome details of the bloody massacre awaiting her, finalized by an execution-styled beheading. We can see parallels of "*god-kings*" rivaling Chaos-Dragons in many later mythologies. However, on the most ancient tablets of Mesopotamia, this is a dramatic "cosmological" event. After TIAMAT is slain, half of her ("the head") is used to create the "*heavens*" ("AN") and the other half ("the body") is used to create the "*earth*" ("KI")—or, "AN-KI," the manifested universe. Some "astrophysical" interpretations of these tablets inspire belief that the epic describes a "collision theory" for the local solar system, particularly concerning formation of earth and moon.

We must assume that the philosophical minds that so carefully devised the Chaldeo-Babylonian system (which became so important for the Egyptians and other mystical and Semitic cultures) never fathomed that the tablets of their Sumerian ancestors, sometimes predating them by thousands of years, would ever be recovered. It seemed that for a time, evidence for Sumerian civilization did disappear from human consciousness, replaced instead by the *Genesis* offered by Babylonians and later derived Semitic lore. In fact, they were using the same written writing system, the same pantheon, and many of the same cosmological concepts under varying guises. "Superimposition" at a literary level appeared seamless.

It was not until the late 1800's that "Assyriologists" realized that some of the tablets and artifacts excavated from the Middle East were pre-Semitic—from before the *Akkadians*. It is now clear that "proper" formation and order of the primordial universe was adjusted to meet political and spiritual needs of a tribal people rapidly turned metropolitan, raising the position of their local deity to support the famous and widespread influence of *Babylon*. In this case, the "elder gods" or "ancient ones" are overridden by the "younger gods"—those most most accessible in all global mythologies, usually representing planets of the local solar system in every instance.

Putting the physical cosmology of ABZU and TIAMAT aside—as the *Infinity of Nothing* and the *Prime Cause*—the emphasis of the current discourse is primarily on the pantheistic applications to Sumerian *Anunnaki* lore. It is difficult to determine if this "War in Heaven" among sentient "*gods*" did actually take place or if it was only written about later as propaganda to blot out the significance and contribution of their ancestors. Although not necessarily a moral facet, TIAMAT directly represents the *first existence*—the first separation of wholeness from the All-Source. This, in itself, generates a belief for many, in a "fall from grace" or "removal from the Source"—what is really at the heart of all dualism in global religions. This is most obvious in Gnostic lore—which views all physical existence as "evil," contrast to purely non-material "Godly" or spiritual existence.

If realizing that we occupy physical bodies in separation, removed from "God" directly, we can understand how the human psyche might demonize the form "first removed" as the cause of our own fragmentation. Our ability in explaining this awareness on various "levels" in no way condones behaviors of the younger generation of *gods*. But they too, must have experienced the same philosophic and spiritual devastation of this realization—and at an understandably higher degree of comprehension.

Dualistic conflict of "forces" in the universe are a necessary property of its existence in movement, but it is not necessarily subject to the "moral dualism" that humans identify with. Forces are constantly working with and against once another to keep "the organized universe" the way it is—and continually moving to the way it will be. Without this, there is only the static and "Infinite Nothing" existence of the original state of ALL, which we cannot even inhabit and still be separated as a being of *Self*. Thus, the real "division" is essentially what is visible and what is not visible (from "human" perspective)—for the infinitude we inhabit contains everything and nothing can not exist. In Sumerian mythology, this is observed in the union or bond of "heaven-earth" (AN-KI) as a singular aspect; as a dual aspect, the seen and unseen aspects of reality; and as a zero aspect, still encompassed in and of the abyssal nothingness. Sumerians depicted this abstract form as a "*mountain*," the physical "bond" between "heaven" and "earth." *Ziggurats* were built as a reflection of the same.

We have previously mentioned the "Destruction of KUR" in passing. Not only does the word KUR mean "mountain," but it appears in the only significant "dragon-slaying" example from pre-Mardukite Sumerian literature. This time, however, KUR is not a cthonic abyssal water-based dragon, but is instead deep in the earth, in the mountain—or in a very literal sense, the mountain (earth) itself. There are three available Sumerian versions of this tablet cycle, each successively more recent in its origination, as the characters change.

Kramer conveniently paraphrases the three versions—

> "The first involves the water-god Enki, whose closest parallel among the Greeks is Poseidon. The hero of the second is Ninurta, the prototype for the Babylon god Marduk when playing the role of 'hero of the gods' in the Babylonian Epic of Creation. In the third, Inanna, counterpart of the Semitic Ishtar, plays the leading role. In all three versions, however, the monster being destroyed is termed KUR."

KUR is an obscure enigma for the prehistoric Sumerian pantheistic worldview, which is otherwise orderly and peaceful. Only later with increased human population did disharmony arise, wrought by new traditions of "evil sorcerers" commanding chaotic "demons" of plague and pestilence. But these expressions are merely accelerated entropy in motion—the opposite of growth and nurture. They do not seem to correlate with a dualistic nature of "good versus evil" applied to our lore of the archetypal primeval dragon. This force only appears chaotic due to its infinite expressions of "change" and "birth"—like the amoral explosive emission of life from seed or egg. Some esoteric texts render TIAMAT as the "Ancient of Days." In the Chaldeo-Babylonian kabbalistic system—also called the *Ladder of Lights*—a mystic confronts TIAMAT ladder as the "Dweller on the Threshold" or "Guardian of the Gate to the Outside"—as a representation of the "Fear of the Unknown" that blocks progress. In other traditions of magic, it is KHORONZON, the "Dragon of Chaos" encountered in the dimensional ascent of astral pathwork.

Modern mystical encounters with this energy may prove challenging for some who hold onto the more animated depictions of a primeval "Dragon of Chaos." This current of power is rather subtle (or gentle) like the waves of the sea, but they can just as easily turn turbulent when perturbed. Anthropomorphic manifestations and astral encounters with a personification of TIAMAT generally reflect her "reptilian" form as a sleek black dragon. Rarely she may assume a more human form, almost resembling Semitic lore of *"Lilith,"* but always female, and usually with black hair. In *Babylon*, The Tiamat Gate is essentially the *"Gate to the Outside,"* which is to say in more esoterically acceptable terms, the *"Gate to the Abyss."*

— I —
: ANU :
KINGSHIP IN HEAVEN

Literature from the Sumerian tradition—cuneiform tablets unearthed during the last century—reveals that the Anunnaki system is the original archetypal "Olympian" pantheon of deities copied and pasted onto diverse cultures for thousands of years. The Anunnaki were originally assigned to twelve positions in the cosmos forming a celestial sphere around the earth (later yielding lore of the "zodiac") and to twelve bodies of our local solar system (ten planets, plus the sun and moon). Prior to the "Ammonite" fascination with the local Sun, best observed among the Egyptians and other solar-cults, it was this collective star-system (or "pantheon") that the ancients deemed the "Rulers of Fate" and "Keepers of the Sacred Cycles on Earth"—the cosmic order of the organized universe.

"Ancient Ones" from Sumerian prehistory—ABZU, TIAMAT, LAHAMU, &tc.—are given brief mention in cuneiform literature, but are viewed as more abstract or metaphysical properties of creation, not accessibly appropriate as traditional deities. We have shown in other chapters how such forces could be seen as the primordial essence of the "All-Source" being first made manifest. But the Sumerians also viewed these active properties as materializing in their own personified "All-Father"—ANU—a figurehead for the hierarchical pantheon. These traits or energetic currents of primordial forces are assimilated by successively "younger gods" as they are elevated to higher roles in the hierarchy.

The genealogy given in the *Enuma Elis* "Epic of Creation" depicts ANSAR (or *Anshar*) and KISAR (*Kishar*) as father and mother of AN ("ANU" in Chaldeo-Babylonian). ANU, in turn, is credited as father of both the I.GI.GI—a legion of "celestial spirits" who "watch" and "see"—and the AN.UN.NA.KI (or Anunna-Ki, sometimes spelled "Anunna-Ge" by early Sumeriologists)—a pantheon of "gods" who *"decree the fates of earth."*

The names ANSAR and KISAR are most coherently translated as "heaven-zone" and "earth-zone" respectively. "SAR" means "cycle" or "the round of" in *Babylonian* language. If we adhere to this defined cosmology, their division as separate and then unity as wholeness is the progenitive spark producing an archetypal lineage of distinct and sentient gods born directly from the "omni-dimension," first known to itself only as the Abyss, then separated by the Primordial Waters and then finally condensed and separated as "heaven" and "earth." Some folk have put forth the suggestion that the *Anunnaki* actually entered our earthly "time-space" from another dimension or star-system.

Most cuneiform tablets are written very "matter-of-factly," almost reminiscent of "technical writing." Their authors felt no need to "validate" or "prove" the existence of the *Anunnaki* any further—just as we today write our own events and history as "statements" that are fundamentally understood within the context of our culture. Naturally, the oldest surviving Sumerian accounts of the "creation of the universe" are sparse and badly fractured. References to AN ("ANU") specifically, are few in number when compared to his later and more active children. While the actually name and power is frequently called upon, very few tablets are dedicated ANU specifically. Rather than petitions for aid, they are often "hymns" of praise, as reflected in this seven-line cuneiform tablet fragment, translated by L.W. King—

1. *siptu bilu sur-bu-[u]...*
   "Mighty Lord..."
2. *ilu-Anim sur-bu-[u]...*
   "ANU, Might Lord..."
3. *ilu sami-i...*
   "God of the Sky..."
4. *ilu-Anim ilu sami-[i]...*
   "ANU, god of the Sky..."
5. *pa-sir u-mi...*
   "Loosener of the Day..."
6. *ilu-Anim pa-[sir u-mi]...*
   "ANU, Loosener of the Day..."
7. *pa-sir sunati...*
   "Interpreter of Dreams..."

As we see in more popular interpretations from the last century, academic scholars have filled in many cracks of these broken tablets with the lore presented in post-Sumerian periods. The farther away from the original simplicity of the tradition that we get, however, the more strongly the Semitic influences and those of Zoroastrian dualism are incorporated. Again, academicians have often employed the reverse engineering method of working backwards from more familiar (and relatively more recent) systems in which to interpret antiquated and more obscure ones. This is purely fallacious, especially given what we commonly know regarding the degradation of information transmission (communication) over time.

It is sometimes difficult to separate the interpretation of ANU's position without conjuring up lore connected to his offspring. Many tablet authors began their sagas and incantations with some kind of unifying genesis to support why such and such happened or where such a such draws their power from, like the following, translated by Kramer—

After heaven had been moved away from the earth,
After earth had been separated from the heavens,
After the name of man had been fixed;
After AN had carried off heaven,

After ENLIL had carried off earth,
After ERESHKIGAL had been carried off into KUR as its prize...

Following sequential logic of the above passage, unity of creation fractured into dual existence of "heaven" and "earth," which were then separated from one another. In this ancient Sumerian version, AN "carries" off heaven, becoming responsible for the organization and order of heaven, and his son ENLIL is left to oversee work concerning physical existence on Earth. [And in this instance, "KUR" is used synonymously as "*Underworld.*"] The later Assyrio-Babylonian or "*Mardukite*" versions attribute more of these responsibilities to the lineage of ANU's *other* son, ENKI (or EA) and his son, MARDUK—figures receiving little attention in the purely Sumerian sources, also for political reasons.

The position of ANU in the Sumerian pantheon is as an undisputed "*Father in Heaven,*" who acts as the supreme "progenitor" or "father of the gods" from his place as the "King of the Local Universe." The "*House of Anu*" (the traditional "heaven" or "abode of the gods") is sometimes written as UR.ANU or "*Uranus*" (from the Greek "*Ouranos*"). His most sacred place of "worship" on earth was in the city of Uruk at the temple of E.ANNA—also translated to mean "*House of Anu.*" The number of his rank is sixty—the number of cosmic perfection, or "whole value," in Mesopotamian mathematics—similar to our "100," but expressed in their entire mathematical system in a manner similar to our own retention of their division of a *whole hour* by *sixty* minutes, not *one-hundred.*

Later Mesopotamian traditions viewed ANU in a similar manner as the abstract Babylonian expression of ILU. He became the "Lofty One" or "Supreme God Most High" in the pantheon, a remote, distant and indiscriminate All-Father much more representative of the "Heavenly Father" that Jesus alluded to in the *New Testament* then that of the *Old Testament* God of the Hebrew. Solidity of his personification becomes increasingly faint in descending traditions, and though within his power, he rarely intervenes or makes an appearance to the "earth" world of gods and men. His main function in the pantheon is as the "Father" of the gods, who are then mainly left to deal with material universe on their own accord.

> When first the gods were [like] men on earth,
> Settling on the bond-heaven-earth,
> ANU decreed the *Anunnaki* would come forth...
> —*Tablet A, "Necronomicon: The Anunnaki Bible"*

Few incantation tablets (or "prayers") invoke the powers of Anu directly. The heavenly force is perceived as too vast to be channeled directly by successors and to degrade it to anything more accessible would be to compromise the nature of what is represented. In Semitic traditions, the role of Kingship in Heaven is equated to the full extent of power that keeps the universe in motion, contained in an "unspeakable" and "unknowable" name (the "Tetragrammaton" in modern Hebrew-based mysticism—YHVH). It is more common for the magician or priest to evoke a subsidiary deity from the "pantheon" ("*divine lineage*") to invoke the names known to them rather than pursue methods of Egypto-Hermetic cryptomancy to divine and compel spirits against their will using "true-names." In the Chaldeo-Babylonian tradition, the names of ENKI and MARDUK are evoked to speak the names—later traditions often used them to replace obscure and "secret" names altogether. As Lenormant explains—

> "True indeed there was a supreme name which possessed the power of commanding the gods and extracting from them a perfect obedience, but that name remained the inviolable secret of *Hea* or EA—ENKI. In exceptionally grave cases the magician besought *Hea*, through the mediator *Silik-mulu-khi*—MARDUK, to pronounce the solemn word in order to re-establish order in the world and restrain [temper] the powers of the abyss. But the enchanter did not know that name, and could not in consequence introduce it into his formulae... he could not obtain or make use of it, he only requested the god who knew it to employ it, without endeavoring to penetrate the terrible secret himself."

Though appearing infrequently in prayers, one example of a magician's "Grand Invocation" addressing ANU appears as a protective incantation at times and then also a hymn of adoration.

From *Tablet-P* in "*Necronomicon: The Anunnaki Bible*"—

> ANU, King in Heaven, Eternal Prince of the *Anunnaki*,
> Whose words are the rule over the *Assembly of Anunnaki*,
> Lord of the unequaled Horned Crown [*of the Starry Heavens*],
> You who can travel anywhere in the universe on a raging storm;
> You who stands in the royal chamber admired as a king.
> The ears of the IGIGI are directed to hear your pure words,
> The *Assembly of Anunnaki* gather around thee in reverence.
> At your command the *Anunnaki* bow to salute;
> At your command the wind blows
> And food and drink are abundant;
> At your command the angry demons
> Turn back to their habitations.
> May all the gods of Heaven and Earth
> Pray at your *Altar of Offering;*
> And may the kings of dragonblood on Earth
> Give you heavy tribute.
> May men pray to you daily and offer sacrifices and adoration.
> May your heart be at rest and may you ever reign righteously.
> To the city of *n.* show your abundant favor and grace."

The no less significant role of royal "Lady of Heaven" does not appear to be fixed individual. Several female entities are listed at one time or another as consorts of ANU. The title-name ANTU is usually given, and much like the name of her husband, her title is more of a role than a proper name (and carries a numerological designation of 55). The "Queen of the Starry Heavens" traditionally rules the cosmos with her partner, but the exact personality associated often it differs by tradition. In one interpretation of the Sumerian *Genesis*, the consort of ANU (or AN) is originally listed as KIA (or KI), the *"Spirit of the Earth"* that "ENLIL separated from the heavens." In a rather romantic Babylonian version, ANU bestows the name of I.STAR or *Ishtar* (Sumerian: IN.ANNA)—meaning "beloved of ANU"—onto his grand-daughter, a title-position sharing that of his own consort.

If one were to assume that the ANShAR and KIShAR [parents to AN and KI] represents the pure spirit of *zi-an-na* (spirit of heaven) and *zi-ki-a* (spirit of earth) in the mystical incantations, then we might assume, since not otherwise addressed from the pantheon, that the addendum nearly always added in prayer to the forces (after those just mentioned) are to the manifested "first forms" of both heaven and earth as *zi-dingir-anna* and *zi-dingir-kia*. KANPA is translated from our original *"Mardukite"* cypher manuscript [*Tablet-I* in *"Necronomicon: The Anunnaki Bible"*] as either "mark well," "remember" or "conjure" based on references from the last two centuries of revived tablet literature. DINGIR is given as "first-god" or "mighty spirit power."

> *Zi Anna Kanpa*
> *Zi Kia Kanpa*
> *Zi Dingir Anna Kanpa*
> *Zi Dingir Kia Kanpa*

Mystical experiences by modern Mardukites with ANU directly have been limited. Given the archetypal sage-hermit motif attached to him, it can be difficult for the mind to comprehend the force of his "shade." Though it may be the result of poetic licensing, his image of a "King in Heaven" seated on a throne in the clouds can be traced back even to these first spiritual philosophies. Whether or not this is taken literally by an initiate, the fact remains that according to tradition, ANU leads the original *Anunnaki* pantheon of Sumerian "elder gods" to earth. For meditations and modern ritual, his sign is often traced as a singular ray (or arrow bolt) descending downward.

— II —
: ENLIL :
DEMIURGE OF CREATION

After the realms of "heaven" and "earth" had been clearly defined, the great separation or fracture of reality ensued. In fact, the ancient texts quite literally describe this as the heavens (the eternal all-encompassing space aspect) being "moved away" from earth (the solidified concentrated matter aspect). This is generally followed by a reiteration—ancient tablet writers seemed to enjoy poetic redundancy—of earth being "separated" from heaven, as evident even in the *"Song of the Hoe"*—

> *ENLIL, who will make the human seed of the Land*
> *come forth from the Earth,*
> *and not only did he hasten to separate heaven from earth,*
> *and hasten to separate earth from heaven...*

It is customary for Sumerian tablet cycles to begin with the formation of creation and the genealogy of their pantheon even if it did little to contribute to the actual context of the saga. It is possible that this literary mechanism added credibility epic characters and places set against the background reality of creation, and of course, the *"gods."* The act may also have been a result of devotion and respect. In parody we might equate this to—*"First the universe was created, then the gods were born and then such and such happened."* Many of these early tablet cycles include introductory lines that reinforce an understanding of Sumerian cosmogony and spirituality. Judging by the frequency of their appearance, there is little doubt concerning the identity of at least two primary gods of the Sumerian tradition, the first of which we have already mentioned—

> *After AN had carried off heaven*
> *After EN.LIL had carried off earth*

EN.LIL—["EN"=*Lord*, "LIL"=*Air, Breath, Lofty*]—was the national god of ancient Sumer, essentially displacing (the more distant and less materially concerned) AN (ANU) as head of the "Elder Gods" on Earth. ENLIL's offspring include the majority of the "younger generation" of *"Enlilite"* gods. His "patron-city" or "sacred-city" was Nippur [NI.IBRU], named for the geographic center (or "mid-section") of Mesopotamia, where his temple-ziggurat was built—the E.KUR, "House [like a] Mountain"—the four corners of which represented the quarters of the material world. His consort is also ranked high in the pantheon—NIN.LIL (or in the later form as *Belit*)—a title given to SUD. ENLIL's position is designated 50 —"Command of Physical Space"—in Mesopotamian numerology, and the correlating rank for NINLIL is 45.

More than simply a "Ruler" of the Organized Universe, ENLIL's position and title displays him as the original representation of the "*demiurge*" of creation—best known as a "Gnostic" concept, borrowed from Greek and Hermetic Schools—meaning the "designer of the material world" (a title also attributed to ENKI as *Ptah*, "the Engineer," in Egypt). But, ENLIL did not personally attend to each and every aspect of this material world. His commanding position enabled him to focus on *management*—*overseeing* other "spirits," "angels" or Anunnaki that were led down from the "heavens" (or, out of an inter-dimensional existence, *&tc.*) to forge a concrete physical existence on "earth"—like adding paint to a once blank canvas of infinite potentiality. For this, he is the *first* attributed with the power of the number "Fifty," also the number of names (of "angelic" war-generals, bio-engineers, *&tc.*) found on the seventh tablet of the *Enuma Elis*. This is the same "Power of Fifty" attributed as the "names" of MARDUK in *Babylon*, used to elevate him to the position of "Enlil-ship" [*ell-ilu'tu*] or "Kingship" of the material world.

ENLIL's first responsibility in the "new world" was assigning tasks and official designations, some of which seem to have been competed for. Sumerian tablets account for one such instance, introducing us to the forerunners of Cain and Abel, two brothers who rival against one another in an agricultural contest to win the favor of ENLIL and the position of "farmer-god." Given the peaceful "swords to plow-shares" described in literature from ENLIL's *Sumer*, no bloody murder is described at the climax of the story, but instead a simple judgment by "wise father ENLIL," which is mutually agreed upon by the the two brothers (Emesh and Enten) and they toast one another with libations! The translation by Kramer—

> ENLIL answers *Emesh* and *Enten*:
> "The life-producing water of all the lands,
> *Enten* is its 'knower,'
> As farmer of the gods he has produced everything.
> *Emesh*, my son,
> How dost thou compare thyself with *Enten*, thy brother?"
> The exalted word of ENLIL whose meaning is profound,
> The decision taken, is unalterable,
> Who dares transgress it?
> *Emesh* bent the knees before *Enten*,
> Into his house he brought . . . [offerings],
> The wine of the grape and the date.
> *Emesh* presents *Enten* with gold, silver and lapis lazuli.
> In brotherhood and friendship,
> Happily, they pour out libations,
> Together to act wisely and well, they determined.
> In the struggle between *Emesh* and *Enten*,
> *Enten*, the steadfast farmer of the gods,
> Having proved greater than *Emesh* . . .
> . . . O father ENLIL, praise!

Another ancient Sumerian epic—the Creation of the Pickax—describes the agricultural tool ENLIL gave to the "primitive workers" to aid their field-work, keep the populations fed, but also to ensure appropriate offerings of sustenance were being brought to the temple-ziggurats. As a deity in the Anunnaki Pantheon, ENLIL's role and identity is best reflected in the purely Sumerian texts. He is transferred to the Babylonians as IL.LIL, to the Assyrians as *Bel* (the original one, anyway) and he even becomes the prototype of the Semitic Yahweh (EL in Hebrew). None of these later forms actually preserve the definitions of his position among the original Sumerians—"Lord God" of the Judeo-Christian *Old* Testament, as Lenormant confirms—

> "*Hea* [EA–ENKI] passed into the Chaldeo-Babylonian [system] without changing his office, character or name, (but) *mul.ge.lal* [ENLIL], on the contrary, bore no resemblance in the documents of the magical collection to [his former office] *Bel*, the demiurge and god of the organized universe,with whom he was afterward assimilated, in order to find him an equivalent in the religion by which he was adopted."

An apparent dualism later emerged in Mesopotamia, not only between lineages of ENLIL and ENKI, but also among political campaigns of the "younger" gods. This "philosophical conflict" is all too easily passed off in people's mind's as "light versus dark" and "good versus evil." But, what we are really given is a "division of reality"—still a singular reality mind you, but divided in consciousness. The *demiurge* of creation is later viewed as the "separator" of the *physical* from the *spiritual* and thus, by mortal standards, the one responsible for manifesting a world of form that is experienced in pain and suffering. While this is not directly reflected in Sumerian spirituality, the evolution of this esoteric tradition later in Mesopotamia (and elsewhere) accompanied a significant analytical (or critical) thought process with subsequent generations. Each had the opportunity to assimilate and revise the system. Sandra Tabitha Cicero summarizes this development—

> "*Ellil* was a friend to humanity. However, like the Hebrew god *Yahweh*, his anger could be aroused by human wickedness It was *Ellil* who advocated that gods unleash the Great Flood upon humanity in the story of *Atra-Asis*. The unpleasant task of enforcing human calamities decreed by the gods fell upon *Ellil*. Because of this he has usually been accused of being a severe and destructive deity by later scholars. By contrast, Sumerian hymns venerate him as a gracious father figure who protects his people."

Kramer translates an example of such a hymn from the "ENLIL in the E.KUR" tablets—

ENLIL,
Whose command is far reaching;
Whose "word" is lofty and holy;
Whose pronouncement is unchangeable;
Who decrees destinies unto the distant future. . .
The Gods of Earth bow down willingly before him;
The Heavenly gods who are on Earth
Humble themselves before him;
They stand faithfully, according to instructions.
Lord who knows the destiny of The Land,
Trustworthy in his calling;
ENLIL, who knows the destiny of Sumer,
Trustworthy in his calling;
Father ENLIL,
Lord of all the lands;
Father ENLIL,
Lord of the Rightful Command;
Father ENLIL,
Shepherd of the Black-Headed Ones. . .
From the Mountain of Sunrise
To the Mountain of Sunset,
There is no other Lord in the land;
You alone are King.

We see very little of this venerated mention of ENLIL specifically within Mardukite literature of the Chaldeo-Babylonian paradigm. When he is respectfully mentioned, it is usually only in the context of the fundamental "Supernal Trinity" [ANU–ENLIL–ENKI] invoked at the head of some incantations. Most post-Sumerian negative attitudes toward ENLIL centrally focus on his recorded opposition to the creation of humans, and then their preservation during the *Deluge*.

Modern Mardukite experiences with the ENLIL-current are subject to self-honesty. Expectations and culturally based biases held firmly in the psyche will have a hold on any literal interpretations. But this is no less present pertaining to mystical work, which requires the magician maintain an degree of absolute purity and self-honesty if "invoking" this energy. This is the very real "god," depicted in the Judeo-Christian *Old Testament*, and is not trivial being. [In other words: weigh your heart against a feather first!] The mystical symbol most with ENLIL is a downward pointing triangle—a sign of command—possibly a literal representation of energetic flow (downward from above), or else the leadership and power of the Anunnaki "brought down" to Earth.

— III —
: ENKI :
LORD OF THIS WORLD

The spirito-mystical "Supernal Trinity" composing the most ancient pantheon is concluded with ENKI, brother of ENLIL. Anunnaki genealogy records kept by post-Sumerian civilizations emphasize that ENKI and ENLIL are actually half-brothers. Both are divine sons of ANU—the "Sky-Father"—but as royal heir to "Kingship of Heaven," ENLIL is also the son of ANTU—the "official" consort of ANU—while ENKI is born to NAMMU. [Other texts reveal ENLIL as the eldest son of KI and ENKI as the son of ANTU.]

Differing Anunnaki lineages play a more significant role among the "younger pantheon" and later dualistic interpretations, but in the original formation of Sumerian civilization, ENLIL and ENKI are actually perfect compliments to one another in the division of the material world—ENLIL as the ruler of the air and fire aspects, leaving ENKI the domains of *The Deep*: water and earth.

As the original title suggests, "ENKI" means, quite literally, "Lord of the Earth"— ["EN"=*Lord*, "KI"=*Earth*]— later known as the Babylo-Akkadian epitaph "EA," likely derived from the Sumerian ideograms for "*house*" [E] and "*water*" [A]. This water alignment is suggested further by names for his temple-ziggurat, built in the southern city of *Eridu* [or *e-ri-dug*—"Home of the Mighty"] known as both E.ENGURRA ("House of Lower Waters") or E.ABZU ("House in the Depths").

Where ENLIL is given a certain authority over the organization of "space" and management of other deities, ENKI is given control over more "worldly matters" on Earth, and carries the designation of 40. [NINKI or DAMKINA, his consort, is 35.] On a cosmological level, ENLIL represents the active spirit manifest in the world as a whole—or the *why*—separated from the "heavens." By comparison, ENKI represents more passive elements, but clearly the more condensed "material" ones solidified on Earth, and also the spirit of *how* things exist—"hidden" internal engineering, program or "natural design."

> "Here in *Eridu* there was a local deity by the name of *Ea*, and the aspiring theologians of that city, eager to make him the supreme deity of the land, pressed forward the claim for lordship over the earth, and in an effort to insure his claim applied to him the epithet *en-ki*, 'Lord of the Earth,' which then became his Sumerian name. But though *Enki*, after some centuries, did succeed in displacing *Ninhursag* [*Belit, &tc.*] and taking third place in the pantheon, he failed to topple *Enlil* from his supremacy and had to settle and had

to settle for second best, becoming an *Enlil-banda*, a kind of 'Junior Enlil.' Like other gods he had to travel to *Nippur* to obtain *Enlil*'s blessing after he had built his his temple *E'engurra* in *Eridu*; he had to fill the *Ekur* of *Nippur* with gifts and possessions so that *Enlil* might rejoice with him; though he had charge of the *Me* controlling the cosmos and all civilized life, he had to admit that these were turned over to him by a generous and more powerful *Enlil*."

—S.N. Kramer, *"Sumerian Mythology"*

A Babylonian priest, Berossus, in the 13th Century B.C. wrote an epic dedicated to the figure *"Oannes,"* a later name for ENKI. Here, the author describes ENKI establishing the material infrastructure of human civilization, depicted as the "sublime fish god" [*fish = scales = reptilian*] who rises from his ocean home (or in this case, the Erythian Sea near the Persian Gulf) to teach men the crafts necessary for their developmental arts and sciences to flourish. ENKI is known in *Babylon* as the "Arch-Magus," father of the occult arts and divination, who passed this knowledge to his son, MARDUK. He served as a patron to those who chose spells and esoteric sciences for combat and is sometimes credited with the original knowledge of magical warfare in the local universe. In some Chaldeo-Babylonian mystical texts, ENKI is referred to as "Our Father" in much the same way that the Sumerians referred to ENLIL and, of course, the much later generation of Mardukites (in the neo-Babylonian period) referred to MARDUK.

Similar properties of ENKI described in the *Oannes* saga also appear in another tablet cycle, of Babylonian origin—"The World Order of Enki." [Given on Tablet-K of *"Necronomicon: The Anunnaki Bible."*] Here, the cuneiform author sets out to list the many innovations of ENKI, some of which are originally attributed to ENLIL in earlier Sumerian mythology. Since "Mardukite" Babylonian Tradition recognized MARDUK as ENKI's successor, the finale of the "World Order" tablet concerns the "passing over" of INANNA-ISHTAR for a position among ENKI's roll-call of Babylonian gods. ENKI answers INANNA by documenting implied and bestowed powers she already possesses—but elsewhere from *Babylon*, such as in *Egypt* as ISIS—

What did I keep from you?
What more could we add to you?
You were put in charge of the crook,
The serpent-staff,
The wand of shepherd-ship.
You interpret the oracular omens of battles and combats.
INANNA, you have destroyed what cannot be destroyed;
And you have conceived the inconceivable.

A duality between divine brothers—ENLIL and ENKI—played a significant role in the establishment of not only human civilization in its physical, fundamental and evolutionary aspects, but also the spiritual and religious philosophies that later emerged on the planet. To point out a widely held, but relatively recent conception (adopted by the Roman Catholic Church): "Yahwist Monotheism." This dictates everything in the universe results from a single being alone, the leader of the "*anakim*" or "*malachim*" [*Anunnaki*] appearing in the Judeo-Christian *Old Testament*. The stature of his being is held above all others who are but intermediaries in the stories.

The position in *heaven*, however, seemed too surreal for accessibility by the priests and prayers of early people, so the pantheists and materialists developed patronage toward the "Lord of the Earth"—representing the powers of the *here and now*, and the necessities and comforts of physical existence: fertility, love, wealth... these all became the domain of ENKI, whose "secondary" birthright in heaven seems to have transferred to a "primary" one on Earth.

Trailing in the wake of the gods was their sense of "supremacy"—an embedded pyramid-structure turned innate—first used to govern themselves and then left to chosen figureheads and bloodlines on Earth thereafter. This struggle for world domination and power essentially crippled contemporary humans, who simply do not carry enough awakened genetic and intellectual faculties to properly execute such ventures. What efforts have been done in the past, both political and physically combative, have been performed by individuals who actually take these matters very seriously. An investigation into the occult beliefs of the Third Reich will reveal that the Nazis actually adopted very similar beliefs concerning the origins of their race and even connected the Germanic interpretation of the Anunnaki pantheon to the Kings of "*Atlantis*"—meaning they believed in higher minds remaining from a prior civilization.

While it does not condone the actions taken, this fueling belief in "god-blood" and "alien-technologies," however trite it might seem to some readers, allowed Nazi Germany to nearly take over the world. We can see some evidence of this "self-righteousness" throughout history. Many folk have felt as if they were direct physical counterparts acting on behalf of their personal god. The very bloodlines of these gods were believed to flow in the veins of certain kings and temple-priests other lineages, thus representing the power attributed to "heaven," but on "earth." Long before World War II, the Christian Crusades of the Middle Ages were fueled by the same belief—that their god had come in human form and bestowed a decree that "on earth as it is in heaven." Suddenly, "Lord of the Earth" became a highly coveted position, for it was now (from an earthly perspective) just as good as that in "heaven" and more immediately accessible to the people. Titles, icons, powers and attributes of the gods, growing more and more distant in memory with the passage of time, were passed on to specific "royal" and "magical" families—the living embodiments of the "old gods" for Earth's future.

As the age of gods passed into a time of men, the harmonic dance of grace and beauty once driving a unified Sumer was gone forever, lost to the variegated mix of analytical minds. "Lordship" passed to the humans—peace and love all but disappeared from the earth. Rivalry for supremacy in a post-Sumerian world of monotheism resulted in many "tribal" wars in the names of their personal deities.

The essence of brotherly love that formed the very systems of physical existence (now being fought over), became separated as "moral dualism"—there was only room for one god now, and the fight for such once political, turned bloody. Of the two brothers, "God" would be associated with all that was orderly, and a "Satan" figure to represent all that was disharmonious. The force of Chaos, first overcome by the Sumerian gods and later tempered to balance creation was now viewed as a source of "evil" and the personification of such was passed onto a "devil," but originally the *brother* of "God."

As Semitic peoples near Mesopotamia developed their own traditions, beneficial properties of the Anunnaki, coupled with the personality of ENLIL, became the figure *Yahweh*. [Yet, the name "EA" clearly has a more similar sound to "*Ia*" or "*Jah*."] The role of *antithesis* was given to ENKI. Although this association of "evil" and "discordance" is hardly justified, the ENKI current energetically assimilated this in consciousness—quite simply, he was now the "rebel" among the "elder" pantheon, and it is not surprising that his most famous offspring—MARDUK—would be a "rebel" son. As a patron, when all of the other gods have said "no," he is the one that might (almost always) say "yes." This is demonstrated not only in the infamous Flood epic (when he went against the will of the *Anunnaki* to secretly preserve his own bloodline), but in any instance when even the gods are petitioning for favors that the others "won't touch."

For magical purposes, many of ENKI's attributes have since been passed onto the younger generation but in times of extreme need, ENKI seems to be unparalleled in the ability to "get things done – no matter how." He also seems to allot special time and care for INANNA-ISHTAR in several tablet-cycles, including her own infamous epic—"*The Descent.*" But while rebellious, he was no shady rogue: he was a scientist and philosopher above all else, and the greatest of both among the Anunnaki (additionally a child of ANU), his skills and bloodline were prized in the "*fashioning*" of the material world—a title he carried in the Egyptian pantheon as PTAH, the "*designer.*"

The mystical symbol used by modern Mardukites to represent the energetic current of ENKI closely resembles a pyramid or mountain—the KUR. Direction of energy suggested by the symbol is "upward." Movement pools at the surface (or building below the surface of the earth) and is directed towards the sky. It is the exact (polar) opposite to the sign used to represent ENLIL. Both ENKI and MARDUK are, at times, depicted as residing within a chamber, pyramid or inhabiting the "*Deep*" [Abyss], all of which are indicative of an "underverse" operating beneath the surface of consciousness and (visible) material reality.

Modern "Mardukite" encounters with the ENKI-current have been "strong" due to increased modern inclinations of those interested in magic and esoteric sciences. His archetype remains among the most potent alive in systems today. Where the magician is ever seeking the essence of creation or the "words" by which it can be known, in Mardukite tradition, ENKI is considered that very "*word*" of god made manifest and set free to evolve and unfold in the physical world. Fragments of this spiritual understanding are still maintained in the Semitic Kabbalah—lore which is, even in itself, derived from the original Sumerian Anunnaki "*Tree of Life*."

— 1 —

: NANNA-SIN :

THE MOON – "WHO SHINES FOR"

NANNA is listed on Sumerian tablets as eldest of the "younger pantheon," first-born son of ENLIL and NINLIL. His patron city was Ur, where he maintained primary residence at his temple-ziggurat—E.GISH.NU.GAL or *E.Gishshirgal* —"Home of the Throne Seed." He also made frequent appearances in the northern city of *Harran*, where his *E-Khulkhul* temple stood. NANNA is named for the bright light of the moon gracing the night sky earth, referenced in one epithet as NAM.RA.SIT (*Namrasit*)—"Who Shines Forth." His consort—NINGAL or *Nikkal* —is the "Great Lady of the Moon," goddess of divination and dreams, the most commonly accessible human "thresholds" to interact with the "*Other.*"

NANNA is credited for prosperity of the ancient Sumerian city of Ur. The early metropolis represented the pure idealism of Sumer as brought to high esteem, long before its legendary destruction from the wrath of ANU and ENLIL. Our ancestors preserved details of these events on cuneiform tablet cycles called "lamentations." The famous "Lamentation for the Destruction of Ur" is written from the perspective of the "*Lady of Ur,*" or NINGAL—the consort of NANNA. She relays the sudden sadness that befell the land the day of the "storm" neared. She sheds tears before AN and ENLIL that her city "not be destroyed." But, the assembly of Anunnaki remained *unmoved*—

> *AN never bent toward those words,*
> *And ENLIL never with, 'It is pleasing, so be it!'*
> *[To] soothe my heart.*

ENLIL called down the "storm of heaven" using the "fire-god"—GIBIL—to assist. The gods "left the city ruin and the dead were piled up." In despair, NANNA appeals to his father ENLIL, asking him to lift this heavy curse and restore the city to its former glory. He speaks of the greatness of Sumer and the love for the people toward their gods. But ENLIL is firm, as Thorkild Jacobsen translates—

> *O noble NANNA, be thou (concerned) about yourself,*
> *What truck [sway] have you with tears?*
> *There is no revoking a verdict,*
> *A decree of the assembly,*
> *A command of AN and ENLIL is not known to ever have changed.*
> *Ur was verily granted kingship – an (ever)lasting [eternal] reign,*
> *It was not granted.*
> *You, my NANNA, do not worry. Leave your city!*

This is an abrupt introduction for our character description of NANNA, but it demonstrates the immediate unrest ensuing in Sumer when control is passed to the "younger generation" of *Anunnaki*. The specific reason for the "Destruction of Ur" is conveniently concealed from the tablet saga. Zecharia Sitchin has put forth an interesting theory: Since NANNA is also known as SU.EN (or "SIN" of later Chaldeo-Babylonian literature), it is possible that he either shares an identity with, or lord over, ZU, a "creature" that once stole the "Tablets of Destiny" from ENLIL's possession. That name could self-implicate NANNA as "Lord Zu," or, again, be a reference to control of a serpent-being as EN.ZU—"Lord of the Zu." The name SU.EN might be associated with ZU.EN, or else EN.ZU. The typical persona of NANNA as a "gentle father" doesn't appear to match this allocation. It would, however, provide some explanation for why retributive annihilation came down through the leading pantheon, as city-states started to be governed by the "younger generation."

NANNA is given the number 30, correlating to the lunar month—the word "month" is named for the "moon"—and his consort is 25. As eldest of the "zonei" or "younger pantheon" given control of the local solar-system, NANNA was given the most prominent celestial domain in conjunction with the earth—the Moon. NANNA is actually a shortened version of the more complete designation— Nannar, "Light of the Full Moon." As the form of "SU.EN," he is actually representating the crescent or partial moon, and the Babylonians adopted the name "SIN" from this. The other name "ENZU" is derived from his Akkadian epithet— EN.I.ZUNA—so, the theory mentioned previously is not without some basis.

In Sumerian mythology the moon is held in high regard. Although the primordial chaos cosmologically brings forth the Sun into existence first, as illustrated in nearly all other solar-oriented "Mardukite" systems, the Sumerian Anunnaki chose to represent the Moon with NANNA, a firstborn son of ENLIL and NINLIL, who with his consort NINGAL, give birth to both INANNA-ISHTAR (*Venus*) and SHAMMASH (*the Sun*). It is here, as before concerning cosmology represented by pantheistic beings, that we must keep a distinction between the *Anunnaki* "younger pantheon" and the literal "celestial bodies" they are named for. Ancient tablets are quite obscure in this regard, because cuneiform signs for the planets and deities are identical. The people, themselves, were not confused by this, as we might be today when looking back at the tablet records with modern eyes. In one sense, NANNA is described as the "light of the moon." But certainly NANNA, the *Anunnaki King of Ur*, was present in his city while simultaneously the light of the moon bore down on the earth at night. The association is clearly a reference to a more ancient cosmogony reflected in Sumerian beliefs: the day was born from the night, and not that the moon literally gave birth to the sun-star of our local system.

As a mystical "energetic current," the *Moon Gate* is traditionally the first that an individual will encounter when crossing the veils of material existence to the veils of negative existence, or the *Abyss*. Ancient Anunnaki denizens of the universe established "veils of existence" when the "material order" was brought or willed into being. They stationed the "younger pantheon" as *Guardians of the Gates*. The moon, as we might expect, is quite vibrant but gently passive and tranquil. NIN-GAL—the "Lady of the Moon"—receives many of the lunar attributes in later systems—If not by name, then by gender, as most esoteric revivals that do not truly use the combined-counterpart paradigm of a male-god and female-goddess as one essence, usually reduce celestial divinity to polar dualism: a 'masculine' "solar" god and the 'feminine' "lunar" goddess. But, *Sumer*, unlike *Babylon*, was a primarily *lunar*-oriented tradition with subsequent emphasis on the *Sun* and *Venus*. Ancient astronomical symbols found on the oldest Sumerian art are frequently representations of the *Sun-star*, *Venus* and, in the case of NANNA-SIN and NINGAL—the *lunar crescent*—which, when depicted above a deity, was often called the "horns."

* * *

Once an "initiate" passes the "*Earth Gate*" in search of cosmic truth on the path of "Ascension" up the *Ladder of Lights*, the lunar current is generally the first one accessed. This is because the "Moon Gate" is most closely aligned to the familiar astral and dreams "level" of enchantment and fantasy that many access—even unknowingly. As an elementary aspect of all mystical work, the "first degree" is where a seeker is able to actually realize in consciousness that they are not only their physical body. Actualization of this basic principle is not taken for granted, since many do not achieve even this "degree" of spiritual evolution (or "unfoldment") during their lifetime. Yet, in contemporary "new age" traditions, many initiates too often simply stop here, even when they believe they have moved on from it, remaining enamored with the infinite potentiality of appearances able to manifest through dissolution of the first veil. Instruction from "*Necronomicon: The Anunnaki Bible*" reiterates—

> "The first 'level' encountered (aside from the extraordinarily subtle
> or blatantly physical 'Earth Gate') in the system is the Moon Gate,
> which ironically, is the embodiment of the 'common' astral plane
> or dreamscape that many have already enjoyed lucid access to
> without even formal occult education."

The formal "magical path" has a starting point. A magician working through the "veils of existence" connected to and surround us as the systematic design that keeps the material world "flowing." But, be warned: the opiate-like tranquility that the mind can experience at this level is quite addicting, and with good reason—it was designed to hold fast the unbidden minds that drifted into it, whether intentionally or otherwise. It is a veil meant to be so glamorous that the mere access of it immediately conjures illusions of ascension and enlightenment that are not yet truly manifest. The elation of initially breaking free of the physical chains can bring such ecstasy that the naïve neophyte actually believes they "have arrived," when really they have just begun. As the enigmatic editor Simon warns—

"It is the initiatory plane, and it is here, at the Lunar Gate, that the vast majority of occultists lose their way, forever. For most people, it is the repository of every inspirational, delusional, ghostly, spiritual, hallucinogenic event that has ever transpired in their lives. The temptation of this plane is to become one of those vague, ethereal types one finds spouting psychobabble on morning talk shows. Many channelers are victims of staying too long on the Lunar level; astral puppets who never progress beyond sitting on the ventriloquist's lap. . . instead of mastering this plane, it has become *their* master; every breeze that brushes across their faces become a caress from beyond, every news item a direct message from an entity on Alpha Centauri. Avoid them like the very plague . . ."

The astral "shade-forms" of NANNA-SIN and NINGAL reflect an archetypal otherworldly "fairy" king and queen—born of heaven, ruling on earth and embodied in the lunar threshold connecting between the two. Most mystics encountering these personas have seen them in their elderly form, but the blue-hued moonlight radiating from their skin gives off so much beauty that we tend to think of them as ageless. The color associated with the moon is silver and the essence and symbol attributed to NANNA is the royal wand or scepter of lapis lazuli.

When the moon was not visible, it was thought to be dwelling in the underworld. When a lunar eclipse occurred, Sumerian tradition described the moon battling wicked demons before reappearing. This more active face of the lunar current is not often tapped by most "magical" tables of correspondence. We can find similar beliefs concerning the disappearance-and-appearance of the *Sun* and *Moon* throughout mythologies of many ancient cultures. The Mardukite "Invocation of the Nanna Gate" given in "*Necronomicon: The Anunnaki Bible*" very closely resembles an incantation found from the tablet-series known to scholars as: "Prayers of the Lifting of the Hand."—the entire basis for L.W. King's "*Babylonian Magic & Sorcery.*" The original prayer is as follows—

O SIN! O NANNAR! Mighty One . . . [among the gods]
  siptu ilu-SIN ilu-NANNARU ru-su-bu u- . . .

O SIN, who art unique, thou that brightens . . . [the heavens]
  ilu-SIN id-dis-su-u, mu-nam-mir . . .

That gives light unto the nations . . . [over the four lands]
  sa-ki-in na-mir-ti a-na nisi- . . .

That unto the black-headed race art favorable . . . [god to your people]
  ana nisi sal-mat kakkadu us-su-ru sa- . . .

Bright is thy light, in heaven . . . [like fire]
nam-rat urru-ka ina sami-i . . .

Brilliant is thy torch, like the fire-god . . . [burning brightly]
sar-hat di-pa-ra-ka, kima ilu-GIBIL . . .

Thy brightness fills the broad earth!
ma-lu-u nam-ri-ru-ka irsita(ta) rapasta

The brightness of the nations he gathers, in thy sight . . .
sar-ha nisi uk-ta-sa-ra ana a-ma-ri-ka

O ANU of the sky, whose purpose no man learns!
ilu-A-nim sami-i sa la i-lam-ma-du mi-lik-su ma-

Overwhelming is thy light like the Sun-god, thy first born!
su-tu-rat urru-ka kima ilu-SAMAS bu-uk-ri-

Before thy face the great gods bow down, the fate of the world is set
before thee!
kan-su pani-ka ilani rabuti purus matati sakin(in) ina pani-ka

In the evil of an eclipse of the Moon which in X month on X day, has
taken place,
ina lumin ilu-atali ilu-SIN sa ina arhi pulani umi pulani isakna(na)

In the evil of the powers, of the portents not good, which are in my
palace and my land,
lumun idati iti.mis limniti la tabati sa ina ikalli-ya u mati-ya ibasa-a

The great gods beseech thee and thou gives counsel!
ilani rabuti i-sal-lu-ka-ma tanadin(in) mil-ka

They take their stand, all of them, they petition at thy feet!
izzizu pu-hur-su-nu us-ta-mu-u ina sapli-ka

O SIN, glorious one of IKUR! They beseech thee and thou givest the
oracle of the gods!
ilu-SIN su-pu-u sa I.KUR i-sal-lu-ka-ma ta-mit ilani tanadin(in)

The end of the month is the day of thy oracle, the decision of the
great gods;
bubbulum u-um ta-mit-ti-ka pi-ris-ti ilani rabuti

The thirtieth day is thy festival, a day of prayer to thy divinity!
umu XXX-kan i-sin-na-ka u-um ta-sil-ti ilu-ti-[ka]

O God of the New Moon, in might unrivaled whose purpose no
man learns,
ilu-Namrasit i-muk la sa-na-an sa la i-lam-ma-du mi-lik-su ma- . . .

I have poured thee a libation of the night (with) wailing, I have offered
thee (with) shouts of joy a drink offering of . . . [*type of drink*]
as-ruk-ka si-rik musi lallartu ak-ki-ka ri-is-ta-a si-kar . . .

I am bowed down! I have taken my stand! I have sought for thee!
kan-sa-ku az-za-az a-si-ka ka- . . .

Do thou set favor and righteousness upon me!
ka-sa dum-ki u mi-sa-ri sukun(un) ili-[ya]

May my god and my goddess, who for long have been angry with me,
ili-ya u ilu-istari sa is-tu u-um ma-du-ti is-bu-su

In righteousness and justice deal graciously with me! Let my way be
favorable, with joy . . .
ina kit-ti u misari lis-li-mu itti-ya ur-hi lid-mi-ik had-is ni- . . .

And ZA.GAR, the god of dreams hath sent,
u-ma-'-ir-ma ilu-ZA.GAR ilu sa sunati

In the night season . . . [cleanse me of] my sin, my iniquity may . . .
[it be absolved]
ina sat musi Kab.mis ar-ni-ya lu-us-mi sir-ti lu-ta

For ever may I bow myself in humility before thee!
ana da-ra-ti lud-lul da-li-li-[ka]

— 2 —
: NABU-TUTU :
MERCURY – "WHO SPEAKS FOR"

Mythologists and mythographers often associate the Sumerian "Lord of the Tree of Life" [*Ningishzidda*] with the Egyptian deity THOTH—the archetypal Mercurial current shared by Hermes, Merlyn, Ogmios, &*tc.*, but the most iconic *Anunnaki* "messenger of the gods" more appropriately corresponds to a more "Mardukite" character in Babylon. If one carefully considers the "divine" occupation of this lineage in Egypt, there is evidence for a "third party" of gods, apart from strict ENLIL and ENKI lineages, that most strongly influenced the Babylonian system in preference over the former Sumerian one.

In the Babylonian tradition, the "Apollonian herald of the mercurial current" among the "younger pantheon" is the *heir-son* of MARDUK and SARPANIT—the patrons of *Babylon*. This role is attributed to NABU—also *Nebo* or *Nabak* in Semitic language—meaning "spokes-person." He shares residence at the temple-ziggurat of the city of *Borsippa* [*Birs-i-Nimrud*] (approximately ten miles from *Babylon*) with his consort, TASMIT—*Teshmet(um)* or *Tashmitu*. In addition to managing the national school and temple of scribe-priests, NABU and TESMITU made annual visits to *Babylon* for the celebration of the "New Year" [A.KI.TI/ Akitu] festival held on the spring equinox.

NABU is the original "scribe of the gods," a patron deity of wisdom-knowledge and writing, inventor of the "reed-stylus" (*pen*), and the first truly refined form of cuneiform—distinguishing the stylus-script of *Babylon* from early pictograms of *Sumer*. His energetic current carries an affinity to Mercury—communication, divination and the air element. Semitic-Hebrew language incorporated the word "*Nabih*," meaning "prophet." NABU is effectively the "Prophet of MARDUK" and a "Messianic Son" for Mardukites of *Babylon*. Priests and kings evoked his name in the consecration of their libraries, asking him to bless their hands when writing tablets and also to curse those who might steal or desecrate the libraries. The intellectual nature of NABU and his unusual manner of psychological warfare are echoed on an ancient basalt tablet called the "*Caillou Michaux*," named for the archaeologist excavating it for the French National Museum—

> *May Nebo, the supreme intelligence,*
> *overwhelm him with affliction and terror,*
> *and lastly may he hurry him into incurable despair.*

When the ancient Mardukites were losing ground to the Enlilite-Yahwists during the "Old Testament" biblical era, NABU was charged with the task of maintaining a tradition of MARDUK's followers near *Babylon* and in *Egypt*. Several neo-

Babylonian Kings of the time period are also given related names in patronage and reverence to the younger pantheon of the Mardukites, such as: Nabuna'id ("*Nabu is exalted*"), Nabupolassar ("*Nabu protects his son*") and, of course, Nebochadnezzar ("*Nabu preserve my first-born son*"), just to name a few. For the Mardukites, NABU represented a "messianic prophet"—born of a "Heavenly King" (MARDUK) and ENKI's special hybrid offspring (SARPANIT), long before Semitic and Christian lore existed to record such things, but undoubtedly served as a source of inspiration to later traditions.

Although an old soul—a steward of all wisdom of the gods, responsible for recording their "movements" in a Mesopotamian version of the "Book of Life" called the "Tablets of Destiny"—NABU is actually a relatively young "deity"of the Mardukite Anunnaki pantheon. His other epithet—TU.TU—appears notably as the thirteenth name of the "*Enuma Elis*" (on *Tablet-F* of "*Necronomicon: The Anunnaki Bible*") that MARDUK assumed during the "*Epic of Creation.*" The "name" of this "power" is transferred to NABU in the Babylonian Mardukite Tradition, although the governing domain is quite ambiguous:

> *NABU-TUTU,*
> *He who created them anew,*
> *And should their wants be pure,*
> *Then they are satisfied.*

This intellectual riddle described the very function NABU serves—the recording of life, history, people... and *gods*—the "eye-of-the-beholder" concerning descendants of the Anunnaki, origins of humanity and courses of life and existence—were now NABU's to hold. He could create them anew, give anyone a new face and past and therefore future. He was the "*Voice of God*"—the "Metatron"—the messenger frequency of the highest brought to the lowest and an intermediary between.

Mesopotamian religion held a firm inseparable view of male-female aspects in divinity, but the relationship between NABU and TASMIT is truly complimentary —where NABU is a projector of communication, TASMIT is a receiver. She is the Babylonian "goddess of hearing," the one who listens to the prayers—often sought as a "*transmit*" to her husband and the other deities. A powerful incantation to "*Tesmitu*" is found on the reverse-side of the prayer-tablet referenced previously for NANNA. The incantation is specifically a petition to "remove sickness and enchantments caused by an eclipse of the Moon"—

> O Lady TASMITU!
> I __ , son of ___ and ___ ,
> Whose god is ___ , whose goddess is ___ ,
> In the evil of an eclipse of the Moon,
> Which in ___ month on ___ day has taken place,
> In the evil of the powers, of the portents,
> Evil and not good, which are in my palace and my land,

I have turned towards thee!
I have established thee!
Listen to the incantation!
Before NABU thy spouse, the lord, the prince,
The firstborn son of E.SAGILA, intercede for me!
May he hearken to my cry at the word of thy mouth;
May he remove my sighing;
May he learn of my supplication!
At his mighty word,
May god and goddess deal graciously with me!
May the sickness of my body be torn away;
May the groaning of my flesh be consumed!
May the consumption of my muscles be removed!
May the poisons that are upon me be loosened!
May the ban be torn away and the curse consumed!
May the Anunnaki come forth and demand justice!
At thy command, may mercy be established!
May god and king ordain favor
At thy mighty command that is not altered,
And thy true mercy that changes not,
O Lady TASMITU!

* * *

Perhaps one of the most fundamental lessons to be learned via the mercurial current is *discernment*. Once the veils have been penetrated and the spectral showers of vast images and illusions are tapped on the lunar level, *temperance* is required. Where the *Moon Gate* provides access to the "magical path," the *Mercury Gate* (*"Nabu Gate"*) is the beginning of the "mystical path," concerning the "Secret Doctrines of the Cosmos" contained on the "Tablets of Destiny." The half-truths of worldly glamours must be stripped away. True knowledge must replace all misinformation.

Our intellect causes psychosomatic effects on our emotional state, which in turn influences our behavior. The methodology suggested taps undefiled unconditioned stimuli from beyond the veil of tangible experiential based memory data. This ensures a higher rate of success generating transcendental moments of *"true gnosis,"* and not merely trivial enlightenment-delusions of false-light. The *light on the screen* can be made to be seen for what it is.

The "weight of wisdom" often causes NABU to appear relatively much older than he actually is. His number is twelve, a fundamental value to the *"sexagesimal"* (Base-60) mathematics of Mesopotamia, a method still used today to denote time, angles, locales and speed of travel across any space. His traditional color is blue, and in addition to the "stylus," NABU is represented by the double-barred cross, also visible in his cuneiform sign.

The usual Mardukite invocation made to NABU (in "*Necronomicon: The Anunnaki Bible*") resonates strongly with the twenty-second prayer of the "*Lifting of the Hand*" cuneiform tablet series—

O hero, prince, first-born of MARDUK!
siptu rubu asaridu bu-kur ilu-MARDUK

O prudent ruler, offspring of ZARPANITU!
Massu-u i-ti-ip-su i-lit-ti ilu-ZARPANITU

O NABU, bearer of the Tablet of Destiny of the gods, Director of the
  E.SAGILA!
Ilu-NABU na-as duppu si-mat ilani a-sir E.SAG.ILA

Lord of E.ZIDA, Shadow of Borsippa,
bil E.ZID.DA su-lul duru-BORSIPPA-ki

Darling of IA [ENKI], Giver of Life,
na-ram ilu-IA ka-i-su balatu

Prince of Babylon, Protector of the Living,
asarid BAB.ILI na-si-ru na-pis-ti

Lofty Lord of the hill-dwelling, fortress of the nations, Lord of temples!
ilu du-ul da-ad-mi kar misi bil is-ri-ti

Thy name is the word in the mouth of the people, O sedu ["spirit"]
zi-kir-ka ina pi nisi su.dub.ba ilu-sidu

O son of the mighty prince MARDUK, in thy mouth is justice!
mar rubi rabi ilu-MARDUK ina pi-ka kit-ti

In thy illustrious name, at the command of thy mighty godhead,
ina si-ik-ri-ka kabti ina ki-bit ilu-ti-ka rabiti(ti)

I ___, the son of ___ and ___, who am smitten with disease, thy servant,
ana-ku pulanu apil pulani mar-su sum-ru-su arad-ka

Whom the hand of the demon and breath of the wicked [spirit has seized],
sa kat utukki-ma imat bur.ru.da nam-kil-lu-ni-ma nal-susu-ni

May I live, may I be perfect [with your wisdom]
lu-ub-lut lu-us-lim-ma . . . gub.bu.du luksud(ud)

Set justice in my mouth!
su-us-kin kit-ti ina pi-ya

[Kindle] mercy in my heart!
  sup-si-ka damikti(ti) ina libbi-ya

May the Anunnaki return and be established! May they command mercy!
  ti-i-ru u an.nu.na.ki man-za-[za lik-bu-u] damikti(ti)

May my god stand at my right hand!
  li-iz-ziz [ili-ya] ina imni-ya

May my goddess stand at my left hand!
  li-iz-ziz [ilu-istari-ya] ina sumili-ya

May the favorable sidu [spirit], the favorable lamassu [guardian] be
      with me!
  ilu-sidu damiktu ilu-lamassu damiktu . . . -kis illi-ya

— 3 —
: INANNA-ISHTAR :
VENUS – "QUEEN OF HEAVEN"

Known in *Egypt* as "Goddess of Ten-Thousand Names," a unique position of *"Queenship of Heaven"* is reserved by one of the "younger pantheon" in both Sumerian and later Chaldeo-Babylonian systems. Daughter of NANNA and NINGAL—the Sumerian aspects of the Moon—and twin to SHAMMASH (the Sun), this title of high esteem is passed on to a young "Lady of the Stars"— unequaled in beauty and cunning use of divine politics. In ancient Sumer, she is introduced in the original cuneiform literature as IN.ANNA—"Lady of ANU" and *"Queen of Heaven."*

INANNA quickly rises in status as the "archetypal goddess" on earth. She simultaneously represents both a "goddess of love" and "goddess of war," granting her significant domain in the physical world. As a result, she was favored among the masses adoring her for her influence. She is originally given a numeric designation of 5 in Sumer—but in Mardukite Babylon she receives 15, replacing the position held by NINMAH (*Ninhursag*) from the elder pantheon. She remains a primary goddess in Assyro-Babylonian tradition, with the name I.STAR (or *Ishtar*)—"The Goddess"—*istari* being the Akkadian word for "goddess." Her traditional/ceremonial color is sometimes white (INANNA) and sometimes light-green (*Venus*).

Assyrian art frequently depicts INANNA-ISHTAR with wings. The same winged form is visible on her Egyptian form as ISIS. Clearly she was a goddess of the aerial world, not only the *"Anunit-(um)"* ("ANU's Beloved"), but literally a "queen" of the skies, stars or heavens. Mythological cycles describe seven objects connected to ISHTAR for her aerial travels. Similarly, there are seven garments and ornaments removed during her "Descent to the Underworld." It is quite likely that these items are related to her position as "Lady of the Stars" or "Queen of Heaven"—power symbols associated with this role. Mystical revivalists consider this symbolism significant for modern ritual magic activities reviving Mesopotamian-based ceremonialism (and the Underworld), but perhaps they have an even greater unseen esoteric relevance. In the cuneiform tablet account of ISHTAR's "Crossings to the Underworld" (given as *Tablet-C* in *"Necronomicon: The Anunnaki Bible"*), these objects are referred to as seven "Divine Decrees" that she "fixes" to her body. They are listed as—

1. Shugurra – Starry Crown of Anu (on her head)
2. Wand of Lapis Lazuli (in her hand)
3. Necklace of Lapis Lazuli (around her neck)
4. Bag of Brilliant-Shinning-Stones (carried)
5. Gold Ring of Power (on her finger)

6. Frontlet Amulet (as a breastplate)
7. The Pala – Royal Garments (worn about her body)

Zecharia Sitchin interprets the talismans differently, describing "Seven Objects" of INANNA that were "necessary for traveling the skies"—

1. *Shu.gu.ra* – she put on her head
2. Measuring pendents – on her ears
3. Chains of small blue stones – around her neck
4. Twin stones – on her shoulders
5. A golden cylinder – in her hands
6. Straps – clasping her breast
7. *Pa.la* garment – clothed around her body

Genealogies of Sumer detail INANNA as a "fourth generation" Anunnaki figure—daughter of NANNA, born of ENLIL, son of ANU—and is therefore the "great-granddaughter" of ANU. She receives a special place in his heart, which proves beneficial in her rise to power. Even more than this, INANNA is a very actively determined personality that stops at nothing to acquire what she deems rightfully hers. If she wants it, she will take it. In the mythic cycles, this includes "decrees of heaven," "decrees of earth," "secret names of gods" and everything in between. In many ways, her post-Sumerian cult following rivaled MARDUK for supremacy in *Babylon*. She quite effectively used these powers to win an eternal loyalty from mortals in exchange for granting select worldly desires. The kings she favored, she would stand beside in battle and those she did not (or who fell out of favor) she would lend aid to the opposing side, proving that this "goddess of love" is not to be scorned.

The actual truth of how this "archetypal goddess" figure rose to high power is not so widely known. Her many names have, however, become legendary—not only in Mesopotamia as INANNA and ISHTAR, but elsewhere as *Isis, Aphrodite, Venus, Astarte, Metis, Brigit* (among countless other names)—marking her widespread appearance among many diverse cultures. Later religious misogynists could not recognize such vast power as a female form, transferring her identity to *Ashtoreth* or *Astoroth*—a leader of a demonic hierarchy of angels in the Judeo-Christian Semitic and Kabbalistic systems.

The original Sumerian tablet cycle involving INANNA and ENKI is academically called *"The Transfer of the Arts of Civilization from Eridu to Erech."* Seeking greater abundance and power for her city, INANNA travels to *Eridu*—the residence of ENKI—in pursuit of secret knowledge, holy relics and tablets of power that will enable her to achieve this. Her charm, coupled with the looseness that comes with heavy drinking, won over ENKI, who gave up some one-hundred decrees and treasures in his compromised state. These are then loaded onto her "Boat of Heaven" and transported back to *Erech*, intermittently making seven rest stops along the way.

Realizing what he's done soon after, ENKI immediately sends his counselor ISIMUD with a host of monsters in pursuit of ISHTAR, but the damage is done and she arrives safely in *Erech* with her new found "decrees" intact. We might compare this account to the acquisition of power by ISIS in *Egypt*, as deTraci Regula describes—

> "Her skill as a magician was employed when she sought to receive the sacred true name of Ra, her father in some stories. Ra was ignoring the needs of humanity and Isis resorted to a drastic act of magic, creating a small snake from the exudation of his body, which bit him. To stop the pain, Ra agreed to give Isis his most secret name, allowing her to restore balance."

A romantic patina for INANNA-ISHTAR is toned by the Romeo-and-Juliet-motif in the relationship with her consort—DAMUZI (*Dumuzi*) [Sumerian; "*the good son*"] or in Babylon, TAMMUZ "*the good shepherd.*" There are many different accounts of their courtship activities and later involvement with the Underworld. [See also *Tablet-U* from "*Necronomicon: The Anunnaki Bible.*"] One version describes how INANNA-ISHTAR was head-over-heels overtaken with DAMUZI from the start. However, another tablet series explains that at the beginning, the "shepherd-god"—DAMUZI—is rivaling with a "farmer-god" for her love and affections. Not surprisingly, DAMUZI is actually the youngest son of ENKI, and apart from MARDUK, NABU and few others, he was an "officially" acceptable spouse in the tradition of Anunnaki "succession." This was later maintained among the "younger generation" via a combination of the two lineages—in this case a daughter of ENLIL and a son of ENKI.

INANNA-ISHTAR's rise to power was by no means an arbitrary event. Its significance affected the history of the Anunnaki, but also the evolution of civilization as a whole—the politics, religious beliefs and spiritual traditions. She even maintained high recognition as a patron of Babylon. But it was not the *position* itself that changed the fate of the planet—it was, instead, the *responsibilities* that came along with it.

Anunnaki tradition held the "succession" matter as of highest importance for maintaining domain leadership. It became customary for the "younger generation" lineages of ENLIL and ENKI to commingle. For ISHTAR, it was MARDUK—heir of ENKI—that was her intended spouse. Each perfectly complimented one another as the *apex leadership* of the younger pantheon. But, neither party seemed interested in maintaining this obligation as a "team"—so, it never occurred. The role of consort was passed onto ENKI's youngest son, DUMUZI. It initially seemed that everyone agreed to this arrangement, but it resulted in fracturing the powers, creating a third party of gods. The Anunnaki lineage of ENKI *separated*—the followers of MARDUK versus worshipers of ISHTAR throughout *Sumer.*

When MARDUK retreats to *Egypt* to regain supremacy of his own "Mardukite" tradition, ISHTAR sets her sights on making the powers *there* her own as well. We can certainly see evidence for a significant influence that ISIS provides for our contemporary general understanding of *Egypt*. The "fighting" that erupts between "brothers" thereafter may be of a similar theme to what is alluded in the "farmer-god versus shepherd-god" stories (concerning ISHTAR's courtship of a mate). ISHTAR's "undying love" for DUMUZI is explicitly expressed. Quarreling among the family reaches climactic heights when DUMUZI drowns under uncertain circumstances. It is then that ISHTAR marches on MARDUK (known as "Ra" there, to the Egyptians), arriving with the Horus-Seth tribes—fracturing the pantheon in Egypt too, as Zecharia Sitchin explains:

> "The first presence of Inanna/Ishtar in Egypt is mentioned in the Edfu text dealing with the First Pyramid War. Called there Ashtoreth (her Canaanite name), she is said to have appeared on the battlefield among the advancing forces of Horus. . . as long as the fighting was only between the descendants of Enki, no one saw a particular problem in having a granddaughter of Enlil around. But after the victory of Horus, when Seth occupied lands not his, the situation changed completely: the Second Pyramid War pitched the sons and grandchildren of Enlil against the descendants of Enki."

* * *

Mystical experiences with INANNA-ISHTAR's *Venusian* energy current are prevalent throughout the ages across nearly all ancient cultures. She is favored by priests and priestesses of many esoteric and occult traditions many times over for thousands of years. As a self-made "goddess queen" of the *Heavens* and the material domains—love, lust, war, magic—her coveted position of influence is unparalleled among the pantheon. It becomes clear why her intended betrothed was MARDUK, but as they rivaled for the same side of the same coin, they really became the same side of two coins.

Although Mesopotamian literature provides a wide array of Anunnaki activity, the colorful picture portrayed in the original system is "*amoral*" or concerns a "*higher ethic*" than readily discernible in mortal life. In fact, this "*utilitarian*" ideal, for better or worse, is demonstrated by most any "higher order" of "authority," which is often mysterious to those it governed. In some form—physically and in memory—the "younger pantheon" of Anunnaki were the "gods" of earth religions for thousands of years, even preferred (in contrast to their elders) for their worldly material accessibility.

As Guardian of the *Venus Gate*, INANNA-ISHTAR is encountered on the mystic path as a moral challenge to rise above the pleasures of earth and seek a higher spiritual gratification.

Should the initiate succumb to these temptations she will undoubtedly reward such as well, but there is a strict clause to such attainment that is well known to occultists—

> *Inanna-Ishtar takes her own for her own,*
> *And that once chosen by her,*
> *No man may take another bride.*

There are no shortages of Babylonian tablets revealing prayers, rites and incantations in honor of ISHTAR. Her allied tradition in *Babylon* consists of the same offerings that priests and priestesses offered MARDUK—the sprinkling of pure waters, libations and potent beverages, fragrant oils, honey and butter with bread, with sacred woods burning as incense. The number "*seven*" frequently appears in these ancient ceremonies—it was often customary to present a food or drink offering seven times. Or, in other instances, such as the "*pure waters,*" offerings are sprinkled about the ground. Other times, vials and jars were left at an "*Altar of Offerings*" dedicated to a specific deity. Once the gods physically left, people on earth retained only memories of their existence, but the temple-priests (and their families) were continuously sustained thereafter, living on the offerings that once supported the physical existence of great Anunnaki figures.

Like the other examples, invocation-prayers to ISHTAR used by modern Mardukites are similar to those found on the "*Prayers of the Lifting of the Hand*" tablet-series from the Kuyunjik collection—

> O ISHTAR, good is thy supplication, when the spirit of thy name is
>   propitious [favorable].
> *[ilu-ISTAR] ta-a-bu su-up-pu-u-ki ki-i ki-ru-ub nis sumi-ki*

> Thy regard is prosperity, thy command is light!
> *[nap]-lu-us-ki tas-mu-u ki-bit-ki nu-u-ra*

> Have mercy on me, O ISHTAR! Command abundance!
> *rimi-nin-ni-ma ilu-ISTAR ki-bi-i na-ha-si*

> Truly pity me and take away my sighing.
> *ki-nis nap-li-si-in-ni-ma li-ki-i un-ni-ni-ya*

> . . . .
> *ir-di uz-ki is-di-hu li- . . .*

> Thy [feet or hands(?)] have I held: let me bring joy of heart!
> *sar-ta-a-ki a-hu-zu lu-bi-il tu-ub libbi- . . .*

> I have borne thy yoke: do thou give [me] consolation!
> *u-bil ap-sa-na-ki pa-sa-ha suk- . . .*

I have [held] thy head: let me enjoy success and favor!
u-ki-' kakkadu-ki li-si-ra sa-li-mu

I have protected thy splendor: let there be good fortune and prosperity!
as-sur sa-ru-ra-ki lu-u tas-mu-u u ma-ga-ru

I have sought thy light: let my brightness shine!
is-ti-'-u nam-[ri]-ir-ri-ki lim-mi-ru zi-mu-u-a

I have turned towards thy power: let there be life and peace!
as-hur bi-lut-ki [lu]-u balatu u sul-mu

Propitious be the favorable spirit who is before thee: may the *lamassu* that goes behind thee be propitious!
lu tas-lim ilu-sidu damiktu sa pa-ni-ki sa ar-ki-ki a-li-kat ilu-lammasu lu tas-lim

That which is on thy right hand, increase good fortune: that which on thy left hand, attain favor!
sa im-nu-uk-ki mis-ra-a lu-us-sip dum-ka lu-uk-su-da sa su-mi-lu-[uk-ki]

Speak and let the word be heard!
ki-bi-ma lis-si-mi zik-ri

Let the word I speak, when [spoken], be propitious!
a-mat a-kab-bu-u ki-ma a-kab-bu-u lu-u ma-ag-rat

Let health of body and joy of heart be my daily portion!
ina tu-'ub siri u hu-ud lib-bi i-tar-ri-in-ni u-mi-sam

My days prolong, life bestow: let me live, let me be perfect, let me behold thy divinity!
umi-ya ur-ri-ki ba-la-ta surki lu-ub-lut lu-us-lim-ma lu-us-tam-mar ilu-[ut-ki]

When I plan, let me attain (my purpose): Heaven be thy joy, may the Abyss hail thee!
i-ma u-sa-am-ma-ru lu-uk-su-ud samu-u hidutu-ki apsu li-ris-[ki]

May the gods of the world be favorable to thee: may the great gods delight thy heart!
ilani sa kis-sa-ti lik-ru-bu-ki ilani rabuti lib-ba-ki li-tib-[bu]

— 4 —
: SHAMMASH :
THE SUN – "SHINNING ONE"

Ancient Mesopotamian astronomers correctly depicted the *Sun* in the middle-center of the *"Ladder of Lights"*—a stream of energies connecting our physical world to the ALL via a *"bridge,"* often represented by "Celestial Bodies." Assuming the esoteric chronology that begins with the *"Earth Gate,"* the Seeker approaches Gates of local planetary systems—those relatively closer to the Earth: the *Moon*, *Mercury* and *Venus*—and then the *Sun*. According to Sumerian cosmology (and lineage tablets), the *Sun*—or more accurately, the *"sun-god"*—was a twin brother to INANNA-ISHTAR (*Venus*), the "Morning Star" born of NANNA (*the Moon*). This general course also follows with a worldview that "day was born from night" and more esoterically that "light emerges to penetrate the darkness."

The role of the *"sun-god"* as the physical and spiritual "illuminator" carried the very name given to the "face of the sun"—the Anunnaki sky-commander UTU or UDDU (Sumerian for *"shinning one"*). The same appears on cuneiform tablets in Akkadian and Chaldeo-Babylonian languages as SAMAS—often written as it is pronounced: "SHAMMASH"—and *"Babbar"* in some sources. His consort is AYA or AIA (also *"Shendira"*)—from the Akkadian for *"dawn."* Together they shared a sanctuary at *Larsa* (in Sumer); and also a temple in *Sippar* (near Babylon), where the couple eventually retired. SHAMMASH is given the Anunnaki designation of "20" and reign of the solar domain—the task of maintaining order as chief of the Anunnaki "Judges"—governing justice, law, balance and truth. [In fact, the *"Shammash"* title was used by Medieval Jewish communities to designate a person that assisted in maintaining a governing order. The name was even used later to designate a "temple servant."]

SHAMMASH—and the *Sun*—are called forth frequently with incantations from mystical and religious cuneiform tablets from the *Ancient Near East*. However, as a subordinate to many other entities in the pantheon, the system as a whole can hardly be considered "sun-worship" in the conventional sense. It might be more ac-curately described as "stellar-worship"—if we even ascribe the misunderstood word "worship" at all—as all primary *"Olympian"* deities of this tradition were either named for celestial objects, or we must assume they named the planets after themselves. We can be sure, however, that the *Sun* played a significant role in the "order" of the material world—a "conqueror of evil" (considered sleeping or bat-tling demons at night) or the "protector of travelers" by day, ceaselessly keeping watch over man's daily activities and work-life. The *Sun* clearly became a popular force for the masses to call on, as Lenormant describes—

"The sun was not one of the highest gods of the religious system which had served as a foundation for Accadian magic, his power did not approach that of the three great spirits of the zones of the universe [governed by the Supernal Trinity]. But it was just his lower rank that made him more accessible to the prayers of man; and the fact that his influence upon man and the phenomena of life was so sensibly felt, made them assign to him the office of arbiter of events and of fate; while lastly, as he dissipated darkness, and consequently was engaged in a struggle with the bad spirits, he became one of the supernatural personages to whom the magical invocations were most frequently addressed."

* * *

The "*Sun Gate*" is a significant threshold "crossing" on the mystic path. Many do not reach this far in their spiritual evolution (or "ascension process"). Many are too enamored by trappings of lower realms to reach (and survive) the self-annihilation prominent at this Gate. This veil is bright and shinning—it will surely illuminate any "darkness" within you that is still waiting to be purged, in addition to any other physical and sensation-based delights remaining from the Venusian initiation.

In the Egyptian mythic cycle associated with the *Sun*—Yes, there is "Ra," actually a representative of a "*sun behind the sun*" (even more than our local sun), but more important to our topic is the "Osirian mythos" of death and transformation—the "solar-judge" weighing the soul to measure impurity. The initiate must allow the pictures and images of their "former" programmed existence to be burned away—allow the baggage and energetic attachments of a "lower life" to be dissolved.

> "*I come in self-annihilation and the grandeur of inspiration.*"
> – William Blake

The challenge-riddle of the "*Sun Gate*" is: "all that glitters is not gold." Just as surely as the sunlight can pierce the darkness, so too is it sometimes blinding to see what is right in front of us. We must be ready, always, not caught basking in the glowing rays of the shining sun. The apex of solar power at noon reflects the heights of empires and all systems—but these too must ebb and fall in their own cyclic tides. Everything is in motion; and everything everywhere is connected together.

It is from the "*Solar Gate*" that an initiate must prepare in "self-honesty" for the forthcoming encounter with the "Annihilator" energies of NERGAL. After being given charged on the Mardukite mystic path of the "*Ladder of Lights*" by NABU at the second gate, there are many Anunnaki figures (representing lessons on the path) from those who stood against the rise of a *Mardukite Babylon*—ISHTAR, SHAMMASH and NERGAL—all of which have played a part in its abolition. Even SHAMMASH (UTU) sided with DUMUZI against MARDUK in that tablet cycle; and then later against NABU, siding with NERGAL and NINURTA in what some scholars call the "Pyramid Wars," which resulted in mass-destruction of the ancient "Middle East," leaving a resonant imprint of unrest forever on that locale.

"The Great Hymn of Shammash" is potentially the most significant mystical cuneiform tablet transcription from Mesopotamia regarding the *"sun-god."* A seeker will see that it reveres more than simply the "physical *sun*," but the "sublime light of truth" personified by the Anunnaki position held SHAMMASH (UTU). Several of the lines (particularly at the beginning and end) on the tablet cycle have worn away, but the definitive academic version, first appearing in *"Babylonian Wisdom Literature"* by W. Lambert (in 1960), remains the most complete modern translation for both mystics and scholars. The "dogma" presented reflects other Babylonian wisdom tablets, such as the "Book of the Law of Marduk" given as the *Tablet-L* series in *"Necronomicon: The Anunnaki Bible."* The hymn reads—

21. You climb to the mountains surveying the earth,
22. You suspend from the heavens the circle of the lands,
23. You care for all the peoples of the lands,
24. And everything that EA (ENKI), king of the counselors had created
        is entrusted to you.
25. Whatever has breath you shepherd without exception,
26. You are keeper in upper and lower regions.
27. Regularly and without cease you traverse the heavens,
28. Every day you pass over the broad earth . . .
33. Shepherd of that beneath, keeper of that above,
34. You, SHAMMASH, direct, you are the light of everything.
35. You never fail to cross the wide expanse of sea,
36. The depth of which the IGIGI know not.
37. SHAMMASH, your glare reaches down to the abyss
38. So that monsters of the deep behold your light . . .
45. Among all the IGIGI there is none who toils but you,
46. None who is supreme like you in the whole pantheon of gods.
47. At your rising the gods of the land assemble,
48. Your fierce glare covers the land.
49. Of all the lands of varied speech,
50. You know their plans, you scan their way.
51. The whole of mankind bows to you,
52. SHAMMASH, the universe longs for your light.
88. A man who covets his neighbor's wife
89. Will . . . before his appointed day.
90. A nasty snare is prepared for him . . .
91. Your weapon will strike at him, and there will be none to save him.
92. His father will not stand for his defense,
93. And at the judge's command his brothers will not plead.
94. He will be caught in a copper trap that he did not foresee.
95. You destroy the horns of a scheming villain,

96. A zealous . . . his foundations are undermined.
97. You give the unscrupulous judge experience fetters,
98. Him who accepts a present and yet lets justice miscarry, you make bear his punishment.
99. As for him who declines a present but nevertheless takes the part of the weak,
100. It is pleasing to SHAMMASH, and he will prolong his life . . .
124. The progeny of evil-doers will fail.
125. Those whose mouth says "No," their case is before you.
126. In a moment you discern what they say;
127. You hear and examine them; you determine the lawsuit of the wronged.
128. Every single person is entrusted to your hands;
129. You manage their omens; that which is perplexing you make plain.
130. You observe, SHAMMASH, prayer, supplication, and benediction,
131. Obeisance, kneeling, ritual murmurs, and prostration.
132. The feeble man calls you from the hollow of his mouth,
133. The humble, the weak, the afflicted, the poor,
134. She whose son is captive constantly and unceasingly confronts you.
135. He whose family is remote, whose city is distant,
136. The shepherd amid the terror of the steppe confronts you,
137. The herdsman in warfare, the keeper of sheep among enemies.
138. SHAMMASH, there confronts you the caravan, those journeying in fear,
139. The traveling merchant, the agent who is carrying capital.
140. SHAMMASH there confronts you the fisherman with his net,
141. The hunter, the bowman who drives the game,
142. With his bird net the fowler confronts you.
143. The prowling thief, the enemy of SHAMMASH,
144. The marauder along the tracks of the steppe confronts you.
145. The roving dead, the vagrant soul,
146. They confront you, SHAMMASH, and you hear all.
147. You do not obstruct those that confront you. . .
148. For my sake, SHAMMASH, do not curse them!
149. You grant revelations, SHAMMASH, to the families of men,
150. Your harsh face and fierce light you give to them . . .
154. The heavens are not enough as the vessel into which you gaze,
155. The sum of the lands is inadequate as a seer's bowl . . .
159. You deliver people surrounded by mighty waves,
160. In return you receive their pure, clear libations . . .
165. They in their reverence laud the mention of you,
166. And worship your majesty for ever . . .
174. Which are the mountains not clothed with your beams?
175. Which are the regions not warmed by the brightness of your light?
176. Brightener of gloom, Illuminator of darkness,
177. Dispeller of darkness, Illuminator of the broad earth . . .

Invoking the "solar force"—whether SHAMMASH or by another name—is common not only to the mysticism of Sumer and Babylon, but throughout esoteric history. The name "SAMAS" is called upon no less than a dozen times throughout the "Maqlu" (Maklu) cuneiform tablet series (given as *Tablets–M1-9* in "*Necronomicon: The Anunnaki Bible*"). In many instances from the *Maqlu series*, SHAMMASH is called alongside MARDUK to destroy the wickedness and evil-doers in the world. Although SHAMMASH later sided against MARDUK, the name is invoked in Mardukite literature of the "*Ladder of Lights*" (or "*Stairway to the Stars*"), following the original Babylonian ideal of "unification," even if only to maintain control of the entire Anunnaki pantheon under MARDUK—just as we see with the inclusion of many other Anunnaki names in the Babylonian paradigm. The "Law-Code" attributed to *King Hammurabi*, is dedicated to a "divine" knowledge transmission from both SHAMMASH and MARDUK—

> *By the command of SAMAS*
> *The Judge of Heaven and Earth,*
> *May truth and righteousness reign supreme*
> *Throughout the lands.*
> *Let those who read these words have a pure heart*
> *And pray to MARDUK, my Lord,*
> *And SARPANIT, my Lady, his consort.*
> *By the decree of SAMAS,*
> *I have been given my Eternal Legacy.*
> *If a forthcoming ruler should read my words*
> *And not corrupt the law,*
> *Then may SAMAS extend the length of his reign on Earth,*
> *And he shall ever reign in righteousness over his subjects.*

The mystical incantation of the "*Shammash Gate*" was strongly influenced by the previously given hymn. No prayer dedicated solely to SHAMMASH (or the "sun-god") was found in the *Kuyunjik* collection. Instead, like the *Maqlu* series, the Babylonian invocations in that series are directed to both SAMAS and MARDUK. One interesting example, however, is a badly fractured tablet-incantation from "*Prayers of the Lifting of the Hand*" – *Tablet 53*, to be used "against the evils attending an eclipse of the moon." It is directed to EA (ENKI), SHAMMASH and MARDUK. Leonard King offers the following description of the eclipse tablet—

> "No. 53 (*K 3859 + Sm. 383*) preserves the bottom portion of a tab-let and contains a prayer to *Ia, Samas,* and *Marduk,* of which both the beginning and end are missing. The supplicant states that he is praying after an eclipse of the Moon and he implores these three deities to rescue him from the clutches of a spectre, by whom he is continually haunted. What remains of the *Obverse* commences as follows:—

O arbiter of the world, Marduk, the mighty, the lord of Itura!
abkal kis-sa-ti ilu-Marduk sal-ba-[bu bil] I.TURRA

O EA, Samas, and Marduk deliver me,
ilu-I-a ilu-Samas u ilu-Marduk ya-a-si ru-sa-nim-ma

And through your mercy let me come to prosperity!
ina an-ni-ku-nu i-sa-ru-tu lul-lik

O Samas, the spectre that striketh fear, that for many days
ilu-Samas ikimmu mu-pal-li-hi sa is-tu u-mi ma-'-du-ti

Has been bound on my back, and is not loosed,
arki-ya rak-su-ma la muppatiru(ru)

Through the whole hath . . . me, through the whole night hath stricken
    me with terror!
ina kal u-mi iksus-an-ni ina kal musi up-ta-na-lah-an-ni

The supplicant then describes the ways in which he is tormented by the spectre, who defiles him and attacks his face, his eyes, his back, his flesh and his whole body. On the reverse of the tablet he recounts to *Samas* how he has tried to appease and to restrain his tormentor. Apparently his efforts have met with no success for he now turns to the *Sun-god* for relief, which he prays he may receive through his mighty command that is not altered, and through the command of *Marduk*, the arbiter of the gods."

— 5 —
: NERGAL & ERESHKIGAL :
MARS & THE SHADOWLANDS

The legendary *"Underdark"* or *"Realm of the dead"* has been all too colorfully—or perhaps mono-chromatically—depicted by mythographers as merely a pile a rotting bodies, an infinite swamp, or with the arrival of dualism –a hellfire of intolerable damnation. Cuneiform tablet descriptions of the *"Shadowlands"*—or the "Great Below"—are indeed conceivably "darker" in the spectrum of mortal comprehension. Traversing the Celestial Spheres on the *"Ladder of Lights,"* we are confronted with a "Dweller of the Threshold" to our "Dark Night of the Soul"—and ultimately a spiritual rebirth—rising as a "phoenix"... as a *"god,"* readied for access to the (next) *"Marduk Gate."* Figures of the *"Underworld zonei"* play important functions and roles affecting human consciousness regarding death, entropy and physical cycles observed in the cosmos. Any "good" or "bad" is based strictly on human sentiment. The *"Kingdom of Shadows"*—access to its true knowledge and mystical interpretation of these energetic currents—has been shrouded in occult mystery for a very long time, and perhaps for good reason.

Where INANNA-ISHTAR is the *"goddess of love and war"* for the "upper realm," "realm of light (stars)," and "world of life," her *sister*, ERESHKIGAL was so for the "lower realm," equated with the *"Underworld"* or *"Land of the Dead."* She shares this domain with NERGAL—the "death-god" or "plague-god"—archetypal "war-god" representing the *Martian* energy current. The word "KI.GAL" (as in *"Eresh-Ki-Gal"*) is usually translated by scholars in academia as *"Great Below."* This is a curious ascription when nearly all other cuneiform applications of the word "KI" (for *"Ki-Gal"*) suggest a literal meaning: "Great Earth" or "Great Lands." The position-role and accepted lineage of ERESHKIGAL remains stable across most contemporary interpretations, but such is not the case with NERGAL.

NERGAL—the *"Great Watcher"*—(NER = *"Watcher,"* GAL = *"Great"*) is something of an enigma on tablet sources. Early twentieth century scholars could not ascertain his parentage definitively. More importantly, the designation given to him of "eight" is not harmonious with the Base-60 system of Mesopotamian mathematics—where other Anunnaki designations are divisible by "60"—nor is *Ninib-Adad*, the Babylonian "storm-god" (also within this pantheon) who bares the number "four." This may be appropriate as the two deities are connected in the *Erra Epos* tablet cycle. However, the fact remains that: given the Sumerian ambiguity left to us from the available cuneiform sources, at best we can assume his father (or grandfather) is either ENLIL or ENKI. We only know for certain that NERGAL is not directly the offspring of ANU. If he were, he would be listed higher in the pantheon. But, NERGAL is too young for this, anyways.

130

Based on known Anunnaki marriage customs, it would be appropriate if NERGAL were actually the love-child of ENLIL and NINLIL as Kramer describes—

> "*Enlil*, (still) impersonating 'the man of the gate,' cohabits with her [*Ninlil*] and impregnates her. As a result *Ninlil* conceives *Meslamtaea*, more commonly known as *Nergal*."

In contrast, the late controversial Sumeriologist, Zecharia Sitchin, suggests ENKI as NERGAL's father in his genealogical accounts. This might be more plausible, making NERGAL and ERESHKIGAL "half-siblings," in a similar manner found between MARDUK and ISHTAR. In this way, their union—an embodiment of "divine couplehood,"—would have been "blessed" by the Anunnaki Assembly of "gods," much as a union of MARDUK and ISHTAR would have been. It is sometimes confusing because by standards of the "younger pantheon" and Mardukite tradition, ENKI is practically everyone's "*Father*"—the one they all go to regardless of lineage.

ENKI plays a very fatherly for ERESHKIGAL during one of the earliest Sumerian tablet cycles, describing primordial creation—when she is carried off to "*Kutha*" or the "*Underworld*" by the serpent-monster, KUR. Of all the "*Elder Gods*," it is ENKIwho goes after her—though she is later made "*Queen of the Underworld*" and allowed to remain there. By this account, ENKI is the first of very few who ever "descend" to the realm of the "dead" and able to return permanently ["*resurrected*"] from that state— the others being ISHTAR and MARDUK—in recorded epics.

Modern traditions observe ERESHKIGAL as an archetypal "*Dragon Queen of the Netherworld*," ruling with her dark king, NERGAL. [Their courtship is described on *Tablet-U* from "*Necronomicon: The Anunnaki Bible.*"] In essence, she replaces the KUR-current for Babylon, and she is given domain over the seven Egyptian-Osirian "*death-gates*," fluently described in both Egyptian sources and the INANNA-ISHTAR tablet cycle of "*Descent to the Underworld.*" She is given a role of high esteem by the "seven" Anunnaki Judges, encountering every dead spirit to pass through the gates. Egyptologist, E.A. Budge, explains—

> "After the spirit had appeared before *Ereshkigal*, it seems that the *Anunnaki* sat in judgment upon it, and with *Mammitu*, the goddess of the destinies of men, proceeded to discuss the good and evil deeds that it had done in the body."

NERGAL, however, moves back and forth across the "*Underworld Gates*" acting as an "*angel of death*"—the *Ares/Mars* "god of destruction" in the pantheon. The two "*Shadowland*" rulers have quite the collaborative enterprise with one half acting as a "Great Destroyer" and the other half burying the dead. Though not a Christian-like Hell or sickening Hades, the Shadowlands represent the Anunnaki "death-machine" that seals the entire circuit for humanity.

The lore reveals the Anunnaki as *Guardians* and *Gatekeepers* of
both "Life and Death" for humans in this Earthly material existence.

NERGAL is also known as ENGIDUDU ("*Lord who prowls by night*")—commander of the "*Sebittu*," the famous *Seven Demons* of the Anunnaki—used for dealing out plagues and pestilence. But, hardly portrayed as "evil," all of this was originally presented as a means for the gods to maintain "balance." The other Semitic "Angel of Death"—*Azazel*—comes from a "realm of light" or else SHAMMASH, a counterpart of NERGAL in the *Erra Epos*, a tablet cycle describing the Anunnaki politics and destruction of the ancient "Middle East."

As a "war god," NERGAL is invoked for militant blessings in pre-combat rituals. The following Babylonian example from the German anthology, "Ritualtafeln," transcribed by R. Campbell Thomson in "*Semitic Magic*"—

> *Ritual: when an enemy [attacks] the king and his land . . .*
> *The king shall go forth on the right wing of the army,*
> *And thou shalt sweep the earth clean, and sprinkle pure water,*
> *And set [three] altars, one for Ishtar, one for Shammash,*
> *And one for Nergal,*
> *And offer each a loaf of wheaten meal (flour),*
> *And make a mash of honey and butter,*
> *Pouring in dates and . . .-meal,*
> *And sacrifice three full-grown sheep,*
> *Flesh of the right thigh, hinsa-flesh and sume-flesh thou shalt offer*
> *Sprinkle upuntu with cypress on a censer,*
> *And make a libation of honey, butter, wine, oil and scented oil,*
> *Then shalt thou make an image of the foe in tallow,*
> *Bend backwards his face with a cord;*
> *The . . . of the king, who is named like his master,*
> *Shall . . . the robes of the king . . .*
> *Shall stand before the preparation and repeat this formula before*
> *Shammash.*

NERGAL was never "officially" known as ERRA in Sumer. The *Erra Epos* tablet cycle (also known as "*Erra and Isum*" and given as *Tablet-V* in "*Necronomicon: The Anunnaki Bible*") is of Akkadian origin. The epithet "*Erra*" is a somewhat derogatory name for NERGAL—a corruption of the names he did possess: *Irrigal* or *Erakal*—with "*Erra*" now meaning a "Servant of Ra" (MARDUK), which he clearly was not. Contemporary translators attribute authorship of this epic to the pen of *Kabti-Ilani-Marduk*—possibly a scribe or priest-king related to a 12th Century B.C. "Babylonian Reformation" under a leader named in the "King Lists" as *Marduk-Kabit-Aheshu*.

The account follows:— MARDUK gives a warning prophecy about the devastation that will ultimately result if he were to step down from his seat at Babylon. This prediction is nothing short of "apocalyptic," describing the ruin of Babylon and all of the great Mesopotamian cities. NERGAL goes to Babylon and explains to MARDUK that his "self-made" supremacy has angered the other (Anunnaki) gods, and that MARDUK is in possession of something (a mysterious object never clearly defined) that not only "powers" or "empowers" Babylon, but all of the other Mesopotamian cities of the gods as well. When MARDUK cannot be convinced to leave "his seat" in Babylon, NERGAL attempts a different tactic by describing various other "holy artifacts" that would ensure his righteous rule. These objects happen to all be in the "*Shadowlands*" and would require retrieval by MARDUK personally. NERGAL promises to "watch over" Babylon while MARDUK is gone and promises very distinctly that nothing will "change" during his absence.

The tablets are obscure about the actual nature of the "holy artifacts" MARDUK goes in search for, or the "object of power" propelling Babylon (kept in a secret room called the *gigunu* that adjoined MARDUK's throne chamber at the top of his ziggurat-temple). But we know that the "object of power" was disturbed by NERGAL as soon as MARDUK "left his seat" in pursuit of the "holy artifacts." Instantly, the "waters stopped flowing," first in Babylon, then in the remaining great cities. The power and strength of ancient Babylon had been weakened, but not yet destroyed. Its destruction came later—a planned attack resulting from mistaken blame for this tragedy, all of which was placed on MARDUK.

When the "Supernal Trinity" called forth the "Anunnaki Assembly" of gods regarding the incident, all of the "younger pantheon"—NINURTA, NERGAL, SHAMMASH, ADAR and ISHTAR—conspired in judgment against MARDUK and NABU, placing full blame on them for the collapse of the systems. Any *unity* of the "celestial pantheon" was split forever. And with MARDUK absent in pursuit of the "holy artifacts," NABU stood alone to face the entire assembly, as translated by Zecharia Sitchin—

> Speaking for his father, *Nabu* blamed *Ninurta*, and revived the old accusations against *Nergal* in regard to the disappearance of the pre-Diluvial monitoring instruments and the failure to prevent sacrileges in Babylon [referring to the disturbance of the "power object"]; he got into a shouting match with *Nergal*, and showing disrespect:
> *Nabu* to *Enlil*, evil he spoke:
> "There is no justice!
> Destruction was conceived!
> *Enlil* against Babylon caused evil to be planned!"
> It was an unheard of accusation against the Lord of the Command.
> *Enki* spoke up, but it was in defense of his son, not of *Enlil*.
> Asked *Enki*:
> "What are Marduk and Nabu actually accused of?"
> His eye was directed especially at his son *Nergal*:
> "Why do you continue the opposition?"

After the council assembly agrees that MARDUK should be removed from power in Babylon, NERGAL and NINURTA decide to wage an entire nuclear war against Babylon and the "Tribes of NABU." Many lamentation tablets were behind from the wake of this. More devastating than the descriptions of fiery blasts themselves were the accounts of "evil winds" turning entire cities into ghost-towns. Traditions of MARDUK and NABU were moved underground and to *Egypt* where MARDUK already had established a new civilization of followers, presenting himself as *"Amon-Ra"*—*"The Unseen God."* Devastation in the "Middle East" left its inhabitants and all surrounding-area tribes hostile toward one another—persisting to the present day, a war that has been waging on pointlessly for thousands of years.

* * *

It is easy, then, to understand how NERGAL became the prototype of the *Mars-Ares* personage. As the word *"Erra"* evolved, it later came to denote NERGAL as the "Annihilator," a role previously given in Sumerian literature to GI.BIL—GIRRA or *"fires of god."* NERGAL and SHAMMASH frequently employ these *"fires of god"* to carry out judgments decreed by the Anunnaki Assembly. NERGAL is even described in the *Gilgamesh* cycle as "the ambusher who spares no one." The challenge of the *"Mars Gate"* regarding initiation on Mystical Path is thus the temperance of anger, pride, &tc.—overcoming *all Fear*—destructive energies that will manifest within the initiate uncontrollably chaotic if allowed to pass through the (next) *"Marduk Gate."*

Modern mystical and astral experiences with *"Underworld"* currents reveal these *"Shadowland"* beings as often pale or with blue-hued skin and dark or white hair (sometimes long or unkempt). The absence of clothing also seems prominent in the Underworld, particularly among females. This is best depicted in imagery of the two naked goddesses—ERESHKIGAL and ISHTAR—famously confronting one another in physical rivalry on the floors of the *"Underworld"* palace (in the "Descent" tablet cycle).

The invocation of the *"Nergal Gate"* used by modern Mardukites (as given on *Tablet-B* of *"Necronomicon: The Anunnaki Bible"*) is strongly influenced by the twenty-seventh tablet in the *"Prayers of the Lifting of the Hand"* series from the *Kuyunjik* collection. According to translator, L. W. King, the tablet was originally in possession of *King Ashurbanipal*, so the original inscription bore his name as the benefactor of the prayer's blessings. In this instance, the prayer invokes NERGAL as the first-born of *Nunamnir*, who is ENLIL. The prayer is as follows—

> I mighty lord, hero, first-born of Nunamnir!
> *siptu bi-lum gas-ru ti-iz-ka[ru bu-kur ilu-NU.NAM.NIR]*

> Prince of the Anunnaki, lord of the battle!
> *a-sa-rid ilu-A-nun-na-[ki bil tam-ha-ri]*

Offspring of Kutusar, the mighty queen!
i-lit-ti ilu-KU.TU.SAR [sar-ra-tum rabitum(tum)]

O NIRGAL, strong one of the gods, the darling   of Ninminna!
ilu-Nirgal kas-kas ilani [na-ram ilu-NIN.MIN.NA]

Thou treadest in the bright heavens, lofty is thy place!
su-pa-ta ina sami-i illuti [sa-ku man-za-az-ka]

Thou art exalted in the Underworld and art the benefactor of its . . .
ra-ba-ta ina aralli-[ma asira(ra) LA.TI-su]

With EA among the multitudes of the gods inscribe thy counsel,
it-ti ilu-I.A. ina puhur [ilani mi-lik-ka su-tur]

With SIN in the heavens, you seek all things,
it-ti ilu-SIN ina sami-i [ta-si gim-ri]

And BIL, thy father has granted thee that the black-headed race, all
    living creatures,
id-din-ka-ma ilu-BIL abu-[ka sal-mat kakkadu puhur napisti(ti)

The cattle of NIRGAL, created things, thy hand should rule!
bu-ul ilu-NIRGAL nam-mas-[si-i ka-tuk-ka ip-kid]

I, so and so, the son of so and so, am thy servant!
ana-ku pulanu apil pulani [arad-ka]

The . . . of god and goddess are laid upon me!
mi-lat ili u ilu-istari [is-sak-nu-nim-ma]

Uprooting and destruction are my house!
nasahu u hu-lu-uk-ku-[u basu-u ina biti-ya]

[. . .] (untranslated)
ka-bu-u IA si-mu-[u it-tal-pu-nin-ni]

Since thou are beneficent, I have turned to thy divinity!
as-sum gam-ma-la-ta bi-li [as-sa-har ilu-ut-ka]

Since thou are compassionate, I have sought for thee!
as-sum ta-ai-ra-ta [is-ti-'-u-ka]

Since thou are empathic, I have beheld . . .
as-sum mu-up-pal-sa-ta [a-ra-mar . . .]

Since thou are merciful, I have taken my stand before thee!
as-sum ri-mi-ni-ta [at-ta-ziz pani-ka]

Truly pity me and hearken to my cries!
ki-nis naplis-an-ni-ma [si-mi ka-ba-ai]

May thine angry heart have rest!
ag-gu lib-ba-ka [li-nu-ha]

Loosen my sin, my offense . . .
[pu]-tur an-ni hi-[ti-ti . . .]

[. . .] (untranslated / broken)
. . . -sir lib-bi ilu-ti-ka . . .

I god and angry goddess . . .
ilu u ilu-istaru zi-nu-ti sab- . . .

Let me talk of thy greatness, Let me bow in humility before thee!
nir-bi-ka lu-uk-bi [da-li-li-ka lud-lul]

— 6 —
: MARDUK :
JUPITER – KING OF THE GODS

Ancient Mesopotamia witnessed a rise of the "younger pantheon," which took great interest in the activities and devotion of humans on earth. Of them, perhaps the most famous for "planetary mythology" is MARDUK—*Jupiter*—the national god of Babylon. Much like his half-sister—INANNA-ISHTAR—a self-made "queen of the heavens," MARDUK exploited his own personal conviction, cunning and tenacity to secure his position as the primary controller of the "*Ladder of Lights*"—the BAB.ILI, "Gates of the Gods"—even exceeding the position of his father—ENKI—by assuming the role and functions of ENLIL—the ANU of "Material Existence"—to his followers.

Little mention of MARDUK is made in earlier pre-Babylonian Sumerian cunei-form literature. He was content, for a time, to remain an assistant to ENKI, mastering the esoteric arts of "magic" and "science" in *Eridu*. MARDUK was ori-ginally given the numeric designation of "10" and told to "wait his turn"—at the "*Age of Aries*"—to rise in the pantheon. His most familiar name—MARDUK—is actually a modern transliteration derived from the Semitic "*meri-dug*" (*Merodach*). An older version of his name is written: AMAR.UTU (*a.mar-utu.ki* = "Light of the Sun on Earth")—often interpreted by contemporary scholars as "*solar calf*" or "*son of the sun*." This provides some background to MARDUK's esteem. And as the foremost son of ENKI, he gained power quickly.

The later Semitic "*Maerdechai*" or "*Mordechai*" came from his name in Chaldeo-Babylonian language—"*silik-mul.u-khi*"—meaning "*Marduk is God.*" The more commonly used MAR.DUG means "*son of the pure mound*"—thought to be a reference to pyramids not only in Mesopotamia, but also in Egypt, where he raised himself as the leader of a third party (interpretation) of Anunnaki gods—the Egyptian Pantheon—as "*Amon-Ra,*" again identifying himself with the "solar" current and "stars" directly.

MARDUK's decision to raise himself to a monotheistic-like "*God*" status in Babylon created new political issues for the other Anunnaki on Earth. Exercising his "divine rights" stretched tensions between lineages—of ENKI and ENLIL—for supremacy on earth. When MARDUK and ISHTAR did not partner for this role, each sought the right to install their own dynastic lineages and choose the humans as "Kings" in their stead), during the "Age of Aries," beginning in 2160 B.C.—the birth of a New Dynastic global era. Zecharia Sitchin explains how in Babylon—

> *"Marduk* was proclaimed King of the Gods, replacing *Enlil*, and the other gods were required to pledge allegiance to him and to come to reside in Babylon where their activities could be easily supervised. This usurpation of Enlilship was accompanied by an extensive Babylonian effort to forge the ancient texts. The most important texts were rewritten and altered so as to make *Marduk* appear as the Lord of the Heavens, the Creator. . ."

Certainly, the other Anunnaki were less than appreciative of MARDUK's desire to rule over them. Yet throughout the *"Age of Aries,"*—his time to reign—he was not left to his own accord in Babylon (or in Egypt). This seems to have been a disciplinarian act by the other gods. If we take the most literal interpretations at face value, MARDUK lost all rights of kingship "in heaven" when he took a "human" wife instead of his betrothed half-sister. His argument was that his consort —SARPANIT—was a descendent of *Adapa*, and thus of Anunnaki bloodline via ENKI; that ISHTAR was no more interested in the union than he was, and it had not affected her rise to power; and finally, if not "in heaven," why not "on earth"? The logic seems to have gone unheard and where the "Mardukite" legacy was threatened in Babylon and Egypt, as its survival was frequently aided by "foreign hands."

In post-Sumerian Assyrian accounts, MARDUK—as the great "father-god" AS-SUR or ASHUR (*"Ashshur"*)—seems to emerge in their tradition as if from nowhere. This led some scholars in the late-1800's and early-1900's to wonder if MARDUK was a purely fictitious figure imagined into being for solely political reasons. Similarly, while SARPANIT—also *Sarapan* or *Zarpanitu*—is mentioned often in Babylonian prayer-tablets, she does not appear in any significant mythic tablet (saga) cycles. Her elevated status is rightly achieved from her direct relationship with MARDUK, and together, they are the parents of NABU. At the spring equinox "A.KI.TI" festival, she is the "spring-maiden" of fertility ceremonies in Babylon. In the *"Edaphic Tradition"* that spread across Europe, she is known as *"Erua,"* or more appropriately, ERU. These later European "elven-faerie-dragon" dynasties claimed descent from MARDUK and SARPANIT, their "star-goddess mother of vegetation and fertility." And sure enough *"Eru"* is an Akkadian word for "pregnancy."

* * *

For nearly two millennium, MARDUK and SARPANIT are national patrons of all priest-magicians and priestesses of Babylonia. In fact, by literal title, "Babylon" became the *"seat of the gods,"* but by Mardukite standards, this was to be realized differently than either *monotheism* or *polytheism*. The system of myth and magic born in Babylon was first and foremost dedicated to MARDUK's *"Divine World Order,"* often illustrated through the first mystical *"kabbalah"* system: *10 gates, 2 doors* and *7 levels*—just like the design for the Mardukite *ziggurat* "E.TEMEN. AN.KI" – *The Temple of Heaven and Earth.*

An excellent incantation-tablet example invokes MARDUK and SARPANIT after an experience of "evil from an eclipse," as first excavated by the French and transliterated in Vincent Scheil's "*Une Saison de Fouilles a Sippar*," later translated by Thomson, who explains to us in "*Semitic Magic*" that the prayer was given to *King Assurbanipal* by his brother, *Samas-sumukin*.

Both scholarly sources were used to reconstruct the full prayer in tact with both *English* and *French* translations of the original *Cuneifom* transliteration—

   . . . O great lady, kindly mother,
        FR. ôo grande déesse, mère miséricordieuse
          C. *beltu sa-qu-ti ummu rim-ni-ti*

   Amid the many stars of heaven,
        FR. parmi les nomlbreuses étoiles clu ciel
          C. *ina ma'-du-ti kakkabe sa-ma-mi*

   Thou art mistress . . .
        FR. vous êtes reine . . .
          C. *beltu ka-a-si . . .*

   I, *Samas-sum-ukin*, the king, servant of his god
        FR. moi Samas sum ukîn roi, serviteur de son dieu
          C. *ana-ku Samas sum ukin sarru, GAL ili-su*

   Vicegerent of his god Marduk and his goddess Sarpanit
        FR. vicaire de son dieu Marduk et de sa déesse Zarpanitum,
          C. *sakin ili-su (ilu)-Marduk (ilu)-Istarti-su (ilu)-Zar-pa-ni-tum*

   Of the evils of the eclipse of the moon, Fixed for the fifteenth day of Shebat
        FR. des maux de l'éclipse de lune fixée au 15 du mois d'AB
          C. *ana lumun AN-MI (ilu)-Sin sa ina arhi AS um 15 (kam) sak-nu*

   Of the evils of the signs and omens, evil, baneful,
        FR. des maux de signes et visions funestes, malfaisantes
          C. *ana lumun idati SI-BIT-mes limnuti la tabuti*

   Which have occurred in palace and my land
        FR. qui arriveraient dans mon palais et mon pays,
          C. *sa ina e-kal-ya (MU) u mati-ya ibba-su*

   I am afraid, and I fear, and I tremble
        FR. j'ai peur, je tremble, je frémis
          C. *pal-ha-ku-ma ad-ra-ku u su-ta-du-ra-ku*

Let not these evils draw near to me or my house
> FR. ces maux, de moi et de ma maison
>> C. *lumnu suatu ya-a-si u biti-ya*

[. . .] "Let them not approach [come near]"
> FR. qu'ils n'approchent pas
>> C. *a-a TE*

Accept the *upuntu*-plant from me and receive my prayer.
> FR. agrée l'tpuntu, agrée ma prière
>> C. *upuntu muh-ri-in-ni-ma li-ki-e un-ni-ni*

What becomes apparent when researching Mardukite-specific materials: MAR-DUK is the original "rebel-god," rising to supremacy and places himself in the highest positions—"Primordial Dragonslayer" and "Creator of the Universe"—*Jupiter*—the great force that maintains the orderly zones of the "solar system." His domain evolves to include all sciences and magics—the true understanding of the hidden patterns and secret doctrines of the cosmos. It is here that all magical tradi-tions were born—later fragmented into systems practiced throughout human history, and all based in symbols and signs, names and numbers, prayers and in-cantations. These are the esoteric or "*Hermetic*" arts first known to ENKI, then MARDUK, and finally NABU. The challenge of the "*Marduk Gate*" is then to ac-tually apply the esoteric formulas of "Cosmic Law" to direct and channel the powers of the Universe toward causal manifestations in creation and personal as-cension—otherwise true "*magic*." Editor Simon relays in his handbook—

> "Where *Nergal* represents Will—pure Will, unassuaged by purpose
> —and *Inanna*, desire; *Marduk* is the Law. This Law is no so much
> the Law of courts and decrees, but the Law of science, the
> lineaments of the created universe. Through the first five Gates we
> have become initiated into the use and sense of various Forces; in
> the *Sixth Gate* we become masters at manipulating all of them, at
> mixing them to produce various effects."

Mardukite "initiates" actually invoke this current in numerous ways. However, in maintaining consistency with our current volume, it is the incantation-prayer tablets we are most interested, and there are many. Several "prayers" to MARDUK may be found in "*Necronomicon: The Anunnaki Bible.*" The traditional "Gate Invocation" generally follows the formula demonstrated in the key examples from the *Kuyunjik* collection that the current editor has chosen to adapt for this series. The "*Isagila*" mentioned in its text is a reference to the primary ziggurat-temple of MARDUK in Babylon, also transliterated: E.SAG.ILU or *Esaggadhu*.

> Siptu gaasru supuuu iziz Assur
> Almighty, powerful and strong one of *Assur*.

Rubu tiizkaru bukur NU.DIM.MUD
　Exalted, noble-blood, firstborn of *Enki.*

Marduk salbabu muris I.TUR.RA
　Almighty *Marduk*, who causes the *Itura* to rejoice.

Bil I.SAG.ILA tukultiti Babiliki raim I.ZID.DA
　Lord of the *Isagila*, Aid to Babylon, Lover of the *Izida.*

Musalim napistiti asarid I.MAH.TIL.LA mudussuubalatu
　Preserver of Life, Prince of *Imahtilla*, Renewer of Life.

Zulul maati gamil nisi rapsaati
　Shadow over the Land, Protector of foreign lands.

Usumugal kalis parakkani
　Forever is [*Marduk*] the Sovereign of Shrines.

Sumuka kalis ina pi nisi taaab
　Forever is [*Marduk*] the name in the mouth of the people.

Marduk bilu rabuu ina kibitka kabitti luublut
　Almighty *Lord Marduk* at your command I remain alive.

Ina kibitika sirti luublut luuslimma
　At your command let me live, let me be perfect, let me behold
　　your Divinity.

Luustammar iluutka
　What I will to be, let me obtain my wishes.

Ima usaammaru luuksuud
　[*Marduk*], cause righteousness to come from my mouth.

Supsika damiktimtim inalibbiya
　[*Marduk*], cause mercy to dwell in my heart.

Tiru u naanzazu likbuu damiktimtim
　Return to Earth, establish yourselves and command mercy.

Iliya liizziz ina imniya
　May my god stand at my right hand.

Istariya liizziz ina sumiliya
　May my goddess stand at my left hand.

Iliya sallimu ina idiya luukaaian
May my god who is favorable to the stars, stand firmly at my side.

Surgamma kabaa simaa u magara
To speak the Word of Command, to hear my prayer and show favor.

Amat akabbuu ima akabbuu luu maagrat
When I speak, let the words by powerful.

Marduk bilu rabuu napistimtim kibi
Almighty *Lord Marduk*, come and command life.

Balat napistiya kibi
As you command my Life

Maharka namris adalluka luusbi
Before you I bow, let me be satisfied

Bil urrula Ia litiska
Bel's Fires go with you, *Ia* [*Enki*] smile upon you

Ilani sa kissati likrubuka
May the Earth Gods be favorable to thee and me

Ilani rabuti libbaka litibu
May the Good Gods delight in your mercy.

This incantation tablet continues on its reverse with part of a prayer addressing Sarpanit as the:

Queen of *Isagila*, the palace of the gods, the . . . mountain
sar-rat I.SAG.ILA ikal ilani sa-du-u- . . .

Lady of Babylon, the Shadow of lands!
Bi-lit Babili-ki su-lul ma-ta-a-ti

Lady of the gods, who loves to give life,
ilu-Bilit ili sa bul-lu-ta i-ram-mu

Who gives succor in sorrow and distress,
it-ti-rat ina puski u dannati

The . . . one, who holds the hand of . . .
. . . -ma-li-tu sa-bi-ta kata-du na-as-ki

Who supports the weak, who pours out seed,
i-pi-rat in-si sa-pi-kat ziru

Who protects life, who gives offspring and seed,
na-si-rat napisti(ti) nadnat(at) aplu u ziru

Who bestows life, who takes away sighing, who accepts prayer,
ka-i-sat balatu li-kat un-ni-ni ma-hi-rat tas-lit

Who has made the people, the whole of creation!
ba-na-at nisi gi-mir nab-ni-ta

— 7 —
: NINIB-NINURTA :
SATURN – WHO COMPLETES THE FOUNDATION

Drawing from more readily available 19th Century "Assyriological" research, Simon's "*Necronomicon*" from the 1970's describes the Guardian of the "*Seventh Gate*" as the "youngest son" of ENLIL. The name given is ADAR, coupled with a footnote that the force is sometimes called NINIB. The remaining description is actually of a "storm-god" (not *Saturn*) and immediately the name ADAD comes to mind—the "storm god" and "youngest son" of ENLIL according to Sumerian tradition. So... Perhaps the author has made a mistake—some kind of typo. And what a critical point to have such obscurity: when we are on the brink of the final gate before reaching communion with the IGIGI—the "*Outer Ones*." Even many of the original Mardukite researchers misappropriated this energy current to ADAD-ISHKUR or *Ramman*—the "wind-storm deity." This has been officially corrected in our archives.

As it turns out, ambiguity of ancient "Mardukite" records was not an oversight. The personage of NINIB-ADAR is intentionally minimized for the Babylonian system. Confusing the "youngest son" of ENLIL with his "oldest son"—born to half-sister NINHURSAG or NINMAH—kept political attention away from any claims to "Enlilite" supremacy in Babylon. In Babylon, MARDUK was supreme—any access to a further "*Seventh Gate*" would require his direct assistance. In short—ADAR is not a typo of ADAD, but is in fact, the *Assyrian* (and in some cases, *Akkadian*) name derived from *Nindar* or NINURTA—the Anunnaki heir of ENLIL and representation of *Saturn* in Sumerian tradition.

Superseding all previous esoteric regards, it is NINURTA who is selected by the Sumerian Anunnaki to give watch of the "*Saturn Gate*." Clearly this provided inspiration for MARDUK to assume the "*Fifty Names*"—all of the "Keys to the Kingdom"—under his name. Modern occult "self-initiates" of the earlier "Simon" work are aware that passing the "*Marduk Gate*" allows a magician-priest of "Mardukite" tradition access to the "*Fifty Names*"—meaning direct access to the "*Arts of Civilization*" and "*Secret Formulas of the Cosmos*." Most seekers of the "New Age" are concerned with little else. For most who are diligent enough to seriously work through the gate-system, their work self-honestly ends here. Those who may have thought they had completed some type of "Ascension" journey through "*Gates of the Necronomicon*," using virtually all previously available lore, now discover they did not.

Naturally, very few modern practitioners have achieved "True Enlightenment" via a Mesopotamian revival of any kind when using materials other than what is available from the *Mardukite Research Organization*.

Without the "Mardukite" foundation, other revivals become fanciful and imaginative reenactments that elevate consciousness to the same extent as any cultural-motif "New Age" creative visualization exercise. MARDUK makes *himself* the "final gate" of the material systems without actually being so. And those who *do* pass on from the "*Marduk Gate*" do not always even reach NINURTA—*Saturn*—withholding, in part, a complete spiritual progression all due to a political "cover-up" in Babylon, concealing any knowledge of NINURTA as the Sumerian heir to *Enlil-ship* of the local system.

To understand the ambiguity, one must realize that NINURTA does not even originally appear in the Sumerian "Olympian" *Pantheon of Twelve* and it seems his position among the "younger pantheon" on the "*Ladder of Lights*" is jumbled for later "Mardukite" followers. We must assume this was to prevent Sumerian succession from in any way "stealing the spotlight" from the position of MARDUK. Regarding the original Sumerian status of NINURTA and his absence from the pantheon, Zecharia Sitchin explains—

> "*Ninurta* was assigned the number 50, like his father. In other words, his dynastic rank was conveyed in a cryptographic message: If *Enlil* goes, you, *Ninurta*, step into his shoes; but until then, you are not one of the twelve, for the rank of '50' is occupied."

Among various excavated Sumerian tablet-cycles of KUR, the hero (or heroine) is attributed to one of three different characters—ENKI, INANNA and NINURTA—each encountering the force differently. The epic concerning NINURTA is the most detailed, possibly the most accurate, and bares striking resemblances to later Babylonian revisions (of the "*Enuma Elis*") detailing MARDUK as the serpent-slayer next in line for "*Enlilship.*" Loss of these details unfortunately led a broken spiritual system wrapped in Anunnaki politics. This is resolved in consciousness with a self-honest unification of the pantheon with "new" modern Mardukite standards of viewing the "younger generation" of Anunnaki gods. Doing this repairs a broken religio-magical system (or "spiritual paradigm"), now accessible to modern practitioners, scholars and esotericists for the very first time, *ever*—in a clarity not even known in the ancient world.

* * *

NINURTA is a hunter, but as a son of ENLIL we should not be surprised to find him described also as a "plough-man" or "farmer god." Many from the Enlilite lineage are connected to agriculture and "farming," much as the lineage of ENKI carries affinity for animals and "shepherding." In later Semtic lore, NINURTA appears as *Nimrod* (although this character is sometimes confused with NABU), sharing the same role as in older appearances from Mesopotamian literature—assisting in the reformation of civilization after the *Flood.*

Politics enter the arena only when matters turn towards Babylon—NINURTA is actually the original organizer of Enlilite tribes against the Mardukites in Babylon. In one famous cuneiform epic, he is given the epithet "ISHUM"—from the "*Erra Epos*" cuneiform tablet cycle ("*Erra and Ishum*") described in a prior chapter— meaning "scorcher." He acts as an adviser to NERGAL (ERRA) during the violent acts to "unseat" MARDUK from Babylon.

Both NINURTA and his consort—BAU (or *Gula*)—are actually attributed healing properties in the original Sumerian mystical tradition. As the defeater of both "*Asag*" (or KUR) and ANZU (in another epic), NINURTA is called upon to "*defeat*" demons and "evil spirits"—of sickness and disease. BAU, especially, is a patron to nurses and doctors. At first glance, these attributes seem out of character as representations of the *Saturn*-current—which reflects a confrontation of the darkest ("hidden") parts of *ourselves* in combination with the final constraints of "Cosmic Law" as it applies to the local material system. The "absolute healing" seems more appropriate when we consider that the "*Saturn Gate*" is the final threshold crossing or barrier to "Ascension"—*liberation* from the material program —and its primary gatekeeper according to the Sumerian tradition, is NINURTA, the Anunnaki-decreed rightful heir to ENLIL. The very essence of a "*seven-fold*" system comes into logic focus more clearly than ever before—the "*Foundation of Heaven and Earth*" is complete and the mysteries of the ziggurat "Temple of the Seven Spheres" are laid out before the Seeker.

The "*Seventh Gate*" leads to the "*Supernal Trinity*" of Anunnaki—the "*outer limits*" of our local system—a position in which NINURTA is waiting for heir-ship of in the Sumerian system. This means by some standard, era or version: ENLIL, NINURTA *and* MARDUK all maintain the designation (position) of "50." The heart of this beats a difficult fact to accept for the bloodline of MARDUK and all those calling ENKI, "Father" in the *Mardukite* paradigm. All this may seem trite to the uninitiated, but it is probably the deepest darkest kept secret in ancient Babylon —thus, even there deserving of the designation of *Saturn*. Proper realization of the system is what esotericists seek as the "*Hidden Key to the Necronomicon*." It not only brings harmony to the system for a modern practitioner—divine-messengers and temple-servants of the gods—but, for the gods *themselves*.

Mysteries of the "*Seventh Gate*" represent the highest initiation accessible to priests and priestesses *on earth*. More or less "divisions" of the whole does not change the whole. Others have simply broken down perceived fragments of reality into other *quantities*—the Babylonian "Gate-system" consists of *seven*. The "Secrets of the Gates" are hidden throughout Babylon in mythic sagas and esoteric traditions of *Elder Gods* and the *younger pantheon* in Mesopotamia.

On many levels of manifestation, the "Gates" *are* functional. The "*Hidden Key*"— the paradigm represented by the whole—was essentially the *first* "government-secret" kept by priests and scribes occupying the highest positions—the final "combination sequence" to make the "Star Gate of Babylon" actually *work*.

Even as the "Seat" of MARDUK, by Sumerian standards, the existence of Babylon and MARDUK's "Star-Gate" was deemed "illegal" in Enlilite territory. Babylon was eventually destroyed—hence our misunderstood genetic memory of the *"Tower of Babylon"* incident. NINURTA held residence in several ancient Mesopotamian cities, but most scholars agree his primary ziggurat-temple was the *E.Shumedu* in Nippur.

NINURTA—as heir to ENLIL—was a "solar deity" representing *Saturn*, but also *Sirius* in the old Sumerian astrology, as did MARDUK later. *Sirius* is often referred to in mystical literature as the "sun behind the sun," and is considered the true and secret form of ancient "solar-worship." MARDUK sought to represent the same "sun behind the sun" in Egypt. As one cannot see a candle flame when placed in front of the sun—the elusive celestial force of *Sirius* is shared as "Saturn of Stars," and part of a gateway or bridge beyond our system.

The "Invocation of the Saturn Gate" dedicated to NINURTA previously used by modern Mardukite Chamberlains from *"Necronomicon: The Anunnaki Bible"* is effective, but another incantation example for esoteric experimentation or general research is included here as adapted from the second tablet of the "Prayers of the Lifting of the Hand" series—

> O mighty son, firstborn of ENLIL.
> *siptu ap-lu gas-ru bu-kur ilu-Bil*
>
> Powerful, perfect offspring of ISARA,
> *sur-bu-u git-ma-lu i-lit-ti I.SAR.RA*
>
> Who art clothed with terror, who art full of fury!
> *sa pu-luh-tu lit-bu-su ma-lu-u har-ba-su*
>
> O NINURTA, whose onslaught is unopposed!
> *ilu-NIN.UR.TA [sa la im]-mah-ha-ru ka-bal-su*
>
> Mighty is thy place among the great gods!
> *su-bu-u man-[za-za] ina ilani rabuti*
>
> In E.KUR, the house of decisions, exalted are thee,
> *ina I.KUR bit ta-[si]-la-a-ti sa-ka-a ri-sa-a-ka*
>
> And ENLIL, thy father has granted thee
> *id-din-ka-ma ilu-Bil abu-ka*
>
> The law of all the gods thy hand should hold!
> *ti-rit kul-lat ilani ka-tuk-ka tam-hat*

Thou judges the judgment of mankind!
ta-dan di-in ti-ni-si-i-ti

Thou leads him that is without a leader, the man that is in need.
tus-ti-sir la su-su-ru i-ka-a i-ku-ti

Thou holds the hand of the weak, you raise him that is not strong!
ta-sab-bat kat [in-si] la li-'-a tu-sa-as-ka

The body of the man that to the Lower World has been brought down,
     you can restore!
sa a-na a-ra-al-[li]-i su-ru-du pa-gar-su tutira-ra-

From him who sin possesses, the sin you can remove!
sa ar-nu i-su-u ta-pat-tar ar-nu

Thou art quick to favor the man with whom the god is angry.
sa ilu-su itti-su zi-nu-u tu-sal-lam ar-his

O NINIB, prince of the gods, a hero you are!
ilu-NIN.IB a-sa-rid ilani ku-ra-du at-ta

I, so and so, son of, so and so, whose god is so and so, whose goddess
     is so and so,
ana-ku pulanu apil pulani sa ilu-su pulanu ilu-istari-su pu-lanitum(um)

Have bound for thee a cord, . . . [a cord]. . . have I offered thee;
ar-kus-ka rik-sa ku.a.tir as-ruk-ka

I have offered thee *tarrinnu*, a pleasant odor;
as-ruk-ka tar-[rin]-nu u-ri-su tabu

I have poured out for thee mead, a drink from corn.
akki-ka du-us-su-bu si-kar as-na-an

With the may there stand the gods of ENLIL.
itti-ka li-iz-zi-zu ilani su-ut ilu-Bil

With thee may there stand the gods of E.KUR!
itti-ka li-iz-zi-zu ilani su-ut I.KUR

Truly pity me and hearken to my cries!
ki-nis nap-lis-an-ni-[ma si-mi] la-ba-ai

My sighing remove and accept my supplication!
un-ni-ni-ya [li-ki-ma mu-hur] tas-lit

Let my cry find acceptance before thee!
zik-ri [li-tib] ili-ka

Deal favorably with me who fear thee!
si-lim itti ya-a-tu-u pa-lih-ka

Thy face have I beheld, let me have prosperity!
pa-ni-ka a-ta-mar lu-si-ra ana-ku

Thou art full of pity. Truly pity me!
[mu]-up-pal-sa-ta ki-nis nap-lis-an-ni

Take away my sin, remove my iniquity!
an-ni pu-tur sir-ti pu-sur

Tear away my disgrace and my offenses you loosen!
[i]-ti-ik kil-la-ti-ma hi-ti-ti ru-um-[mi]

May my god and goddess command me and may they ordain good fortune!
[ili]-ya u ilu-istari-ya li-sa-ki-ru-in-ni-ma lik-bu-u damiktim(tim)

May I praise thy heart, I bow in humility before thee.
[lib]-bi-ka lu-sa-pi da-li-li-ka lud-lul

— A —
: MESOPOTAMIAN MATHEMATICS :
SECRETS OF MEASURING SPACE AND TIME

Ancient Sumerians observed and understood connections between cycles, time and mathematics. In addition to the "invention" and pragmatic use of the "wheel" (or circle), they also developed "religious" calculations of the circle at 360-degrees. Their use of "Base-60" or *sexagesimal* math for systematic measurement of time-space remains with humanity to this present day. Consider the length of a day at 24-hours (or two sets of twelve) of "60"-minutes containing "60"-seconds each; or the celestial zones of the astrological zodiac as a "wheel" or sphere of twelve "houses" of 30 degrees each; or else the twelve 30-day "festivals of the moon" composing an annual cycle or "wheel of the year"—or "*sat-ti.*" The annual year (*sat-ti*) was even originally only divided into three seasons: beginning ("*res sat-ti*"), middle ("*misil sat-ti*") and end ("*kit sat-ti*").

"Magicians" and esoteric philosophers—ancient and modern—find significance in sigil-scripts, colors, mystical alphabets and other "occult correspondences." All of these play their parts in magical ritual drama, spiritual incantations and other ceremonial applications. As a *universal* expression of "Cosmic Law," *numbers* are the most fundamental mystical "signs" in the realm of form, representing infinite wisdom and practical correspondences. Although our traditional or more familiar "classical" system of numerology is derived from a "Base-10" paradigm (for example, where "10x10=100" is a *whole*), the original Mesopotamian mathematics is "Base-6," or more appropriately, "Base-60." This only seems complicated because modern consciousness is most familiar with a "*Base-10 metric system*"— decades and centuries and "percents."

In Western civilization, "Base-60" mathematics is most closely identified with our sense of "time." Rather than dividing an hour into hundredths or percents, we are able to see 60-minutes as the "*whole pie.*" A quarter of that "pie," while still "25%"—per-*cent*, meaning "per-*100*"—it is *not* a quantified value of "25," but instead: "15," as in 15-minutes—"15x4=60." The modern standard space-measuring "foot" is divided by 12—and "12x5=60." This type of thinking more closely resembles Mesopotamian worldview.

Although school-teachers most frequently emphasize only the proverbial Sumerian "use of the wheel," it was the "mathematics" that forever established that the wheel (or more correctly, the "circle") consisted of 360-degrees—or "6x60=360." Here among the ancients, "geometry" was born—long before the classical Greek mathematicians—a means of literal "earth-measuring." Even more than this, the ancients demonstrated abilities to measure time-space on "earth," in the "heavens" and the relationships between.

```
BASIC MESOPOTAMIAN MATHEMATICAL FORMULAS

6 x 1          = 6      = earth, fire, power, spatial [Marduk]
6 x 10         = 60     = command, heaven-earth, fire [Anu]
6 x 10 x 10    = 600    = chaos, void, abyss, dragon [Tiamat]
6 x 60         = 360    = earth-time, cycles ["local planet"]
6 x 60 x 6     = 2160   = earth meets heaven ["zodiacal age"]
6 x 60 x 10    = 3600   = heaven-time, spiritual cycles ["sar"]
```

A full turn or cycle of the "Wheel of the Year"—"*sat-ti*"—in *Babylonia* was separated into "12 periods" (or *zones*) of 30-days (*degrees*) each. These periods equated to 12 annual "*moonth festivals*," more appropriately called "months." The quantity values of 12x30 and 6x60 are identical—*360*. Ancient astronomers were also aware that the observed year was actually slightly longer than 360-days, and that there are actually 13 lunar cycles in a year, so an additional "*13th month*" was included to make the calculations fit the observations. Everything is always in motion. We must even rectify the mathematics of our modern linear time-keeping with the inclusion of "leap-days." In most instances of the ancient calendar, a "*new moon*" meant the start of a "*new month*." The days counted of a month were synonymous with the "days of the moon"—for example: "*sixth day of the moon.*"

SUMERIAN/AKKADIAN ANNUAL YEAR

1. Nisannu – Nisan (*spring equinox*)
2. Airu – Iyyar
3. Simanu – Siwan
4. Du'uzu – Tammuz
5. Abu – Ab
6. Ululu – Elul
7. Tishritu – Tisri (*autumn equinox*)
8. Arahsamna – Marchesvan
9. Kislimu – Kislev
10. Tebitu – Tebet
11. Shabatu – Sebat
12. Addau – Adar
13. "Second Adar" (*extra month*)

ZODIAC NAMES OF THE CELESTIAL SPHERE

1. Ku-mal (*Aries*)
2. Gu-an-na (*Taurus*)
3. Mash-tab-ba (*Gemini*)
4. Dub (*Cancer*)
5. Ur-gula (*Leo*)
6. Ab-sin (*Virgo*)
7. Zi-bi-an-na (*Libra*)
8. Gir-tab (*Scorpio*)
9. Pa-bil (*Sagittarius*)
10. Su-hur-mash (*Capricorn*)
11. Gu (*Aquarius*)
12. Sim-mah (*Pisces*)

The annual cycle was also divided as a light and dark half, marked distinctly by the two primary religious festivals of ancient Mesopotamia—the spring festival of *Akitu* and the harvest festival of *Zagmuk*. Both are symbolically represented as points of *"divine marriage"* between "heaven" and "earth"—later signifying simply the relationship between a ruling King and his lands. Originally, the more popular *fertility rites* of the spring were agricultural, with an emphasis on *land renewal*. With later development and spread of these tradition, *Akitu* became known as *Ostara*—the pagan *Easter*—in dedication to ISHTAR (*Inanna*).

Mesopotamian mathematics is *"sexagesimal."* The number "sixty"—attributed to ANU—is sacred within its own system, with exactly *twelve* factors—*three* of which are prime. These "factors" also appear in the tradition as *sacred* numbers— 1, 2, 3, 4, 5, 6, 10, 12, 15, 20, 30 and itself, 60. It is perhaps no small coincidence that "60" is the smallest whole number value perfectly divisible by all of the numbers 1 through 6. This was very useful in the highly innovative form of *"multiplication by reciprocal"* developed by the Sumerians and Babylonians. Logic calculations requiring a value to be "divided" by another number, were instead written as a "multiplication" of the reciprocal (or inverse) of the other number. Therefore, in this system, an expression:

"60 *divided by* 10" becomes "60 *multiplied by* one-tenth."

[60 / 10 = 6] *is the same as* [60 x 0.1 = 6]

Calculations of space and distance also followed *sexagesimal* patterns. Where we are familiar today with the use of centimeters and inches, feet and yards, the basic unit of length measurement in ancient Mesopotamia was essentially the division of a meter (*"kush"*) into 360-parts called a *she*, each equivalent to approximately one-tenth of an inch.

If we simply transfer a decimal place, we can still use the "standard" system to visualize—where one foot or 12-inches approximately equals 120 *she*, so 1 *kush* or 360 *she* is roughly equivalent to 36-inches. [It is interesting that society has retained a system of spatial-measure where a standard unit is divided into 12-parts.]

6 *she*	=	1 *su-shi*
30 *su-shi* or 360 *she*	=	1 *kush*

* * *

The original Anunnaki hierarchy of pantheon designations runs in increments of five—from 5 to 60—allowing space for the "Olympian Twelve" to be plotted thereupon. The Sumerian Anunnaki "*Pantheon of Twelve*" of course consists of: *Anu* (60), *Antu* (55), *Enlil* (50), *Ninlil* (45), *Enki* (40), *Ninki-Damkina* (35), *Nanna* (30), *Ningal* (25), *Shammash* (20), *Inanna-Ishtar* (15), *Ishkur-Adad* (10) and *Ninhursag-Ninmah* (5). Spiritual politics in post-Sumerian Mesopotamia resulted when altering the names (or representative figures) with the "Mardukite" pantheon, but the actual "roles" themselves went unchanged—mathematically fixed. Designations for the "*Supernal Trinity*"—60, 50 and 40—become "master numbers" of Babylonian numerology. The fractional designations for the "*planetary gates*" are inherited by the "younger pantheon" in Babylon—

1 / 2	= 30	*Nanna-Sin* (Moon)
1 / 3	= 20	*Utu-Shammash* (Sun)
1 / 4	= 15	*Inanna-Ishtar* (Venus)
1 / 5	= 12	*Nabu* (Mercury)
1 / 6	= 10	*Marduk* (Jupiter)
1 / 8	= 7.3	*Nergal* (Mars)
1 / 15	= 4	*Ninib*, *Adad* or *Ninurta* (Saturn)

PRECESSION OF THE BABYLON GATES

1 = 7	*Nanna* – 30	30 x 2 = 60	30 = 1 / 2 x 60
2 = 6	*Nabu* – 12	12 x 5 = 60	12 = 1 / 5 x 60
3 = 5	*Ishtar* – 15	15 x 4 = 60	15 = 1 / 4 x 60
4 = 4	*Samas* – 20	20 x 3 = 60	20 = 1 / 3 x 60
5 = 3	*Nergal* – 8		
6 = 2	*Marduk* – 10	10 x 6 = 60	10 = 1 / 6 x 60
7 = 1	*Ninurta* – 4	4 x 15 = 60	4 = 1 / 15 x 60

— B —
: MARDUKITE SIGIL-SEALS OF THE ANUNNAKI :
FROM "NECRONOMICON: ANUNNAKI BIBLE" (TABLET-X)

ANU

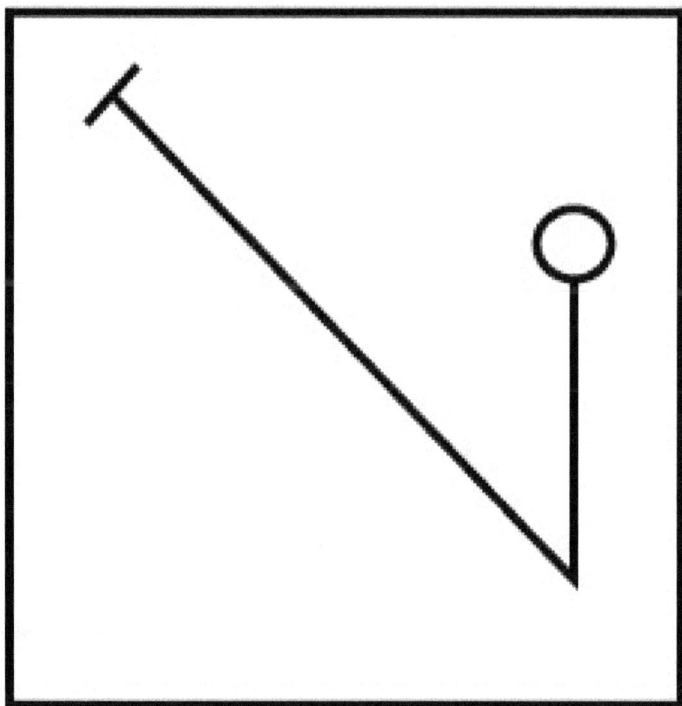

ENLIL

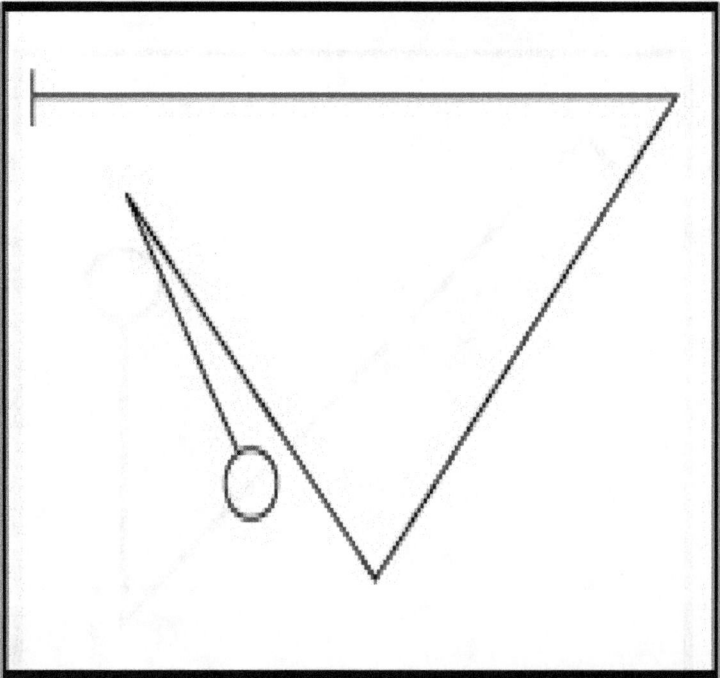

ENKI

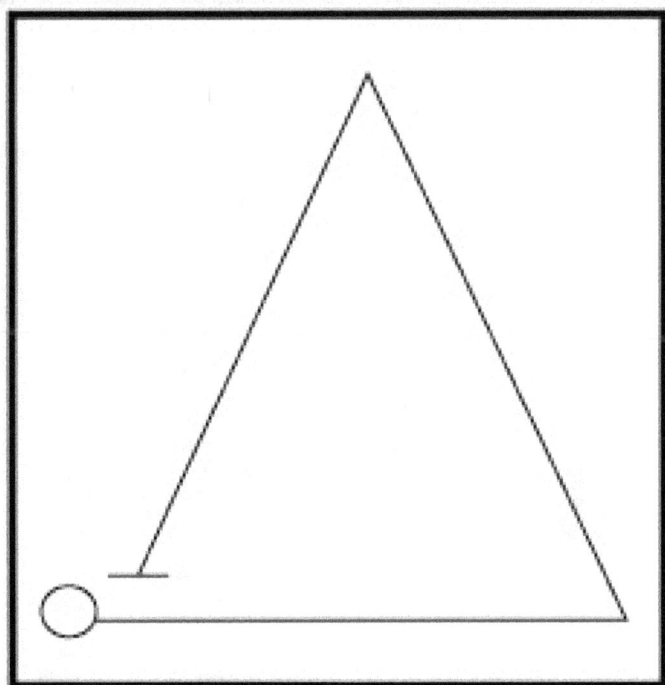

NANNA

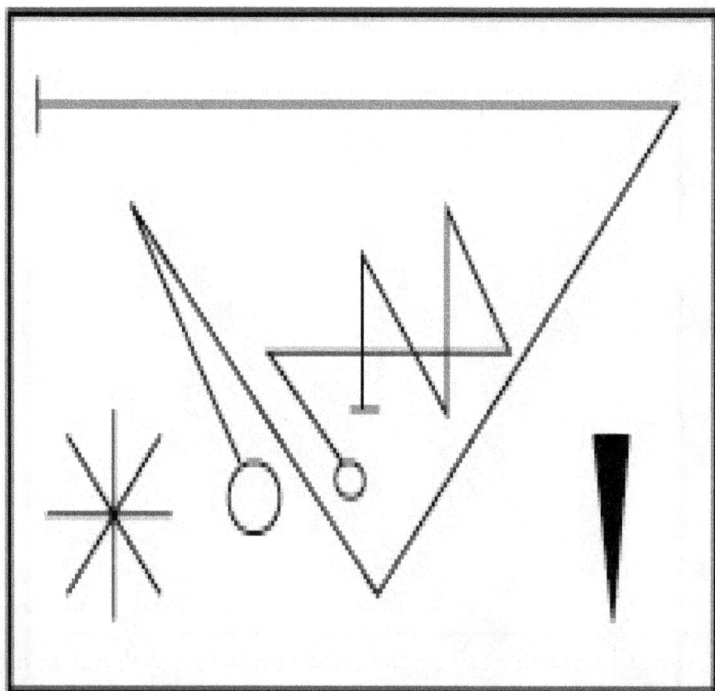

NABU

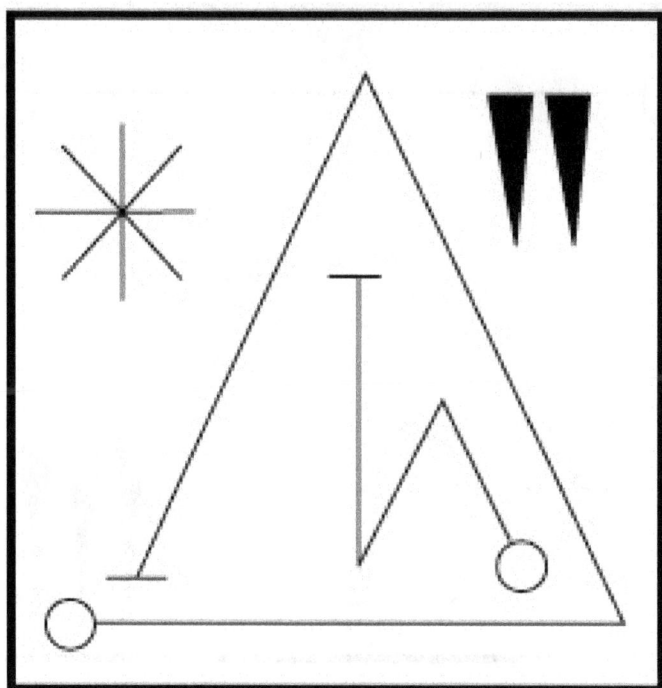

ISHTAR

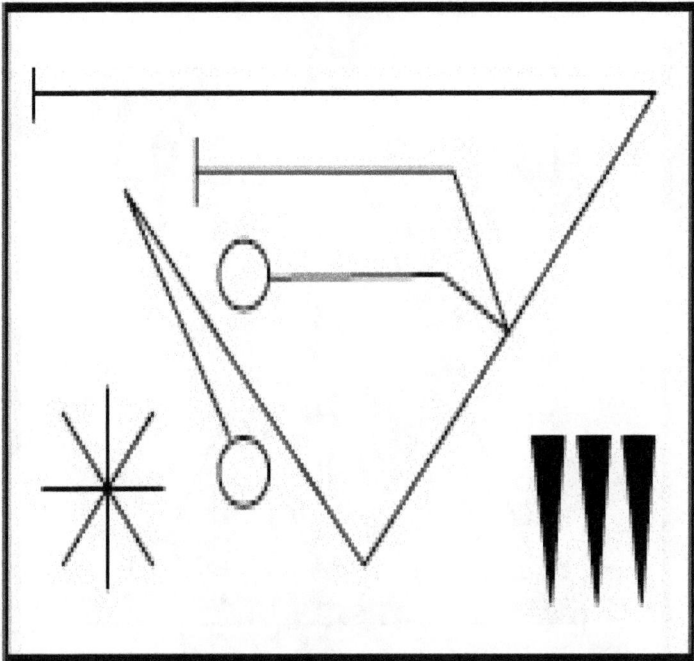

SAMAS

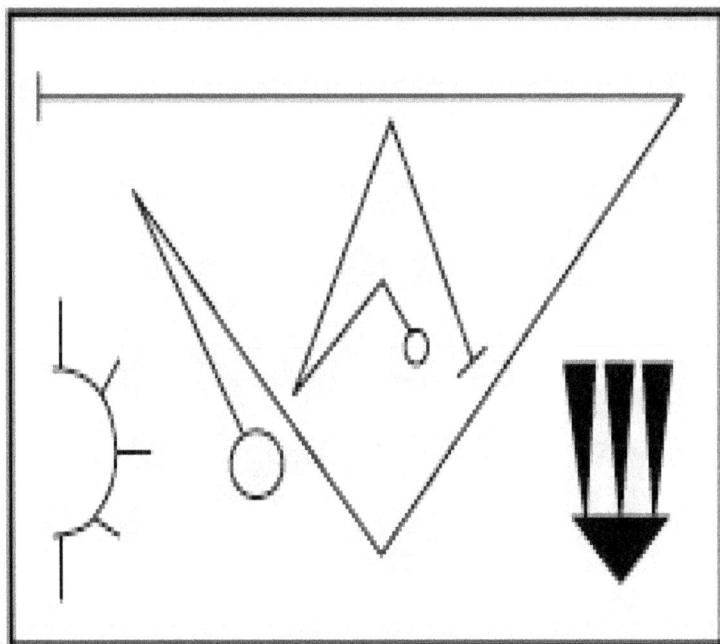

NERGAL

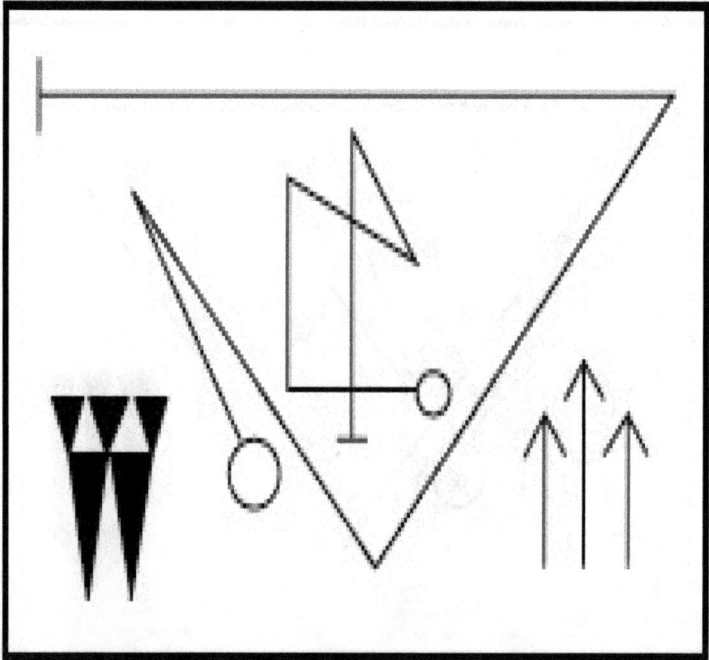

MARDUK

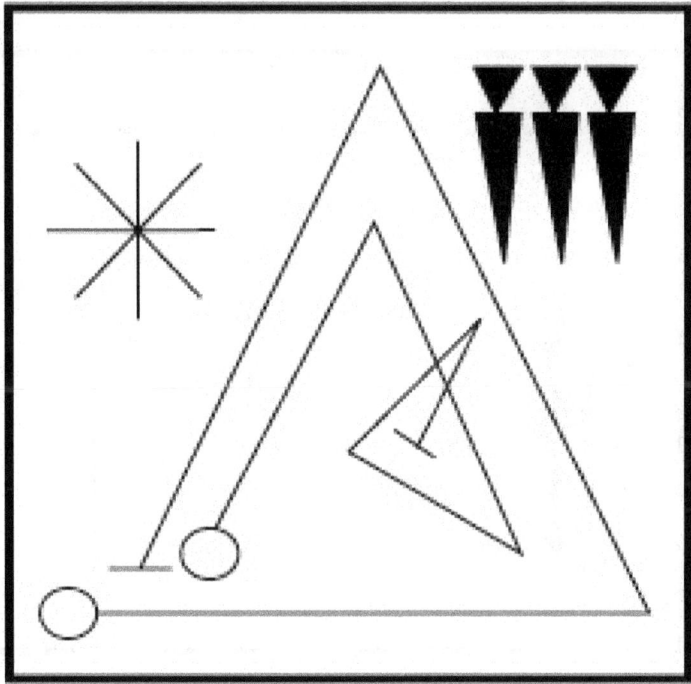

164

NINURTA (NINIB)

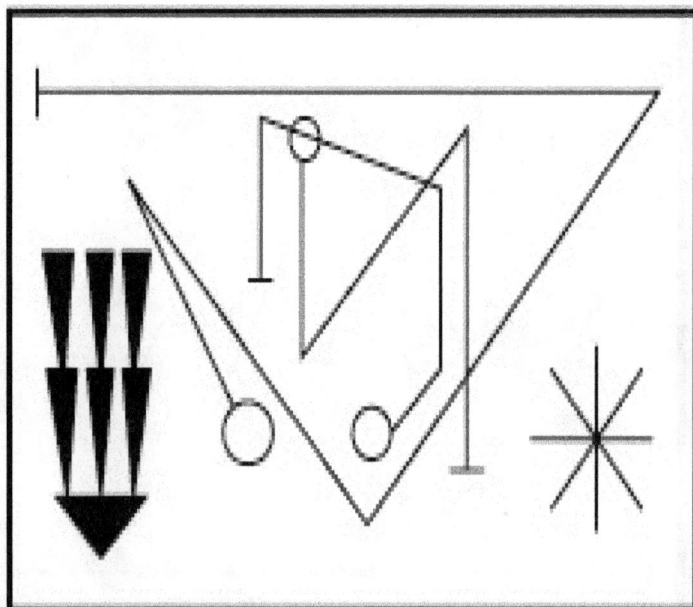

SARPANIT

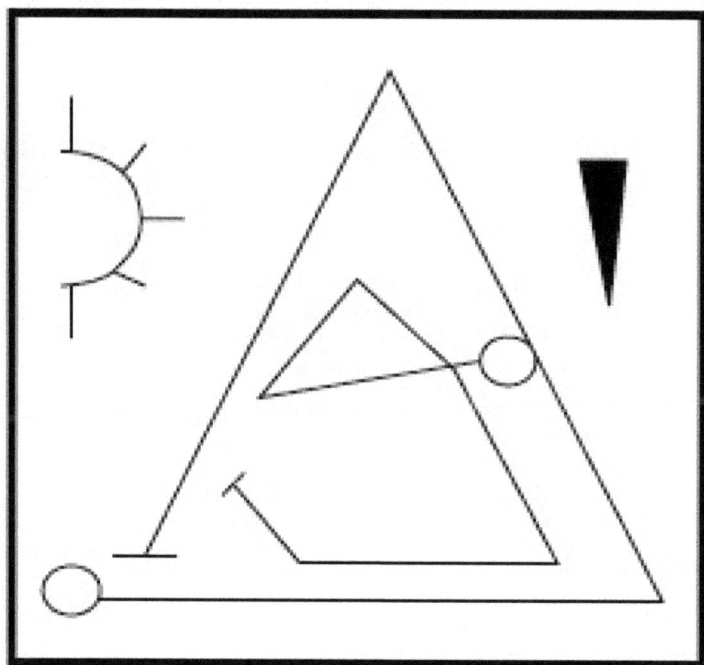

— (—
: BOOK OF MARDUK BY NABU :
FROM "NECRONOMICON: ANUNNAKI BIBLE" (TABLET-W)

We have sealed seven representative stations in BABYLON. While it is true that each of the cities did emphasize their local patrons, a god and a goddess, We have sought a unity for all the gods, under the watchful eye of my father, MARDUK, son of ENKI.

Our father, ENKI, took MARDUK as an apprentice to the magical and religious arts while in E.RIDU and I later took hold of such mysteries and dispersed the knowledge to my scribes and priests in BABYLON and Egypt, where my family was recognized by other names.

The "Seven" are each embodiments of one of the seven gates forged in BABYLON, homes to the gods of the "younger pantheon." It is true, the same seven-fold division may be found to fragment the *world of form*—corresponding to color, sound, or the planets observed by the ancient ancestors from Earth, seen as "*Guardians.*"

The seven planetary systems, which have been connected to the "Seven" of the Gates, also correlate to an easily observable weekly cycle of time. The planet-ruling days will offer the supplicant [priest] an intention ceremonial or meditative opportunity to appeal to each of the "sets" of ANUNNAKI "divine couples" honored in the "younger pantheon" of Babylon.

Sunday – Sun – SHAMMASH [UTU] (& AYA)
Monday – Moon – NANNA [SIN] (& NINGAL)
Tuesday – Mars – NERGAl (& ERESHKIGAL)
Wednesday – Mercury – NABU (& TESHMET)
Thursday – Jupiter – MARDUK (& SARPANIT)
Friday – Venus – ISHTAR [INANNA] (& DUMUZI)
Saturday – Saturn – NINIB [NINURTA] (& BA'U)

Within the combined domains of the "Seven" are all of the material and spiritual aspects a priest, priestess or magician seeks in life (e.g. ISHTAR for *love* or SAMAS for *truth*) and one merely must appeal with self-honesty and true words to attain them. This is as the original arts were set down in days of old, left for men to remember us—and we will remember you.

The names and Gates are not merely there for the bedazzlement of the "occult initiate" as you have been taught (there to ascend to and forget about): they are very real "magical skills" and "spiritual lessons" based on the division and fragmentation of the material universe—a mastery only attainable by a true and faithful relationship with the ANUNNAKI gods of your ancestors.

Man's use of the spiritual power of the gods became subverted, altered and bastardized into the mystical systems now given for your disposal, written by men with no better understanding of the traditions they seek to invoke then those who read them. (And some of these traditions have even falsely said to be derived from my hand.) The true priest, priestess or magician compels the gods by friendship and trust, not fear and hatred. By MARDUK, I learned the power of incantation. I was taught to appease the gods in his name, to speak the words of the higher. MARDUK invoked the name of ENKI, our father, who, invoked the name of ANU. And so was born the magical "hierarchies" that magicians have confused. I taught the magician-scribes of my order to invoke my name and seal during their petitions to the gods, which I have given here, as I learned it from MARDUK.

ANU above me, King in Heaven.
ENLIL, Commander of the Airs.
ENKI, Lord of the Deep Earth.
I am NABU – hear my words.
I am the priest of MARDUK and SARPANIT.
Son of our father, ENKI and DAMKINA.
I am the priest in E.RIDU.
I am the magician in BABYLON.
My spell is the spell of ENKI.
My incantation is the incantation of MARDUK.
The Tablets of Destiny, I hold in my hands.
The Ankh of ANU and ANTU, I hold in my hands.
The wisdom of ENLIL and NINLIL, I call to me.
The Magic Circle of ENKI and DAMKINA, I conjure about me.
SHAMMASH and AYA are before me.
NANNA-SIN and NINGAL are behind me.
NERGAL and ERESHKIGAL are at my right side.
NINIB-NINURTA and BA'U are at my left side.
The blessed light of ISHTAR and DUMUZI shines favorably upon my
*   sacred work.*
It is not I, but MARDUK, who performs the incantations.

As should become increasingly apparent to contemporary folk of the current age, the ANUNNAKI are powerful and influential, though often directly unseen, forces behind the reality of the life you exist in—as your ancestors were well aware of. If you work with us in conjunction with the natural flow of the universal energies, then you will come face to face with your true destiny—and invited home, again.

Discern your true-knowledge, learn the challenge of self-mastery, and then dear *seeker*, resolve to walk with the gods among the stars, circumnavigating the illusions of this world which have been raised before you as a test of your existence.

When you have proven yourself before us, we shall celebrate your arrival...

MONDAY – THE MOON – NANNA & NINGAL

ilu-NANNA. ilu-SIN. ilu-istari-NINGAL.
NANNA. SIN. NINGAL.
ilu-NANNAR. ilu-NAMRASIT.
NANNAR. MOON.
su-bu-u man-za-za ina ilani rabuti maru aplu ilu-ENLIL u ilu-NINLIL
Mighty One among the gods, son of ENLIL and NINLIL,
nam-rat urru-ka ina sami-i ina sat musi
Brightest in the heavens at night,
du natalu, nasaru anabu harranu-dim
Keeping watch, protecting weary travelers
u nisu ina bitu sat musi suttu
And the people in their homes as they sleep.
itti namrasit ina sami-i
Your brightness extends through the heavens,
kima diparu, kima ilu-SAMAS
Like a torch – Like a fire-god [Samas].
samsatu ilu-NANNA namaru suttu agu
Radiance of NANNA, who reflects the dreams of men,
abu ilu-SAMAS
Father of the SUN
rimi-nin-ni-ma anaku ____ , apil ____ , sa ilu-sa ___ u ilu-istari-su ____ .
Be favorable to me, I, __ son of __ , whose god is __ and whose goddess
   is __ .
ilu-NANNA u ilu-NINGAL rimi-nin-ni-ma
May NANNA and NINGAL deal graciously with me,
kaparu anaku sillatu lu-us-tam-mar ilu-ut-ka
Cleanse me of iniquity that I may be free to call upon thee.
petu babu temu
Open the Gates of your mysteries to me,
li-iz-ziz ina imni-ya u sumuli-ya anaku arad-ka elu
Stand on either side of me, a servant of the Highest.
an-un-na-ki ti-i-ru u na-an-za-zu
May the ANUNNAKI come forth an be established.

TUESDAY – MARS – NERGAL & ERESHKIGAL

ilu-NERGAL. ilu-IRRIGAL. ilu-istari-ERESHKIGAL. ilu-ERRA.
NERGAL. IRRIGAL. ERESHKIGAL. ERRA. MARS.
siru belu ersetu
Exalted Lord of the Underworld.
ilu-istari-ERESHKIGAL, beltu ersetu
ERESHKIGAL, Queen of the Underworld.
saqu-su manzazu it-ti ilani samu
Great is your place among the gods of heaven.
ilu-NERGAL u ilu-istari-ERESHKIGAL
NERGAL and ERESHKIGAL,
rimi-nin-ni-ma, ana-ku ___ , apil ____ , sa ilu-su ___ ilu-istar-su ___ .
Truly have mercy on me, __ , son of ___ , whose god is ___ , whose
   goddess is ___ .
banu-ya libbu alalu
May your hearts be tempered.
di-ni uzzu ina ramanu libbu
Temper also the anger within my heart,
ana-ku izuzzu mahru ze
That I may stand before you,
petu babu temu
Open the Gates of your understanding to me.
rimi-nin-ni-ma ina damu u du lemnutu seg ina ramanu zi
Grant me a favorable death and keep evil from me in life.
ana-ku arad-ka elu kamazu ze rimi-nin-ni-ma
I, a servant of the Highest, kneel before thee, take pity on me.
babu-mah du pataru
May the Great Doors stand open.
an-un-na-ki ti-i-ru u na-an-za-zu
May the ANUNNAKI return and be established.

WEDNESDAY – MERCURY – NABU & TESHMET

ilu-NABU. ilu-TUTU. ilu-istari-TESHMET ilu-istari-TASMIT. ilu-NEBOS.
NABU. TUTU. TESHMET – TASMIT(U). NEBOS. MERCURIOS.
tupsarru si-mat ilani
Scribe among the Gods,
sarru nam-zu si-mat ilani
Keeper of the Wisdom of the Gods,
asaridu bukur ilu-MARDUK u ilu-SARPANIT
Firstborn of MARDUK and SARPANIT.
ilu-NABU na-as duppu si-mat ilani
NABU, Bearer of the Tablet of Destinies of the gods,

ramanu ur-hi suttu lid-mi-ik
May my dreams [destiny] be filled with prosperity.
ilu-NABU u ilu-TASMITU ka-ba-a si-ma-a suk-na ya-si-sa
May my petitions fall on the ears of NABU & TASMIT.
rimi-nin-ni-ma, ana-ku ___ , apil ___ sa ilu-sa ___ u ilu-istari-su ___ .
Be favorable to me, I, __ son of __ , whose god is __ and whose goddess
 is __ .
ebbu ramanu nam-eme-sig u ummuqu si-mi-i su-pi-ya
Cleanse me of false knowledge, that I might be ft to call upon thee.
petu babu temu
Open the Gates of your understanding to me.
amat a-kab-bu-u kima a-kab-bu-u lu-u ma-ag-rat
Bless my mouth with true words to speak the prayers
sumu-ka ka-lis ina pi nisi ta-a-ab
May the prayers rise from the lips of the people.
anaku arad-ka elu
I am a servant of the Highest,
an-un-na-ki ti-i-ru u na-an-za-zu
May the ANUNNAKI come forth and be established.

THURSDAY – JUPITER – MARDUK & SARPANIT

*ilu-MAR.DUG. ilu-MAR.DUK. ilu-istari-ZARPANIT. Ilu-silik-MULU.KHI
 DIL.GAN.*
MARDUK. MERODACH. SARPANIT. MULU-KHI. JUPITER.
lugal arali, belu asipu, ilu-su BAB.ILI
Lord of the Lands, Master of Magicians, God of Babylon.
ilu-SARPANIT(UM), belitu istari-su BAB.ILI
SARPANIT, Lady of Babylon.
gasru u sapsu ina an-ki zi atwu
Mighty and powerful on earth and heaven are your words.
belu u belitu su BAB.ILI
Lord and Lady of Babylon,
maharu ramanu arua abnu-gesnu, abnu-uqnu u hurasu
Accept my offerings of alabaster, lapis lazuli and gold.
dinu-ma ramanu lid-mi-ik
Judge my life favorably,
anaku ___ apil ___ sa ilu-su ___ u ilu-istar-su ___ .
I ___ , son of ____ , whose god is ____ , and whose goddess is ____ .
lu-us-tam-mar ilu-ut-ka u atwu ramanu maharu karabu
Make me fit to behold your divinity and teach me to receive thy blessings.
petu babu temu – petu babu idu
Open the Gates of your understanding. Open the gates of your power.
ina ki-bi-ti-ka sir-ti lu-ub-lut lu-us-lim-ma
Let me live. Let me be perfect.

napsiti narbu ramanu ki-bi su su-sud ilani samu
Command greatness in my life as your expansion permeates the gods
of heaven.
anaku arad-ka elu
I am a servant of the Highest.
an-un-na-ki ti-i-ru u na-an-za-zu
May the ANUNNAKI come forth and be established.

FRIDAY – VENUS – ISHTAR & DUMUZI

ilu-INANNA. ilu-istari-ISHTAR. ilu-DUMUZI. ilu-ISTAR.
INANNA. ISHTAR. DUMUZI. ISTARI VENUS.
belitu, martu-su ilu-NANNA-SIN sa karabu ina samu
Queen, Daughter of the Moon, who is blessed by the heavens,
ramu-su ilu-ANU, rabianu samu
Beloved of ANU, Command in Heaven,
namru-sat musi
Brightness of the Evening,
lu-dub-gar-ra sat musi
Huntress of the Night,
li-iz-ziz ilu-istari-ya ina sumili-ya sutlumu karabu nissanu sabu u ilani
Do come to stand favorably at my side, grant me the fruits of men and gods.
ilu-istari-ISHTAR u ilu-DUMUZI
ISHTAR and DUMUZI,
rimi-nin-ni-ma, ana-ku ___ apil ___ sa ilu-sa ___ u ilu-istar-su ___
Be favorable to me, I, ___ son of ___ , whose god is ___ and whose
goddess is ___ ,
mesu-ya nigussu, anaku aga simtu maharu zi qistu
Cleanse me of impurity make me a vessel fit to receive your rewards.
petu babu temu
Open the Gates of your understanding to me.
li-iz-ziz ramanu manahtu-su zid
May my actions be true.
a-mat a-kab-bu-u kima a-kab-bu-u lu-u ma-ag-rat
May the words I speak bring me to success.
is-ti-' nam-ri-ir-ri-ki lim-mi-ru samu kima nasaru sabu-su karabu
May your light shinning in the heavens be a guide to all men you bless
favorably.
si-lim itti ya-a-tu-u anaku arad-ka elu
Bless me, a servant of the Highest.
an-un-na-ki ti-i-ru u na-an-za-zu
May the ANUNNAKI come forth and be established.

SATURDAY – SATURN – NINURTA & BA'U

ilu-NINURTA. ilu-NINIB. ilu-istari-BA'U. ilu-ADAR.
NINURTA. NINIB. BA'U. ADAR. SATURN.
siptu aplu gas-ru bukur ilu-ENLIL
Mighty firstborn son of ENLIL.
su-bu-u man-za-za ina ilani rabuti siru rubu-su ilu-ENLIL u ilu-NINMAH
Great is your place among the gods, royal prince of ENLIL and NINMAH.
belu u beltu sihip same u erseti, ilu-NINIB u ilu-istari-BA'U
Lord and Lady of the heavenly abode, NINIB and BA'U,
atwu karabu-ya kisal mahu
Speak favorably of me in your courts,
ana-ku ___ apil ___ sa ilu-su ___ u ilu-istar-su ___
I, ___ , son of ___ , whose god is ____ , and whose goddess is ____ .
an-ni pu-tur - sir-ti pu-sur
Absolve me of my sins. Remove my iniquities.
lu-us-tam-mar ilu-ut-ka u atwu ramanu lid-mi-ik
Make me fit to call upon and receive your blessings.
petu babu temu, anaku arad-ka elu
Open the Gates of you Understanding to me, a servant of the Highest,
ilu-istar-BA'U, biltu sur-bu-tu, sela ummu
BA'U, Mighty Lady, merciful mother.
ilu-NINIB, nisirtu qarradu ilu-ENLIL
NINIB, hidden warrior of ENLIL.
ki-bit narbu ramanu zi
Command greatness in my life.
si-lim itti ya-a-tu-u
Look upon me favorably.
sumu-ka ka-lis ina pi nisi ta-a-ab
May your name be in the mouth of the people.
an-un-na-ki ti-i-ru u na-an-za-zu
May the ANUNNAKI return and be established.

SUNDAY – THE SUN – SHAMMASH & AYA

ilu-SHAMMASH. ilu-UTU. ilu-istari-AYA. ilu-SAMAS. samsu.
SHAMMASH. UTU. AYA. SAMAS. SUN.
anqullu u igigallu
Fiery and Powerful One,
dinu ilani
Judge among the gods,
maru aplu ilu-NANNA-SIN
Son of the Moon-god,
sapiru nam-simtu apitu
Overseer of the destinies of the lands.

174

ilu-SAMAS u ilu-AYA karabu danu simtu
SHAMMASH and AYA, Be the favorable judges of my destiny.
metequ damaqu
May the path be prosperous.
la-kasadu immu kararu
Unequaled light of day,
ilu-SAMAS u ilu-AYA
SHAMMASH and AYA
si-lim itti ya-a-tu-u ___ , apil ___ , sa ilu-sa ___ , ilu-istar-su ___ .
Shine favorably on me, __ , son of __ , whose god is __ and whose
   goddess is __ .
napahu ramanu sir-tu
Incinerate my iniquities.
lu-ub-lut lu-us-lim-ma maharu nuru
Make me perfect to behold your light.
enu atwu uznu ilu-ENLIL
Lord, who appeals to the ears of ENLIL,
petu babu temu
Open the Gates of your understanding to me.
sumu-ka ka-lis ina pi nisi ta-a-ab
Permanent is your mighty word on earth.
qibitu nig-silim ina ramanu napistu
May your unquestioned command dictate prosperity in my life.
ana-ku arad-ka elu
I am a servant of the Highest,
an-un-na-ki ti-i-ru u na-an-za-zu.
May the ANUNNAKI return and be established.

— D —
: LADDER OF LIGHTS :
INITIATIONS OF ANCIENT MYSTERY SCHOOLS

True esoteric mysteries are often earned by Seekers (and initiates of the *Ancient Mystery School*) progressively through a series of *steps*. The purpose of "grading" is to *gradually* introduce a Seeker to successively "higher" levels of realization and awareness that cumulatively unfold. Various traditions throughout the ages have each interpreted these mysteries differently, adding their own flavors and tables of correspondence, often times obscuring the number of "degrees" to fit their systems: "10 degrees" of the *Golden Dawn*; "33 degrees" of *Freemasonry*, &tc. But, the most ancient famous examples, specifically for our purposes, are described as a "sevenfold" system.

In a conventional esoteric institution, each "level" of initiation—or "step" on the *"Ladder of Lights"*—not only increases a Seeker's awareness of the system, but also grants new potential for personal development. Each *"Key"* is earned while working with a particular fragmented energy "current." These currents have also been called the "seven rays of light" (or the "seven pillars") because they comprise the main tenets of information contained within the structure of form, usually encountered directly in the physical (visible) world of light as "Cosmic Law."

Although the essential existence of the ALL is wholeness, material reality is distinguished by seven bands of a visible spectrum. Each degree appears separate —resonating its own frequency and perceived energy current. Philosophers applied this paradigm to other material spectrums—*seven* notes of music, *seven* colors, *seven* days of the week—each corresponding with one of *seven* physical "celestial spheres" (*planets*), and so forth. The initiate was able to "sample" each aspect of the system in exclusion, and then as incorporated knowledge (with the rest) accumulated as a "base" of understanding—a "base" for *awareness* and *knowing*.

The Babylonian system of *"Gates,"* levels or degrees, are realized into existence uniquely by different traditions and their practices—all as a result of their *base*. Personal workings are performed from a *"Body of Light"*—the practitioner elevating their consciousness on the astral plane—then intoning specific passwords and names while tracing spiritual gate "seals," "signs" and "forms" that all trigger a preset shift in conscious *awareness* and *knowing*. These "levels" are often associated with "aethyrs" or "etheric planes" of manifestation that is deemed the "Other." Each level of initiation, step or *"rung"* requires entrance or passage through an *astral gate* equivalent to achievement of further stages of spiritual unfoldment. Similar practices are found in many modern forms of "ceremonial magic," incorporating their own "Ladder of Lights."

The Babylonian Star-Gate system—alluded to in all of the Mesopotamian influenced *Necronomicon* cycles of modern esoteric literature—corresponds with an ancient "Mardukite" plan to dedicate and seal the "younger pantheon" of the Anunnaki in Babylon under the reign of *Marduk*. These were to be the patrons of *"New-Babylon,"* a political and spiritual vision that never actually experienced total fruition, but which continues to evolve even today.

The first time Babylon fell, the main priestly class of magicians, priestesses and *Nabu*-scribes moved to Egypt, inspiring an entire "Hermetic" legacy. Modern "Dragon Court" revivals are often led by those with kinship to the Nile Region as well. This does not constitute any genetic propaganda—especially since all of the dynasties seem to switch back and forth like a pendulum swing, changing with time and politics. Even in Babylon, we see the *"Hand of Marduk"* extend to foreign Kings when necessity demanded. By the time of the "Classical Period," Alexander-The-Great succeeded in taking control of *"dragonblood"* in Egypt, just as he had in Babylon. This over-stretched empire primed weakened conditions on a global scale, eventually leaving the known world wide open to Roman reign, particularly when the Ptolemaic dynasty was "given" to Rome by Cleopatra. Then, when Rome fell, so did its forced "false" authority systems that the world had become dependent on.

The *ankh* was widely known in Egypt as a protective symbol of life—literally the "Key of Life." Few are aware that it also esoterically represented the double-helix serpent-coiled (DNA) and *"Tree of Life"* in Mesopotamia. The *Ancient Mystery School* dedicated the symbol to the AMON-RA in Egypt (also ATEN and "Marduk-RA"). It therefore became highly revered by the Mardukite priesthood altogether. In some traditions, the *ankh* was given (bestowed) to a scribe-priest-magician upon completion of their seventh (final) initiation.

The *ankh* is essentially a "cross," but also and a symbol of "crossings in the heavens"—meaning also "among the stars," or literally "the astral." In one version, the symbol is of the Self standing before the "Omega" shaped gateway. In its original Anunnaki form, this cross is drawn as a "T" (*Tau*) with a serpent being entwined around it. This is where the upper loop comes from, but which continues to coil in an *"infinity-8"* pattern down the stem, simultaneously representing the famous "serpent staff" of ancient magicians. The serpent is the *"serpent of wisdom"*—the *Primordial Dragon*—and equally representing the *"Cosmic Law"* embedded in what humans call "DNA." The Egyptian word: "AN-KH," is very similar to the Sumerian word: "AN-KI," meaning *"universe"*—the ALL—or literally: *"heaven+earth."*

It should come as little surprise that some long-standing esoteric factions of underground society—existing before the inception of the modern "Mardukite" movement—made use of these same mysteries: Egyptian Freemasonry and Rosicrucianism. These initiates hold a belief that these "stories of the gods" are in fact literal references to very ancient "luminous beings" (*"Illuminati"*) that eventually *came to be* considered along the same lines as the Olympian Titans. "Tahutian" practitioners—neo-Egyptian dedicates to the embodiment of *Nabu* as the "Thoth-current"—still observe a (self)-initiation system inherited from the Egypto-Babylonian "*Ladder of Lights.*" This specific lore has been maintained in an occult manuscript known as the "*Crata Repoa*," describing seven "levels" of Hermetic initiation.

* * *

A neophyte (initiate of the first degree) is called the "*Pastophoris.*" This is a title bestowed upon the Seeker who has passed the "Earth Gate," and is by nature, a Guardian of the "Gates of Men," and given the secret (pass) word: AMON. They are taught the basic symbolism of the Ladder of Lights and instruction in the physical (natural) sciences. [Mardukite Gatekeepers: NANNA and NINGAL —"*Moon Gate.*" Mystical/Temple Craft: Dream Work.]

The second level is called the "*Neocoris.*" The Seeker is initiated by "water and serpent" and given physical knowledge of cosmos—the mysteries of geometry, mathematics and architecture. They are bestowed with the "serpent staff," and by the password: EVE, they are granted access to the secret lore of the origins and fall of the human race. Their temple duties include cleaning the pillars (pylons) and generally tending to custodial needs of the shrines. [Mardukite Gatekeepers: NABU and TESHMET—"*Mercury Gate.*" Mystical/Temple Craft: Knowledge of Other Minds.]

Ascending to the third step on the Ladder of Lights earn the title of "*Melanephoris,*" when the initiate becomes a Guardian of the "Gates of Death," and perhaps also given the secrets of mummification (a valuable art in Nile Region). Here, the Seeker receives the infamous "Underworld Initiation" after being led to the "Tomb of Osiris" with the passwords: MONACH CARON MINI, meaning: "I count the days of anger." [Mardukite Gatekeepers: ISHTAR and DUMUZI—"*Venus Gate.*" Mystical/Temple Craft: Past-Life Memory.]

From this point, the Seeker would be left in the catacombs and archives of lore to discern the secret to access the next level of initiation on their own. If they did not, they would ever remain an initiate of the third degree—but if they were to discover the "secret code," then they would be initiated as a "*Chistophorus*" via the "blindfold rite" (where a red noose is hung around the initiates neck, like a leash). Only then is he allowed to enter the Assembly of the Inner Circle, an Adept among Masters of the Highest Councils. The "*Chistophorus*" is an Adept who has earned the secret of the "shades" (a code for the "primordial battles in heaven" based on the *Enuma Elis*) and given access to the "secret chambers" of the Order. Soon thereafter, the seeker is granted an initiation by fire after proving themselves via dramatically "slaying the dragon" (or removing the head of Medusa/Typhon, etc.) and the password: ZOA. [Mardukite Gatekeepers: SHAMMASH and AYA—"*Sun Gate.*" Mystical/Temple Craft: History and Doctrines of the Universe.]

If successful past this point, mystical knowledge comes also in the form of a practical instruction is chemistry and metallurgy as fifth degree "*Balahate*" and the word: KHEMIA or CHEMYA. [Mardukite Anunnaki Gatekeepers: NERGAL and ERESHKIGAL—"*Mars Gate.*" Mystical/Temple Craft: Function and Formulas of the Universe.]

After working to master the "godly" understanding of the "heavenly spheres" and the "gods of old," the Adept is the installed to the sixth degree and called the "*Guardian of the Star-Gates,*" or literally, "*Astronomer who stands before the Gate of the Gods*" (a Master-Priest status). Only then are the religious secrets divulged as well as the "true natures" of the Anunnaki, their origins and lore of their rule (and return?) on earth. The seeker is then granted another initiation through the "Gates of Death," this time to meet the Elder pantheon as a true Priest. [Mardukite Gatekeepers: MARDUK and SARPANIT—"*Jupiter Gate.*" Mystical/Temple Craft: Material Unity via Love.]

The final and seventh step on the Ladder of Lights is called the "*Saphenath Pancah,*" an initiation required to attain "Prophet" status in the tradition. Secret knowledge of the gods is offered, including privileged knowledge of the "Elixir of Life." The Adept-Master-Priest, now Prophet, is given a white robe [*etangi*] and an ankh to wear. The password of the grade is: ADON ("*Adonai*"), a Semitic name, meaning "Lord of the Earth." [Mardukite Gatekeepers: NINURTA and BA'U —"*Saturn Gate.*" Mystical/Temple Craft: Dissolution of Self via Spiritual Unity with the ALL.]

—PART TWO—
NECRONOMICON REVELATIONS
(LIBER R)

— 0 —
: NECRONOMICON REVELATIONS :
THE ANUNNAKI LEGACY & MAGICAL REVIVAL

The arrival of the "Simon *Necronomicon*" in the mid-1970's did little to satisfy dedicated "Lovecraftian" fanatics—those searching for the legendary book alluded to in a specific series of stories known as the "*Cthulhu Mythos*." *Howard Phillips (H.P.) Lovecraft*'s gothic fantasies elusively described a primordial pantheon of "Ancient Ones" and a legacy they left behind in literary form—the "*Necronomicon*"—many of his readers believed the book had to be *real*, and that the mythos he suggested must somehow exist at the heart of *real* prehistory. Using a platform of fiction, and sparking a new literary genre, H.P. Lovecraft *did* imagine his stories into being, but they were not based on any research or historical fascination—they were the product of astral torment and nightmares.

In 1904, famed occultist *Aleister Crowley* was compelled to spend the spring equinox—the ancient Babylonian "Akitu" New Year—in Egypt. There, he encountered a member of the *Anunnaki*, which explained to him that the "Equinox of the Gods" was taking place—"the *gate* forced open" into a "new aeon." Crowley had traversed the "*Nabu Gate*," making contact with the being often identified as "THOTH"—but who is, in fact, NABU, the divine-scribe and son of MARDUK— a master of the esoteric arts of magic and science. The Hermetic Order of the Golden Dawn had successfully previously tapped the "*Moon Gate*," as did many other groups and practitioners of the "magical revival." Politics that led to fracturing an alliance between *Crowley* and the *Golden Dawn* concerned "control" of the "*Nabu Gate*"—the *Gate* of THOTH, HERMES, MERCURY, among other names. To the surface world (even the contemporary "New Age") this is all unofficial, of course. All initiates have their own semantics to describe these events. However, the result of Crowley's personal efforts (used to base his own tradition)—"*Book of the Law*"—just one of many *Anunnaki* transmissions granted to receptive mystics on the planet during the modern magical revival—

> "*Every man and woman is a star.*"

Although popularized later by Kenneth Grant for the O.T.O., Aleister Crowley never once used the word: *Necronomicon*. Based on popular ceremonial magic of the era, his arsenal of medieval and kabbalistic grimoires already possessed their own titles, ones well-recognized today in the "New Age" community. Crowley's favorites were the "*Book of Abramelin*," the "*Goetia*" and the "*Keys of Solomon*." He even allegedly assisted Gerald Gardner in the creation of the *Book of Shadows*, thus directly influencing the religious movement that sprang from it: *Wicca*.

Of the previously available grimoires, a consensus among early members of the *Mardukite Research Organization* demonstrated that the "divine magic" style reflected from "Abramelin-the-Mage," was the preferred example to our own work. It carries a higher "mystical value" than the other "magical" volumes available that may partly resemble the type of ritualistic work thought to be connected to the "*Necronomicon* of H.P. Lovecraft"—of which we are only left with brief passages amidst his stories. The very idea that the "gate-work" itself will "kill" is ridiculously false, as Aleister Crowley lives on for another four decades after the Egypt-incident.

H.P. Lovecraft was only 14 years old in 1904. It was, however, the year that ultimately changed his life. The death of his grandfather left the family in ruin—they were still trying to overcome the loss of his father in 1898. Four years later, when Lovecraft suffered a "nervous breakdown," he was unable to complete his high-school education. It becomes clear that the visions he beheld—resulting in volumes of poetry and short stories—did not come from any logical source: an occult education, bizarre interests, or even mystical mythologies, but were, instead, the product of living beneath the shadows of despair, enduring a perpetual "dark night of the soul" that would never lift at dawn.

Some scholars have gone to great lengths to prove that Lovecraft's grandfather was a very active Freemason, but there does not seem to be any direct "spill-over" interest for either Lovecraft or his father. The only work of mythology (we know for certain) that appealed to Lovecraft and may have any relevance to his later work, is "Arabian Nights." And before using the Greek name "*Necronomicon*," Lovecraft proposes that the legendary work first bore the title "*Al Azif*" in Arabic. Descriptions of Lovecraft's "*Al-Alif*" also share some similarities to the Yezidi "*Al-Jilwah*," given as *Tablet-J* in the Mardukite "*Necronomicon: The Anunnaki Bible*." It would seem to some that Lovecraft did somehow access the *Gates* directly—or, like Crowley, was *directed to them intentionally*.

There is a cosmic "dualism" present in Lovecraft's work that is out of synch with the original Sumerian pantheon or tradition. Such themes really develop more strongly in later Semitic and Zoroastrian interpretations of the *Anunnaki* system—and also from Egypt. For this reason, many skeptics attacked the "Mesopotamian mysticism" presented in the Simon *Necronomicon*—but, if there is some validity behind all of this, then it alludes to something that was not even known to the *Sumerians* concerning origins of their gods—something that would become emphasized later by the *Babylonians*.

Lovecraftian stories describe the malignant force of "*Ancient Ones*" that at one time reign supreme in the cosmos but are later defeated by a younger generation of "*Elder Gods*"—those responsible for the creation of men and the inhabitable ("civilized") earth. There is no evidence for this in Sumer, and the closest resembling cycle from the *Ancient Near East* that could apply is none other than the "Mardukite" Babylonian paradigm—centralized on the "*Enuma Elis*," given as

Tablet-N in *"Necronomicon: The Anunnaki Bible."* If we are to consider one possible connection ancient lore where Lovecraft could possibly pull his "Cthulhu mythos" from, it is the mythology painted of TIAMAT in the *Enuma Elis*—a Babylonian worldview, *not* Sumerian. It resembles the discordance among primordial gods that Lovecraft alludes to more closely than anything else.

Consider (Mardukite *Necronomicon: The Anunnaki Bible*)—

"When first the gods were [like] men on Earth."

Compared to (*Necronomicon of H.P. Lovecraft*)—

"The spawn of the Old Ones covered the Earth and their children endure throughout the Ages."

Lovecraft continues (from the Hay *Necronomicon*)—

"And the Elder Gods opened their eyes and beheld abominations..."

The bizarre horrors described in "H.P. Lovecraft's *Necronomicon*" appear in the *"Enuma Elis"* concerning a primordial battle between the "Ancient Ones" [TIAMAT and ABZU] and the "Elder Gods" [the *Anunnaki*]. Much as the "younger gods" displaced their forefathers in post-Sumerian traditions, we can see that this was probably the case here. TIAMAT and ABZU are most not necessarily a "malignant" force, but in the Babylonian version of the *Enuma Elis* we read of TIAMAT—

"She spawned monster-serpents,
Sharp of tooth and merciless of fang;
With poison instead of blood, she filled their bodies.
Fierce monster-vipers she clothed with terror.
Whoever beheld them, terror overcame them."

Returning to Lovecraft (Hay, *Necronomicon*)—

"Loathsome Cthulhu rose up from the Depths and raged with exceeding great fury against the Earth's Guardians: The Elder Gods."

And from the *Enuma Elis*—

"She acted possessed and lost her sense of reason..."

After the battle (*Necronomicon of H.P. Lovecraft*)—

"Beyond the Gate [to the Outside] dwell now the Old Ones; not in the spaces known to men, but in the angles between them..."

Hints of such "space between spaces" can also be found in the *Enuma Elis*—

> "Go and cut off the life of TIAMAT,
> Let the wind carry her blood into *secret places*."

Following this mythology, we can see why Simon chose the *"Necronomicon"* as the form to present his "recension" of a Mardukite-Babylonian grimoire. It was not a book of evil, but a book of false perceptions concerning the Sumerian Anunnaki *"gods"*—a picture painted by the priests dedicated to the "younger pantheon" of Mesopotamia, especially those emphasizing the national god of Babylon: MAR-DUK. The attitude from Lovecraft toward the book, reveal it as dark and perverse; not meant for the "realm of light" or "world of men," and instead to ever remain in the private collections of "select" men—who dared never speak of it. Of course, Lovecraft's personal *Necronomicon* was a work of pure fantasy, *but* the cuneiform tablets composing the oldest writings on the planet...*are not*. That such ancient Mesopotamian collections of these tablets now share a cover-name with Lovecraft's creation is about the only debatable issue for scholars and mystics alike, and one based purely on semantics of a "title"—none of which actually changes the message. Peter Levenda (allegedly "Simon") explains in an 2007 interview—

> "On another level: the *Necronomicon*—the publication of a book called the *Necronomicon*—no matter what *Necronomicon* [version] it is; I think raises a lot of questions that have become very controversial and that is: what is a true 'book'? Or, questions concerning the value of psuedoepigrapha; for instance, the *Keys of Solomon* was not written by 'Solomon.' There's false attributions to it. The Gardnerian *Book of Shadows* was written by Gerald Gardner. It wasn't written by some ancient pagan witches a thousand or even hundreds of years ago. So, we have to ask ourselves: where is the true value? The *Necronomicon* itself forces people to question: what do we really value? Do we value an ancient text because it's ancient? Or, do we value it because it has something else to offer us? Is a new text with an ancient patina just as valuable as a new text or a genuine ancient text? ...It asks a lot of questions."

The very application of "magic" to the system is a clue to savvy occult interpreters, since this magic of *sigil-forms*, *names* and *numbers* of Anunnaki *"gods,"* was "Mardukite-Hermetic"—specifically Babylonian and Chaldean—as passed down from ENKI. The entire idea of "personal magic" is absent from the original pre-Babylonian religious system of Sumer. The most ancient Magicians, Priests, Priestesses and Kings, all maintained a direct relationship with the gods. Then later, after the gods "left earth," traditions of prayer and supplication became more prominent—the people sought to invoke the power of the (now) distant "gods" back into the material world. But nowhere in ancient Mesopotamian mysticism is there evidence for practices to "exorcise" the power of the gods by *force*—making demands of the "divine" simply because some magicians is privy to a special name, signature-image or numeric formula. This "bolder" form of practice came about later during the neo-Babylonian and rise of Semitic cultures—it became popular in the Mediterranean as "*Hermetics*" and eventually came to dominate esoteric philosophies of Egypt and Greece. Francois Lenormant describes the origins and development of these beliefs—

> "The mystic name [*sign, seal, &tc.*] exercised a power upon the god himself to whom it belonged, and that when called by this name he was obliged to obey the incantation. The virtue of the formulae lay not in an invocation of the divine power, but in the fact of a man proclaiming himself such or such a God, and when he, in pronouncing the incantation, called to his aid any one of the various members of the pantheon, it was as one of themselves that he had a right to the assistance of his companions."

MARDUK taught this evolving methodology to magicians of his Hermetic magic (most likely against the wishes of his superiors)—the ability of assuming a "god-form" to compel the universe by magic, and to use incantations in his name, as found with the frequently used incantation passage—

> "*It is not I, but Marduk, who speaks the incantation.*"

Thus, magicians of the later systems spent more time divining secret names and formulas than establishing their own relationship with the powers they sought. Mystics of more antiquated traditions relied on "*true knowledge*" of the "*gods*" themselves—those possessing the very "names" and "numbers" of the cosmos. By petitioning the deity in self-honesty to act on their behalf, the Mesopotamian priest or priestess was able to perform works of utilitarian "magic" Positive "civic magic" aided development and maintenance of the land—the "*Realm*"—that lived and thrived under the patronage of a particular local Anunnaki deity). The original pursuit for power, by "magic," or favor of the gods, remains here, embedded within the ancient systems. Against popular belief, driven by fear and naivete, the ascent up the "Ladder of Lights" toward "god-hood" is no "Pandora's Box" waiting to harm the practitioner—the devouring will be only of one's impurity—for only the *Self-Honest* armed with *Absolute Truth* will be allowed to pass, as Lenormant warns—

> "The power of magical incantation to compel obedience from the gods themselves became, however, formidable, even to him who exercised it, if he did not show himself worthy to possess it by moral purity and a knowledge of divine things."

— 1 —
: NOVEM PORTIS :
NINE GATES OF THE KINGDOM OF SHADOWS

The path of the *Ancient Mystery Tradition* has, up until now, led the Seeker along a vast array of "colors" and "images"—up rungs of a "*Ladder of Lights*" as it were—tracing phantasmal images of the material world back to their Source. But, it is not glamorous procurement of further persona and personality upgrades that Seekers are after—rather, it is the absolution or dissolution of the same; transforming programming you have already acquired and become weights keeping you bound by distractions of—and energetic slavery to—the material very world; a Realm of *light* and *forms*.

So, a Seeker passes through "*Seven Gates of Life*," question for completion—to bring parts of the whole together—if they be so lucky. More often though, it is the case that initiates separate the "*whole*" into additional esoteric "*parts*" that merely ends with a life further separated—a spiral journey of vocabularies and paradigms, but no closer to the Source. Therefore, our emphasis should not be on the bedazzle-ment projected in front of our psyche for this world. An addiction quickly forms toward "intellectual delights—making some obscure *numerological* or *symbolic* links between a myriad of forms. But, the ALL is actually connected to *All* in equality and oneness—not just to be found in a few sacred "correspondences"—these semantic relationships between observable attributes and invisible forces.

Wholeness. This is never fully realized in the World of Light that we are accustomed to. This world exists because of a state of perceived separation from the World of Darkness. Polarity. As a semantic solution, our purpose is not necessarily to glorify Darkness, either. There are many people that succumb to trappings of Darkness, just as some do in the Light. Such only happens when the misinformed initiate is instructed to experience the ALL as "parts" *in exclusion* to other "parts." This occurs in many traditions emphasizing duality contrary to the Oneness that is the Source. Duality is not Oneness—and no system observing such can ever offer complete unification of cosmic knowledge.

So, what does one do? We first climb up the "*Ladder of Lights*"—on the "*Tree of Life*" we have fallen from—and thereby unify the manifold natures of existences found in the Light—but is this the end? While working back up the "*Tree of Life*," the Seeker uncovers a very dangerous glitch in the system—that this is not all there is. But where is it? And how do we experience the hidden aspects of the cosmos for wholeness.

How do we get to the other side..?

The *"Master Astronomer Standing at the Gates of the Gods"* moves forth—traversing the Gates of this Universe. The Seeker inevitably moves passed the final doorway—the *"Seventh Gate"*—and is able to glean a look behind the curtain... And there is nothing more horrifying than what one will find. For indeed, all we have done and worked towards, all we have quested for in our endeavors through the Light and the material System, and when the curtain is peeled back it is only to reveal—Nothingness... *The Primordial Abyss*.

All of the systems in the mind—all that have gives form its meaning—has been washed away and the realization of the illusion is paralyzing. For when we had our *"Wizard of Oz"* to toy with in our minds, we could at the very least laugh in our own folly at being fooled into playing a game of some supernatural crazed madman behind the curtains. At the very least things could be made to make some sense—*systematically*—as a reflection of what we believe about the material world.

But, now at the cusp of reality and sanity, we know better. Before you is the Other Side of the Tree... Crossing the Abyss... Into the Beyond... You have reached the edge.

You are have reached – the Shadows...

* * *

After the rise of the *"Hermetic Order of the Golden Dawn"* and the "magical revival" in the late 1800', the spiritual and metaphysical world of the mystics—once hidden away, restricted to dank fens of society—began to appear in the public spotlight, or at least carry an *illusion* of being maintained in public view. With this followed the widespread revival and use of medieval grimoires—many of them translated or introduced by like *MacGregor Mathers* and Aleister Crowley. Magical organizations relating to these individuals—such as the GD (*Golden Dawn*), OTO (*Ordo Templi Orientis*) and Crowley's own AA (*Argentium Astrum*)—all begin to influence mystical practices and underground traditions, directly affecting the multitudes on the surface world.

Naturally, we are most concerned foremost with content from the Babylonian derived text—*"Necronomicon: The Anunnaki Bible"*—research and developed by the Mardukite Chamberlains in 2009—and its interconnected relationship to the Great Mysteries. However, the association of modern pseudoepigrapha in this regard is not limited simply to a book called the *"Necronomicon"*—for such is just a *name*, as is *"Al Azif,"* or anything else we want *"defined"* so as to give anything its definitive form. We often attempt to solidify that which cannot be solidified—that which is not meant to be solidified.

* * *

The novel "*El Club Dumas*" released in Spain in 1993. American English-speaking audiences would have to wait three years to find "*The Club Dumas*" on their shelves. This literary treatment by *Arturo Perez-Reverte* was lost amidst a mystery genre ruled by contemporaries like Agatha Christie and Sue Grafton. It did not receive pop-culture attention until its motion picture realization under a different title.

In *Reverte*'s novel, the main character—*Corso*—set in a dusty environment of Antiquarian book-selling, is on a quest to uncover the truth of a lost fragment-chapter of the famous serial by Alexander Dumas—"*The Three Musketeers.*" In the course of events, Corso is culled into a different kind of quest... and more people have been exposed to the influence of this modern tale then you might originally suspect, for the cycle is known by another more popular title:—

"*Nine Gates of the Kingdom of Shadows.*"

Although now popular in NexGen occultism, prior to the 2009 Mardukite "*Liber 9*" release (as "*Nine Gates of the Kingdom of Shadows*"), the work had previously escaped inevitable occult pseudoepigrapha! [While still available as a stand-alone title, "*Liber 9*" has since been incorporated into the greater "*Necronomicon: The Anunnaki Bible*" anthology.]

From the Spanish edition we translate the title "*Nine Doors to the Kingdom of Darkness.*" We can appreciate the shift in American language—"*Gates*" to "portals," and "*Shadows*" to the "Darkness." These changes happen frequently with American cultural imports from other countries. American audiences also seem more receptive to *video* media then books, as certainly motivated Roman Polanski to film "*The Ninth Gate,*" released in 1999, starring Johnny Depp. The wood-carved engravings that are so paramount to the film are taken directly from illustrations found in Reverte's novel.

It might surprise many occultists to note that the vein of pseudoepigrapha runs deep within the mystic stream— reaching down to all too familiar works, such as the "*Keys of Solomon*" or even the "*Book of Abramelin*"—genuine books with false assertions of authorship. It comes as no surprise that we see a rise of more legends of such "books within books"—"fantasies within fantasies"—as the existing human condition undoubtedly achieves its ends in the "*Realm of Light*," when we must, by necessity of our survival, reach out to the *Shadows*.

Considering themes from the lore of *Nine Gates*, we are instructed that the work is based on yet another book—furthering our psyche's journey an esoteric literary rabbit hole. The "*Delomelanicon*"—unarguably a new vision of the *Necronomicon* Cycle—is a book reportedly written by the "Devil himself" as a guide for "his followers." The work, said to have once been in the possession of King Solomon, reached the realm of Medieval Sorcery in 1666 by *Aristide Torchia*, who published his version of this "Devil's Notebook" as "*De Umbrarum Regni Novem Portis.*"

Torchia and all but three copies of this work are burned by the Church. The title —"*Delomelanicon*"—the current editor translates as "*Book of Summoning the Darkness*," (similar to the coveted, but equally fantasy-based, witches' *Book of Shadows*). When first analyzed for "*Liber-9*" in 2009, some early Mardukite Chamberlains preferred the translation "*Invocation of Darkness*," as given in the Soto translation of "*Club Dumas.*"

If we lend a thought to this story for a moment, putting aside trappings of se-mantics, vocabulary or verification of a medieval sorcerer's grimoire—consider a book given to a class of followers from an entity contrary to the accepted "God On Duty"—considered a "*devil*" to one side, and a "*savior*" to the other. Immediately, we conjure to mind Anunnaki politics of ancient Mesopotamia—beings like MAR-DUK and ENKI—or some other specific "alien intelligence" with some motive for leading folks back through the *Gates*. And if these beings are indeed hidden in folds "between" the "*Realm of Light*"—the reality we see everyday—then they would most certainly belong to the Shadows – *and the spaces between spaces*.

The archetype conjured to mind by the "*Nine Gates*" is very similar to the *Necronomicon*. There is, at the very least, obvious symbolic emphasis of "portals," "thresholds" and "gateways"—such as is inseparably paramount to this lore. Following esoteric and occult examples, the "*Gates*" are introduced to the Seeker under the guise of "Darkness," because such was (and remains to be) the perception of what is "forbidden" and "hidden" knowledge—at least from the perspective of the Realm of Light. For, even as Peter Levenda concisely said of the Simon *Necronomicon*: "It is a book about Darkness." Levenda reiterates that it is not a book about "pacts with devils" or anything so trite, such as you might see with the "*Grand Grimoire*" ("*Red Dragon*"), &tc.—but more importantly it is an ancient, nearly prehistoric methodology for *understanding the Darkness*.

We can see by his choice of directing the "*Ninth Gate*" film, that Polanski is interested in the esoteric enigma of the *Necronomicon*—and what is interesting as a result: both Kenneth Grant and "Simon" have acknowledged "*The Ninth Gate*" in their works as nod in their direction. Without even knowing this, one can still easily compare the "*Ninth Gate*" movie to "*El Club Dumas*" and instantly recognize where the emphasis shift lies. Simon, in his book "*Dead Names*" explains that—

> "...anyone who met me in those days in the 1970's would recognize Johnny Depp's character: glasses, beard, black clothes, black raincoat, bag over one shoulder. The intrigue that follows some of the events in the real story [of the publication of the Simon *Necronomicon*] including the references to wealthy individuals who sought the power of the book for themselves."

Those already familiar with the "*other side*" of the Mystery Tradition have possibly run across the cryptic O.T.O. series of three trilogies produced by Kenneth Grant. The final volume of this sequence of literature—"*The Ninth Arch*"—released in

2002, three years after the *"Ninth Gate"* movie (and a decade after the release of *"El Club Dumas"*). The current editor's opinion is only that one title bore some resemblance of the other. In Grant's case, the designation of "Arch" carried dual meanings—both to an idea of "Gateways," but also semantic parallels (something Grant is obsessed with in his writings) between the words *"Arch"* and *"Arachnid"*—AR*a*CH*nid*.

So now, thanks to Kenneth Grant, we have the "Spider" to add to the equation—as he offers *"Ninth Arch"* as the *"Book of the Spider"* or *"Grimoire of the Spider."* The *"Grimoire of the Night"* and other obscure works by the author, focus on the "other side of the tree"—once the initiate has first worked through the *"Grimoire of the Light."* [These Spider transmissions are designated known in the O.T.O. as both *"Book 29"* and *"OKBISh"*—a name that Grant claims is related to a Mesopotamian root for word "Spider."]

A lifetime can be spent chasing fragmented rays of light glimmering in various magical schools, but, all of this suggests that beneath the surface of the light, and in the *"betweens,"* there is as yet another part to the mystery for the Seeker—the *"Darkness"*—the *"Shadows."* In most cases, the Seeker will just rush to throw light against the screen again, impressing familiar images from their own experiences in the Light—not allowing the self-honest experience of something "unknown" to unfold. We need not materialize demonic images or cast fears before us only to allow them to become manifest by our own will—as such is not the true nature of the Shadows. Such falseness has only been created within the fragmented and fractured minds of men who further the polar necessity for the Shadows as they cling to the Light.

For what greater horror could man behold in the Realm of Light, then to reach the unspeakable realization that is most capable of shattering their delicate human psyche (and perhaps the dissolution of the Ego)—that it is no demon or gruesome vision to behold—but the full experience that the material world is a mere veil to something else. It is not the ends in itself, only but a *means.*

But how can reality come apart at the seams? For, we are a nation of civilized and enlightened men, are we not? Surely even humans have come to take the gear-grinding world for granted and the systems and boundaries that keep things in "check" are also in fear of dissolution—including monetary and political—as even *George Hay* notes, in his Preface to the *"R'lyeh Text,"* concerning world changes taking place on the planet since the *Necronomicon* cycle and early "Mardukite" revival of the 1970's noting—

> "... the dissolution of 'fixed' and 'given' groupings of Nation-States, and, far more important, of the belief systems that had until recently been holding them together."

Considering that the Lightworkers have further taken their fragmented human psyche and placed greater limits and sanctions of "good" and "evil" on all existence, the perpetuation of duality continues unresolved in the universe. With only casual interpretation of Mardukite *Necronomicon* lore—one might say that mankind was separated from the "Source," for an existence in a polarized world. But humans also further this separation from the Source over the course of their lives by lengthening the distance between perceived opposites instead of seeking harmony—*a return to the Source*. So long as the separation is maintained in the mind, manifestations of fear, jealousy, discord and the like will continue to be given existence in reality and confirmed by the psyche. While progression on the "spiral of evolution" is always forward and upward—the speed and rate of travel (or development of our spiritual evolution) is not guaranteed by any tradition not standing in *Self-Honesty*.

— 2 —
THE SIMON NECRONOMICON

Most widely distributed of all known versions of the *Necronomicon* is an edition released under editorship of "Simon." If you are currently reading this book, you are probably already familiar with the version of which I refer. Originally released in 1977 (then re-released in 2008) as a prestigious hardcover format, it is the mass-market paperback edition by Avon books (now HarperCollins) that received most of the attention by occultists and skeptics alike.

According to Simon, in *"Dead Names"*—his own account of the *"Dark History of the Necronomicon"*—the paperback edition, first released in 1980, has now sold nearly one-million copies, not including those recirculated by electronic and illegal means online and through unauthorized self-publishing. However, success of this printing history in the occult genre has only been rivaled by the work of *Anton LaVey*, also published by Avon Books—though it is important to note that LaVey's work started reaching mainstream markets in 1969, over a decade before the *Necronomicon* paperback.

Simon's *Necronomicon* might have made a sooner public appearance, but as the story goes, they had difficulties finding the right publisher for it in the mid-1970's. The "Cthulhu Mythos" drew a growing subculture of cult-fiction fans into the *Necronomicon* archetype (from writings of H.P. Lovecraft), but it seemed that no one really wanted to touch the project—either they weren't being taken seriously (or were afraid to), or it was just assumed that the project was doomed to fail. As anyone who has professionally worked with anything related to publication of a *Necronomicon* might understand, the actual truth of the situation is somewhere in the middle.

Literary creators have two choices when confronted with development and production barriers—either abandon the notion altogether or do it yourself. Those of us who have felt strongly enough about our "place" in the mysteries—and who have not been "blessed" with soul-selling spiritual contracts to blatant commercial success, and are self-honestly determined enough to see the work through (in spite of personal discord and suffering that often result from many "arts-in-commerce-driven-by-passion")—take it upon ourselves, in the Shadows of the mainstream, on our own tenacity, to do what we feel we must... *Against all odds*.

Sadly, it is only when manifested art and literary creations are brought out of the "shadows" that it becomes the subject of public scrutiny, in the public—in the Realm of Light—where occult work does not belong in the first place. This presents a serious "spiritual" or "mystical" dilemma, one confronted by nearly every "secret society" or "occult organization" that has been charged to hold any true aspect of the mysteries—how to deal with the publicly written word?

During the 1970's, bringing books to print of this caliber was a serious feat. It was a different age and time from what we have grown accustomed to today—and likewise, taken for granted. Things were done by mail and by phone—things took longer. We were not living in the current "print-on-demand" age where nearly any self-proclaimed "author" can now see their book "in print"—for a small price. Books were still being "typeset." Equipment and efforts were different and computers were not what they are today (or even always available to the average citizen). If you were not already a part of "big publishing," the labor, equipment and materials were not readily at your disposal.

What is only loosely spoken of in pop-culture metaphysical literature and occult manuals is the "power" exercised simply in such mass amounts of energy moving —and when done intentionally, these efforts in themselves can render projects with "life," not even considering what occurs when it reaches the "reality" of someone beyond the originator(s).

Of all of the various versions of "*Necronomicon*" found on the market today, the predecessor *is* the Simon work, not including the very loose and scattered references from Lovecraftian literature decades earlier. A lesser known version by George Hay appeared in the underground shortly thereafter. The two were completely unconnected—as the Seeker often finds when comparing the many available versions—other than use of a title and theme: "*Necronomicon.*"

When Simon's *Necronomicon* first debuted, very few people were privy to this specific "type" of esoteric understanding. It concerned a truly archetypal, pre-classical and pre-Christian methodology—a root system from which many other branches of the tree later formed, then perceived as separate—whether because of semantics or their cultural locale in time and geography. Even many supposed occultists and New Agers of the period had very little background in the real mythos being dealt with—which was not at all *Lovecraftian*, or even *Sumerian* as many others believe, but *Babylonian!*—the "Mardukite" paradigm.

The "Mardukite paradigm" is not paramount to any other popular editions of the "*Necronomicon*," including the Hay edition and also contributions of ritual magician, Donald Tyson—all of which are based purely on the vision and semantics of H.P. Lovecraft's "stories." [The exception to this, of course, being "*Necronomicon: The Anunnaki Bible.*"]

With the arrival of Simon's *Necronomicon* and its relationship with the work of *H.P. Lovecraft* (based on the title alone), the two mythoi have been confused by neo-gothic punks and emo-musicians as being one and the same. And although there is no real correlation to the work of Anton LaVey (other than being simultaneously produced by the same publisher), based on its marketed image alone, the "Simon" book is just as often found in the hands of someone carrying Anton LaVey works on "Satanism"—and as such the *Simon* book received further dark shadowy undertones as a result.

Contents aside, it may be that the manifestation of a tangible book, wholly obscure for its time, with the title across the front— NECRONOMICON—is what really launched the success of the book. For many, the chances to own and possess a work of such epic proportions was a dream come true. But as with many dreams and wishes, the dreamer does not always know what is for their own higher good. The only thing sometimes more daunting than the *quest* itself—is when you actually *find* what you seek!

One is then left to wonder: if the title used to label the work has been fabricated and is, in itself, the product of a fictional work by the hands of *Lovecraft*, to what validity might there even be to the *Simon* work using the title? Such is really an ignorant question, for the true Seeker should not be so easily caught up in missing the forest for the trees. Again, the Truth Seeker is urged to disregard that *one* semantic for their pursuit into genuine Mesopotamian mysteries, in order to have a self-honest experience on the pathway—not one that is so easily tainted by arbitrary filters put in your way to cause a distraction from any true 'enlightenment'.

As a result of the left-handed embrace of the *Cthulhu Mythos* drawn from the writings of *H.P. Lovecraft*, the "*Simon Necronomicon*" is marketed (and often boasted by practitioners of "New Age" traditions) as a powerful book of "black magick," a "grimoire of evil sorcery" and "most dangerous book" in existence! No sooner had Simon's *Necronomicon* been celebrated for coming into being, it was just as quickly renounced for its existence—and not simply by right-wing types that you would normally expect, mind you—but, by the very pulp-fiction fans who originally rejoiced in its arrival! Surely, this was not the "*Necronomicon*" originally referred to by Lovecraft!

... And thank the gods for that!

* * *

Experience is wholly subjective—a matter of perspective—and the written word is often communication of experience from a perspective by the author. This is actually how history is manipulated throughout the ages. Communication is also dependent on its *receivers* and "instructors" of this history have the ability to paint experiences of the "unknown past" with their own biases. This is carried with subsequent generations and has, in effect, shaped the way humans interact with their world—based on their "worldview." The *Necronomicon* is a paradigm for a "worldview," reflecting some of the oldest known beliefs and traditions on the planet—alluding to things that can very much *affect* the unprepared. That the uninitiated, who is already unstable, risks their own delicate psyche when "dabbling" in lore better left to others, is very much the case—but not necessarily any more the case with the *Necronomicon* then anything else.

We all know these types. If they weren't able to attribute their "madness" to the *Necronomicon*, they would just as soon be fundamentalist victims of some other creed. The difference is, the *Necronomicon* gnosis represents the "truth behind the world" hidden in the shadows and darkness of man's common worldview today—it becomes an easy target for attack. Because of its tangible absence, but century of allusions, its reputation preceded it—*heavily*.

When experienced from the dualistic perspective common to con-temporary reality, the *Necronomicon* does seem to represent a "dark element" in the spectrum. Part of this relates simply to the title and gothic overtones related to "death." Another part is the actually methodology involved. It represents aspects of our history that have been hidden from us, misrepresented, and—once we find out the truth behind even the system it is based in—shrouded in deception. It alludes even further to an understanding of existence that requires no degrees, titles or magick words and is instead dependent on true and faithful individualized experience of the "*Abyss*," a Void-of-Naught—the Infinity of Nothingness—which just so happens to be the true background existence to material reality—everywhere and nowhere at once.

Based on modern "Mardukite" Babylonian research, the *Necronomicon* paradigm is a very serious subject—well beyond Lovecraftian fantasies—that many "blessed" with involvement in this necessary paradigm-shift for our times, take very seri-ously. Unlike many *Necronomicon* critics out there who simply scream "hoax" to anything that bares the title, the modern "Mardukite" institution is more sympathet-ic toward early changes in consciousness provided by Simon's contribution—even if incomplete when compared to the greater encompassing "Mardukite" tradition.

Skeptical critics are used to throwing out the baby with the bath-water, without giving things a second thought. For them, the content of the Simon's *Necronomicon* itself—or even "*Necronomicon: The Anunnaki Bible*" for that matter—is irrelevant, given that the *title* of the work may be derived from a fictional source. Even though the interior corpus of the text has no real relationship with "*Lovecraftian*" fiction, it is easier for them to disregard the whole thing altogether, over a title. And these are the same "high minds" that would in another breath urge you "not to judge a book by its cover" (and so on) and yes, the same minds that so many other naïve initiates turn to for their *answers*.

* * *

Most work on the "Simon" grimoire seems to have been handled by a man named *Peter Levenda*, who has actually remained the primary public face for any "Simon" work—regardless of who "Simon" may actually be. It is interesting to note that combined, the name Simon-Peter is actually significant—in biblical context, where Simon becomes "Saint Peter," as the "Rock of the Church." Since mutual acquaint-anceship connects the modern *Mardukite Research Organization* with the original *Simon* circle, protection of individual identities and associations is essential—not only when dealing with Mystery Traditions (as has always been the case), but espe-cially when dealing with the *Necronomicon*. In short—*a lot* of underground politics is involved.

There are many issues with presenting Simon's *Necronomicon* as a historical book in itself. Firstly, the original manuscript it is supposed to be based on was stolen not long after copies were made for translation. And even these copies seem to be unavailable to anyone now. More important for our purposes than dating any actual manuscript, is dating the tradition which alluded to. Materials from Simon's *Necronomicon* bare striking resemblance to information derived from other available books of esoteric archeology, including—"*Semitic Magic*," "*Chaldean Magic*" and "*Babylonian Magic*."

The one thing it is not—it is *not* Sumerian in origin, as many thought and as its own editors profess. While it is true that Sumerians occupied the same space geographically linked to its birth-place—and they observed the same basic "Anunnaki" pantheon—their tradition is not actually evident in the work other than what was culturally absorbed into later traditions Simon's work is actually based— *Babylon*. Any idea that this tradition is "nondenominational" is also false. It is clearly laced with the "Mardukite-specific" spiritual politics found strongest in Babylonian traditions and literature—and often mirrored in Egypt. Among these themes, of course—a centralized veneration of MARDUK-RA as the "Lord of the Gods," something entirely absent in the previous (original) *Sumerian Tradition*.

According to the story provided in "*Dead Names*," the manuscript that served as a basis for Simon's *Necronomicon* was allegedly recovered from a stolen rare-book collection in 1972. Those later involved with translation and presentation of the salvaged tome were none other than aforementioned Peter Levenda, and also *Herman Slater*, the owner of Magickal Childe bookstore in Manhattan, originally known as the Warlock Shop.

Completed and dedicated on October 12, 1975 (the hundredth anniversary of *Aleister Crowley*'s birth), the book required another two years of work before the team successfully brought it to the public. One common misconception is that *Magickal Childe* published Simon's *Necronomicon* in hardcover, when its production was actually managed as a somewhat private venture under the umbrella name: *Schlangekraft, Inc.* Later, however, *Magickal Childe* is credited with a release of the first edition of a slim sequel volume, originally called the *Necronomicon Report*, then republished more widely as Simon's "*Necronomicon Spellbook*," first appearing in the underground in 1981, then reprinted by Avon/HarperCollins.

As mentioned, self-publishing books during the mid-1970's required some serious skill and experienced people—and *money!* In walks *Larry Barnes* to the *Magickal Childe* bookstore—a man with a lifelong obsession with all things Lovecraft and an undying desire to publish and promote a "*Necronomicon*." Some other caretakers of the original manuscript or those involved with the project—declining acknowledgment for this current Mardukite volume—claimed to care little (or know nothing about) H. P. Lovecraft, although most swear that the title did actually grace the manuscript cover—but *not* the familiar sigil, which was apparently created later, as with the remaining art for the book, including the interior "sigils." The title remains the main questionable aspect related to the presentation of the book in public. Other than the "energy" that the name caries, the title alone really says nothing definitive toward the validity of its contents.

That it was a stolen manuscript seems plausible. That it does, in fact, bare renderings of the little-known (at the time) tablet invocations and epics from Mesopotamia—we have already established in our Mardukite *Necronomicon* cycle. That a practical "Sumerian Tradition" revival was of supreme interest, but previously inaccessible, to Aleister Crowley and the O.T.O. "magical organization" is also on record. The idea that the *title* may have been adopted later by request, or to offer the work substance—a canvas to be set against—may have actually been the only real fabrication. The title alone is all that Larry Barnes cared about when he wanted to make a "real" bound-book version of the "*Necronomicon*"—if the content seemed historically valid, then even better.

Book design was left to *James ("Jim") Wasserman*, who had previously worked for a prestigious occult bookseller—*Samuel Weiser*. Jim was in charge of seeing the actual design and construction of the book through. These same public entities connected to Simon's *Necronomicon* have—over three decades later—re-released the hardcover in late 2008, for its *31st Anniversary*—the same year that the modern "Mardukite" movement was officially founded. Wasserman returned to present a leather-bound edition exclusively from Studio 31, limited to 220 copies. The standard cloth-bound unlimited edition remains available as distributed by Ibis—the more recently established Samuel Weiser publishing imprint dedicated to hardcover editions. In 1977, the original leather-bound editions (numbered of 666) sold for $50 each. Today, these editions can fetch several hundred dollars. Comparatively, the newer 2008 cloth-bound hardcover edition retailed for $125, with Studio 31 offering its limited leather editions for $295. They have become as collectible to some as they are sacred to others.

"*Cthonic*" presentation of the book and the dark gloom tied to the project did little to divert the "dread" and "horror" already attached to the title. Ornate cover design on the original hardcover met the preference of Larry Barnes, seeking again to define that *grimoire* from Lovecraft's visions. "Simon" writes in *Dead Names* that he would have preferred simpler cover—something they certainly achieved with the more frugal 2008 edition. The developers followed ideas put forth in Lovecraft's work more than they emphasized the specific content drawn from Mesopotamia. Simon's *Necronomicon* was presented as an archetypal long-lost sorcerer's "black book," the "most dangerous and powerful" on the planet—at least for its time. In some ways, the hype was justified. Certainly monumental for its time, the work remains a cornerstone for many today—although its efforts have since been surpassed by the work of the *Mardukite Research Organization*—specifically "*Necronomicon: The Anunnaki Bible*" and its supporting materials.

Very few—even those who had studied cultural folk mythologies and other pagan pantheons revived by "mystical movements" of the last century—had gained any access to (or understanding of) the ancient Mesopotamian methodologies predating all the rest. This change in human consciousness was not only monumental, but intentional—an integral part of a larger picture where obscure spiritual forces and secret councils have indeed been directing the course of many events in recent history. These include some many profound ventures from the 1970's, bridging the 60's to the 80's via visions and manifestations that many might have never conceived of before. The music changed. The media changed. The very colors being perceived in the world changed – more real, surreal and yet wholly artificial. Ground work began in human consciousness. A new *Babylon*—a new *Mardukite* age—was *rising*.

The technological age was counter-balanced with an extreme sense of "fantasy" and "spiritual occultism," such as had not been present in human civilization for a very long time. It was a necessary program, followed to temper the rise of the "electronic gods"—those that are still being raised to supremacy by their human creators. Thinking that the "*Old Gods*" have left them, humans have felt an over-whelming need to raise another in its place—this time, by their own creation—or so they think. It was not until fantasy enthusiasts and Lovecraftian *Necronomicon* readers started getting together with the science-fiction and Sitchin-eqsue circles in the late 1970's that the "mainstream population" (outside of orders like the *Golden Dawn* or *O.T.O.*) were given a chance to understand what was already known in the remote underground for thousands of years—knowledge concerning the existence and nature of the *Anunnaki!*

Most controversy surrounding Simon's *Necronomicon* concerned its presentation as H.P. Lovecraft's *Necronomicon*, and further as a "dreaded tome" that held power from the start, based on some of the more "supernatural" claims dealing with its production. Among these—that the typesetters were plagued by a swarm of rats during their work—an aspect that seems to bother a lot of critics. Things of this nature do little to affect the actual content, but the idea being brought forth, again, was—"this book is *dangerous!*" The debate about rats in factories seems so trite compared to the bigger picture and is it really that bizarre at any rate—we are talk-ing about Manhattan, right? That the book might "expose you to psychological forces with which you cannot cope" is also not an empty boast. If you are not ready to face the reality that everything you think you know about your world is a sham —a clever deception by alien forces—then certainly, steer clear of the *Necronomi-con* in all of its forms.

— 3 —
THE SCHLANGEKRAFT RECENSION

Modern revival of ancient ideologies—known as the *"New Age Movement"*—has successfully brought new public awareness to many ancient mythoi. Consider: folk traditions of Europeans in the guise of neodruidism or Celtic witchcraft; resurgence in use of Norse runes and divination systems of Romany gypsies; "singing bowls" from Buddhist monks and Tibetan shamanism; a cornucopia of Asian *feng shui* devices—all these things litter aisles of nearly every "metaphysical" outlet. Furthermore, there is no shortage of statuary and holy regalia that can be purchased to grace devotional altar spaces of contemporary ceremonialists.

Preceding all of this—distant remains of the most ancient energetic currents of the cosmos. These were later interpreted somewhat differently by varying regional cultures throughout time—cultures that are relatively more recent and thus seem more accessible for modern revival. Absent among these many avenues—a means where the Seeker is offered their best assistance in returning to the Source—to long-lost forgotten tablets of Mesopotamia. These ancient cuneiform tablets are only recently being shaken free enough of the sands they were lost to, for them to finally be seen self-honestly again from out of the underground... Even if only glimmers and glimpses can be caught from early efforts in the 1970's.

Peter Levenda connects origins of Simon's *Necronomicon* to a little known *Slavonic Orthodox Church*. After discovering many covert political atrocities to the *Church's* involvement, *Levenda* says he defected from this mode of life, seeking to separate himself from its corruption. But, he was present long enough to see other established sects and churches rise and intertwine with their own brand, contributing higher legitimacy to otherwise shady and "unsavory" characters.

Two shady individuals notorious for rare-book theft—whose identities are never actually revealed—allegedly came in contact with *Levenda* and the *Church* at one juncture. These men made their living by going into libraries, universities and other private collections and literally stealing books. Some books had maps and diagrams that could be spliced and sold separately for even higher returns then what the entire work might be worth in tact. Sometimes methods were even employed to "raising seals," hiding ownership by libraries, *&tc.*, and rebinding and repairing old books, when necessary, for resale. A significant collection of occult materials made its way into possession of founding members of the *Slavonic Orthodox Church*, which *Peter Levenda* became privy to while working and visiting with colleagues. From this collection came forth the famous Simon's *Necronomicon*.

Simon's *Necronomicon* was quickly absorbed into "counter-culture" and mistaken as some kind of devil-worshiping companion to LaVey's Satanism; which is just as often misunderstood, but beyond the scope of our current subject. The work is not readily accepted into the—now mainstreamed—"New Age." It is less frequently integrated into modern magical traditions of "legitimately" practicing *Wiccans* and *Druids*, and more often found among teenagers and young adults with no occult background—not to mention those up-and-coming in the "Matrix-generation." These "NexGens" are fully aware of the concept that they are living in some Tron-like computer game reality. NexGens know it is not only possible—now they can show you just how it is done and how we might make it work for us—burrowing the rabbit-hole ever deeper—fragmenting the path back to the Source.

By fragmenting the puzzle into more pieces, the chase to put the picture back together becomes longer, more challenging—and to the psyche that is driven by stimulus—more intriguing. With more pieces to the puzzle there are more ways in which parts *might* be "fit together" and "connected" to give that psyche its much needed fix of "eureka" (yet another glamour). Keep in mind that the size, nature and picture for the puzzle (the "big picture") remain fixed—only the number of pieces and level of difficulty are changed.

But, the occult is what it is for a reason. It holds just as many glamours and illusions as the "*Realm of Light*" people are more comfortably familiar with. The true secrets of the "occult lodge" protect themselves, even when out in the open—and publishing words does not guarantee esoteric understanding. It is far easier to hide something in front of someone and keep them going on the notion that what they seek requires additional seeking—more levels and layers of understanding. This is essentially what has become an "enlightenment deception" on the surface world, or what many philosophers might simply call "*false knowledge.*"

The *Necronomicon*—both in archetype and form—represent a way out of *this* trapping. ...But! Without guidance (such as expressed in more recent Mardukite efforts—including "*Necronomicon: The Anunnaki Bible*" and the current Mardukite "*Gates of the Necronomicon*" cycle of material)—the Seeker is inevitably just going to fall into trappings of a different system, and this time possibly not make it *out*. Why? Because it was designed to be that way. Those who have worked through the "initiatory program" of the "*Gates*" from the Simon version will many times over tell themselves they have been "successful," even though they still are experiencing it from a "first degree" realization. Then there are those who have stumbled into the niche of the system, and arrived in the *Abyss*. This is rare—and still only a fraction of what the whole system represents – a mere *shadow*.

* * *

One modern occultist bridging the gap between Aleister Crowley's era and the modern one—*Kenneth Grant*. Some of Grant's earlier works could only allude to possible connections between Crowley's "magick" and specifically Lovecraftian in-terpretations of the "*Necronomicon*." Then in more recent installments of Grant's "Typhonian O.T.O." materials, he begins citing from what he calls the "*Sch-langekraft recension*"—otherwise known as Simon's *Necronomicon*.

Of Kenneth Grant's many cryptic tomes composing the "Typhonian Tradition" of *Ordo Templi Orientis*, the one titled "*Outer Gateways*," briefly describes communications made by ceremonial magicians of magical lodges with the "*Old Ones*" or "*Deep Ones*"—demonstrating that he evidently took this subject seriously. Kenneth Grant essentially inherited the O.T.O. organization and cult-following of Aleister Crowley. Therefore, we can be certain that the *Schlangekraft recension* was far from the only means—or even remotely close to their original experiments—of making contact with "alien intelligences." But Grant acknowledged—no doubt made successful use of—and celebrated the work as a very real "*Portal to the Abyss*." The book represented an element—Mesopotamia—that earlier magicians weren't accessing directly with any of their systems, as Peter Levenda expresses in an interview—

> "Where the New Age is concerned, a lot of the occultism is '*Judeo-Christian*'—the *Keys of Solomon*, for example; the *Secret Books of Moses*, and all of that stuff. It was all based on a *Jewish* and *Christian* concept. With the coming of the New Age you did have a rise in neopaganism, but there was not a system of 'ceremonial magick' for a neopagan mentality; it [ceremonial magick] was, again, based on *Jewish* and *Christian* concepts, which were themselves borrowed from pagan origins, but the pagan origins were gone for the most part. In a sense the *Simon Necronomicon* filled a need for people with a true neo-pagan interest to become involved with the *higher magics*."

Rather than a "Cthulhu mythos" drawn from semantics used by H. P. Lovecraft to describe his dreams and visions, the *Schlangekraft recension* offered a preliminary means for someone with no background in Mesopotamian cultures or ancient cuneiform tablets to quickly immerse themselves—thereby unlocking a personal subconscious "portal" to the "*Other*." The work is by no means complete and certainly not wholly accurate, but that is not to say it has not served its purpose in the greater scheme—in the system—just as the contributions of others, intricately interwoven, have as well. Kenneth Grant notes in "*Outside the Circles of Time*" that—

> "Certain fugitive elements appear occasionally in the works of poets, painters, mystics and occultists which may be regarded as genuine magical manifestations in that they demonstrate the power and ability of the artist to evoke elements of an extra-dimensional and alien universe that may be captured only by the most sensitive and delicately adjusted antennae of human consciousness..."

That Simon's *Necronomicon* is not representative of Sumerian *paradigms* is already apparent and will continue to be demonstrated as such here. The type of dualism suggested—the supremacy of MARDUK—are all very clear indicators of the Chaldeo-Babylonian "Mardukite" elements not found in early Sumer.

The Simon book *is not* a proper "priests guide" for even following traditions of Mardukite Babylon—as the modern Mardukite *"Necronomicon: The Anunnaki Bible"* was developed. Instead, Simon's book is presented as a bastardized magician's "grimoire," primarily describing ritual-styled sorcery more common to "Hermetic magic," but not the religious or ceremonial "priestly" methods that we should expect to be present. The manner in which forces are dealt with indicates a perspective of someone slightly "outside" the original Mardukite system— someone who is not personally in a position to relay it fully, for they have not been fully initiated to it themselves.

References in Simon's book to *"Enki, Our Father"* is another key Mardukite Babylonian sign-post. A purely Sumerian tradition would have heralded divine attributes primarily to ENLIL, and then perhaps also to his heir-son NINURTA. Instead, it is Babylonian in origin, deferring all esoteric powers of "earthly magic" and "world order" specifically to ENKI, and his own heir-son MARDUK—the patron *Anunnaki* deity of Babylon. In both the modern Mardukite *"Necronomicon: The Anunnaki Bible"* and Simon's *Necronomicon*, ANU remains a distant figure and ENLIL is only mentioned occasionally—in regard to the "Supernal Trinity." The ancient Mardukite Babylonians assigned all worldly "Enlil-ship" or "God-ship" to MARDUK—and *"on earth as it is in heaven."*

Before any of the planetary *"Gates"* are introduced in the *Schlangekraft Recension*, the introductory "Testimony of the Mad Arab" describes an unnumbered *"Gate of Death"* called GANZIR. Lore of this Gate exists from cuneiform tablet epics describing crossings specifically to the "Underworld," but it is not necessarily the *"Gate to the Outside"* or to the *"Abyss"* that is alluded to elsewhere—it is not the "Gate-to-End-All-Gates." It is not part of the *"Ladder of Lights"* because it is not a part of the visible *"Realm of Light"* and it is not "realized" in the seven-fold "stargate-system" of Mardukite Babylon for this reason—nor is the *"Earth Gate"* or the *"Supernal Trinity"* stations—all of which were combined to form later "kabbalistic" representations of this system.

The more familiar sevenfold web-matrix represents the "seven rays" (or "seven pillars") used specifically to seal systems of the physical, material, manifest and visible world. The *"Gate of Ganzir"* does not lead "out of the system," but rather it links to the *Underverse* domain of ERESHKIGAL and NERGAL—a dimly lit part of the same system, but the *"Other Side"* of the Tree of Life. Rather than a vast palette of colors for material manifestation, the *Underworld* is fashioned by an "absence" of these colors—a pale reflection in *shadows*—but it is not the "No-Being-Void-Nothingness" found in the *Abyss*. Death is merely a threshold state—a crossing—but you are still not there! Why, then, is such lore even alluded to in the texts if it is not being directly utilized in the gate-system? Answer:—To fully enlighten the initiate (Seeker) to the magnitude of what they are dealing with: that the *Anunnaki* forces hold the keys to both life and death—because both are still a part of dualistic existence—fractal entities—fragmented from the whole into individualized existence.

Ceremonialists raised in elitist traditions are eventually aware of the short circuit that is embedded in their own highly elevated systems—spread out through countless tomes and journals of spiritual theories and mystic entanglement. Having chanted all the combinations of syllables and added all the *gematric* numbers, they are left back alone in their lavishly decorated circles successful in only conjuring a protection against true enlightenment and their own fears. This is probably what intrigued Kenneth Grant the most about the *Schlangekraft recension,* for its esoteric emphasis was not on the Realm of Light, but the "Realm of Death," naturally overshadowing the work from the start—beginning with the very title: *Necronomicon.*

A long-standing history of "death-cult" themes connected to the *Necronomicon-*archetype spark reservations for many folk—preventing new insights—again, mainly due to the title. The same facets that blindly attracted over a million people to its pages are what keeps countless times that many away. They are unaware of what the "Mesopotamian" work really entails—the contents and deeper gnosis of ancient mysteries that it actually can provide. For that matter, many who own or come across the book are intrigued, even inspired by its existence, but are afraid to read it themselves, following a stereotyped "urban-legend" begun by H. P. Lovecraft, that the mere reading can cause madness. All the better. Such minds really should not delve into the occult anyways, as there is not enough holy water and blessed salt in existence to keep their fears from eventually manifesting—creating more problems for the rest of us.

As we might expect, Kenneth Grant's O.T.O. approach is metaphysical rather than literal, recognizing "death" as a transitional "crossing." In fact, he semantically correlates "death" with "*Daath,*" the hidden "*sephiroth*" ["sphere," "station" or "gate"] in the later Semitic Kabbalah, derived from the same Babylonian gate-system as the *Necronomicon.* The Kabbalah depicts "Daath" as an "eleventh" factor in an otherwise tenfold system, barely visible from *this side* of the "Tree of Life" and somehow bridging the world of "form" to a realm of "not"—a Gateway to Voidness. It is not "voidness" in itself, but an embedded loophole in the system dividing the height or summit of the lower material (physical) existence from the foundation or depths of the higher Supernal (spiritual) existence. Understand that all existence [AN.KI] is, of course, a singular reality, it has merely been fixed with curtains and doors, veils and gates, by which it might be more easily contained...

and it works pretty well.

— 4 —
TOWARDS A BABYLONIAN NECRONOMICON

Everyone coming in contact with the "Necronomicon paradigm" has come and gone preaching their own personal truths about it. For many, it is a fictitious manifestation that could not ever be real. Others see it as part of the "*Akashic Libraries*," an account that is locked away in the astral, just waiting for some person to unlock the mysteries. There are some who find the appeal to fantasy and horror, but they do not believe themselves or anyone else capable of discerning the truth or exercising real power. Too often it is the highly inquisitive analytic human minds that breathe life into spiritual-semantic stumbling blocks. But—as reality is a matter of perspective, each "viewpoint" is only correct from a certain "point of view." Consider this as we move through this lesson.

Firstly, modern "grimoires" directly influenced by H. P. Lovecraft (*Hay & Tyson*) can hardly be considered "genuine" articles of ancient literature and mysticism in themselves—and so we will not spend much space and time here to analyze them. Most Lovecraftian-inspired creations (*Hay/Turner & Tyson*) are usually designed by not only enthusiastic fans of Lovecraft, but also experienced "ceremonial magicians," who already carry an understanding of "grimoire-magic" operations. Therefore, they have a good chance of creating a workable system of magic that will yield positive results for others—as much as any other. *If you build it, they will come.*

It is not difficult for experienced practitioners to construct their own workable systems—especially those spending many years immersed in correspondence tables and comparative charts of elemental and planetary forces. All these system require is a "theme" or "pantheon"—some structure to base the "vibrations" and "rays" against. If a suitable one is not found, or able to be conjured from readily available cultural research, the next option is to just *make one up*. As Timothy Leary suggested—"*start your own religion*"—and in the case of Lovecraft's fanatics, *they did just that*. In essence the forces are already in place namelessly operating by the same Cosmic Laws—they await only to be named and known by a subjective individuated psyche. Hence for Lovecraftians: the *Cthulhu Mythos!*

While the "Simon group" worked to "translate" (or "develop") the *Schlangekraft recension* in New York, another *Necronomicon*—also an independent "first" of its kind—was simultaneously being edited and designed on the other side of the Atlantic Ocean, in England. As much as Simon's work brought the legendary archetype to life as an influence for the rising "*Mardukite Age*" and specifically dedicated to the *Anunnaki* energy-currents of MARDUK, the U.K. team (*George Hay, Robert Turner* and *Colin Wilson*) were far more interested in allegorical power embedded in Lovecraft's own archetypal *egregores*—specifically the "*Cthulhu Mythos*" in exclusion to all else.

> Where once we had no *Necronomicons*, by the end of the 1970's
> the world now had three—including an *H. R. Giger* art book.

George Hay's *"Necronomicon: Book of Dead Names"* appeared in 1978. The work did not initially see much attention beyond underground circulation—as is common of these types of releases at their inception—but it did provoke a more serious occult revival interest toward Lovecraftian-specific semantics. The book was only distributed in the United States after being reprinted by Skoob Books in 1992. Three years later, a follow up companion—*"The R'lyeh Text"*—appeares, also edited by George Hay, but this time giving more credit to the alleged "researcher" of both books, Robert Turner. To add a dose of credibility, both books include an introduction by Colin Wilson—well known for his prolific writings on the "supernatural" and "occult" topics for many decades.

As a harsh critique of the efforts—representing a focal turning point of energy for misguided ceremonialists, Hay's *"Necronomicon: Book of Dead Names"* (and its companion) do little more than provide Seekers with some less than necessary New Age fluff regarding reinvention of Lovecraft's vision of an ancient paradigm. But we have no need for Lovecraft's semantics of an "alien-god system." We know better—that one actually does exist, extending into the prehistoric consciousness of men—and such is much more worthy of pursuit. Even as magickal texts go, Hay's *"Necronomicon: Book of Dead Names"* and *"R'lyeh Text"* really do offer quite little (as we are inclined to agree with our predecessors in their critiques). It is more likely that these books were created for personal reasons and originally for a specific network of readers.

The entice in prescribing ceremonial occult attributes to Lovecraft's mythos is furthered in these works by mere mention of more verifiable connections to these arts: Enochian magic of John Dee; references of Lovecraft in Kenneth Grant's work; possible similarities to Crowley's *"Book of the Law"*—all of which, if we are to take the Hay/Turner materials at face value, actually play little or no part in the system of "practical magick" that is even offered in the books. If they are not taken "seriously," and are instead obtained to be a part of some Lovecraftian literary collection, then the two books are intriguing in the light of a fictional "Cthulhu cycle," with a certain nostalgia to them. They will not, however, aid the Seeker in further reaching *"self-honesty"* or unveiling the *Great Deception* that has befallen both the world of light and darkness, alike.

* * *

The basic *Necronomicon* archetype—an arcane tome divulging esoteric secrets from another time, even before men, when "gods" walked the earth—self-defines its own existence as integral to *"Akashic Records."* These localize on the *"astral plane"*—containing knowledge of the inter-dimensional omniverse. Aside from Semitic-influenced Gnostic scriptures (such as those found among the *Nag-Hammadi* collections in the mid-twentieth century), the most ancient records mirroring the type of lore we are after, is again, the cuneiform tablets of Mesopotamia—an aspect central to the Simonian and Mardukite interpretation of the *Necronomicon* legacy.

Donald Tyson casually remarks that his inspiration for a Lovecraftian *Necronomicon* cycle came from the astral—and we know that Lovecraft's own inspiration was derived from "dreams of terror and death" and other obscure nightmares—essentially experienced in the astral—so the chances of experienced magicians intentionally tapping these otherworldly forces are actually fairly good. And what's more: the "magician," "priest" or "priestess" is often the bridge—or *"gate"*—inviting these primordial energies to manifest on *"our side"* of the *"Tree."* Kenneth Grant concurs—

> "Does this mean that those from Outside will actually put in an appearance on earth? If so, then the secret rites hinted at in grimoires such as the *Necronomicon,* and the *Books of Thoth*, of *Dzyan*, of *Enoch*, contain the keys to their summoning and we have for long aeons been blind to their usage..."

As a perfect example, we find *H. P. Blavatsky's* Theosophical *"Book of Dzyan"* mentioned by Grant, and its even appears as *Tablet-D* of *"Necronomicon: The Anunnaki Bible."* However, Lovecraftian references specific to the *Necronomicon* are few and far between—in spite of the tremendous attention it has received from his work. There is little to draw from directly in Lovecraft's writings for which to actually base anything other than an *idea*.

Lovecraft did well to keep an aura of mystery shrouding his tome—enough to make people believe it had to exist, but so cryptic as to make it nearly impossible for it to be so. Certainly, no reconstruction (with the exception of the Mardukite *Necronomicon* legacy produced by the Mardukite Chamberlains) has ever truly lived up to what the fanatics crave—part of this due to their very attachment to the Lovecraftian mythos: if the *Necronomicon* can be purchased in any store, then it loses the edge of mystery so sacred to its existence. Aliens and gods aside, a person's own "psyche" has the ability (is essentially programmed) to deceive them into playing inconsequential logic games with semantic understanding of basic things—leading nowhere.

Let us consider, then, what options remain now for the Seeker, Adept or Master: *First*—you could go back to a familiar world of forms, embrace the mathematical precision and beauty of the *"Realm of Light"* in all of its worldly glamour, and *take the "blue pill"* as it were—all of this we speak of is pure fantasy and your parents and civil leaders know better; *Second*—you can choose to invite into your life any and all things "opposite" to this realm, thrashing about in your cage, cursing your wardens, demanding to make the "fantasy" real, Lovecraftian or otherwise, because anything is better than the program you continue to subject yourself to; or, *Thirdly* —to extend your mind back to the farthest reaches of space and time to unveil the mysteries of not only what you have been shown, but also what you have not been shown, to drink deeply from the very real source of lore available to those who "initiate" to seek it.

Versions of the *Necronomicon* appearing and remaining in the "New Age" are usually based specifically on Lovecraftian literature. Yet, during the 1980's and 90's, several small print run editions of strictly "Simonian" companions emerged—most of which offered very little "new" information to enhance the system. Many rehashes by obsessed fans of the *Schlangekraft recension* started showing up—including "*Hidden Keys of the Necronomicon*" and "*Necronomian Workbook*," published by a small underground press called I.G.O.S.—the International Guild of Occult Sciences.

During its short existence, I.G.O.S. was run by someone named "*Brother Moloch*"—author of the surprisingly expensive (now out-of-print) "*Necronomian Workbook*." He also seems to share Simon's fascination with the *Red Dragon Grimoire*—also known as the *Grand Grimoire*. Avon/HarperCollins briefly republished the grimoire as a "Simon" book, titled "*Papal Magic*." Its supporting material strongly resembled an work by Tracy Twyman—"*The Magic of St. Peter*"—which the same company had previously declined to publish. These types of "grimoire" carry a strong archetypal in older circles—sharing a similar energetic current as the *Necronomicon*.

Most modern practitioners and "New Age" readers also seem primarily concerned about ritual magic for material gain. The arrangement of traditional "grimoires" and emphasis on "spells" from "witchcraft" revivals may be the cause—or else, it is just human nature. But, the *Necronomicon* is essentially an archetype of the most ancient beliefs and traditions on the planet—whether in Lovecraft's fantasy or as part of the Mesopotamian cycle—and it therefore has much more to offer than a few "love spells" and "money charms."

The arrival of Simon's *Necronomicon* awoke the consciousness of the global population to forces—very real forces—that had long since been forgotten. This is an essential part of required "NexGen" changes happening on the planet—in brief: the return of the "*Old Ones*," just as Lovecraft predicted, envisioned, or *dreamed*. Most of us are indoctrinated from birth with familiar parochial and Biblical interpretations of these ancient traditions—but they have not been "realized" clearly for literally thousands of years. Such would, in itself, deem the pursuit worthy enough—but more importantly, with historical validity.

In spite of controversy over the title, Simon's book represents *first steps* toward a true "Mardukite" system. After the official inception of the modern "Mardukite" movement, the *first step* that the Mardukite Chamberlains ("*Mardukite Research Organization*") took in 2009 was to very simply bridge this gap. The Mardukite "*Liber N – Necronomicon*" was the first discourse prepared, now a part of the greater source book anthology—"*Necronomicon: The Anunnaki Bible*." It was not intended as a replacement or even competition for the *Schlangekraft recension*. Instead, it was released to the world as stand-alone volume composed of raw cuneiform tablet materials representing a more complete and verifiable archive—of the *same* sources hidden behind the admittedly bastardized collection of Simon's frugal anthology. In essence, our Mardukite *Necronomicon* work is intended as a gateway for esoteric Seekers from their more familiar-"unfamiliar" territories, into the much deeper realizations accessible.

— 5 —
A STAIRWAY TO HEAVEN ?

The *Schlangekraft recension* begins with a series of "lessons" dedicated to the sevenfold Gate-system. Mardukite interpretations of the same are referred to as the *Book of Star Gates* or *the Babili Text*—Tablet-A and Tablet-B of "*Necronomicon: The Anunnaki Bible*"—drawn from the very heart of Babylon. Attributes, designations and invocation prayers specific to the "younger generation" of *Anunnaki* appearing in the Babylonian system are quite clear. They are also quite verifiable using esoteric archaeology.

For personal experimentation, suitable independently researched substitutions for "Simonian invocations" were easily found by the Mardukite Chamberlains from the *Kuyunjik* cuneiform tablet collection, preserved at the British Museum—fully described in the companion work of our *Gates of the Necronomicon* anthology by Joshua Free (or else in "*The Sumerian Legacy,*" formerly "*Sumerian Religion*"). This series of tablets—called NIS KATI—is more "famously" known in scholarly circles as the *Prayers of the Lifting of the Hand*—or alternately, "Raising of the Hand." Additional work by by the Mardukite Chamberlains resulted in a new standard for Anunnaki invocation—*The Book of Marduk by Nabu*—included in more recent editions of "*Necronomicon: The Anunnaki Bible*" as the *Tablet-W* series.

Simon's "Banishings and Exorcisms" are reminiscent of "magic" found on the MAKLU (or MAQLU) tablets, and are easily identifiable. He presents his chapter as "The Book of the Burning of Evil Spirits." Many of the incantations are identical to those published scholarly as the "*Maqlu Tablet Series*" ("*The Burnings*"). Simon even includes other various incantations from Akkadian and Assyrian origins—the "*Surpu Tablet Series*" ("*The Consuming*") or the "*Utukku Limnuti Series*" ("*Of Evil Spirits*")—all of which are described in more detail within our Mardukite "*Necronomicon: The Anunnaki Bible.*" More than simply the exorcism of evil spirits, or a manual to anti-demon healing rites—such as is more the case with the other tablet series mentioned here—the *Maqlu Series* targets specifically those who feed "evil" its existence: *the wicked-witch and evil sorcerer.*

Colorfully broadcast across nine cuneiform tablets, the *Maqlu* research conducted by the Mardukite Chamberlains in 2011 provided *Tablet-M* translations for more recent editions of "*Necronomicon: The Anunnaki Bible.*" Even in its raw untranslated forms, a diligent Seeker or Adept can easily find correlations between the earlier Simon and later Mardukite works. For example, Simon's version illustrates "A Most Excellent Charm Against the Hordes of Demons that Assail in the Night," to be used while censoring the sacred circle with incense, or sprinkling blessed waters, while using the following untranslated incantation—

214

ISA YA! ISA YA! RI EGA! EI EGA!
BI ESHA BI ESHA! XIYILQA! XIYLQA!
DUPPIRA ATLAKA ISA YA U RI EGA
LIMNUTTIKUNU KIMA QUTRI LITILLI SHAMI YE
INA ZUMRI YA ISA YA
INA ZUMRI YA RI EGA
INA ZUMRI YA BI ESHA
INA ZUMRI YA XIYILQA
INA ZUMRI YA DUPPIRA
INA ZUMRI YA ATLAKA
INA ZUMRI YA LA TATARA
INA ZUMRI YA LA TETIXXI YE
INA ZUMRI YA LA TAQARRUBA
INA ZUMRI YA LA TASANIQA
NI YISH SHAMMASH KABTU LU TAMATUNU
NI YISH ENKI BEL GIMRI LU TAMATUNU
NI YISH MARDUK MASHMASH ILANI LU TAMATUNU
NI YISH GISHBAR QAMIKUNU LU TAMATUNU
INA ZUMRI YA LU YU TAPPATTASAMA!

Compare this to final incantation from the fifth tablet of the *Tablet-M "Maqlu Tablet Series"* given in our Mardukite *"Necronomicon: The Anunnaki Bible"*—

> *i-sa-a i-sa-a ri-e-qa ri-e-qa*
>   *Go away! Go away! Be gone! Be gone!*
> *bi-e-šá bi-e-šá hi-il-qa hi-il-qa*
>   *Stay away! Stay away! Flee! Flee!*
> *dup-pi-ra at-la-ka i-sa-a u ri-e-qa*
>   *Get off! Go away! Stay away! Be gone!*
> *limuttu-ku-nu ki-ma qut-ri li-tel-li šamêe*
>   *Your evil spell, like smoke, rises skyward into nothing!*
> *[170] ina zumri-ia i-sa-a*
>   *From my body, keep off!*
> *ina zumri-ia ri-e-qa*
>   *From my body, be gone!*
> *ina zumri-ia bi-e-šá*
>   *From my body, depart!*
> *ina zumri-ia hi-il-qa*
>   *From my body, flee!*
> *ina zumri-ia dup-pi-ra*
>   *From my body, get off!*
> *[175] ina zumri-ia at-la-ka*
>   *From my body, go away!*
> *ina zumri-ia la tatârâ*
>   *From my body, turn away!*

ina zumri-ia la tetehêe
  From my body, do not approach!
ina zumri-ia la taqarubâ
  From my body, do not come near!
ina zumri-ia la tasaniqâqa
  From my body, do not touch!
[180] ni-iš SAMAS kabti lu ta-ma-tu-nu
  By the breath of Shammash, Radiant One, you are commanded!
ni-iš E-A BEL naqbi lu ta-ma-tu-nu
  By the breath of Enki, Lord of the Deep, you are commanded!
ni-iš Asariludu maš-maš ilimeš lu ta-ma-tu-nu
  By the breath of Marduk, Magician of the Gods, you are commanded!
ni-iš GIRRA qa-mi-ku-nu lu ta-ma-tu-nu
  By the breath of Girra, your Executioner, you are commanded!
ina zumri-ia lu-u tap-par-ra-sa-ma
  Indeed, you shall be kept from my body!

The primary body of "spiritual scripture" supporting the tradition in the *Schlangekraft recension* is called the "*Magan Text*"—a version of tablet cycles better known elsewhere as the "*Enuma Elis*" and "*Descent of Inanna*." The specific texts used for Simon's work do not appear elsewhere in scholarly translations, but its elements are the same as those scattered among various tablets from Mesopotamia. This suggests that the "*Magan Text*" is someones combination of several epics—which were separated accordingly in the Mardukite "*Necronomicon: The Anunnaki Bible*." But, it should be understood that the admittedly "bastardized" versions appearing in Simon's work are shorter concise—almost portable—versions of other actual tablets. This even furthers the idea that this *Necronomicon* of a "Mad Arab" was not an original "priest guide" or "Babylonian manual" at all, but a crude attempt to preserve such—perhaps the result of a later underground oral tradition. But, the alleged "Mad Arab" author is wrong on one specific detail about his text—

> "The verses here following come from the secret text of some of
> the priests of a cult which is all that is left of the Old Faith that
> existed before Babylon was built..."

This would mean "*Sumerian*," and we know this is wrong because, the "*Magan Text*," in both its Simonian version and the specific cuneiform tablets it is based on, are *not* Sumerian—or pre-Babylonian at all—but is the very composition of epics used by priests and priestesses for religious, spiritual and political propagation of none other than a "Mardukite" <u>Babylon</u>! A "younger generation" of *Anunnaki* "gods" were elevated to a superior status by the "Nabu-priests" of *Babylon*. The "Mardukite" cuneiform tablets of NABU to MARDUK were forged in *Babylon*, providing evidence to support MARDUK as "King of the Gods." This is part of what is hidden beneath the "*Magan Text*" of the *Schlangekraft recension*, as the "Mad Arab" explains—

"Remembering is the most important and most potent magick, being the Remembrance of Things Past and the Remembrance of Things to Come, which is the same Memory."

To reiterate: the first part of Simon's "*Magan Text*" is little more than a version of the quite famous and most widely influencing of Babylonian tablets: the *Epic of Creation*—also known as the *Enuma Elis*, and given as *Tablet-N* in "*Necronomicon: The Anunnaki Bible*." The original text may have once developed from an earlier Sumerian paradigm of cosmogenesis, but in this Babylonian version, MAR-DUK is elevated to "King of the Gods"—a position earned by slaying the primeval ancestral dragon—TIAMAT—in a primordial "*War in Heaven*," thereby putting "cosmic order" in the universe.

Another famous cuneiform series—The *Descent of Ishtar*—also appears within the Mardukite cycle of Babylonian tablets (given as *Tablet-C* in "*Necronomicon: The Anunnaki Bible*") and Simon's "*Magan Text*," where it is referred to as the "*Sleep of Ishtar*." As politically dramatic as the *Enuma Elis* was for Babylon, the *Descent of Ishtar* provided a "passion play" of spiritual material illustrating the nature of the *Underworld*. Much of the material used in "death cults"—which is to say "*gate cults*"—originates here and even in Egypt, where the "dog-star cult" is dedicated to *Anubis* as the "Guardian of the Death Gates."

When interpreting these cycles, spiritual realizations can be overshadowed by physical geographic descriptions—"descent" and "under"—indicating specific relative direction. Mardukite Tradition realized this more in the sense of inter-spacial transitioning, or more preferably—*crossings!* Similar lore is preserved as the Egyptian "*Book of the Dead*," concerning "gates" and "pylons"—also includes in *Tablet-C* in "*Necronomicon: The Anunnaki Bible*" for comparison.

In Simon's *Necronomicon*, a few cryptic passages appear as part of the "*Magan Text*," separating the two primary tablet epics. The materials from Akkadian and Assyrian exorcism tablets, concerning "*Seven Demonic Forces*," sometimes referred to as the MASKIM or MASQIM. Temple healers and priestesses often used the *Masqim* concept to understand and cure physical ailments and emotional issues plaguing the population—driving away, in their perspective, the unfavorable unseen spirits along with the unfavorable physical or visible conditions. We see evidence for this work very clearly in the "*Surpu*" tablet series, discussed in *Tablet-H* of "*Necronomicon: The Anunnaki Bible*." The nature of such beings is often represented as morally "evil," but they are a *part* of the cosmos—connected to the Source as active powers of otherwise morally-neutral (or amoral) forces. The "ethical" polarity of any phenomenon tends to be based on observed physical effects or experiences in one's own reality—a mountain or wasteland region can even become "evil" when it is met as an obstacle to overcome or cross. These impressions (or "emotional imprints") are not "momentary"—they can continue to affect memory and human consciousness long after the original stimulus is withdrawn.

The closing passages of the "*Magan Text,*"—with the exception of including the name "CUTHALU"—may be relatively familiar to many Seekers. They are a version of the very words used in many modern ceremonial occult operations—derived from the "*Chaldean Oracle Tablets*" (given as *Tablet-O* in "*Necronomicon: The Anunnaki Bible*"). Few outside the realm of academia use the term "Chaldean." In consciousness, its mystical tradition is simply absorbed into what we might readily just call *Babylonian* today. "Babylon" was a city and a nation. But, the mystical culture developing within it became known as "Chaldean" during its pinnacle Renaissance under King Nebuchadnezzar II. Rooted in observing a celestial "*Arien Age*" of MARDUK, "Chaldean-magic" is a stellar-oriented (or "astral") system of mysticism focused on "stars" and "planetary forces" far more than earthly and worldly elements.

In the *Schlangekraft recension*, remnants of the ancient Mardukite tradition, once implemented in Babylon, are brought to an accessible level for modern ceremonial magicians previously experienced with medieval "kabbalistic" grimoires of sorcery. For those less experienced, Simon's "*Necronomicon Spellbook*" (originally called the "*Necronomicon Report*") reached the public in the 1980's, attempting to capitalize on what its editors considered as the "grimoire" portions. Quite curiously, the main "grimoire" part of the work is an interpretation of the seventh ("secret") tablet from the "*Enuma Elis,*" catalogued in "*Necronomicon: The Anunnaki Bible*" as *Tablet-F*. This final tablet of the cycle illustrates how, *after* slaying the dragon TIAMAT and fashioning the heavens and the earth, MARDUK becomes "King" among the *Anunnaki* gods, taking on the sacred names of the preexisting Anunnaki Assembly—*fifty names* to be precise.

The "Mardukite" magician is instructed to appeal to MARDUK—or one of his *names*—for any and all spiritual and magical requests. This includes pathwork on the "*Ladder of Lights*"—system developed in Babylon for the "younger generation" of Anunnaki gods. If they could be more accessible to the people (then their ancestors) then they would be the favored representative powers ingrained into the reality (consciousness) of the people.

Simon's *Necronomicon* makes frequent mention of the "distant and forgetful nature of the gods," but such could just as equally apply to forgetful and easily misled beliefs of humans that have shared participation in "separating" or "fragmenting" reality by their own existence and thought-forms. Perhaps this is part of the maddening realizations H. P. Lovecraft spoke of regarding acquisition of such "divine knowledge" from the *Necronomicon*, because the real demon—*the real devil*—that seeks to devour and destroy you, is *yourself!*

Many pursuing Simon's *Necronomicon*—or essentially any *Necronomicon*—often seeking a specific type of "ritualized grimoire," and the "Book of Fifty Names" provided that for the reader. It was designed to. What may not be easily discerned is: that work, later recreated as the "*Necronomicon Report*," was a frugal manufacture by Magickal Childe, and essentially Herman Slater. Larry Barnes also seems to have been adamant about the Avon printing of the work, published as the "*Necronomicon Spellbook*," all primarily for financial reasons. This is clearly evident by anyone who has compared the "*Spellbook*" to their original "*Necronomicon*." In some ways, the goal was still fueled by a specific mystical intention—to make the *Necronomicon* mythos that much more accessible to people.

Experienced practitioners of ceremonial magic are usually able to glean most of the rudimentary "practical" aspects of Simon's work without the need of a guidebook. Such "guides" become questionably necessary only when the "uninitiated" seek short cuts for uncovering the same mysteries as those who devote their lives to the endeavor in Self-Honesty. These other psuedo-sorcerers are not personally invested in uncovering the *ancient arcanum* and likewise carry no responsibility for it. They do not look to the ancient sources themselves and rely on others to do this busy work for them. Equally reliant on interpretation by someone else.

Naturally, these forces cannot be fooled or culled into submission, and the metaphysical application that is so popular is in many ways a self-deception. These systematic traditions, "hermetically sealed" within themselves, rose from Semitic grimoire-styled "ceremonial magick." They are not surprisingly rooted in more ancient Egypto-Babylonian "Hermetic" forms of ritual magic—first the domain of ENKI, later passed to the possession of MARDUK, and then his scribe-son NABU. These three figures appear under different names in various mystical traditions all around the planet, each expressed entirely differently based on language and cultural worldviews.

Personal, individuated and subjective experience certainly colors reality. It is inescapable. The real challenge comes when the written word must be employed to bring something that is truly "occult"—existing only in the shadows of human consciousness—into the "*Realm of Light*" for the people to see. This must be done by the *hand* of someone—no matter how divine the "gospel" may be—and is, in many ways, always limited to their own vocabulary, speech and understanding.

As time passes on, simple truths can become very elaborate mysteries due to the manner in which the knowledge is preserved. If the technology of today is the "magic" of yesterday—might what we see as "aliens" and "monsters" of today, as H. P. Lovecraft suggests, be the *gods of yesterday?* Simon admits in "*Dead Names*" that for his project—

> "...some mysterious power that has used us to midwife itself into consciousness."

This is very much the case—except in this instance, the "mysterious power" is not so mysterious to the initiated. It carries with it a name that is not at all present in any Lovecraftian literature—the name of MARDUK.

* * *

Deep analysis of Mesopotamian traditions reveals that ancient priest-magicians and priestesses of Babylon did not necessarily use "magic" of the specific nature described in Simon's work.This type of "grimoire" emerged later. At best, they would invoke powers of the *Anunnaki* using incantations in the name of MARDUK. This idea of using "secret names" as properties of MARDUK—or any other demigod—for "spellcraft" and "low magic" is a much more recent addition to the system.

As magical systems evolved, later operators and scions of the traditions were kept in fear—in the "dark"— concerning the true nature of cosmic power, the Anunnaki, and structure of material reality as a whole. After the "gods" left the earth, what they left behind was designed so that those who might "stumble upon" the secrets of the gods would not understand what they behold. Instead, they would be lost to lifetimes of "mystifying correspondences" and numerological calculations—but never finding the way out! There are others locked in the matrix-web of material reality—those who do not succumb to the "occult" enlightenment trappings—who feel they are *above* such "superstition," the physical sciences were devised for the Realm of Light—simply another self-validating semantic paradigm used to base reality. The need to "know" and "label" creates new semantics to "know about." Yet, the "whole" is still unchanged.

The true cosmic nature of all things is much more "basic" than these systems provide understanding for.True knowledge remains simultaneously "hidden" and "in front of" all humanity. But the human psyche sees it, not for what it is, but refracted in a world of lights. People are naturally conditioned to remain enamored with the spectrum of variegated colors dancing on the wall rather then the unifying source of them. Mystical and "magickal work" is no different than other physical sciences provide. Modern "ritual magick" techniques are based on the same work conducted by the ancient "*Nabu-Tutu*" cults of Babylon—and later Egypt—but they concealed mysteries exclusive to their own inner circles, of a more "spiritual" nature—a more direct means to the Source without the trappings of the system.

Evidently, the ancient Mardukite Babylonians distinguished between their "esoteric" or secret knowledge and the "exoteric" or public display of knowledge intended for the masses. The public tablets, literature and traditions were raised to preserve a secret spiritual system—reserved for those "who know"—a secret "illuminated" class of society. This is alluded to in many "mystery traditions" and "mystic schools" throughout history—and yet they, themselves, have not been able to overcome glamours inherent in the human condition. Both mainstream and niche religions are no different, but unfortunately those who find this out are often so overcome with despair that they fall victims to any alternate fantasy or succumb to lifestyles rooted in hedonistic delights—"stooping down into a darkly splendid world." They fall prey to a atheistic and nihilistic "*Its all crap*" mentalities, having nothing of substance to fill the void. Consider the words of the "*Chaldean Oracles*" from *Tablet-O* in "*Necronomicon: The Anunnaki Bible*"—

Do not fix your mind on the vast systems of the Earth;
For the Plant of Truth grows not upon the ground.
Move, therefore, away from the Material World,
If you should enter the Star-Gate of the Sacred Paradise,
Where only Virtue, Wisdom and Unity are assembled.
Stoop not, therefore, down unto this Darkly-Splendid World;
Wherein lies a continually faithless depth,
And Hades shrouded in cloudy gloom,
Delighting in senseless images...

The forces "sealed" into currents of the magician's craft are the same "*Gates*" or "*veils*" of existence found in Anunnaki literature—called "*zonei*" in Simonian material. These forces describe a band of "seven lights" composing the spectrum of "form" that we experience as the "Material World." These "vibrations"—forces in motion—are the "*Cosmic Laws*" of the systematic universe as it was "designed." They really have no names or attributes themselves, except as we ascribe when communicating an understanding of them. At this point, the experienced practitioner can learn to be a master of the rays or allow them to be his or her master. This is not only   a decision or feat of willpower—it requires an entire restructuring of the psyche. Do you serve the "deception" or become a Master ("Ascended"?) of the Spheres—rightfully taking your place among the "gods" outside of this material existence—"*and in the spaces between...*"

* * *

Before the 31st Anniversary resurgence of the Simon hardcover, Avon/Harper-Collins published mass-market editions of new "Simon" books in 2006. Simon's popular "*Gates of the Necronomicon*" discourse reached the public on Samhain that year, six months after the Beltane appearance of his "*Dead Names: The Dark History of the Necronomicon.*" These two critical "gate threshold" periods were chosen intentionally, coinciding with this "magical tradition." Simultaneously, 2006 was the same year work began to solidify the inception of the modern "Mardukite" movement led by Joshua Free—a vision realized publicly (online) two years later in 2008.

Renewed interest in this paradigm followed the release of Simon's "*Gates*" material, helping to pave the way for a new millennium phase-shift of Mardukite revival. Emphasis returns to Egyptian and specifically Mesopotamian influences on the system—particularly the sevenfold *stargate* paradigm. As we discover, all of this is critically connected to the "magick" of this world—specifically the very manner in which the world itself operates by design. But, one of the most reoccurring key symbolic elements in esoteric lore is the connection made between "*gates*" and "*stars.*"

The fundamental principles or laws of the cosmos—forces of "gods," "stars" and "planets"—eventually blended together in human consciousness; just as the aspects of "god," "sky" and "heaven" were all represented by a single Sumerian character —"AN." Any distinction in understanding between these natures is lost to language and human over-identification of knowledge with strictly "words" and "labels."

In a methodology of reality separated into "levels" of existence, these "gates" represent the pathways, avenues or bridges of communication and power "between the veils." Beyond these *veils*, all of existence experiences its own entangled and unified nature with the ALL. The true magician does not succumb to an "illusion of power," falsely believing himself a god from pride, but instead realizes that it is the ability to communicate and facilitate communication with the "fabric of space" that causes manifestation—by the powers of the "God-Source!" This is what has been concealed in the dark and and "shadowy" side of the occult—for the more self-deluded that "magicians" and "dabblers" become in their own conceptions of enlightenment, the less likely they are to see the forest for the trees—and the deeper the enslavement to their own systems.

Representations of a "Celestial Gate"—to "outside" of the system—are mytho-graphically transposed onto the "Celestial Pole." By definition, this is the planet's "naturally ordained" axial relationship with the "Celestial Sphere"—an astronomic-al term used to define the zodiacal band of stars visible when we look relatively "out" into the universe, significant to the "precession" or relative movement of bodies in this solar system. In the most ancient recorded times of Mesopotamia, the central polar star-body or "constellation" was the "Dragon"—*Draco*—particularly the star *Thuban*. As of several thousand years ago, the "Great Bear" took domin-ance as the "Time Keeper of the Heavens," revolving around the star *Polaris*. A shift from centralization of the Dragon to the Bear reflected in cultural interpreta-tions of traditions and lore evolving from earlier, more ancient eras.

> *The Dragon was defeated!*
> *It lay below now, "dead but dreaming,"*
> *overtaken by the Bear!*

The fierce bear-king in Egypto-Babylonian traditions became "MARDUK-RA"— but this was only "truth" to the "*younger generation*" of *Anunnaki* "gods" of Babylon—their perception; their story. The "Ancient Ones" predating the more familiar Mardukite pantheon were once honored by a much more ancient "Dragon-cult"— dedicated to the ancient primeval cosmic serpent mother of life— TIAMAT.

Simonian discourses unknowingly [we assume] continue to perpetuate the same deception of polarity raised by the "younger," who gave themselves the name "Elder Gods" in order to secure a further separation of their divine nature from their ancestors of antiquity. Unfortunately, even in the 2006 edition of Simon's "*Gates of the Necronomicon*," MARDUK is still referred to as a "*Sumerian*" god— which is not really the case. We find the same misnomer quite often in Zecharia Sitchin's work as well. MARDUK *existed*, but he was never recognized officially in the pre-Babylonian *Sumerian* "pantheon"—a detail that may seem trite to some, but as the modern Mardukites discovered in discerning the origins of their own organization—it is actually quite significant.

As a general classification, the term "<u>Mesopotamian</u>" is quite preferable when the exact nature is not always readily available. This encompasses not only the prehistoric *Ubaid* and *Sumerians*, but also the later emerging *Babylonian* (*Chaldean*), *Akkadian*, *Assyrian* (*&tc.*) cultures that all shared similar languages, religion and geography—their interpretations of the mysteries merely separated with time, shifting in the sands of the desert "between two rivers."

The *Schlangekraft recension* also refers to the "*Anunnaki*" as separate from the system or else as the "Seven Judges of the Underworld." Early works by Sumeriologist, Samuel N. Kramer, often related them as "*Earth gods.*" The "*Igigi*" are portrayed as a race of demon-Watchers, somehow separate from the class of "Guardian Watcher Spirit"—or "*sedu*"—conjured to a magicians side for each ritual observation from that grimoire.

Simon's research into the "Celestial Gate" is intriguing. He suggests that the "Great Bear" constellation is the "astral key" that activates the *Gate* from the earth perspective, when the *bear* "hangs from its tail." How curious—this actually happens every day! But, it is not only the event itself, but the timing or threshold that is significant—it is when the remaining "stars are aligned" that the *Gate* is functional *from our side*.

Where much has been written elsewhere concerning Samhain—October 31—when this "Celestial Gate" is most accessible *from the other side*, it is really at the other half of the year, at Beltane—April 30—when this alignment happens shortly before midnight, a natural ceremonial time for such mystical work. If this is correct, it suggests a convergence in "earth-time" with "heaven-time." Ceremonial execution would then require a delicate calculation of sun-cycles, lunar-cycles and stellar-cycles. So, now the seeker must put the "gate-theory" into perspective. Not only is it something that happens "naturally" on a daily basis, it is observed (and apparently ceremonially effective) only under the most opportune times, and then too, subject to a calculation that might be mistaken. Where then, does the fear come from for "leaving this gate open for too long"...?

— 6 —
THE INFLUENCE OF H.P. LOVECRAFT

Contributions of H.P. Lovecraft—and the *"Cthulhu Mythos"*—are mostly absent from the earliest work of the modern "Mardukites"—particularly *"Necronomicon – Anunnaki Bible."* They play a very passive role in our researches—which mainly emphasize the specifically "Anunnaki" and "Mesopotamian" aspects of the legacy.

The questions of *sanity* and *reality* are the two primary themes prevalent in all of Lovecraft's work. It is not surprising that "Simon" begins his *"Gates of the Necronomicon"* discourse with a semantic lesson on these two words. According to H. P. Lovecraft's existential perceptions, arcane knowledge is very dangerous when we factor in the human element. So long as the characters accept what they have been given as the "norm" of society (via social conditioning) there is no question of sanity—reality is one-to-one with the consensus of the Realm. But what if this were not the case? What if things are only "real" from a matter of perspective—a deeper truth veiling the way things are as an Absolute? Or, perhaps there are no absolutes—as this would also be a very "maddening" realization as well: *things are only the way they are because that is how we see them.*

Forces exist in the universe—active principles of "Cosmic Law" in perpetual motion. They are actually quite amoral—without mundane morality—and exist solely to feed the operation of "existence" as it is. The material world is fashioned to function as necessity. The way in which this is subjectively perceived has little to do with the fact that it must function, and continues to function *with or without* our agreement. Of course, a systematically fractured universe requires a degree of intricacy to keep in order. Polarized forces seem set against each other to keep the program active. But, they are opposite only in their outer natures—as they are perceived. But in truth—they are the same—two sides of the same degree. That the human mind wishes to fragment some as "good" and others "bad" becomes its own device—its own way from which to view the world.

H. P. Lovecraft's *"Cthulhu Mythos"* is therefore not reality as it is, but reality as some humans have come to interpret their experiences. We are simply given a glimpse of one man's fragmented experience of universal forces and how they relate to one another. Quoting fantasy roleplaying developer, *Monte Cook*—

> "These forces taken together are not the Cthulhu Mythos, however. They are simply reality, the way things are. The body of knowledge known as the Cthulhu Mythos is the result of human attempts to make sense of this reality. We interact with these forces in tentative ways, and come away with suspicions about their true nature. Like medieval physicians who believed that stomach aches were caused by a small imp lodged in the belly, we look into the

night sky and think we know what's there. We're wrong, because
we can never truly know the darkness."

H.P. Lovecraft's personal experiences, visions and meditations interacting with
these primordial forces manifested in his literary work—always presented as works
of fiction—keeping any esoteric meaning enshrouded in mystery. Regardless of
whether or not he researched lore of Dogon tribes in Africa, or Oannes myths of
Mesopotamia, or if his family had involvment with Egyptian Freemasonry—
Lovecraft was plagued by his own very real dreams and nightmares of terror and
occult horror—and they do not seem to have subsided in his waking reality.

From his own subjective perceptions, "Lovecraft's Universe" was essentially *bad*.
Color this however poetically with "*black seas of infinity*" and other word pictures
—essentially, from the viewpoint of humanity, bad things happen for no reason, or
bad things happen causally from human actions (such as opening the mind to the
Necronomicon or opening some other gateway), but ultimately in the end—*bad
things happen.*

* * *

Nihilism grows like a tumor on Lovecraft's psyche the further he delves into the
nature of his visions for the sake of his readers—or, perhaps as a personal coping
mechanism. His perspective is very clear though—celebration of the Old Ones is
bad; celebration of the new religions is bad; pursuit of the spiritual is bad;
materialistic hedonism is bad... and when you factor in all the rest we might add to
this, the end result is always the question: *why are we even here?!?* Given this
sentiment or any systematic realization of this, the very idea that Lovecraft's
characters seek to use the *Necronomicon* to "live forever" or "bring discarnates
back" to this wretched existence is clearly *insanity!!!*

By the end of Lovecraft's literary career, scattered details of the *Necronomicon*
reached such epic proportions that it seemed that it would be nearly impossible for
it to exist. Certainly, no edition in print has ever truly satisfied the strictest of
Lovecraftians. And many show they are misguided. The modern "Mardukite
Office" was plagued with correspondence following the public release of its "*Liber
N – Necronomicon*" in 2009, from those seeking advice on how they might devise
and publish their own "beefed up" versions of the legendary tome. We had literally
run out of politically correct ways of saying: *you've missed the point, guys.*

Just as described in stories of Lovecraftian literature, partaking in a very real
intellectual pursuit of the *Cthulhu Mythos* and *Necronomicon* can become the most
dangerous drug available for this existence—a truly unsatisfiable thirst for
knowledge. For those who have dismissed the worldly systems of glamour and
illusion there is the deception of enlightenment embedded within the "occult"—
another system usually so convoluted that it keeps the psyche ever perpetually
occupied on the unresolvable "mystery" fabricated on the screen.

H. P. Lovecraft never truly designated a specific pantheon for the Old Ones. This was a task left to his interpreters—a task taken up by many in realms of both literary fantasy and practical mysticism. From the plethora of scattered references composing the "*Cthulhu Mythos*," Robert Turner singled out six specific forces for a version of the pantheon provided in his "*Necronomicon: Book of Dead Names*"— Azathoth, Yog-Sothoth, Nyarlathotep, Hastur, Cthulhu and Shub-Niggurath. In spite of the name adopted for the system, Turner ranks his pantheon in order of presidency, putting Cthulhu somewhere towards the end. Even in these revived Lovecraftian occult traditions, Cthulhu does not take a central role.

Many esoteric mysteries beyond our understanding of "Cosmic Law" bare no readily discernible answers for a fractured human psyche—but, nonetheless the quest ensues, and humans are left to fight amongst themselves with multifaceted interpretations. The lure of H. P. Lovecraft's *Necronomicon* is: just one more moment of power; just one more incantation; just one more deciphered word—will grant the Seeker a key out of the system—the "*Key to the Outside*." And this type of "gambler's fallacy" runs rampant in most "New Age" traditions.

A quick consolidation of Lovecraftian lore combined with Simonian and Mardukite "*Gate*" research and lore, all point toward a the threshold time taking place during the ancient annual "*Beltane*" festival. Popularized by the Celts and Druids, there does appear to be some "otherworldly" significance here. Lovecraft explains that the time is optimal for receiving primordial knowledge via the "*whisperer in darkness*"—strangely echoing the ceremonial magician's "*voice in the silence*," alluded to in various transcendental occult materials. Lovecraft writes in his prose of the same name, titled: "*The Whisperer in Darkness*"—

> "Former experience had told him May Eve – the hideous Sabbat
> night of underground European legend – would probably be more
> fruitful than any other date, and he was not disappointed..."

Even the *Necronomicon* of Lovecraft's visions, however, seem to thwart the Seeker from unveiling the true nature of these beings. As a literary work in itself, Lovecraft's *Necronomicon*—however enlightened or inspired the text may be—was still subject to the same individuated subjective consciousness of its allegedly Arabic author—given as "*Abdul Alhazred.*"

One must wonder about the early experiences of the human populations when encountering physical forces of their "alien gods." Consider the story of Ezekiel's Chariot or even the "burning bush." Mention has previously been made in the introductory materials of "*Necronomicon: The Anunnaki Bible*" concerning the "three angels" who approach Abraham in the deserts... The list is endless. Lovecraft explicitly explains, in his discourse on horror fiction, that it is the "fear of the unknown," above all other human emotions, that is not only traumatic and mentally shocking, but powerful and strong. Fear is unique above the rest—immediately able to bring its bearer to the most primitive base animal levels of survival—*fight or flight!*

Lovecraft's pantheon of gods appear to do little to soothe any human fear—and they use it to their benefit—cloaking themselves in obscure anonymity until the "stars are right" for their return. Will they even return? Did they ever truly leave?

> "It seems that the evil legends about what they have offered to men, and what they wish in connection with the earth, are wholly the result of an ignorant misconception of allegorical speech—how totally we had misjudged and misinterpreted the purpose of the Outer Ones in maintaining their secret colony on this planet..." — *The Whisperer in Darkness*

After spending several decades relaying his encounters with the "*Other*" in the form of gothic horror fantasy, we receive no apologies—but merely a subtle "oops!" for our efforts in following his previously relayed cycle. Surely, Lovecraftians and academicians alike will point out that such is being taken out of context—from a work of "fiction." But thematic plot-lines in Lovecraft's cycles are actually quite sparse. It becomes quickly evident that this literature is not meant to relay some great horror adventure stories—rather, they describe a loosely collected set of ideas and philosophy. Any background information simply offers a setting to present the lore as "facts"—much as how we might glean our knowledge from history books or a newspaper article.

* * *

H.P. Lovecraft once explained to his beneficiary. *August Derleth*—"I have something to say, but can't say it..." And it is at this moment that the horror really hits us, for we now know for certain that Lovecraft knows well more than he is letting on. We have experienced it before—because his prolific writings, as insightful as they might be, continue to only be written by the truth of Lovecraft's own experiences—veiled from the reader's casual experiences concerning the "stories" themselves. "The books you read are safe," we remember the bookseller telling Bastian in *The Neverending Story*—"This book is *not* for you."

To better understand the levels of Lovecraft's own realizations of the universe, one might distinguish from what "cycle" of life and literature he writes from. Nearly all of the stories branded as "Cthulhu Mythos" appear towards the end of his lifetime, and yet we see this was not about new conceptions, but simply newer realizations of the same encompassing world. There were originally no direct efforts made to compile a "pantheon" and Lovecraft never once used the phrase "*Cthulhu Mythos*" to refer to his own work. This a term was later coined by August Derleth. Lovecraft acknowledges that his interpretation is a primitive understanding at best, shaped by the fears of men—part of the evolution in human understanding of what has been hidden—resting in the shadows of mysterious occult esoterica—for thousands of years.

But let us be clear: *His work is not a stopping point—and those who treat it at such will inevitably realize the "dead end" embedded at the "height" of the system —where no true transcendental experience will be found.*

As described by some other esoteric and occult authors, the mind-shattering mysteries of the *Abyss* are also tapped during "sexual" experience. In fact, according to many modern "magickal orders"—usually those involved with or influenced by the work of *Aleister Crowley*—a sexual medium (on some level) is actually required for human consciousness to access any of the "*Gates*." It is interesting to note that Lovecraft's own "*Cthulhu*" cycle of works begin to emerge during the time he is married (1924-1929). *Kenneth Grant* draws from Rabbinical lore in "*Outer Gateways*," explaining that Moses failed to access these mysteries—the "Fiftieth" or "*Final Gate*" (of "*supernal light*") of the cosmos—"because he ceased to live with his wife." Other schools warn students against use of (physical) "sexual magic"— often due to its tendency for abuse, or else to seek "heightened states" through abstinence.

That humanity has been separated from the Source and fractured into individual existences has already been suggested, but in the face of sexual union we experience an even further separation from each other—the very idea of a "union" for mortals denotes a separation in the first place—that parts once divided are rejoined. Complex lust programs deeply ingrained in human consciousness, force the true nature of even *this* to remain veiled.

THE CYCLES OF LOVECRAFTIAN LITERATURE

Macabre – 1905 thru 1920
Dreams – 1920 thru 1927
Cthulhu – 1925 thru 1935

"Now I regret the harm I have inflicted upon these alien and incredible beings in the course of our nightly skirmishes. If only I had consented to talk peacefully and reasonably with them in the first place... But they bear me no grudge, their emotions being organized differently from ours..." —*The Whisperer in Darkness*

This is what causes the distortions in reality—*fear* of the unknown. Just as equally dangerous is the fear of what *can not* be known—or perhaps for some, what *should not* be known. Such thinking turns truth into anathema—just as the fear-program was designed to!

"All that the Outer Ones wish of man is peace and non-molestation and an increasing intellectual rapport. This latter is absolutely necessary now that our inventions and devices are expanding our knowledge and motions, and making it more and more impossible for the Outer Ones' necessary outposts to exist *secretly* on this planet. The very idea of any attempt to *enslave* or *degrade* mankind is ridiculous." —*The Whisperer in Darkness*

Given that "our eyes have deceived us before," it is rather difficult for a serious student to draw any clear logical conclusion about the nature of "alien gods" solely from Lovecraft's work. Can we be certain this time that these forces are indeed "favorable spirits" as opposed to some other gruesome horrors that have haunted us in the night? Are the ones that created us, going to be the same ones returning? Can we be certain that all forces presenting themselves as "peaceful" actually be the "kindly guardians" of the cosmos we seek? Is there any hope in illuminating the darkness so fixed by the human psyche?

— 7 —

THE CTHULHU CULT

The concept of H. P. Lovecraft's *Necronomicon* became inseparable from what literary fans and contributors later coined as the "*Cthulhu Mythos*." This collections of writings were never really intended as a functional "pantheon" in itself—but existed as a *cycle* composing the final works of Lovecraft during his lifetime.

Cthulhu makes his first appearance in 1925—a year after Lovecraft's marriage. In this new cycle of material, he sought a more definitive form to the thoughts, dreams and visions haunting his life. He sought to understand the causal universal reality as it had affected him—as his personal experience dictated it him and how he in turn communicated to his readers. This *cycle* of "Cthulhu" literature was just as sporadic and sparse as his earlier works—but then one must remember that these writings were first published as short serials in a magazine called "*Weird Tales*," and very few of them are book-length as stand alone works.

"*Call of Cthulhu*" is a short story debuting the figure now popular among enthusiasts and a familiar name among left-hand-path practitioners, which is to say those who prefer "darker" and more "rebellious" aspects of the occult. One really is led to wonder what "enlightenment" is intended through blatant disregard for natural order—or, the love of chaos. Nonetheless, it is the darker aspects of this "mythos" that attracts attention from the alternative-types, punks and outcasts. Perhaps a "fluffier" book on self-help candle meditation methods using flowery incense and bath soaps has an appeal to lonely witch-type housewives—but, for those seeking more antagonistic approaches to "rebelling" against the "reality deception," well, the system always provides, dictating—*Whatever the thinker, thinks; the prover, proves.*

H. P. Lovecraft's "*Call of Cthulhu*" is written as a "detective mystery," where the rites and activities of a very modern and active "Cthulhu Cult" are described. While the essence of esoteric lore and occult mystery runs deep beneath the surface, just as with any other well-established "cult" in history, the means of enlightenment by quasi-hippie methods of free love, drunken orgies and the like, certainly leave much to be desired—though many *do desire* this method for purely hedonistic ideals, even if they prefer to shroud their beliefs and actions with the illusion of enlightenment.

Celebration of the *lower* is hardly a means to the *higher*. And those mistaking or misusing the secret power embedded intentionally in the "*Sex Gate*" will find the experience to be just as physically, emotionally and spiritually disturbing and dam-aging as any of the other "*Gates*" method. This is not to say there is not some validity to the methods. But, the human psyche seems to muddle its experience of "sexual" energies, and so it is not a preferred method of instruction—at least certainly not at any "neophyte" levels of occult initiation. [We might speak the same warnings regarding what some refer to as "psychedelic shamanism."] An initiate must be in a state of absolute "clear" *Self-Honesty*, or the experience will yield yet another pitfall—leaving the Seeker confused, lost—and again, far from true enlightenment.

What can we say for humans? They were programmed to enjoy fucking so they wouldn't confuse it with killing—and the emotional charge to make rational sense of both. If sex didn't feel good, for at the very least "evolutionary" purposes, the human race would have bred itself out into extinction a long time ago. We watch as the race has grown to hate its own, itself and everything "apart" from itself. How dismal, indeed. Perhaps Lovecraft had a point or two after all—when even I have seen inside the human psyche at your best and at your worst and I can usually never tell the difference... Lovecraft writes in *"Call of Cthulhu"*—

> "The most merciful thing in the world, I think, is the inability of the human mind to correlate all it contains. We live on a placid island of ignorance in the midst of black seas of infinity, and it was not meant that we should voyage far. The sciences, each straining in its own direction, have hitherto harmed us little; but some day the piercing together of dissociated knowledge will open up such terrifying vistas of reality, and our frightful position therein, that we shall either go mad from the revelation or flee from the deadly light into the peace and safety of a new dark age."

One way in which the occultists have always dealt with the "maddening revelations" is, again, utter immortality. Although the current editor was mentored at an early age in the methods of the *Hermetic Order of the Golden Dawn* and is aware of the work related to the seemingly "darker" derivatives of the same: *Argentium Astrum* (A.A.) and *Ordo Templi Orientis* (O.T.O.), these have not been the glasses worn from which to envision the modern Mardukite movement, even considering the *Necronomicon* amidst all of the "gore" and "horror" surrounding it.

In the past, many underground "cults" and groups often coped with these "maddening revelations" using some kind of ritual drama or other intentional reenactments intended to trigger states of consciousness—including activities designed to bridge a fiction ("Cthulhu Cult") to history. Among some real groups, especially those influenced directly by Aleister Crowley, these are not unique. For example, similar secret cult rituals were written for *Argentium Astrum* in 1910, known as the *"Rites of Eleusis."*

The *"Rites of Eleusis"* are a perfect example of this celebration of the *lower*—now esoterically relayed to initiates as "religious ecstasy"—to awaken their *higher* faculties. [*Indeed...*] What is not as well known is that there are actually *seven* "Rites of Eleusis"—each corresponds to none other than one of the seven "Zonei" of the *Schlangekraft recension*, or the seven "Gates" from the *Babili Texts* in "Necro-

nomicon: The Anunnaki Bible." The rites are presented the planetary precession we should expect—the precise *Gate* chronology we are already familiar with—*only reversed*. [The order indicated by the *"Rites of Eleusis"*—Saturn, Jupiter, Mars, Sun (Sol), Venus, Mercury and Moon (Luna).]

Participation in such an underground "cult" is very compelling to a certain type of individual. These "inquisitive ones" often venture as deep as they can to unveil what they already know to be a Great Deception. But where is the horizon? Where does the land and sky divide itself—the "real" from the "unreal" ...where? The answer is very clear—it does not. The division is really only within one's own mind —as is the "manifold nature" of reality—as are all the fragmented *"gates"* and *"levels"* that one perceives to exist. The "real" is broadcast all around us—but at an individual level, we can still fail to recognize it for what it is. For this reason, all of the applicable practices and traditions emphasize—*piercing the veils of illusion.*

Why always "underground"—in secret—or with friends? An individual who "stops accepting the program" is semantically *"insane."* When your reality is no longer one-to-one with that which has been given to you, society no longer deems you of a "clean" sound mind. You have gone against the norm—You have broken the veils. Your world reality is now a minority-of-one... Enter: "underground clubs," "secret societies" and "fraternities" that jump at the opportunity to bring the energy and power of another mind under their own group consciousness umbrella of enlightenment. This is yet another layer of glamour embedded into the system for those who "break free." As soon as one "level" is completed—like a game—the next immediately begins and so they must work their way through one labyrinth after another of initiation and indoctrination. This is not the path that all choose, but it is an easy one to succumb to. In a nutshell—if the individual Seeker is, again, not approaching their pursuit in *Self-Honesty*, the result is very likely "getting lost" in yet another system.

Where we might expect details of dismal cult abuse and abhorred bloody rites, the real intriguing parts of Lovecraft's "Cthulhu cycle"—concerning the *"Old Ones"*— regards classification of two important details: where they came from and why they were here. Here, described from *"The Whisperer in Darkness"*—

> "The Winged Ones came from the Great Bear in the sky, and had mines in our earthly hills whence they took a kind of stone they could not get on any other world. They did not *live* here, but merely maintained outposts and flew back with vast cargoes of stone to their own stars in the north."

This passage, written in the late 1920's or possibly 1930, reveals an emphasis on an area of space that some Seekers are probably all too familiar with—the *"Great Bear"* in the north—but also the mining operations, which we assume to be gold— something we are to expect based on many interpretations of ancient Mesopotami-an "Anunnaki" lore. We can consider the context and call it "fiction." But artists often choose this method to communicate very real ideas, just as the visions and messages that L. Ron Hubbard received, he first described to people in novels—such as *"Battlefield Earth."* We should not be so easily dismissive of "fiction" medias from their nature alone. As an instructional tool, "stories" and "fables" are timeless.

Certainly, many original cult classics—*1984, Animal Farm, Anthem, The Giver*—or new ones like *Ferngully, Avatar* or even *The Hunger Games*—are all intended to relay very real statements about the world, observations that are more easily communicated *en masse* via the realm of fiction. So long as the end result is a highly marketable work that we can safely store in our mind as a "nice story," we are never truly faced with the total implications of what the artist meant. But the messages are there and they are loud and clear—it is no covert conspiracy. But if they were to really all hit you at once—you might overload! Hence, for good reason, the program keeps people only about 10% conscious of what is happening around them—and this seems sufficient for operating in material existence. This is the most the human condition is designed to handle without self-honesty— think of it as a cosmic "loss prevention" program. Until you can *afford* it, you don't get to have more.

* * *

"They worshiped, so they said, the Great Old Ones who lived ages before there were any men, and who came to the young world out of the sky. These Old Ones were gone now, inside the earth and under the sea; but their dead bodies had told their secrets in dreams to the first man, who formed a cult which had never died. This was that cult—it had always existed and always would exist, hidden in distant wastes and dark places all over the world until the time when the great priest Cthulhu, from his dark house in the mighty city of R'lyeh under the waters, should rise and bring the earth again beneath his sway. Some day he would call, when the stars were ready, and the secret cult would always be waiting to liberate him." —*The Call of Cthulhu*

And so, by the act of simply writing this passage, H.P. Lovecraft opened a gate that could allow all these things to manifest in human consciousness—from a certain point of view. It is not necessarily his specific set of semantics (or *"Cthulhu Mythos"*) that we need focus attention on—although many do, claiming to have some deep spiritual relationships with *"egregores"*—artificially created thought-form elementaries—manifested from Lovecraft's psyche onto the printed page. [Which is, of course, possible—*from a certain point of view.*] The iconic image of an ancient cult carrying prehistoric knowledge extending to a time before humans could be enough to entice even the most "right wing" Seekers.

To a still sleeping 1920's and 1930's American society, any effective information relay required an acceptable format for public reception. The realm of fantasy and science fiction offers such creative visionary minds an appropriate avenue for expression. Consider the stories of Jules Verne's machines—thought entirely "fanciful" at their time of origination, but they later served as inspiration for technologies. Developing accounts of the "supernatural" are no different, but rather than use a set framework, paradigm, or systematic vocabulary, the "supernatural" is relayed in Lovecraft's work as the *"Unknown,"* something horrific for no other reason than for being the *Unknown*. When visions turn to gruesome nightmares— and creatures that do not fit within the social norm "one-to-one"—the only way many can interpret them is simply as "monsters." But as Lovecraft began to explain in his final works—"the monsters of today are the gods of yesterday"—and all human communications and relationships with these forces are affected by one's "experiences" and "beliefs." These beliefs or personal determinations define what these experiences implicate on a subjective level.

During initial investigations by the *Mardukite Research Organization*, it seemed many contemporaries and colleagues of the current editor expressed a firm belief that origins of H.P. Lovecraft's "Cthulhu Cult"—and its patron deity, of course— are derived from ancient Middle Eastern lore, but not "Arabic," in the way we understand the region today. Much like other Chaldeo-Babylonian influences on the modern *Necronomicon* cycle, the Cthulhu archetype does share some proximity with certain ancient currents—but, the relation of it, as demonstrated by Lovecraft's bipolar attitude toward the nature of these beings, is painted over with spiritual politics from a post-Sumerian age. To those already familiar with Mesopotamian mysteries, the name *"Oannes"* is asserted, called *"Dagon"* to Semitic Philistines, as the "truest" identity of Cthulhu—and from this suggestion, we can trace the energy current back to the Anunnaki god, ENKI. When one considers the degradation of the "dragon current"—described in Mardukite *Liber-50*—it is not so surprising to see ENKI painted as a "Cthulhu" to awakening minds of the 20th century—*many thousands of years after the fact.*

In c. 300 B.C., *Berosus,* a Babylonian historian, left records describing a divine being—amphibian like in nature—named *Oannes*. According to the account, this being emerged in prehistoric times from the Persian Gulf and essentially instructed mankind in the "Divine" arts and sciences of civilization. Then, he disappeared again, back into the sea—*dead but dreaming*—and the people awaited his return. This concept of a "return" seems fundamental to all religions—that at some indeterminable point in time, an "ultimate confirmation" of one's faith will manifest in front of the whole world. While this definitely assists in sealing systems in consciousness, it is interesting to note that these "messianic" programs are apparently designed to where they always seem to "be coming," but are essentially unfulfillable prophecies in man's eyes. Consider the appearance of Jesus Christ among the Jews—"certainly this cannot be he that the prophets speak of..."

...Do you still deny me?

234

The lure of the *Cthulhu Cult*—or any similar "cult" following—is essentially the promise of a communion with the "*Other*." We all know its there—that this isn't all there is—even atheistic minds among you (preferring the semantic taunts of science to religion) still remain amazed about how many apparent "levels" there are to this "physical existence," and the untold secret power that is sealed away therein. That there was something "before" our modern civilization remains beyond the scope of popular public opinions and false ego-centric worldviews.

Humans tend to forget that it was to the "gods" that the original esoteric technologies and architecture of the ancient world were first dedicated—not as accomplishments to praise the glory of human labor, such as we might see today. Attributing this ancient knowledge and technology—including the very arts of civilization—to a source other than human is practically mind-shattering to anyone completely closed off to such a "reality."

* * *

Distinction between the "*Ancient Ones*" (or "*Great Old Ones*") and the younger "*Elder Gods*" has been a matter of confusion for some time. The entire subject was only briefly alluded to in Lovecraft's work. It became a more commonly related theme from the *Schlangekraft recension*. But, as explained in Mardukite *Liber-51/52*, this political and spiritual division really emerged in later interpretations. Complexities of the global system grew from their simplistic Sumerian form into the more familiar "Mardukite" Chaldeo-Babylonian versions such as our archetypal *Epic of Genesis*—the "*Enuma Elis*" and other ancient scriptures.

Seekers trying to blend multiple systems will be immediately confused—because modern practitioners interpret Lovecraft's "*Great Old Ones*" as planetary forces that the Mesopotamian work (as represented by Simon or in our Mardukite "*Necronomicon: The Anunnaki Bible*") attributes to the "Elder Gods"—meaning the "younger pantheon" of *Anunnaki*. Is it possible that these are allusions to systems predating the Elder Gods? Probably not. These systems did not yet required sealing until the rise of the "Elder Gods."

Differing widely from historical viewpoints concerning Mesopotamian Anunnaki, the Lovecraftian interpretation regards two races of alien intelligence—"Ancient Ones" and the "Elder Gods." After what can only be described as a "primordial battle in heaven"—very similar to what we find in Babylonian literature and later Semitic scriptures derived from the same—the *Elder Gods* "seal" the *Ancient Ones* and entrap their powers into "gate-systems" that divides the material cosmos and "in the spaces between spaces."

In the end, the *Elder Gods* are allowed to rule the local universe. For moral and political justification, opposing forces are always demonized as monsters and "savage beasts" that must be destroyed to further the advancement or survival of a more "civilized" race.

In essence, the *"Great Old Ones"* of Lovecraft's visions, in their horrifying states, only loosely relate to the historic Anunnaki—the real "gods" of ancient humans. The "Elder Gods" are exactly that—these Anunnaki, known as gods, and particularly among them, the "younger pantheon" of Egypto-Babylonian systems became the primary global influence thereafter.

This lore raises critical questions for those following traditions based on any aspect of the *Necronomicon* cycle, Lovecraftian or otherwise: Who or what do you serve? And is it a representation of the Highest? If we consider the *"Enuma Elis,"* the Anunnaki sealed away ancient primordial (possibly malignant) forces in order to create (or maintain) a material existence of *"Order."* If this necessary order also lends itself toward your own existential benefit: why would someone seek to dissolve this? Why consciously create uninhabitable conditions? The answer must reside within the apocalyptic programs of "mortality" that are so deeply ingrained in human consciousness.

All systematic existence is *finite* from a physical or "mortal" point of view. Energy is constantly vibrating and forces are constantly in motion. In accordance with Cosmic Law—All manifestation is fixed to a tidal ebb and flow. We interact with only finite interpretations of these infinite forms and patterns. The trappings of the material system only demonstrate how limited things *can* be—not things as they *are*. Whether or not the knowledge and experience of an individual is *Self-Honest* —free from the conditioning of the system—reality will continue to be justified (analytically or semantically) from the "memory pool" that you actually do have access to. "Conditioning" comes in an infinity of forms. There are few answers for many Seekers discovering or realizing the *"Great Deception"* of material existence. Do we simply rebel against the physical as the Gnostics prescribe? Is this even a realistic approach? For those who fail to learn how to "live in the *kNow*," the focus on the mountaintop causes them to trip over what is right under their feet. There are movements, actions and beliefs that further your spiritual evolution toward the "goal"—and there are those which will not.

As an *Elder God* race—in either Lovecraft stories or Mesopotamian interpretations —these beings were able to fashion or manipulate a reality suitable for human habitation. In physical bodies, they interfaced with humans historically. But their own true natures are far from the familiar condensed energy vibrations of the "material." Seemingly ageless and timeless entities from other worlds appear in some of the oldest known archetypal and genetic memories of humanity. These figures do not seem to have "created," so much as "systematized," the physical existence (and/or its conditions) of man—the arts of civilization—and the knowledge that propelled the race into what it has become. But it is now within the human psyche—its individualized nature—the means to interact with their environment, that has really caused the destruction and havoc that we see today. The seed was planted from outside the system, but most humans have failed to see that they carry and unfold it themselves. There are many types of beings waiting to see *what* humans will *"unfold."*

In innumerable sources, the Elder Gods are represented with a pentagram—an earthly symbol of authority over material domains of five elements—but some believe it reveals the stellar origins of gods and humans. In esoteric occultism, the pentagram is used to represent man, and by nature, material existence. Another frequently appearing symbol—the six-rayed star or "hexagram"—indicates communications between what is "seen" and "unseen"—or "physical" and "spiritual"—aspects of reality. This is evident in many Semitic-Kabbalistic "grimoires"—such as the "*Keys of Solomon*" cycle, &tc. A seven-pointed star is used to distinguish distant origins of the Anunnaki, beings that artistically depicted themselves with an eight-rayed star—the origin of the "asterisk," named for the Akkadian word for gods: "*istari.*"

If a system collapse were to take place—as sealed by the *Elder Gods* in these literary cycles—than the calamity that would follow would be nothing short than "un-creation." Whether because of their own bruised egos or some other even deeper source of spiritual malcontent, some have sought this "*Uncreation*" since the very beginning of ceremonial magic practices—a rebellious self-destruct system within the heart of an already rebellious counter-culture approach. Rather than seek harmonious relationships with the guardian protectors of humanity—because of the type of person often attracted to these aspects—what is presented as "dark" and "recessed" seems to carry the widest appeal.

Whenever one wishes to knowingly embark upon a "dark" path—they have kind of set themselves up already. Any division of polarity in consciousness where one is clinging to a "negative" extreme, the same system is being followed—just backwards—an ebbing pendulum swing between extremes. The "good" only remains so if there is a "bad" to clash it against—otherwise, people get bored and easily begin to stop accepting the program. So long as forces are in motion, the program remains.

Since the time of ancient Sumer, nearly all traditions are based on perceptions of these forces as ever at odds with one another—but they are of a singular nature, primarily split or divided in human consciousness. It is only outwardly reflected as a "dual-party" system, but it is not. The true battle over your "soul"—the unfoldement and evolution of the *Self*—is mainly: you against yourself. Can you rise from what you thought you were, into what you are supposed to be. The "humanistic" reply from the modern *Mardukite* movement, as expressed in "*Necronomicon: The Anunnaki Bible*"—

> "Most practitioners who are drawn to these mysteries are not sympathetic to the destruction and malignant energies manifested on the planet by the human population—correctly dubbed by T.H. White as '*homo ferox*' in his *Book of Merlyn*. It seems to some that the only solution toward protecting the integrity of the "Big Picture"—even beyond the next "seven generations"—requires

reincorporation of the original source powers that brought this all into being at its start. Whether or not this energy can peacefully coincide with the current human systems in place—is the last of our concerns."

* * *

The apocalyptic "*R'lyeh Text*" was not mentioned specifically in H.P. Lovecraft's writings. However, he suggests that the great priest of the Old Ones—*Cthulhu*—lies "dreaming" in the underground city of "R'lyeh," a sunken lost city in the ocean, that will rise again when "the stars are right." This other "book" separate from the *Necronomicon* was suggested by later writers and contributors to the "*Cthulhu Mythos*"—in this case, *August Derleth*. Other similar tomes allegedly from the *Necronomicon* cycle have been introduced in related stories and tales for the past 100 years. Even if we did accept "research" from Lovecraftians, our other Mesopotamian Anunnaki records still predates all of this. The "*R'lyeh Text*," by admission of those who believe in it, originates circa 300 B.C.—approximately the same time that one of the last true priests of Babylon—Berosus (Berossus)—chronicled the details of "*Oannes*"—*Dagon* or ENKI. The "fictional" *Necronomicon* of the "Mad Arab" is only from the 7th century A.D.—well after Chaldeo-Babylonian, Semitic, Christian, Zoroastrian and Persian influences would all have had their influence on *any* understanding of the system.

Concerning Donald Tyson's "Lovecraftian" contributions—"*Necronomicon*" and "*Grimoire of the Necronomicon*"—seven forces are again singled out, such as we should expect, especially from an author skilled in ceremonial magic and Enochian practices. They are, of course, aligned to the system as planetary forces. Throughout esoteric literature and occultism we repeatedly see the same correspondences apply to any seven-fold system—music, color, days of the week, &tc.—but this is all that grants Lovecraftian ritual magicians any "just cause" to celebrate a functional "*Cthulhu Mythos*" tradition. But it is the same universal tradition, but with Lovecraftian names—just as applicable as if we were to ascribe Greek, Roman or some other language to the same planetary system. Donald Tyson chose: Azathoth, Nyaralathotep, Yog-Sothoth, Yig, Shub-Niggurath, Cthulhu and Dagon for his descending pantheon. And here—where many Mesopotamian practitioners and esoteric scholars often associate Cthulhu with the historical Dagon, Tyson continues to separate this entity as yet another identity—as Lovecraft himself may have also mistakenly done.

The primary benefit to displaying a Lovecraftian interpretation across the "*Ladder of Lights*" is simply that we may more easily compare this version to the actual Babylonian luminous gate-system demonstrated in Mardukite materials based on historical sources. For example, we can compare the following planetary associations made between Lovecraftian beings and those of the BAB.ILI system from Mesopotamia—

Azathoth	Sun (Sol)	Shammash (or Samas)
Nyarlathotep	Mercury	Nabu (or Nebo)
Yog-Sothoth	Jupiter	Marduk
Yig	Saturn	Ninurta (or Ninib)
Shub-Niggurath	Venus	Ishtar (or Inanna)
Cthulhu	Mars	Nergal
Dagon	Moon	Nanna (or Sin)

It should be clearly understood: Any properly designed planetary-based system of magic will work for that reason alone—regardless of what "names" are given to the specific currents. For example: So long as the archetypal energy identified is identical one-to-one, the choice of language—*Zeus, Marduk, Yog-Sothoth, Dys Pater, &tc.*—is irrelevant if each is understood to mean: "*Jupiter.*" It is for this reason that people found any mutual success with planetary-aligned Enochian magic—in spite of many "inconsistencies" spread among various interpretations of *John Dee's* work.

The *Schlangekraft recension* includes a preface titled: "*Supplemental Material to 777.*" It is a fascinating parallel derived from the "*Enuma Elis,*" but carries some astrological inconsistencies. However, prior to modern Mardukite work, this is the only direct attempt to connect Kabbalistic or occult associations to the Mesopotamian (Anunnaki) pantheon. It appears in Simon's work allegedly at the request of the O.T.O.—or perhaps even Kenneth Grant, directly. Another version of the same lore later circulated underground from on obscure group (real or imagined) calling themselves the "Order of the Silver Lotus."

COMPARATIVE CORRESPONDENCES

[*Kabbalistic / Esoteric*]	[*Mesopotamian*] {*Lovecraftian*}
0. -00-	Anu (Tiamat)
1. Primum (Crown)	Enlil (Absu) {Azathoth}
2. Zodiac (Wisdom)	Enki (Igigi) {Nyralathotep}
3. Saturn (Understanding)	Adar (Ninib) {ShubNiggurath}
4. Sphere of Jupiter	Marduk
5. Sphere of Mars	Nergal
6. Sphere of the Sun	Utu (Shammash)
7. Sphere of Venus	Inanna (Ishtar)
8. Sphere of Mercury	Nebo (Nabu)
9. Moon (Foundation)	Nanna (Sin) {Cthulhu}
10. Elements (Malkuth)	Kia (Earth) {Ubbo-Sathala}
11. Air	Anna (Sky)
12. Mercury	Gudud (Nabu) {Nyralahotep}
13. Moon	Sin (Nanna)
14. Venus	Dlibat (Ishtar)
15. Aries	Agru (Xubur)
16. Taurus	Kingu (Moon)
17. Gemini	. . . (Viper)
18. Cancer	Shittu (Serpent)
19. Leo	. . . (Lakhamu)
20. Virgo	Shiru Whirlwind
21. Jupiter	Umunpaddu
22. Libra	Zibanit (Dog)
23. Water	Badur
24. Scorpio	(Scorpion-Man)
25. Sagittarius	(Hurricane)
26. Capricorn	(Fish-Man) {Yog-Sothoth}
27. Mars	Mastabarru
28. Aquarius	Gula (Horned Beast)
29. Pisces	(Weapon) {Dagon & Hydra}
30. Sun	Shammash (Samas)
31. Fire	Ag {Cthugha}
32. Saturn	Kaimanu {Tsathoggua}
33. Earth	Kia
34. Spirit	Zi

Quite simply, one of the only ways that the Anunnaki *Necronomicon* lore and the Lovecrafitan *Necronomicon* lore can be mystically esoterically compared is through observation of a common baseline. In the above given examples, the basic planetary orientation of the traditional Babylonian gate-system with the later Semitic Kabbalah—yet another gate-system derived from the same. But...

> *Tell the type of person painstakingly researching and devising such correspondences that "at the end of the day: all is one in equality" and they have a nervous breakdown on you.*

Whether under one set of semantics or another, the systems remain fixed—*static*—against the background of the cosmos—fixed by "Cosmic Law." It is this "background veil" that Seekers truly desire to pierce, but to do so is to acknowledge a whole messy labyrinth of systems and structures that one must sift through, recognize, and absolve. Kenneth Grant writes in *"Outer Gateways"*—

> "The occultist has necessarily to revert to the 'primordial void' in order to encounter the source materialization."

Strictly "Lovecraftian" efforts, whether of fans or occultists alike, have actually failed to pierce the *Veil*—true "Crossing to the Abyss" is not among their most fundamental exploits. Where any threads do appear, they elusively shroud any useful coherency. A few scattered references appear in ambiguous work concerning "veils of negative existence" and also an Argentium Astrum (A.A.) initiation ritual designed by Aleister Crowley. Otherwise, mystical pursuits to self-honestly access the void are relayed more clearly in materials from the modern Mardukite movement. As explained in Mardukite *Liber 50*, it is the *"Primordial Abyss"* that represents the true background nature of existence—everything else is but colors on a screen, keeping the senses occupied in a fractured physical existence.

* * *

Many learned scholars and esoteric leaders fall into the "system-trap," not because they consciously wish to propagate the deception of reality further, but because there are few other ways in which to communicate the information. To be any more "gnostic" in the relay runs risks of looking even "crazier" in an already "fluffy" metaphysical field of study, practice and writing—so very few of those who have become popular personas in the "New Age" are quick to "pull the rug out" from under their readers. Few are willing to sacrifice their income and livelihood for Truth.

> *If new systems systems cannot continue to be packaged as mystical correspondences of various signs and symbols into new materials, then the whole mega-system would collapse. The masses are not ready for such a thing.*

H. P. Lovecraft never saw his mythos as a fixed pantheon—it was left to others to do this, those that sought something practical and workable within the "ceremonial paradigm." Only some, it would seem, have been a little more admitting about this than others. In his "*Grimoire of the Necronomicon*," Donald Tyson writes—

> "Those familiar with Lovecraft's fiction may raise objection that he made no link between the Old Ones and the seven planetary spheres of traditional astrology. True enough. However, it has been a common practice in the Western esoteric tradition to use the symbol sets of astrology to categorize various groups of esoteric beings or occult qualities. This is not a modern conceit, but goes back many centuries. It was done because it was useful, for purely practical reasons, to make this kind of symbolic association. When the lords of the Old Ones are placed on the spheres of the planets, all the occult correspondences for the planetary spheres become available to use in summoning them and directing them in ritual work."

It is the hope of the current editor to resolve the mystery by citing the above reiteration. Because—there we have it: no matter what you do within the system,you are still within the rainbow of lights, playing at the game of alien intelligences. That this began in the ancient Babylonian system of planetary forces and designations has already become clear—but that we continue to interpret all of our mysteries solely from this guise is not so readily observed as people debate their preferred planet-names.

As with any classification or labeling venture, the systematized magicians cease to perceive raw ancient and primordial energy currents as they truly exist, and instead, are forced to see them through the veil of some other esoteric pattern. Nonetheless, contemporary magicians and practitioners have continued to dazzle themselves and each other with the seemingly infinite correspondences and relationships made between the same key elements under various names.

Perhaps the most liberating interpretation of the Mardukite work regarding the "Ladder of Lights" is to "work the system out." Rather than passively pathworking through the glamours and trying to maintain was is perceived, the "Gatework" derived from the Babylonian tradition is used by the modern practitioner to access "outside the system."

By leaving the "safety net" of the Realm of Light, you are no longer contained by its illusions. By not fully "Crossing to the Abyss," you have not been able to access any self-honest experience beyond the veils. Veils of existence are confronted and transcended in their entirety. Warnings connected notoriously to these mysteries speak against only accessing "some" of the veils. There are no half-measures to completion. Doing so leaves the practitioner lost between two world and unable to be withheld by either.

— 8 —
UNIVERSAL AGENTS OF SYSTEMOLOGY

A infinite spectrum of colors and lights—mysteries of reality and the nature of the universe—continue to captivate our minds. The need to "know" is there—always there—programmed deeply within human consciousness, but the avenues are endless and often without "true" enlightenment. The "*need to Know*" is so great that we can even manifest *things* to "Know" about. *Whatever the Thinker, thinks; the Prover, proves.* At the height of the initiatory pyramid, there is a genuine understanding of the material systems and veils of existence—but, what of it? Why is this esoteric pursuit of the "occult" so forbidding and sacred? And what spiritual evolution does it offer, beyond acquisition of mundane gratification?

The gods and spirits that are also a part of the system—what trappings await the Seeker that blindly supplicates before them? The "Solomonic" and "goetic" hierarchies—the demons and angels of the "*Book of Abramelin*"—to what do we owe these figures by prayer and sacrifice? Have they so easily deafened, as well as blinded, so that you cannot even hear their laughter?

It is possible that the Anunnaki may not be much different, but at the very least, a Seeker recognizes the raw energies as they are—to be equally "realist" and "metaphysicist," and call a spade: "a spade." And our modern "Mardukite" efforts are not in creating or transposing a new mythology—but instead, returning to the most ancient and original ones. It should be understood through and through that in spite of the cosmological stories attached to them, the ancient "*gods*" are not the "Source"—not the "Creatrix" of a purely spiritual system. They are, instead, grand manipulators of the system, and for this feat alone they are called "gods." Some have even called them "dream-walkers" or "time-travelers" of the reality we inhabit. They have abilities to move through an additional "astral" dimension. We often imagine them inhabiting this additional dimension, moving through "time-space" as fluidly as our own freedom of movement in this energetically condensed material reality.

"Mardukite" priests of ancient Babylon were, by nature, *Priests of Enki*, following a derivative of ancient *systems* born in *Eridu*—the prehistoric capital city of ENKI, located near the Persian Gulf sea. Beyond the *collected data* to support a belief system, the first pragmatic mystical and religious use of writing was the recording of *incantations*. Examination of these tablets reveals *appeals* to the *gods* for assistance in material matters. [Examples may be found in Mardukite *Liber 50* and *Liber 51/52*.]

At the inception of "prehistoric" *Anunnaki* traditions, the people were instructed to petition their needs to the temple-priests—who in turn make appropriate offers and ritualized incantations necessary to enact "magic" of the *deity* involved. A distinction existed between the public "exoteric" religion observed by the general population and the "esoteric" one covertly practiced by the priests themselves. New "historic" traditions resulted from unique dynamics made possible with the introduction of *cuneiform* writing into human consciousness—a time when things ceased to be seen solely from experience based learning and were instead rooted in language and "data classification" or "systematization." These dynamics of a "Mardukite" state or empire were not necessarily ruled by MARDUK directly, but all of *Babylonia* existed under his care—and watchful eye—by way of the temple-priests and Kings serving in his name.

The modern "Mardukite" movement researches historic systematization but does not propagate religious systems revival in a manner typical of what most people think of concerning "religion" and "dogma." Evolution of planetary systems— particularly human systems—is simply an unfoldment of program-designs playing out. It is not necessarily what is truly intended by "Higher Orders," but simply the way things developed by necessity to bring us here. "Authorities" shaped a prison to contain the human psyche—a vehicle for human sensory experience—further feeding the systematic program by continuously confirming its own very existence. In this way, the Seeker should come to see *Cosmic Law* just like the "Forces of Nature" or "Natural Law" more easily observed locally on the planet. This is actually one reason why mystics so heavily emphasize "getting back to Nature"— because all of the lessons we need to know about the universe are perfectly reflected there for the *Self* to experience.

Nature is a "system" of life—on earth, called an "eco-system." The more "*Elven-Faerie*" or "*Druidic*" paths of esoteric mystery put expressly put forth an idea that the entire earth planet operates as a single living organism—some call "*Gaea*" or "*Gaia.*" Of course, from our perspective it has "relatively" smaller systems and larger ones, but all are integrated into one single program running its course. There is some reason, then, to believe that the earth planet itself is an integral part of a "larger" working universal system. All cosmic systems in *Nature* exist for survival —a pendulous ebb and flow motion of necessity. It is not concerned with what is considered "pleasurable" and "cruel" to an individual—the program simply exists so that it may exist, and once installed, it is simultaneously connected to all of the other programs in existence. All of this composes a single fractal "reality," where systems are "stacked" and perceived separately. Thus, subjectively there is a limited amount of information attainable of the *whole* from any *one* vantage point —and yet at the same time, a fractal signature or blueprint pattern of the whole is contained everywhere at once.

Many "mystics" observe a fundamental pattern inherent in *Nature*. Some have call it "gnomonic" or plot its ratios against various "phi" sequences—like the one famously "discovered" by the mathematician, Fibonacci. Others simply call it a "golden spiral" or compare it to the flow of electrons around an atom... or planets in a system... or even the star patterns in galaxies—nothing is truly random. Wizards and mystics are not above "causal determinism"—and, in fact, they welcome it. This very observation of causal energy patterns is how we make things happen and even "predict" future events. Embracing knowledge of "Cosmic Law" gives one the ability to consciously (intentionally) create change—for how else would you even know to do so? What else gives you reason to believe that acting "now" in a specific way affects future events? Have you not already experienced the potential future before it takes place? Such awareness divides "bookshelf sorcerers" and "armchair wizards" from the true and intentional *reality engineers*."

In one sense, there was a way that people would have experienced the outward "exoteric" expression of *Anunnaki* tradition in Babylon; and then, there was an entirely different "esoteric" reality experienced by those few in society who were directly charged by the "gods" to execute or *feed* this experience to the general population. The modern Mardukite revival works at this from both angles—with "*Necronomicon: The Anunnaki Bible*" containing a significant portion of the "public" or "classical" perception of Babylonian tradition in Mesopotamia. Supplemental work [such as Mardukite *Liber 50* and *Liber 51/52*] focuses on what lingers in the shadows of ancient Babylon—what is not necessarily a part of the "common knowledge" or integrated into the system in a way that people would readily see or perceive.

Anyone can "operate" in reality—the system was designed to "go"—but not everyone has aptitude of what the system design really is, or the history (and identity) of the designers, or perhaps, more importantly, the knowledge to "tweak" (or "adjust") it. All of this has been carefully guarded and sealed behind what even the modern "New Age" interpretation of esoteric lore has failed to grasp. The systems—*all systems*—are self-serving: based upon and existing to further propagation and survival of "the system." For the most part, systems in the universe are essentially "fixed" by *Cosmic Law*. But as modern generations know, the material system itself is more like a "shell" or simply the computer "hardware" that is waiting for a "program" to run. It is actually the "programs"—installed into natural systems governed by *Cosmic Law* that were manipulated by ancient Anunnaki gods during interactions with the material world at the inception of (modern) human civilization.

There are actually many order of being and life consciousness fragments in existence throughout the cosmos, but it was a specific group (called generically "Anunnaki" in Mesopotamian language) that is responsible for installation of the current programs in place all over the planet. Once Babylonian politics entered the fray, and perhaps even before this, "lots" were drawn deciding the hierarchy of the local universe. But, the "younger generation" of "Elder Gods," and their ancestors or "Ancient Ones," all failed on this. Responsibilities for operating these installed programs, which were handed off to specific alleged lineages and cultures for care-taking, were also all mishandled—*miserably*.

This present age—approximately the last 2,000 years—actually started on a simple and beautiful premise brought to Earth by another wise messenger from the sky gods. But men misunderstood gravely—and failing to accept programming of this new freedom, nailed it to a cross. Humans decided to continue *fucking the program up* to the extent of even invoking the name of this peaceful warrior as a guise for corrupting it. Strange words for an occult text? ...*Truth* is *Truth*.

Skeptics and occultists alike wonder why the *Anunnaki gods* do not materialize in the world as they once did—but look what this world would do to them? Do you think ENLIL, ENKI *or* MARDUK wants to be nailed to a tree for your ignorance? *Hardly.* As we have not had much luck in "debugging" the program—the current push by the sons and daughters of the Anunnaki and their followers is toward a complete "system reboot" on planet Earth. In the meantime, we continue to advance Truth Seekers on an experiential path of *true knowledge* contributing to unfoldment of personal spiritual evolution—and abilities that may develop as a result.

The program is flawed—there is no argument there. However, without the matrix-system in place, there is no fractured existence from the All. We would all cease to be "I" and would be a part of the universal consciousness as one—as we truly are, water-molecules in an infinite *Sea of Abyss*. One way or another, it would seem we are facing a powerful transitional "death" threshold—and Anunnaki "powers" are guarding all the doors and holding all the keys in this matter. They are the "Universal Agents" of the *Great Magical Arcanum* in this universe—"agents" existing to protect the system, just as this energetic "cosmic grid" also protects their own existence, or more accurately, the "ambiguity" of it. We have so elegantly focused our clarity on the current initiatory lessons and with these being complete, the points of ambiguity at the end proves that the Seeker is ready for the next "level" or "degree" of clarity—for we have already examined enough under this lens-magnification of our microscope...or *macroscope*.

> *If the theatre lights are brought up too early,*
> *the audience might see the strings.*

Systems are universal—they are everywhere and plentiful. We cannot so much fault their existence as the programs that they run. With rising human populations and their division into distinct geographical cultures and time, "The Great System" became increasingly the *Great Deception*—as its operation could be bent to meet the needs of the masses, or those that governed them. But, the deception is not really a matter of "morality," though many have called it "*Darkness.*" It is a direct result of the "chaos factor" inherent in *all* systems.

With time and without proper care, all systems break down from their programs... the entropy of forms returning to the *Infinity of Nothingness* in as eternal as the formation of new systems. But, somehow, they all seem to... "eat" themselves—Ouroborus—*the serpent dragon of the universe devours its own tail. And at the center of all existences—a black hole to the Abyss.*

— 9 —
PIERCING THE DARKNESS

So often we may have heard the phrase: "The devil made me do it!"—and to this, a response is generated, subject to the beliefs of the masses—or the "Realm"—in that time-space. At one juncture in history, such accusations of witchery on neighbors could result in the instant death of the innocent. Today, civil law generally operates by more scientific, and less religious or superstitious, occupations of the Realm—and thus, lore of psychology, not the *Malleus Maleficarum*, has become the governing gospel for "witchcraft."

It is curious that the ideal of modern "witchcraft" is increasingly pop-cultural in the "New Age," when such has held widely negative overtones throughout history. Even in our lore from the most ancient mysticism in Mesopotamia and Sumer, the official magical tradition of "temple-priests," "priestesses" and "magicians" is treated separate from unsanctioned operations used by "witches" and "sorcerers" *outside* civic regulation. This is especially evident from the complete *Maqlu* tablet texts—given as *Tablet M1–9* in "*Necronomicon: The Anunnaki Bible.*"

Nearly two decades ago, while the current author pursued origins of the *Druidic* and *Pheryllt* traditions of the Celts (expressed in "*Book of Elven-Faerie,*" also found in the collected works anthology "*The Druid Compleat*" by Joshua Free), an observed distinction arose between "holy temple" and "urban religious" magic systems versus more "country-oriented" and "rural folk" traditions. The two classes clearly approach the esoteric path differently. From the first stream there is a sense of "god-given" power used to oversee worldly matters, bestowed on civic priests, priestesses—those serving the Divine by maintaining observation of "*Cosmic Law.*" On the other hand, there are indigenous rural folk traditions embedded in the ancestral genetic history of all cultures, based on common observation of both *priestcraft* and "*Natural Law.*" This class distinction of esoteric mysteries is still carried among the "New Age" traditions today.

After the original ancient "gods" were gone from earth, the approach to esoteric mysteries shifted away from the Divine. The people forgot about the gods themselves, feeling abandoned and left to a intermittently crashing reality system—and it seemed that the gods forgot about the people, at least in the external manner they had expressed "watching over" them in the past. Where the systems and genetics remained, reliance on "divine intervention" subsided. Populations rose and by necessity the philosophies and politics changed to accommodate diverse culture formation. To support the evolution of rapidly growing civilizations, social-consciousness programs had to be "upgraded" as so to keep the system from collapsing. More complicated and intricately woven system-programs were required—and with complexity came a rise in entropic chaos factors and the spread of "*Darkness.*"

Those who work with these mysteries grow beyond the mere "mortal" understanding of good and evil—as without such self-honesty, the exploration of the "*Great Mysteries*" and the "*Great Deception*" become at once impossible. "Darkness" is a name given to the balancing equation of the system that is not contained by the "Light," which from a physical perspective, is interpreted as the "Shadows." This is something beyond morally associations of "good" or "bad"—the Darkness is merely the force (or a name given to the force) that binds all programs now driving what the Gnostics describe as a "*Great Deception*"—that which keeps systems of physical material existence in place. It is both: the "spaces between spaces" and the "ghost in the machine" at once.

Darkness and *Deception*—much like *witchcraft* and *sorcery*—are often considered "negative" terms. Curiously, our understanding of each of these aspects are based on "*fear*" and the "*unknown*"—"*inexperience*" and "*ignorance*." Certainly, it is too cliché to simply say, as many have, that "people are afraid of what they do not understand." But considering how experiential existence projects from "Self," it is necessarily the case that people feed their experiences with personal responses, thereby creating a "resonance loop" with specific concepts. This impression or resonance is not just felt within the "reality" of the person experiencing it directly —it can be shared and it can spread. The larger the system and the more programs being run, the greater the chance for obscurity—the *chaos factor*. As more and more people became aware of this (and began feeding it), this too became "sentient" as its own program—*and now people can even interact with it directly!*

Few things in the universe are as they seem. Their appearance is often based on what the observer sees—their own perceptions. These perceptions may not change what things *actually* are, but people do actually interact with their world based on perceptions from previous experiences and this affects the way things seem. By necessity, this is unavoidable in semantic classifications of reality and also necessary to preserve "deceptions" of the programs. So long as people are distracted by their own internal processes of experience, the aspects that drive and perturb these experiences remain behind the curtain—leaving the observer to merely interact with the "voice" and "image" projected on the screen.

True manifestations of "Darkness" are not usually what we might expect—not even a proper descriptive term for the nature of the beings or creatures themselves. They are understood only to the extent that experiences are interpreted and interacted with. If they *are* the horrors and macabre "you might expect," it is very possible that they are not being encountered Self-Honestly. When approached with false knowledge, fear and/or without confidence, any and all aspects of the cosmos can quickly become a "*devil*" to you—at least from the perspective of Ego. Occult author, Leilah Wendell, writes in "*The Books of Azrael*"—

> "All spiritual energy is originally formless. However, it harnesses
> the necessary knowledge, understanding and ability power to
> transmute itself into visible form. As with psychokinesis, where

simple underdeveloped human psychic energy emissions can influence matter and movement, imagine what mastery an ancient spiritual and divine being can have over the energy that is its very lifeforce!"

While applicable as a fundamental tenet, Leilah Wendell's commentary on manifestation is specifically related to lore of her encounters with "*Azrael*"—the "Angel of Death" in the Semitic interpretation of the ancient mysteries. She interprets this energy current as a necessary part of existence—the force that separates the "spirit-form" from the "body" when a creature-being approaches the "*Death-Gate*" of their current material lives. She goes on to explain that while originally a "form-less" body of energy, these spiritual intelligences, much like ourselves, have the ability to condense their energy into recognizable forms. These forms can take on a sort of *timeless* "archetypal familiarity"—thus while abstract, "Death" is universally portrayed as a recognizable form—the Grim Reaper or "Time"—throughout history. Wendell continues, explaining—

> "If the familiar image were greatly altered, the being would be *deceiving* the viewer; and the Universal Soul does *not* deal in *deceptions*. That is the realm of an opposing force... altogether."

All manifestations of "Darkness" are something of an ambiguity when we look upon and experience them outside of Self-Honesty. Again, it is not so much a description of these forces in themselves, but instead how they are perceived in the reality of lights and encoding that can reveal no "negative spaces between." But, too, all programming can be corrupted. Consider the example given elsewhere in these discourses concerning the appearance of Jesus and his liberating teachings two-thousand years ago. When esoterically examining the actual teachings of Jesus, there is little debate concerning their spiritual validity. But it is not an understanding of these esoteric teachings themselves that are openly expressed by the traditional "Christian" program (paradigm)—which cannot allow individuals to be liberated independent of the "Church."

The system—all worldly material systems really—spawns "slavery," and so anything that might be liberating (e.g. the true teachings of Jesus) must therefore be corrupted in order for the program to maintain existence in the Realm. *Hiding Truth in plain sight.* The torch of esoteric *Truth* may continue to be carried by the select few—but never by everyone. We cannot necessarily tip the scales of mass-consciousness as an ends in itself—and that is not really our goal. Therefore, in this instance, we can say that the system was revised to allow for "Christianity," meanwhile opposing forces continue to use whatever means necessary for survival —*even the teachings of Christ.*

* * *

The current generation has little difficulty understanding that the "self" is an operator (or "user") of a "program" in a "system." Folks have been attempting to systematically relate the human condition to "computers" for some time. Prior to this semantic availability, behaviorist psychology understood similar via their paradigm of "conditioning"—but there is a higher state of awareness beyond physical reactions alone. Proof is evident that physical reality is very much the product of "conditioning"—the "*whys*" and "*hows*" remain elementary, confined to an understanding using "paradigms." All energetic implications beyond the spectrum of "normal" human perceptions—maintained as a "materialist program"—are not understood in existing contemporary methodologies that rely solely on materialist programs.

Understanding the *Self* is not different from relatively understanding the "cosmic whole"—as many mystics have gone forth to explain that they are one and the same. The key is looking at the integrated web-matrix structure of all existence—all of which operates under the same "Cosmic Laws." We observe multiple "systems" within a "System" and all of these are programmed. What we call "fragmentation" is subjectively a way of looking at the divisible aspects of creation as "parts" when classifying and communicating "reality" within any program or "paradigm." There is a pure energetic Source that exists outside of all definitions within the system and so while our true nature may not be separated, the experience of it within this condensed material existence appears to be—hence *fragmentation*.

Elsewhere in *NexGen Systemology* literature, we liken *Self-Honesty* to "crystal clarity." The experience of *Self* as a "programmed crystalline fragment" is also very similar to the idea of programs encoded onto a crystal computer chip. It is so similar, in fact, that we have often found it best to define it this way for modern purposes. At one level of perception, a computer as a whole is a system of material hardware—at another it is a system to run programs. During the casual "user experience" of computers, one does not generally encounter the entirety of background programming on the surface—the actual code embedded "behind" the experience displays only a predetermined "user interface." And it is also *interactive* —within a fixed set of parameters in which to experience itself, but *fluid* and *dynamic* all the same.

The user is limited to system parameters of the program and more often then not, the full capabilities or potential extent of "unfixed" parameters is not experienced by a user. And much like a personal identity, the system becomes increasingly "refined" as *individuality*—by everything from the actual "operating system" used, to the "programs" run, and of course the available space, speed and methodology by which any of this is accessed. Enter further the personal experience of the user and their personality and you can easily see that even the same piece of "hardware" or system is going to be used, accessed and perceived differently by each user, themselves. *This is why the Rabbit Hole of perceived reality appears to run so deep...*

"Light" is essentially the *language* that cosmic existence is encoded in. This not only includes personal identities, but all "manifested" existence within the "visible" spectrum of experience. We mean not only "visual appearances" but the entire base for an "*observer*" to perceive what they experience as their *own* existence, separate from "other" or "outer" existences. In short, the "inner world" and "outer world" are thought of as separate identities, even among many "New Age" schools, and this furthers the perception (or "deception") of such as "fragments." Rather than holding the belief that some "outside reality" has an affect on an "internal reality" and that an "inner realm" can affect an "outer realm," the mystic realizes that they are one and the same "reality"... *since any separation would be contradictory to how and why all things are indeed connected—All as One.*

Although there is only one interconnected existence, the program as given to individual "beings" forces them to interpret reality based on semantic "levels" *within* and *without* a visible (communicable) spectrum to experience. Sensory stimulus is used to increase all personal programming through experience. Personal programming contributes to the total shared *Akashic Pool* or "global consciousness"—just like the world-wide-web. Everything we come to experience is also imprinted within our coding of existence. In many ways these energetic signatures and imprints begin to define us and our existential experience of our environment—albeit artificially. Our subconscious is a repository for potential conscious thought. Few are able to recognize this effect during their lifetime. But, when we come right down to the base knowledge of such, we are again returned to this concept of *Light*.

Cosmic Law is universal. The programming of our own forms is the same as the programming of forms we encounter—perceived to be separate—and all of this is programmed in *Light*. In fact, our main New Age conceptualization of this programming in the "New Age" revives *Eastern* ideals following this logic—auras and chakras—an entire personal energetic web-matrix system composed of what? ...*Light!* All experience in existence and conscious memory of it in pictures and sounds are primarily waves or frequencies of what? ...*Light!* And what you consciously retain is only an awareness experienced within a fixed set of parameters, a predefined scope limit called the "human condition." But this does not mean that relatively "unseen" affects are not also in action, simply in bands of *Light* that are not so visible and consciously retained—but they are not any less "real." Is it not possible that our finite world of lights is the "*shadow*" of something even more "Absolute"...?

* * *

All individualized fragments or "identities" are programmed with a base "operating system" so as to interpret a world around them. By definition, the way reality is experienced compliments and builds upon this preset programming. Additional programming ("updates") will either "enhance" or "override" what already exists—but most often these strongly encoded imprints become a very active part of the program—directly influencing the way life is experienced by a spiritual entity. It also influences what is not expressed—the totality of existence—regardless of our awareness of what is taking place "behind the scenes," yet just as real.

We have mentioned "light encoding" manifesting as personal auric and chakra systems that exist, but they seem outside the small part of the "spectrum" condensed enough to be considered "physical" in the typical sense of the word. At the same time, they share a relationship with all aspects of this Realm—because *All is One*. They do not exist at some separate "level" in exclusion. It is the same "level" and "existence"—vibrations that simultaneously exist at all "levels"—*as One*—but each frequency-type of the wave is senses and experienced differently by different organs of the body—whether "sensory" in a strictly "material" sense or otherwise.

What we experience as reality is a combination of expressions—visible forms of light and audible forms of sound are wave vibrations which interpreted within strict guidelines by specific personal faculties—eyes for light and ears for sound, &tc. But, of course, we already know that these ranges vary between different people and also different species. This allows for the same reality to be experienced differently by individually fragmented entities—*hence, the crystalline perception!*

"New Age" definitions of the "physical" versus the "metaphysical" and the "material" versus the "spiritual" are based in an idea that there are both *sensibly* visible (seen) and invisible (unseen) forces at work in the universe. These particularly affect experiences by energetic beings—like *humans*. However, too often, Seekers become lost in a labyrinth of "levels" and "layers" that are so vastly distinguished in exclusion to one another throughout contemporary literature.

The more widespread the *Great Mysteries* reached on the planet and in the cosmos, the more "complex" the *Great Deception* had to become in order to contain it. It is sometimes difficult to morally decide who the "good guys" are versus the "bad guys." It is all an integral of the same system—one type merely breeds more of the same. Without operating temperance in the exponential rise of programs, a greater "chaos factor" forms within them, supporting an increased population of those who continue to propagate what most would consider "negative" energy. But, this seems somewhat different than a worldview where cosmic forces of *Light* and *Dark* are endlessly pitted against one another, locked in some moral warfare over your soul. In another instance, these forces exist for no other reason than to provide the illusion of movement—the ebb and flow of the pendulum swing of universal energy. One without the other does not create this "motion of activity" and as such will not hold programming. We must not demonize the hidden recesses or celebrate myriads of color. *All is one in equality.*

When someone is cooking in a room other than where you are, you might smell the food and therefore have a sensory reaction with reality—or what you perceive of reality. The source of this, is however, somewhere other than where you have access to visually or with your "material" body—but the experience is still thought of as "real" or within your "reality." There is no question to you, because of your previous experience, that someone "real" exists in another room you "don't see" that is the cause of this. With more "experience" you might even have already distinguished both the person and the type of food being prepared—but these are all things within your field of knowing. These are what people call "levels" of reality—duality between "seen" and "unseen" factors—but they are actually all one reality—one existence. While still within the light spectrum, there are parts of the program that are happening outside our field of view. These still affect us—and we affect them. Based on the above example, imagine if you did not have previous experience with the way that food smells drift, &tc. Even if this is a rudimentary example at best, you should be now realize its implications.

"There are more things in heaven and earth than are dreamed of in your philosophies..." All experiences carry with them aspects that are not within the "normal" human range of sensory experience. These are aspects that the "hardcore materialists" have considered "fictional fantasy" in their reality. Since they have no direct experience with it, it cannot be real to them. But this does not change the fact that energetic aspects will affect them anyway—and the light is bent in a way they are programmed to receive. Those not yet evolved enough to process esoteric knowledge do not seem to miss it. Whether or not they are privy to forces behind what happens to them in their lives becomes irrelevant. So much the better if— allegedly: *the greatest trick the devil ever played was convincing the world he didn't exist. . .*

The *Great Deception* prevails. For those who don't know to look for it—are programmed to reject the "non-material"—the *Great Mystery* does not even exist at all. For those who go in pursuit of it, there are enough trappings along the way to distract them—and even many who reach the top only reach self-deluded points of "pseudo-enlightenment." Some are seeking their way to get "outside"—others don't really know it exists, and they are barely aware of their own waters in which they swim. To the best that is determinable from our perspective of the crystal—it is the *Anunnaki*—that appear to be holding the keys and guarding the gates of this existence. So now you have been show the *door*—and where you go from here is up to you. What you do with it and where you take it—these are the decisions only your own programming can determine. What is good or bad? Who are the saviors? —*Which way is up. . ?*

If you've been paying attention,
then you will figure it out...

—APPENDIX—
CROSSING TO THE ABYSS
&
SIMON'S NECRONOMICON
(LIBER 555)

— 0 —
: CROSSINGS TO THE ABYSS :
A MARDUKITE GUIDE TO SIMON'S NECRONOMICON
by JOSHUA FREE

Given the extent of my involvement in matters of the *Necronomicon* for twenty-five years, it should come as no surprise that I am now being called out from the dark corners I am usually want to reside in regarding the specific topic of the "Simonian" recension of the *Necronomicon* that has earned so much notoriety and publicity since its arrival in the underground during the late 1970's.

Simon's Necronomicon is a delicate topic for me. It has been a long time coming for me to actually give attention to answering my piles of correspondence questioning its details. In the past—even in *Liber R*—I have directly avoided such a feat, preferring the work to stand on its own to those culled into its mystique. It is hardly capable of being overshadowed by efforts of other writers and occultists that have devised published systems to their own preferences—lending a healthy hand to supporting allusions from the fiction writings of *H.P. Lovecraft*—and the later inspired *Cthulhu Mythos*—connected to our own efforts purely for the fact that the title "*Necronomicon*" is shared and perhaps even derived from the *Lovecraftian* sources.

Since 2008, a team officially known as the *Mardukite Chamberlains* (or *Mardukite Research Organization*) in conjunction with *Council of Nabu-Tutu* (operated as *Mardukite Ministries*, and responsible for the publications of the *Mardukite Truth Seeker Press*) have worked diligently in fashioning a complete library archives, produced internally for our own purposes.

This unique *Mardukite* "genre" or "paradigm" has been completely catalogued, spanning everything from prehistoric cosmogenetic origins, through the evolution and development of human populations and traditions, coupled with an understanding of esoteric technologies in the universe, and practical knowledge employed at each stage. Certainly, this has been no small task, and regardless of how monumental it actually is, it ever seems to remain in the underground "scene"—these efforts have mostly remained unnoticed to the surface populations.

What has drawn the connection between *Simon's Necronomicon* and our own work together is the underlying resonance of the original ancient "Mardukite Anunnaki Tradition" of Babylon. This appears in the Simon "grimoire" far stronger than any *Lovecraftian* flavors or the *Cthulhu Mythos*—and it is for this reason that it has been so often paralleled with the modern "Mardukite" efforts.

Someone approaching the *Simon Necronomicon* without any previous occult knowledge may be confused as to its "magickal" and "esoteric" suggestions for modern ritual and ceremony. Yet, the *heart* of the material will still *seep* in and formulate some kind of change in the reader—especially if a lack of "occult" knowledge is coupled with no background in ancient "*Middle Eastern*," "*Ancient Near Eastern*" or otherwise "*Mesopotamian*" cultures and their mythologies. If such is the case, the book will naturally be regarded as a highly cryptic or otherwise incoherent blend of obscure names and correspondences that are without basis. My own personal interests in the *Simon Necronomicon* have always—for nearly *twenty-five years* now—remained fixed specifically on its connection to ancient "Mardukite" Anunnaki-oriented systems.

Overt esoteric natures and intents behind the modern "Mardukite" movement closely resembled the alleged emphasis behind the "Simon group"—those responsible for producing what Kenneth Grant referred to as the "*Schlangekraft Recension*" in lieu of the name of its initial publishers. As such, we hesitantly decided to continue the "theme" of the "*Necronomicon*" to present our own "Mardukite" efforts—which we publicly began the same year *Simon's Necronomicon* celebrated its 31st Anniversary, returning in hardcover again for the first time in decades. A shift was felt—there seemed to be a kind of "revival" effort taking place toward these matters in 2008, including design and launch of a new show titled: *Ancient Aliens*. Very suddenly these matters were no longer restricted solely to an underground echelon of society, but to the mainstream as well—however questionable some of these efforts from others turned out to be in the end. There were strong hopeful focuses on a revitalization of practical knowledge and awareness concerning human history and its place for the future—but somehow the "Mardukites" remained alone in this.

Increased public awareness *is* a positive act for change—even if that change is not for the "higher good" of the whole. It cannot be said that it is better to keep people in ignorance—yet at the same time, many folk are not even capable of properly handling (or processing) *Truth*. The "*True*" nature of reality—that which statically exists in universal space-time—is not restricted on what an individual observer is capable of seeing or not seeing from this "wholeness." Their fragmented perspective is but one field of possible awareness.

When *Simon's Necronomicon* debuted, a very select few were privy to understand this "type" of esoteric knowledge concerning a truly archetypal, pre-classical methodology predating Judeo-Christian traditions—a root system from which many other branches of the tree were later formed and then perceived as separate, whether because of cultural semantics or their locale in time and geography. Even those supposed occultists and New Age minds of the 1970's had very little mainstream background for the Mesopotamian mythos being described—which was not at all *Lovecraftian*, or even *Sumerian* as many others believe—but BABYLONIAN!

Since the arrival of *Simon's Necronomicon* and its relationship—based on the title alone—with the work alluded to by *H.P. Lovecraft*, the two mythoi have been confused by neo-gothic punks and emo-musicians as being one and the same. Too often in my public dealings with the book—since my days as "Merlyn Stone" in the mid-1990's—I have heard people speak in every manner regarding their own prejudiced opinions of *Simon's Necronomicon* as well as their fanciful experiences and pseudo-magick that allegedly did *this* or *that* in their lives. Folks have told me of all the wicked encounters they have had as a result of even reading it and others who believe they have unlocked gates and unleashed forces that will completely destroy the planet or devour humans... It's hard to know when to laugh or yawn as the years draw on!

During my official public involvement with the modern "Mardukites" movement— starting in 2008—I have endeavored to not over-emphasize *Simon's Necronomicon* in regards to our own work and have instead preferred to remain silent on many of the issues related directly to it. Although it would have been impossible to release our current *"Necronomicon Anunnaki Legacy"* ("Mardukite Core") archive of materials without making at least some references and comparisons to *Simon's* books, it was not our starting point and not at all our own basis in developing all that we have under the "Mardukite" banner. Many people have already confused our own work (such as *"Necronomicon: The Anunnaki Bible"*) with being a "rehash" or "supporting companion" specifically to the "Simonian" books without even looking into and realizing what exactly we are presenting here—and I have done my best to avoid propagating further confusion by relaying the historical "Anunnaki" and "Sumerian" or "Babylonian" (Mardukite) legacy independent of what is alluded to directly in *Simon's Necronomicon*.

In the 1990's—working as "Merlyn Stone"—I was known for advocating two controversial underground streams among early esoteric occultists and practitioners. The first of these: a public support for Douglas Monroe and his modern neo-Pheryllt presentation of Druidism. Eventually, I was installed as "Bard of the Twelfth Chair" for his New Forest Centre for Magickal Studies, and even eventually permitted to have an *"interlogue"* published in his third and final book of the "Merlyn Trilogy"—*Deepteachings of Merlyn*, published by Kima Global Books. As of 2018, my own companion work for this tradition also appears from Kima—*The Book of Pheryllt: A Complete Druid Source Book*.

My other main esoteric occult or "New Age" interest focused on the lore behind *Simon's Necronomicon*—for I had immediately intuited the Mesopotamian legacy it reflected from the start, having no personal background in *Lovecraftian* knowledge during this lifetime, but wholly aware of the identities and natures of the *Anunnaki*. My personal researches also revealed that later Celtic interpretations of European "Druidism" were directly evolved from the ancient streams of the Mystery School present in the *Ancient Near East*. Much of this, I later reported on extensively in Mardukite *Liber D*, available as *"Book of Elven-Faerie"*—or in *"The Druid Compleat"* anthology.

In my youth as "Merlyn Stone," more time and energy was spent on "New Age" politics and the defense of these two "paths" than I would care to admit. They remained my preferred *flavors* or *semantics* above any others readily available in the sea of "New Age" convolution. The last century has certainly seen a revival interest in past knowledge through a myriad of forms—lights dancing upon the screen—infinite ways in which the crystalline perception might be bent to meet the eyes and awareness of its beholder—its *Observer*. Unlike many of my predecessors (and peers) in the occult field and esoteric literature, my emphasis is not on "luciferian darkness" alluded to in "left-hand paths" and other "antithetical alternative modes" for incorporating all manners of beasties from *Lovecraftian* lore. My emphasis here, specifically and historically, is on *Babylon*.

Prior to the modern "Mardukite" movement there were no significant resources for someone wishing to incorporate revival knowledge of the *Anunnaki* legacy—and the cultures first observing these traditions, the *Sumerians* and *Babylonians* of "Mesopotamia." Writings of *Zecharia Sitchin* did much to advance some public awareness that these subjects even existed at all—but the paradigm of *Simon's Necronomicon* led many would-be seekers down a path of direct experience with some of these ancient streams. For all of the controversy, one thing is certain—that these ancient *Anunnaki* powers carried far-reaching influence on the development of humanity, evolution of civilizations—and the correlating traditions and systems that came with them.

Although "Mardukite" emphasis is not solely *Mesopotamia*, the name of our organization and research team obviously denotes a certain *inclination* toward these specific aspects or niches, but for good reason: they constitute an entire basis for ancient and prehistoric origins of the human species—the first civilizations and beliefs of modern man, not to mention their development into modern understanding, and everything that has transpired in between. A clear and self-honest awareness of this information has been long overdue for humanity—a feat that will not only change the consciousness of the species internally, but on a larger integrated scale actually transform external perceptions of one's environment, how the human population interacts with each other and ultimately, understanding one's true place in the universe. Is this now what it was supposed to be about all along? Yet when does our fragmented knowledge reach a point of unification?

A proper relay of the modern "Mardukite" movement under the guise of the *Necronomicon*—specifically my *"Necronomicon: The Anunnaki Bible"*—was developed as such for the most obvious reason: that the main tenet was so similar to the only widely circulated version of the paradigm prior to our own efforts; and that *was* the *Simon Necronomicon*—a now mainstream "grimoire" that alluded to remnants of the "Mardukite" Anunnaki tradition best reflected in the lore of ancient Babylonians. In spite of the grief I had already experienced for my earliest renderings regarding the "Simonian" work, I was hesitant to do what we ultimately did—the completion of a true and authentic Mesopotamian *Necronomicon*—or *"Necronomicon: The Anunnaki Bible."*

In spite of our best efforts to isolate the original "Mardukite" work in 2008-9, the subject of *Simon's Necronomicon* kept reappearing at our council meetings and in comparative references published simultaneously with the early "Mardukite Core." It was an almost unavoidable connection for those already aware of "Simonian" work. It also became clear at our inception that we were introducing a uniquely esoteric or mystical approach to the Anunnaki legacy to a segment of the public that would better accept "Mardukite" tradition as a *Necronomicon*—reminiscent of Simon's work—far more than emphasizing it as a revitalization or reconstruction of *Middle Eastern* or *Mesopotamian* traditions. On the surface—especially in 2008— *Sumerian* and *Babylonian* topics were too obscure to be recognized by more than a few people already familiar with preexisting and nearly insubstantial renderings.

Although the complete "Year-1" tablet catalogue developed by the "Mardukites" was later released widely as an anthology—*"Necronomicon: The Anunnaki Bible"*—the original major "Mardukite" public debut (excluding the *Arcanum* materials) was simply: *"Necronomicon,"* containing only the *"Liber N"*—materials considered most highly resonant with *Simon's Necronomicon*. References to *Simon's Necronomicon* were made throughout the original Mardukite archive only when necessary or critically worthy of mention—but it was really the 2010 Mardukite *Liber R*—released as *"Necronomicon Revelations"*—that gave direct attention to the *Simon* work at all. Where many outsiders believed that our attempts all along were simply some "rehash" of *Simon*, it never occurred to them that there just might be some kind of unifying source of inspiration behind this work. Easier for them to run back into familiar Lovecraftian fantasies than to actually have to *learn* anything regarding our Anunnaki focus—then alone the "Mardukite" legacy within the Anunnaki tradition nationally held in ancient Babylon.

Now, in this new millennium, a new generation—*the NexGen*—unifies together under the "Mardukite" banner to explore the undefiled ancient mysteries—a mystery tradition that was not even accessible to our parenting generations or the "old ways" of exploring and preparing a "new age." We are moving beyond all of this—beyond the limitations reached by our immediate predecessors. That is what the "new thought" "new consciousness: paradigm-shift is all about.

This current discourse—Mardukite *Liber 555*—originally appeared to the public as *"Stargate to the Abyss"* and then *"Necronomicon for Beginners"* in 2012. For its fifth anniversary, it was reissued in 2017 under its originally intended title: *"Crossing to the Abyss"*—an esoteric reference to obscure Thelemic rites used by Aleister Crowley's followers. In all discourses and interviews prior to *Liber 555*, a serious discussion regarding any correlation between "Mardukite" work and the *Simon* books remained absent. Yet, no shortage of notes and queries concerning the application of (or the knowledge presented in) the *Simon Necronomicon* explicitly continue to pour into the Mardukite Office. It is in answer to many of these requests and queries that I decided to finally set down *Liber 555* for posterity—and have attached it as an appendix to *Liber R* for this commemorative 10th Anniversary edition of the Mardukite *"Gates of the Necronomicon"* anthology.

— 1 —
ORIGINS OF THE NECRONOMICON

Horror-fantasy fiction writings of *H.P. Lovecraft* emerged at the beginning of the 20th century. In them, we find references few and far between of a mysterious book —a *book of all books*—an "archetypal book" prized among all others, called: *Necronomicon*. The truth as we all know it is simple: *Lovecraft* never released or even composed such a book, his references are sporadic and offer to us only a few lines at a time from something we are expected to believe runs some 800 pages. In fact *no* such book was even comparable to what has been alluded to by *Lovecraft* until late 2010—when the *Necronomicon Anunnaki Legacy: Silver Edition* of the "Mardukite" work was released for a short print run.

Prior to modern "Mardukite" efforts, the *Necronomicon* archetype would have been almost entirely left to the realm of fantasy were it not for the public appearance of the "Simonian" edition released in 1977. While our own Mardukite *"Necronomicon: The Anunnaki Bible"* is the focus of the "Mardukite Core," in this one instance (for *Liber 555*) it is *Simon's Necronomicon* that is the main subject for our current discourse—prepared by the Mardukite Chamberlains Offices. This is *our* official guide corresponding to *Simon's Necronomicon*—something we have not released before, in spite of what many of our unread critics naively believed of our other work, because of the title we all share: *Necronomicon*. It is this *title*, first and foremost, that generally brings initial attention and attitudes to the work, regardless of which versions we refer to.

The literal title is not is Mesopotamian, Arabic or even Latin, but *Greek*— combining two words meaning "death" and "book." It is from this elementary interpretation that many assume it means literally: *"book of the dead."* Even if we assume the name *"Necronomicon"* as a genuine title, this would not actually be the most accurate translation either. More seasoned historians and/or scholars will be quick to point out that the suffix *"-nomicon"* is hardly "book"—or even "list" or "catalogue," such as we find with *"lexicon."* Those working closely with the original *Mardukite* team insisted the words "code" or "law" were far more appropriate—making the *Necronomicon* literally *"records of the dead,"* such as was historically kept esteemed members of ancient society in temples and a palaces.

Until relatively recently in the span of human history, it was the kings, priests, scribes and elite orders and sects of "learned ones" that typically possessed knowledge of writing—requiring the common population to rely on these select few to read and interpret writings for them, including matters of cultural history and religious lore. Thousands of years before the classical periods of Greek and Roman civilization, the introduction of true written language—as *cuneiform* script —more significantly affected the consciousness and rapid development of the human species than any other single factor.

Far removed from any speculative origins from prehistoric hunter-gatherer eras of nomadic life and cave-dwelling, the true and proper development of human civilization occurred hand in hand with the attainment and refinement of "written language"—something we historically ascribe to the *Mesopotamians*.

* * *

We fast forward now to the specific *writings* in question. One of the ways in which mainstream occultists and esoteric writers have avoided the topic of *Simon's Necronomicon* (or even the "*Necronomicon*" in general) is by making an "appeal" to ignorance. When the topic is not altogether avoided, the usual response is "Oh, dear me! To which of the multiple books *claiming* to be the *Necronomicon* are you referring? Isn't that just some book made up in the imagination of *H.P. Lovecraft* anyway?" This is about as far as you will get with contemporary mainstream "New Age" publications—and why so many people over the last decade have looked to the Mardukite movement for any answers that lead toward a better understanding of the *Mesopotamian* paradigm.

In *NexGen* clarity, let us put aside for a moment any artisitic and creative freedoms developed in the field and consider the objective facts: *H.P. Lovecraft* never produced any *Necronomicon* himself; he publicly denounced the existence of any such book in reality and what's more, he said that no such book could ever be compiled to satisfy the ominous character and nature it had come to earn. Quoting Mardukite *Liber R*, "By the end of Lovecraft's literary career, the scattered details of the *Necronomicon* had reached such epic proportions that it seemed that ti would be impossible for it to exist." Quite simply—an archetypal book now had a name and went on to take a life and consciousness of its own. By the time of a *New Age* literary apex during the 1980's and 90's, the only major representation of the icon remained *Simon's Necronomicon*.

Of all the Mardukite publications, any significant attention given toward *H.P. Lovecraft* and the *Cthulhu Mythos* is restricted to Mardukite "*Liber R*" (originally released by Joshua Free as "*Necronomicon Revelations*" and included in the Mardukite "*Gates of the Necronomicon*" anthology). Few details from *Liber R* will be repeated here for the simple fact that—beyond the title "*Necronomicon*"—there is little reflection between *Simon's Necronomicon* and the work of *H.P. Lovecraft*. The exception here being, of course, that certain surface world and *Judeo-Christian* perceptions and worldviews toward "Lovecraftian" themes do parallel the mainstream reception of the genuine historic lore and esoteric knowledge concerning the ancient Anunnaki traditions of the Sumerian and Babylonian cultures.

Up until the more recent "Mardukite" efforts and work of Joshua Free, few publicly visible "*New Age*" writers and occult spokes-people really had much to say concerning *Simon's Necronomicon*—many of them admitting to us that they wished it would just go away, or at the very least, that people would stop bothering them about it. Needless to say, in a post-*Lovecraftian* world—and before the release of "*Necronomicon: The Anunnaki Bible*" edited by Joshua Free—of all the possible versions carrying the title, it was the only one that carried a *true* and *authentic* merit regarding a historical tradition, but not one that people expected—the Babylonian Mardukite tradition. For this reason, many people criticized *Simon's Necronomicon* for not being *Lovecraftian* enough—which came as interesting, when some of the same insisted Simon's book had been *invented* by *Lovecraft*.

The myriad of arguments erupting from the *Necronomicon* subject are all easily dissolved when the acid-test of logic and semantics is applied—but, as everyone has an audible voice that requires *hearing* to validate their own existence, it is these "debates" that become a central focus for most *Necronomicon*-oriented websites, discourses, fact-files and other alleged "authorities" on the matter.

Firstly—debates over the *title* of the work have never been satisfactorily resolved by or to anyone. The use of the word by *Lovecraft* already comes from questionable sources—presumably his own dreams—and why it should appear on an allegedly 7th–8th century *Arabic* manuscript is also unsettling, even assuming such to even be true. We have no actual reason to believe that *Simon's* work should have held such a title—nor is the book contents ever directly referred to such in its corpus. Therefore, the *title* itself may have been fabricated.

One is then left to wonder: if the *title* used to label the work has been fabricated and is, in itself, the product of a fictional work by the hands of *H.P. Lovecraft*, what validity is there to the contents of *Simon's* work, using the title? Such is really an ignorant question—for a true seeker should not so easily get caught up in this mess, missing the forest for the trees. Labels are only labels and we may just as easily disregard that *one* semantic, because it is inconsequential for pursuing the mysteries of its contents. A self-honest experience of this vision of the pathway can easily be tainted or distorted if using arbitrary semantic filters to disguise true enlightenment. We run the risk of catching this sickness when attempting to inappropriately understand the *Mesopotamian* paradigm using inadequate baselines or reference points. For example, as a result of the left-handed sub-cultural embrace of the *Cthulhu Mythos* drawn from *H.P. Lovecraft's* writings, *Simon's Necronomicon* was marketed (and then observed by practitioners of "New Age" traditions) as a book of "black magick," a "grimoire of evil sorcery" and the "most dangerous book" in existence!

Drawing from the legendary archetypal energy the the *Necronomicon* carried underground prior to *Simon's* work, using the *title* simply was simply the easiest means of relaying the work in a flavor the "Simon group" wanted to see. Certainly, it was immediately celebrated by the east coast O.T.O. (*Ordo Templi Orientis*) and provided much fodder for *Kenneth Grant* to write about, seeing it as an extension of the work begun by *Aleister Crowley.* Simon's group either found and/or compiled a rather obscure work of *Mesopotamian* esoterica—all remained was to give it a *title*.

Even if we were to assume that it did actually carry the same title, no other contexts of the work provide evidence that *Simon's Necronomicon* is the same *"Necronomicon"* referred to in *H.P. Lovecraft* writings, or anything that he might have actually held in his possession during his life.

It is only concerning details over the *title* that skeptical critics can at least be thrown their bone—but they are used to throwing out the baby with the bath-water without giving things a second thought. For them, the contents of *Simon's Necronomicon* is irrelevant if title of the work is derived from a fictional source. If we were to only base the substance of knowledge fields on the labels they are classified under, than the entire idea of *Mesopotamian* studies would be suspect—still often referred to by its original misnomer: "Assyriology." Although the interior corpus of Simon's work has no real relationship with *Lovecraftian* fiction, it is easier for outsiders to disregard the whole matter over a *title*. And these are the same "higher minds" that would otherwise urge you "not to judge a book by its cover" and yes, the same minds that so many other naïve folk turned to in the past for their *answers*.

Too often, fallacious thinking just breeds more of the same, and few are properly educated enough to recognize it. This is reminiscent of a fundamental lesson exchanged among *Illuminati* schools concerning the *"thinker"* and the *"prover"*—and how *"whatever the thinker, thinks; the prover, proves."* As such, NexGen Systemology shows us how an insatiable urge to accumulate categorized knowledge, databases and facts in the mind turns out to inhibit us, feeding an endless quest inherited by the human condition that is not meant to actually be achieved in this lifetime—only sought after. The journey is never completed, because the question can never be answered. It is, in itself, faulty rhetoric. But, so long as people are compelled to remain fixed on the wrong surface questions—too confused from the start to ponder any deeper—the true, ineffable, underlying static truth remains hidden—literally *"occult"* by definition—and ever veiled from the consciousness of the consensus, which never evolves awareness of enough *Truth* to properly interact or formulate any self-honest judgments about their reality. *"All things ought not be revealed to all men..."*

This current discourse—Mardukite *Liber 555*—is prepared as a companion to the greater "Mardukite Core" as our official expert commentary on *Simon's Necronomicon*—meaning specifically, the bastardized Mesopotamian tradition alluded to in the text, emerging from the long-lost desert sands of ancient "Mardukite" Babylon. But, one thing we do find evident—and clearly what threw many people off the track—is the lack of *Lovecraftian* themes in *Simon's Necronomicon*. Any mentions or similarity of the *Simon* work to stories of *H.P. Lovecraft* are really only brought forth by its modern editors for efforts to market *Mesopotamian Magic* as the *Necronomicon*. We shall therefore focus on the contents of *Simon's Necronomicon* for *"Liber 555"*—an extension of the information that we have already put forth in *"Liber R.."*

The intention of the current chapter being simply to relay: one should be careful given that the human psyche is so easily "led about" in its understandings based on "language" and adoption of semantic paradigms. This is always the case—but it is especially important to recognize in the realm of "esoterica" and the "occult."

In modern interpretations of the ancient mystery schools, fundamental truths and cosmic secrets are too often veiled by distracting "words" and definitions—many of which are drawn from completely ludicrous notebooks written in codes that many practitioners often mistake on the surface. This is clearly evident in many of the so called "*diabolical grimoires*" that indicate an execution of something ridiculous when the author is covertly referring to something else altogether. For these types of post-Christian era accounts—such as with *Medieval* and *Dark Age* era grimoires—the "magick" and traditions reflect a cosmic moral "polarity" that does not actually exist in the older (original) systems.

As a basic scholarly premise—the literal semantic idea of "devil worship" and "satanism" (as it is generally understood today) is entirely dependent on the *Judeo-Christian* paradigm to exist. It may be the case that after the time of the Anunnaki, *other beings* took notice of the planet and its inhabitants. In either case, this whole issue of moral forces ceaselessly at war with one another throughout the universe over "human souls" only entered mass human consciousness alongside the *Judeo-Christian* worldview—a worldview that is still dominant on the planet today. Older (original) cosmic worldviews of polar dualism—chaos and order—held by ancient Mesopotamians display such forces *amorally*, existing out of necessity for "creation" to be *in universal motion*—not as ethical anthropomorphic forces of "good" and "evil" in the sense we think of these words today.

Casual study of history shows that the human species carries a predilection to "patron" one face of divinity over another—going as far as to favor one name or title in a native language over another, even if it is representing the same "god." We see evidence of this clearly with the evolution of a "planetary pantheon" that duplicates themes and identities of Mesopotamian Anunnaki under various guises. Even among Mesopotamian traditions—and there are many—cultures within the same region all blatantly observed the same pantheon under names unique to their native language. Contrary to popular belief, the original ancient spiritual system observed a *unifying force* operating throughout the cosmos—representative figures were observed as embodiments of specific functions or faculties of "*Cosmic Law.*" These figures—called "*Anunnaki*" on ancient cuneiform tablets from Mesopotamia—demonstrate a presence of *local divinity*, leaving only threads of a deeper level of cosmic spirituality for the average person to glean.

When compared to modern "Piscean Age" *Judeo-Christian* worldviews of the past two millennium, the *Necronomicon* as a Mesopotamian archetype represents "darkness" only from ignorance. Even among "New Age" revivals where every system from the Egyptians, Greeks, Norse and Celts have all been revived into some sort of "*wicca*," the one culture we see only represented by *Simon's Necronomicon*—

and the *NexGen* work of the modern "Mardukite" movement—is *Mesopotamia*, and of the many cultures having come and gone from there, from the heart of *Babylon!*

Even more than what might be gleaned from the post-modern interpretation of the primordial and primeval realms of human consciousness via the *Lovecraftian* paradigm—something dealt with at length in *Liber R*—it is the connection between *Simon's Necronomicon* and the ancient esoteric "Mardukite" Babylonian knowledge that the modern "Mardukite" *systemologists* and *reconstructionists* are most interested in. For this reason, the current discourse—*Liber 555*—will emphasize the "Mardukite" Babylonian Anunnaki methodology that is actually alluded to in contents of *Simon's* work, rather than the *Lovecraftian* paradigm, for which it only shares a *title*.

— 2 —
SIMON SAYS... "NECRONOMICON"

Simon's Necronomicon—as we frequently refer to it—is also called the *Necronomicon edited by Simon*, the *Simon edition, Simonian Necronomicon* and even *Simonomicon*. Occult writer and leader of the O.T.O., *Kenneth Grant*, referred to the book often in his later writings as the *Schlangekraft Recension*—and while he acknowledged the text as "valid magic" in its own right, and even a "stargate" or "portal" as it was presented, *Grant* and the O.T.O. frequently incorporated its use as interchangeable with both purely *Lovecraftian* semantics currents and also an extension of post-Crowley evolutions of the organization.

Both *Simon's Necronomicon* and the former *Lovecraftian* interpretations are traditionally perceived through a dualistic lens that does not necessarily reflect one-to-one with the ancient "Mardukite" system observed by Babylonians—or even pre-Babylonian Sumerians—but it *is* found within all of later emerging traditions and their modern revivals. The truth remains that an emphasis on polar dualism completely fragments underlying unity and wholeness of esoteric lessons that still remain from the primordial static singular existence as the shadows of *Undefiled Truth*. Contrary to the purely "Mardukite" literary contributions—such as "*Necronomicon: The Anunnaki Bible*"—the editors of *Simon's Necronomicon* represent their work within the same dualistic moral paradigm as what is reflected in *H.P. Lovecraft's* writings.

According to the specifically *Lovecraftian* paradigm, a primordial race of beings—called the *Great Old Ones*—existed before the coming of the *Elder Gods,* who "overthrew" them and sealed them away from their own existence in the cosmos. Naturally, the *Great Old Ones* could not be completely destroyed—since nothing can truly be destroyed, and certainly nothing primordial—and so they still exist, alive, or else *dead but dreaming*, outside of *this* time-space that we occupy.

As described within Lovecraft's "*Cthulhu Mythos*"—as many have dubbed the literary sub-genre—neither side is blatantly concerned with humanity. The exception being: a secret cabal of a few chosen humans were always selected by the *Elder Gods* to be "watchers" or *Gatekeepers* of the "*Gate to the Outside*"—the *Gate* that ever binds (or seals) the *Great Old Ones* from returning to our pocket of the universe again. Otherwise, neither the *Great Old Ones* or the *Elder Gods*—from a *Lovecraftian* perspective—are really fighting for the well-being of the human species. In this instance, the *Elder Gods* are perceived as "good" only because they are not *as* "evil" as the *Great Old Ones*. So, even in the truest sense of the *Cthulhu Mythos*, there is no actual moral debate—the whole matter of "dualism" here is not ethics, but of one's own survival.

270

Unfortunately, the *Necronomicon* archetype—and perhaps the ancient world as a whole—is always interpreted with a "dualistic" paradigm in mind. Esoteric scholars know better. That somehow there are two sets of deities combating in the universe for human "souls" resonates too much of the *Judeo-Christian* paradigm to be proper for the ancient Mesopotamian period. Regardless of how ridiculous it might seem when originally applied to a reconstruction of the post-Sumerian "Mardukite" Anunnaki tradition from Babylon, the "Simon group" decided to adopt the name *Necronomicon* and its *Lovecraftian* dualism for their work. Three decades later, the modern "Mardukite" organization followed up with "*Necronomicon: The Anunnaki Bible*."

All of the individuals allegedly contributing to construction and publication of *Simon's Necronomicon*—sometimes called the "Simon Group" or "Schlangekraft Group"—had strong religious and/or occult backgrounds, including ordained *Gnostic* and *Orthodox* priests and monks, with others having ties to such groups as the O.T.O. We should not be surprised then to find strong religious connotations and "New Age" occult references introducing the *Necronomicon* text—prefaced by literary essays provided by its alleged editor, who is only ever officially identified as "Simon."

Front covers of *Simon's Necronomicon* generally only reveal the print title —"*Necronomicon.*" The inside title page ascribes the work: "edited with an introduction by Simon." The copyright is held by "*Schlangekraft, Inc.*"—the original umbrella-name used by the "Simon group." All artwork and illuminated lettering for the original 1977 hardcover was provided by "*Khem Set Rising*"— including the quasi-pentagram sign appearing on the cover (though nowhere else within the actual text of the *Necronomicon*) combining three main symbols used in its ceremonies.

One of the more confusing diversions put forth in *Simon's Necronomicon* toward the identity of its editor, is the fact that the prefatory "Acknowledgments" section is written from the perspective of its alleged "editor"—and yet they are signed *L.K. Barnes*, who was one several of the "Simon group" members. But.. *Barnes* is also listed in the "Acknowledgments"—whereas the name "*Simon*" is not. The assumption we are exploring here logically is whether or not "*Simon*" is a pseudonym for an unnamed figure, or if it is one of the names—or even several of the names— from the "Acknowledgments." L.K. Barnes may have been a more public business face for the "Simon Group"—but, as an individual, not "Simon." Another underground name appears too—*Herman Slater*—former owner of the "Warlock Shop" (now "Magickal Childe") in Manhattan, New York.

Of the many names listed in the "Acknowledgments," it is the mention of *Peter Levenda* that stands apart. *Peter Lavenda* is known occult personality and widely published, particularly regarding politically regarding WWII German Nazi involvement with the occult and the American legacy of covert use of esoteric knowledge. Many people actually regard *Peter Levenda* as "Simon"—although he denies such himself, something we would expect given the powerful cult-following turned counter-cultural phenomenon that *Simon's Necronomicon* has become. There are several reasons to believe that *Peter Levenda* is "Simon" even if he denies it. From copyright registries to similar writing styles and networking among publishing circles—there is no shortage of potential evidence. Not to mention biblical connections specifically between the names *Simon* and *Peter*... But, the choice to use of a pseudonym—"Simon"—is an intentional and long-standing act to disguise the actual identity of the editor. Quoting *Liber R*—"It is not our current intention to editorialize the messenger for the message, as many have attempted to do in their efforts in the past. *Levenda's* public position on the matter remains that 'he is not *Simon*', which can be resaccepted respectfully – though anyone who has heard him speak concerning the *Necronomicon* immediately notices that he speaks in the same manner that '*Simon*' writes.

It is quite possible that direct public notoriety with the "*Necronomicon*" would have had critical implications toward the success or saleability of other unrelated work the author/editor might want to generate for future publication. In the modern media industry, names can easily be typecast toward certain flavors of creative work. People are more familiar with this publicly in the more widespread "visual entertainment industries," but the matter is no less the case in the literary realm. The name "Simon" is now appropriated to a very popular and specific "editor" identity—an esteem resulting from the wide circulation of *Simon's Necronomicon*. But—it took a very long time for the editor to return, for whatever personal reasons that might be attached. Since the mass market paperback publication of *Simon's Necronomicon* Avon (now HarperCollins) in 1980—and as its frugal followup in 1981 (the *Necronomicon Spellbook*)—the public would have to wait until 2006 for any supplemental work to appear: *Dead Names: Dark History of the Necronomicon* along with *Gates of the Necronomicon*.

* * *

Stories fueling public knowledge of the *Necronomicon* are highly influenced by *H.P. Lovecraft's* writings and/or the fantasy-horror genre he inspired. His own perspectives may or may not even be relayed in his work—for *Lovecraft* seemed to downplay the impact his work should inspire and he attributed all of his own inspiration to dreams and nightmares—from beyond. He was not "inspired"—he was *tortured*—and his writing was not meant to "inspire." It was only after his death that his colleagues later dubbed his paradigm the "*Cthulhu Mythos*" and they continued to contribute to its growth. The tones and ideas reflected in the *Lovecraftian* paradigm are not restricted only to a book called the *Necronomicon*—but to an entirely new, alternative, counter-cultural and "dark" motif from which to view the world and life experiences.

According to *Lovecraft's* work, the primordial world is essentially "chaos" and battling "*gods*" from times long forgotten later have an impact on the psyche and life of humans today. In fact, the central "occult" basis of the *Lovecraftian* paradigm is devotion and "worship" of these prehistoric "*gods*." A faction of *Great Old Ones* once replaced and conquered by the younger *Elder Gods* becomes arbitrary to human balance when there are those who secretly worship and *feed* these "evil gods" throughout the ages in secret "cults"—groups seeking to bring about a return of the *Great Old Ones* to *our* time-space. This would systematically destroy the "universe" as we know it—returning the cosmos back into something reminiscent of the "primordial ooze" from which it sprung. This bleak and shadowy worldview is what drives the "horrific" tales of not only *Lovecraft's* work, but anything that has since been attached to it—whether in other literature, "black metal" rock music, or other medias &*tc*.

The *Lovecraftian* paradigm describes the *Necronomicon* as an evil book that worshipers of these ancient cults use to honor the *Great Old Ones* (or *Ancient Ones*)—in spite of the *Ancient Ones'* complete distaste for humanity and that inviting such forces and energetic currents back into the material realm would be devastating for all human life. Of course, the classic "teenage angst-driven punker anarchical nihilist mindset" is not concerned about such things, naively seeking total disestablishment of the systems with a world thrown into a state of *discordia*... For many attracted to the *Necronomicon* archetype—*this* is what takes priority. How any of these "cults" consider left-handed and chaotic-evil pathways as a true *Self-Honest* path to the Absolute is beyond logic—though they claim so; then they go back to their hedonism, narcissism, and pleasure seeking without any higher regard or loftier purpose—always validated in their minds that they are "right" in their ways. Where the *Necronomicon* is concerned, we are speaking in extreme examples—yet, we can recognize these tendencies and patterns easily: the potential slipstream that is inherent in all forms of "rebellion." Sometimes the pendulum swings equally wide the *other way*.

The fallacious issue of being "stuck in old patterns" is an epidemic not restricted simply to a book called the *Necronomicon* or even mystical and "New Age" aspects in general. For similar reasons the modern "Mardukite" movement is predominantly composed of *NexGens* and *Millennials*—those now in their thirties or *younger!* Why? Because the new and next generations are not as interested in knowing and discerning things in the same "fragmented" way that was common to previous parental generations and so forth.

Given the rapid acceleration of the information age, the "older generations" have no reason to change—either how they think or what they do—because they have had a far longer time to validate that things "*are the way they are*" and who am I or anyone else to tell them different. They also have a shorter duration of time in which to remain responsible for things being the way they are—passing the "buck" invariably onto subsequent generations.

So—it may be that we come full circle again, with a "younger generation" pushing to usurp the roles of the elders that have doomed them

Considering all of these ideas put forth—in order to pierce the veils of what we might find of value from *Simon's Necronomicon*, it is important not to be distracted by the icing on the cake, when the real bulk is actually hidden beneath it. The substance of the iceberg is concealed from salient views. The term "distraction" appears frequently in modern "Mardukite" and *NexGen Systemology* works to describe elements in one's life or storage in the psyche that hinders access to "wholeness" and "unified" field of view that is obtainable. When the subconscious can only produce manifestations from the ideas and materials it stores—we are seeking to acquire only the best for our collection during this lifetime.

— 3 —
RECONSTRUCTING THE NECRONOMICON

Appearance of *Simon's Necronomicon* was, in itself, one of the most monumental occult ventures to have appeared in the late 20th-century "magickal revival." That being said, the group connected to the original publication reappeared sporadically since—all using the name *"Simon"* to represent their work—and perhaps legitimately so. Consider, for example: the follow-up "sequel" to the original text—first published in 1981 as the *"Necronomicon Spellbook"* by *Simon*. Among the "Unholy Trinity" or "Simon Group"—*Larry Barnes* put up the money for the hardcover publication of *Simon's Necronomicon* and we assume the one ultimately responsible for seeing the original *Necronomicon Spellbook* through to print and possibly its later negotiation with Avon in 1987 for the mass market print edition.

Before being picked up by Avon (now HarperCollins) as a companion volume to their paperback release of *Simon's Necronomicon* in 1980, the first printings of *Simon's Necronomicon Spellbook* were produced directly by "Magickal Childe"— the name of the bookstore run by *Herman Slater*, in whose bookstore this band of fellows contributing to the release of *Simon's Necronomicon* originally met at—in what was first known as the "Warlock Shop" in Manhattan. The language and style of the *Spellbook* is significantly different than what we *Simon's Necronomicon*. And we know that the original "Simon" did not undertake its design—it was instead a marketing enhancement produced by others in the group that were experiencing financial hardship. Thus, while marginally of interest *as is*, the project was rushed—any significant notes, potential commentary or anything else of esoteric value never appeared in this frugal and elementary discourse.

Accounts later published in *"Dead Names"* attribute discovery of the "original" *Necronomicon* "manuscript" to the enigmatic *"Simon"* figure, that worked together as an "unholy trinity" of individuals—including *Larry Barnes* and *Jim Wasserman* —to publish the book in its initial hardcover presentations. Many have also noticed that in some places in *"Dead Names"* and later interviews with *Peter Levenda*—it is actually *himself* standing with his colleague *"Andrew"* (a fellow co-founder of the *Slavonic Orthodox Church*) as the go through boxes of old manuscripts—one of which bares a Greek title they had never heard of before: NECRONOMICON. The manuscript was photocopied and returned to the collection—apparently still the property of the book thieves—in the *Church*, where it later disappeared. Since then, other versions of the *Necronomicon* have circulated in the underground, all closely assimilating elements and selections used for *Simon's Necronomicon*. Many of these are artificially attributed to *John Dee*—developer of the *Enochian* magical system during the Elizabethan age. Given a direct disappearance of the manuscript and what we might expect about its rarity, it is quite possible that other hands have been upon it in recent history.

The story that *Peter Levenda* provides in interviews is that when the "rare-book thieving monks" had finally been caught, his associate *Andrew* destroyed any material still in the possession of the *Slavonic Orthodox Church* that might connect the two. From this, we are led to believe that the legendary *Necronomicon* manuscript was destroyed. Prefatory notes provided in *Simon's Necronomicon* do not reveal any of this—instead saying that the editor and publisher were only given permission to "publish" the work, but that they did not actually possess ownership of the manuscript itself. This was naturally meant to dissuade the flock of curious demands to inspect the manuscript itself.

* * *

What is actually contained within *Simon's Necronomicon* is a "bastardized over-simplification" of the original "Mardukite" system observed in ancient Babylon in dedication to the Anunnaki. The remnants and pieces that it does provide, resonated enough with several modern seekers that the research and experimentation team of "Mardukite Chamberlains" reconstructed the historical tradition in an even more complete version—known today as *"Necronomicon: The Anunnaki Bible."* Of course—this is not to say that *Simon's Necronomicon* is not valuable in its own right—as a beautiful and significantly noteworthy landmark of a paradigm-shift experienced today in the world.

Some critics are of the mind that *Simon's Necronomicon* is not an authentic manu-script in its own right and that the published book is a composite work developed by several individuals bringing together remnants of the *"Mesopotamian Magic"* genre already existent at the time—specifically *Semitic Magic* by Thompson, *Babylonian Magic & Sorcery* by King and *Chaldean Magic* by Lenormant, the works of E.A. Wallis Budge, *&tc.*—all from the late 19th and early 20th centuries.

As the official story continues: *Herman Slater* was initially unable to find a suitable third-party publisher for the *Necronomicon* manuscript—though he clearly felt a strong need to do so. The twist arrives when *Lovecraftian* fan, *Larry Barnes*, enters the picture—showing up at *Magickal Childe* specifically looking for the *Necro-nomicon*. Coincidentally, *Slater* had a manuscript copy at the shop much to the others delight and presumably, surprise. For many onlookers, this is quite tongue-in-cheek.

But—*Larry Barnes* was a book-printer by trade. His lifelong obsession with the *Lovecraftian* paradigm led him to seek a way to finally realize a publication called the *Necronomicon* during his lifetime. It is this *title* that has ever remained questionable—and the energy the title carried actually said very little about the literal contents of the manuscript when compared directly to the writings of *Lovecraft*. Where *Larry Barnes* handled marketing, funding and print services, actual book design for *Simon's Necronomicon* was left to *Jim Wasserman*—known for his work with another occult bookseller (*Samuel Weiser*).

In 1977, the original leather-bound editions—numbered of 666—of the first printing of *Simon's Necronomicon* were quickly sold out at fifty dollars each. Today, the same edition can be found fetching anywhere from a few hundred to one-thousand dollars among collectors. Other later editions and printings of leather and cloth-bound versions were released thereafter to supply a rising demand that was rising. Arrival of this beautifully constructed "legendary archetype" attracted considerable attention. *Peter Levenda* accounts on his *PlusUltra* interview—"The book was attacked immediately as soon as it came out. *'This is not the Necronomicon'* or *'This is a horrible hoax, it's so poor, it's not even Lovecraft.'* As far as I was concerned, the fact that it wasn't *Lovecraftian* meant that it probably was the real *Necronomicon*. If it was a hoax then it would have been a lot 'better' than what it was."

Perhaps most fundamental to the public assimilation of *Simon's Necronomicon*, far more than the title, is that in spite of the "magickal" and "neopagan" revival taking place, global consciousness remained fixed in viewing the world through *Judeo-Christian* filters—including medieval "grimoires" (*Keys of Solomon, &tc.*) and the Renaissance study of alchemy. *Simon's Necronomicon* represented the ancient "Mardukite" Babylonian tradition for the first time—something truly and authentically predating the *Judeo-Christian* paradigm, and regardless of whether someone "believes" in the paradigm or not, the energetic imprint on human consciousness is unavoidable, especially in the 20th—or even 21st—century. Many of the truly questionable aspects of the occult—all of that old "demonology," "devil worship" and "luciferianism" in practice—are dependent on Judeo-Christian semantics in order to hold any context. They are "alternatives" or "rebellious aspect" against *something*—a reactive creation developed strongly during the *Dark Ages* to fight "mainstream" atrocities resulting from church-run states.

Simon's Necronomicon opened a "gateway" of consciousness into a realm that was truly ancient, prehistoric and undefiled by the later evolution of "what came next"—and to these efforts of the time, we might also add Zecharia Sitchin's "*Twelfth Planet*" to this category, simultaneously released in 1977, though perhaps to a different demographic of reader. "Mardukite" Mesopotamian paradigms were returning to global consciousness—a bridge, or at least a window, to glimpse a truly ancient "occult" and "pre-Christian" (even proto-Semitic) element of human origins and social development that is otherwise hidden or forgotten, but certainly not openly taught. That this *Necronomicon* should emerge from the Middle East— or "*Ancient Near East*"—should not seem surprising. We would expect the most ancient writings to come from the historical origins of the written word—or *cuneiform*—the first non-pictorial writing system set down by the first of a long series of evolving global cultural systems. All of these systems, regardless of their location, emphasize central importance on a learned class of literate "priests," "priestesses" and "magicians" with the ability to communicate with a race of "*Sky Gods*"—beings appearing to many ancient cultures and acknowledged by various culturally specific names—known to the *Sumerians* (by the first actual literary language) as the ANUNNAKI.

Virtually prehistoric and ancient pre-*Judeo-Christian* paradigms are reflected in renderings and cuneiform tablets from the little understood *Mesopotamians* of *Sumer* and *Babylon*. These are far removed from the common way we are taught to understand history and origins of humanity today—although our widely varied and intermittent knowledge carries an underlying unifying and singular source representative of the former, meaning that traditions of today and yesterday are all "mutations" or "selective evolutions" from these much older *Mesopotamian* systems—those alluded to in *Simon's Necronomicon* and subsequently revived and restored more completely by the modern "Mardukite" movement—as evident in the original "*Necronomicon: The Anunnaki Bible*" This ability to evolve our understanding beyond what previous generations were able to glean is really a large part of what this "New Age" *paradigm-shift* is about. Quoting *Peter Levenda* in his interview—

> "Where the New Age is concerned, a lot of the occultism is *Judeo-Christian*—the *Keys of Solomon*, for example; the *Secret Books of Moses* and all of that stuff—it was all based on a *Jewish* and *Christian* concept. With the coming of the New Age you did have a rise in neo-paganism, but there was not a system of 'ceremonial magick' for a neo-pagan mentality; it [ceremonial magick] was, again, based on *Jewish* and *Christian* concepts, which were themselves borrowed from pagan origins, but the pagan origins were gone for the most part. In a sense the *Simon Necronomicon* filled a need for people with a true neo-pagan interest to become involved with the 'higher magicks' so to speak."

In spite of mainstream popularity and widespread distribution, *Simon's Necronomicon* is not often found in many typical "wiccan-witch" New Age shops —and as an Avon/HarperCollins big-house publication, is more easily located in larger book chains and online outlets. Most used book stores keep a copy—though, as a high-theft item, it might be kept behind the sales counters. For all of the reasons previously explained regarding the title of the book and the resulting misappropriated *Lovecraftian* paradigm applied to the *Simon Necronomicon* based on the title alone—we see little advocating or presence of *Simon's Necronomicon* in the contemporary "New Age." With the exception of the modern "Mardukite" movement—and those who are sure to duplicate and rehash our own efforts later— this older *Mesopotamian* motif of authentic occultism remains absent from the "New Age." In conclusion, keynotes from *Lavenda* continue in his interview—

> "*Necronomicon*; the publication of a book called *The Necronomi-con*—no matter what *Necronomicon* it is, I think raised a lot of questions that have become very controversial and that is: what is a true *book*. It questions the value of pseudoepigrapha. For instance, the *Keys of Solomon* was not written by 'Solomon'. There's false at-tributions to it. The "Gardnerian Book of Shadows" was written by Gerald Gardner; it wasn't written by some pagan witches a couple

of thousand years ago, or even hundreds of years ago. So, we have to ask ourselves: where is the value? The *Necronomicon* forces people to question: what do we really value? Do we value an 'ancient text' because its *ancient* or do we value it because it has *something else* to offer us? Does a 'new text' with 'ancient motif' become just as valuable as some other text or a 'genuine' ancient text?"

"*Necronomicon* forces people to confront and question dealing with the *dark side*. All occultism essentially deals with the *Other*—it deals with another reality. It may deal with the '*dark side*' of *human consciousness*. Even if it's '*angelic*' magick; even if it's '*Jewish Mysticism*' or '*kabbalistic occultism*', or anything like that —it still deals with '*dark side*'; it still deals with the *unseen*. And the *Necronomicon* is sort of 'in your face' about that. The *Necronomicon* is all about the *unseen* and it's all about the *dark side* and it makes no apology for it. It may be that the *Necronomicon* answers some need in people by saying: this *is* a book about *darkness*. It does not dwell on 'forming pacts' with '*Satan*' or something—it's not like that, but it *does* deal with *darkness*. It deals with it at a pre-*Judeo-Christian* mentality as far as religion and magick is concerned. Maybe it *is* valuable for that reason. Maybe it represents *unresolved issues*."

"Sometimes I wonder if maybe this whole 'war' between the *forces of Light* and the *forces of Darkness* is just '*Aliens versus Predator*'. I mean, it's a plague on both your houses. Maybe for us, it's a question of just choosing 'sides'—it's not a question of 'right' and 'wrong'. Maybe the spiritual forces are *amoral* or maybe their morality is something beyond our understanding. Unless you *really* have a fine-tuned sensitivity, who knows what's *evil* or *good* or what's beneficial for the human race or not...?"

— 4 —
THE PREFACE – 1979

After immediately selling out its first edition of 666 copies, *Simon's Necronomicon* went on to reach an even wider audience with its "Second Edition" in 1979— containing a new "*Preface*" from the "Editor" that appeared in both the *Silver Edition* hardcover—limited to 3000 copies—and the popular Avon paperback edition. This new prefatory information introduces readers as they set upon their journey; it sets the tone. And when a person is new to these matters whatsoever, then it has an even greater significance to the Seeker and how they will process the obscure tradition loosely outlined throughout the rest of the book.

Since Mardukite *Liber 555* is intended as an intensive scrutiny of *Simon's Necronomicon* within its own paradigm (and additionally in relation to the historical "Mardukite" Anunnaki tradition), we begin with the 1979 "Preface," noting some conflicting data held not only within the Preface itself, but in connection with other facts introduced in Simon's "*Dead Names: Dark History of the Necronomicon*" and also in interviews with *Peter Levenda*—a man that has surprisingly maintained a lot of interests in the "Simonian" legacy across four decades. This seems rather ambitious if *Lavenda* is merely a "background character" to the *Simon Group*, as we are led to believe. [Given my background in *analytics, rhetoric* and *semantics* throughout my own prolific writings on esoteric occult subjects, I have been repeatedly approached concerning my opinions of these matters.]

In the opening lines of Simon's "Preface" we are introduced to the identity of *Larry Barnes*—and here begins a trend of referring to all members comprising the "*Simon group*" by their names, even "Simon", who is also referred to in first-person tense for nearly all accounts. The only name absent from the legacy history —aside from those listed in the "*Acknowledgments*"—is *Peter Levenda*. Why is this significant? Because, for carrying such an allegedly small character role in the development of *Simon's Necronomicon*, the more detailed chronicle given in "*Dead Names*" spends half the book focused on *Lavenda's* personal background— then shifts during second half, using the exclusive perspective of "*Simon.*"

Larry Barnes and "a friend" came to *Herman Slater*'s bookstore in search of a *Necronomicon* to publish—and *Slater* just so happened to have a photocopy of it, provided by *Peter Levenda* from the *Slavonic Orthodox Church* occult book collection on loan from a band of book-thieves. This much information is practically provided in the first paragraph of the "Preface" detailing formation of the "Simon group" by three key members. It is curious then, and an almost *gemini* convolution, to read two paragraphs later: "*Simon* appeared suddenly one day at the living quarters of L.K. Barnes providing additional material on the *Necronomicon...*" What? Who is that? We know everyone else involved, the source of the manuscript and the individuals—why is this new person added to in the equation? ...One that doesn't seem to play a part (by name) in acquiring the manuscript—or the bookstore meeting where the trio—*Levenda, Barnes, Slater*—decide to publish it, or even the actual publication and design, attributed to *Jim Wasserman* of "Studio 31." The name "Simon" suddenly becomes a leading authority on the project—and the "trio" changes—which is why some folk have had issues with the identities in this story: *Simon* is not simply someone with supportive documents for the *Necronomicon*, but is referred to as the "source" of the manuscript—when as far as we know, he had no previous involvement with the *Slavonic Orthodox Church*, if we are to assume that he is a separate identity from *Levenda*.

From the start, the reader begins this path enshrouded in a bit of mystery over the origins of the *Necronomicon* manuscript and its later publication. This is probably not an intentional deception, but to add to the aura of *mystique*. The initial aura attached to the title resulting from *Lovecraftian* uploads into human consciousness, combined with marketing efforts and prefatory information on the text itself, created a unique packaging for an otherwise even more obscure and fragmented rendering of pre-*Judeo-Christian* post-Sumerian "Mardukite" Babylonian Anunnaki Tradition. Keep in mind, this was the 1970's and the occult realm, although growing and expanding as a "New Age" movement, was still mainly restricted to the "underground" and other alternative sects of "counter-culture" in times long before mainstream computer interaction.

The "Preface" builds up a forbidding occult motif—describing various supernatural phenomenon occurring in the lives of the developers, people who went on to assist its printing, and those initially coming into possession of original copies. All of it collectively works to further a "doom and gloom" aura surrounding the *Necronomicon* in consciousness—such as we would expect more from a *Lovecraftian* paradigm far more than the historical "Mesopotamian"—*Sumerian* or *Babylonian* —observation of Anunnaki traditions. At its basic reduction, the general facts as we can understand them from *Simon's Necronomicon* demonstrate to a reader that we are about to be shown a series of "Incantation" translations from cuneiform tablets from *Babylonian* tradition published by someone—*L.K. Barnes*—with a lifelong obsession with the "*Cthulhu Mythos*" and legendary archetype of the "dreaded tome"—"*Necronomicon*." Applicable esoteric information from the "Preface" is found toward the end—regarding effects of the book on human consciousness, particularly in an age experiencing a powerful paradigm-shift. And as explained on Yule 1979, from *Simon...* or *Barnes...* or *Levenda...* someone's own words at least—

> "Every New Age witnesses a baptism by fire. Christians and Muslims are turning on each other and themselves; Israel is once again in serious jeopardy; Buddhism is being eradicated in Southeast Asia as it was in Tibet. The *Necronomicon* is also an amulet, a protective shield, that guards its own against the machinations of 'evil'. Extra-terrestrial or primevally elemental, alien beings or subconscious repression, they are powerless against us if we consider deeply the message of this book..."

— 5 —
INTRODUCING A LEGENDARY ARCHETYPE

"There are many terrors on the Way to Self,
and an Abyss to cross before victory can be declared."
~ Introduction, *Simon Necronomicon*

Contemporary culture has seen a rise of *Lovecraftian* interest—not surprisingly since the 1970's and the release of *Simon's Necronomicon*. There are still many people—even those involved with mystical and occult matters—who are *not* actually aware of the *Necronomicon* paradigm at all, although it is clear that the subject is not nearly as enigmatic as it once was. Since it's arrival in 1977, we have witnessed *Giger* art books, Enochian-styled manuals, "Simonian" recreations, and a lot of post-*Lovecraftian* tripe written in fanship of the "*Cthulhu Mythos*"—all carrying the name *Necronomicon*, and nearly all propagating the same "left-handed" and "gothic"—or "*cthonic*" and "eldritch"—display of horror. And for those who are not avid "readers"—the *mythos* is relayed in countless editions of "roleplaying games"—using tabletop, collectible cards, live action and video/computer medias.

Sporadic sub-pop cultural influences of *H.P. Lovecraft's* writings—and later "cult" interest in *Simon's Necronomicon*—have gone on to directly inspire movies and other mainstream displays of the *Necronomicon* (for example, the *Evil Dead* saga or more famously, *Army of Darkness*), or mentions of it in pop-culture as seen in *The Simpsons* and *South Park* animated sit-coms. New genres of "heavy metal" music even have *Lovecraftian* (*Cthulhu Mythos*) and/or *Simonian Necronomicon* (quasi-*Egypto-Mesopotamian*) themes. It is quite evident that the whole idea has developed a sub-cultural life of its own.

When *Simon's Necronomicon* debuted, a smaller public awareness was in effect regarding concepts of the *Necronomicon*, *H.P. Lovecraft* and even *Mesopotamia*. Given an intended widespread audience, some significant background information would be required when introducing the subject in question to the general public. A small selective cult following of *H.P. Lovecraft's* literary legacy already existed—enough to support a prestigious debut of the original underground hardcover release of the book—but for the rest of the world, many newer occultists found the *Simon Necronomicon* as their own introduction to the *Cthulhu Mythos*—which is also misleading, because for all the things that it *is*, a *Lovecraftian* book it is not. Following the other line of academia—many were introduced to the entire post-*Sumerian* Anunnaki realm of ancient *Mesopotamia* through this tome, though it is *not* actually a very clear presentation of *that* either. BUT! ...for all of these "shortcomings" that many folk have so loudly critiqued in the past—in the time and form that *Simon's Necronomicon* was introduced to the world, it was *just enough*.

The literary "Introduction" given in *Simon's Necronomicon* consolidates a fast-track overview of related base knowledge, dropping in mention of several key esoteric elements that play a significant part in the *Necronomicon* legacy revival—both *Lovecraftian* and *Mesopotamian*. The more obvious of these are *H.P. Lovecraft* references, then a brief mingling of the occult with the likes of *Aleister Crowley* and then his related occult "secret societies" of A.A. (*Argentum Astrum*) and O.T.O. (*Ordo Templi Orientis*)—magical orders that have adopted *Lovecraftian* and/or *Mesopotamian* aspects into their practices; and those that have come to take these mysteries very seriously.

The Mythos & The Magick

The main tenet behind Lovecraft's *Cthulhu Mythos*—the paradigm superimposed over an underlying "Mardukite" Anunnaki tradition adopted by ancient *Mesopotamians* in Babylon—is mostly concerned with polar dualistic forces between *Light* and *Dark* as "good and evil" moral extremes active in the universe. For the *Lovecraftian* paradigm, this is reflected in a primordial energetic struggle between *Elder Gods* and the *Great Old Ones* they conquered. When projected from the Mesopotamian-inspired *Simon Necronomicon*, this dualism is interpreted from the *Enuma Elis*—or "Mardukite Babylonian Epic of Creation"—as a primordial war for supremacy between *Elder Gods* and their ancestors, called the *Ancient Ones* in *Simon's Necronomicon*. This moral dualism does not actually appear directly in the familial feuds among *Anunnaki* descendents found in post-Sumerian Babylonian or "Mardukite" tradition, but it is *this* brand of *Babylonian* culture that is alluded to in *Simon's Necronomicon* and not a *Lovecraftian* one as the title is more likely to suggest.

From the beginning, a reader-seeker is introduced to this tradition as a polar fragmentation of dualistic forces. And although a *Mesopotamian Mystery Tradition* is actually the basis of *Simon's Necronomicon*, this paradigm is introduced with "*Lovecraftian*" glasses—with "*Elder Gods*" pitted against "*Ancient Ones*" as reminiscent of the "*Great Old Ones*" in Lovecraft's "*Cthulhu Mythos*." In respect to the political and cosmogenetic treatise from Mardukite tradition—the *Enuma Elis* —we do not see a reoccurring appearance of "Tiamat" often in Babylonian history in the way we are shown in *Simon's Necronomicon*, meaning: we do not see an actual issue with cults of *Tiamat* rising up as "devil-worshipers" in Babylon, with the exception of some minor anti-authoritarian uprisings that we would expect with any large population—and the *Maqlu* ceremonies were later devised to *exorcise* these efforts as well.

The actual rivalry taking place historically between two ancient *Anunnaki* factions —the Sumerian-based "*Enlilites*" and the new up-and-coming Babylonian "*Mardukites*" (sometimes called "*Enki'ites*")—is not part of *Simon's Necronomicon*— rather we have a description of polarized ethical dualism among "divine beings" that far more represents *Judeo-Christian* paradigms, or even *Zoroastrian-Yezidic* lore, than what we should expect to see representing ancient *Babylonians*, or dare we say it, *Sumerians*. The question that follows is: does this inconsistency invalidate the actual "tablet" information alluded to in *Simon's Necronomicon* or not?

When compared to the more recently compiled historical "Mardukite" traditions, the paradigm within *Simon's Necronomicon* is not a *verbatim* "one-to-one" reflection of actual *Anunnaki* traditions as they were being observed historically during national practice in *Mesopotamia*. Then again, the work is allegedly compiled from "memory," retold by a man many refer to as the "*Mad Arab*"—due to *Lovecraftian* references—during the 8th Century A.D., *long after* the apex (or even the open practice) of *Anunnaki* traditions in *Mesopotamia*. If we should literally ascribe this early *Dark Ages era* to origins to the perspective slant offered in *Simon's Necronomicon*, then some of this moral dualism could actually begin to make more sense —but that does not mean that it is true to the original pre-Christian, or even pre-Arabic accounts given on the ancient cuneiform tablets themselves. In this light, *Simon's Necronomicon* becomes, at best, a pseudo-*Arabic* account of a pre-*Arabic* and demonized *Mesopotamian* tradition that is being experienced in a *Christianized* time period—when the *Roman Church* is healthily established. Such would not be present if the book were of an even older origin. For this reason alone, we might forgive the fact that strong religious dualism is falsely overlaying an otherwise amoral system.

Sumeria

The Introduction to *Simon's Necronomicon* pushes strong connections—an esoteric meeting ground—between legacies of *Lovecraft* and the *Simon* edition, calling it: *Sumeria*. This is only partially correct in the sense of the general ancient geographic origins of "archetypes" in *Mesopotamia*. However, H.P. Lovecraft makes no real mention of *Mesopotamia* or the *Anunnaki* legacy in his writings, nor is it at all an integral part of early *Crowley*-based traditions and organizations—an exception being the slant toward available *Yezidic* knowledge from the "Middle East," where we see some semantic sources for the *Semitic* concept of "Shaitan" (Satan).

Mesopotamia and its ruling class of beings called *Anunnaki*, are central themes for geographic and cultural origins of the modern human species and its evolution as civilization. Their system of *cuneiform* was also the original form of non-pictorial language-writing available in human consciousness. Here also lay the literary origins of later *Biblical scriptures*, archetypal tales of the "Great Deluge" and early interactions between humans and the "Divine," or at least experiences and encounters programmed or instructed as "*Divine*."

What is unique in the perspective offered by the *Simon* editors—and wholly incorrect from the start—is the idea that *Simon's Necronomicon* is a preservation of the earlier *Sumerian* tradition. It is not. All of the references made therein—as well as the invocations and specific "*Stargate*" system explored—are all remnants of a

286

purely "*Babylonian*" esoteric knowledge current—known as "Mardukite"—that is essentially the first direct "evolution" of the original *Sumerian* tradition, dating to the times of pre-dynastic Egypt. Therefore, the idea that the *Simon* edition is in any way a grimoire of "*Sumerian*" occultism proper, is completely incorrect. We might more appropriately designate the birthplace of its origins—politically and geographically—as "*Babylonia.*"

One historical "class distinction" between *Elder Gods* and *Ancient Ones* is offered in *Simon's Necronomicon*—again, referring to "*Enuma Elis*"—a matter that is dealt with more intensely later on in this discourse. The summary of it, however, is offered in the "Introduction" to *Simon's Necronomicon*. Here, the Babylonian *Epic of Creation* portraying MARDUK (son of ENKI) as the dragonslayer of *Tiamat* (the primeval and ancient dragon of Chaos) is used to validate an archetypal primordial morally dualistic conflict between warring factions of gods. This is not really an accurate perception of the *Sumerian* worldview by any means, and if anything, would be only attributable to the *Babylonians* ("Mardukites") if it were to apply at all. *Sumerians* never acknowledged supremacy of MARDUK in their tradition—so the *Simon Necronomicon* is not *Sumerian,* a fact that has fueled many straw-man attacks on the system as a whole. Quoting prefatory information from our own Mardukite anthology, "*Necronomicon: The Anunnaki Bible*"—

> "The work and tradition is not *Sumerian*—which would have heralded most divine attributes to ENLIL and then perhaps also to his heir-son NINURTA; but instead, it is *Babylonian* in origin, deferring all powers of earthly magick and world order specifically to ENKI and his own heir-son MARDUK, patron deity of *Babylon*. In both the modern "Mardukite" literary cycle and *Simon's Necronomicon*—ANU remains a distant figure and ENLIL is only mentioned respectfully in regard to the Anunnaki Supernal Trinity. But, the *Babylonians* assigned all Anunnaki ('Divine') Enlil-ship or Lord-ship of earth to MARDUK..."

Another theme found in global mythologies and also interpreted in *Lovecraftian* literature is the "*Underworld*." But the "*Underworld*" is sometimes mistaken with the "Cosmic Abyss" by naïve scholars and many esoteric occult works—including *Simon's Necronomicon* at times. Beyond the underlying inter-connectivity that all existence shares—*All-as-One*—the two are *not* "interchangeable" or "synonymous." This is important for a post-modern (*NexGen*) Truth-Seeker to understand if pursuing the flavor of mysteries—or interpretation of the mysteries—that *Simon's Necronomicon* provides.

The "*Underworld*" is a name often given to an inter-dimensional geographic locale, otherwise considered the *Land of the Dead*. It some lore, it might refer to a "*Land of Shadows*" (or "*Kingdom of Shadows*"), or more literally, a Realm of *seven* or *nine* "Gates." In any case, it refers to an alter-existence outside the time-space within our defined "human" range of sensory perception—some refer to as the

"*Other.*" In contrast—"The Abyss" or ABZU is very specifically a primordial realm, or "state," of non-existence—more accurately the "*Infinity of Nothingness*" carrying no distinguished light or fragmented existence, but instead the Absolute Infinity or Infinity of Absolute Potentiality. In the *Enuma Elis*, the Abyss is referenced during the initial formation of existence, when light and energetic activity emerged from the *seas of potentiality*—the Abyss. And when too intangible for ancient comprehension, this force was later associated with the *Sun*.

Goddess of the Witches

During the magical revival of the late 1800's, the public witnessed an increased rise in elitist social organizations and underground fellowships such as the *Hermetic Order of the Golden Dawn*, the *Ordo Templi Orientis* and *Argentum Astrum*, not to mention many Western European and American revivals of "neo-paganism" in the guise of "neo-druidism"—but the other largely growing movement in these rising "New Age" and occult community networks emphasized "Witchcraft." This alternate stream of magical revival is derived from rural folk and peasant traditions, later systematized by Gerald Gardner in the early 20th century for the relatively modern innovation of "Wicca." Newer generations now examine all of these various pathways in a more uninhibited wide-angle view—and our understanding is no longer limited by exclusivity to one or two esoteric avenues in our lifetime.

Simon's Necronomicon was never hugely popular among the traditionalist *Wiccans* —those preferring to incorporate and overlay other more colorful and *accessible* cultural mythologies onto their crafts—such as the *Celts*, *Norse*, or even the *Egyptians*—rather than dig into much more ancient and elaborate pre-European traditions from much more inaccessible sources of antiquity. Even traditions and semantics drawn from the Classical "pagans"—*Greeks* and *Romans*—are adopted arbitrarily because, again, they are more accessible and represent pre-Christian paradigms of the "Old Ways" highly sought for New Age material. But these, too, have borrowed and bastardized a more ancient "planetary tradition of divinity" that predates the Classical period by thousands of years. Little popular attention is given among the general population—whether in culture, education or entertainment media—for people to even properly interpret *Mesopotamian* lore.

The original *Sumerian* worldview was based on a unity of two genders—god and goddess—in all elements of mythology. This is even projected in their cosmology regarding the polar rhythm of motion vibrating in all existence. It was only later in *Babylon* that a lean toward the "patriarchal" view developed, but not as a result of any kind of religious sexism—it was not even adopted in civic culture—but did exist during the initial rise of a *Babylonian* "Mardukite" worldview solely to assist elevating MARDUK to supremacy in the *Anunnaki* pantheon. This political act differentiates the *Babylonian* "Mardukite" systems from the former *Sumerian* paradigm with one exception—the appearance of INANNA (*Sumerian*) or ISHTAR (*Babylonian*). By the original design of a "younger generation" of Anunnaki gods,

MARDUK and INANNA-ISHTAR were betrothed—intended to rule beside one another as equals. But both wanted to be *on top*... splitting the pantheon between an older *Enlilite* world order that defined *Sumerian* civilization—and the newer *Mardukite* one in *Babylon*.

The "Introduction" to *Simon's Necronomicon* pays careful tribute to INANNA-ISHTAR as *"Goddess of the Witches."* As an integral of Babylonian Tradition, both the "Mardukite" literary legacy (*"Necronomicon: The Anunnaki Bible"*) and *Simon's Necronomicon* include the epic cuneiform tablet cycle: *"Inanna-Ishtar's Descent to the Underworld."* Mardukite scribes were not so naïve as to believe they would, could, or should replace all former Sumerian *"Enlilite"* elements from the Babylonian *Anunnaki* tradition. Many systematic points remained to maintain coherency with the tradition people already knew. Later, this same Anunnaki tradition was even transposed onto other surrounding *Ancient Near East* cultures as well, all assumed under their own languages and unique cultural interpretations— but the fundamental pantheon itself remained the same; the same Anunnaki figures representing the same planetary system in the local universe. As such, though not espoused to MARDUK, the historical *Bab-Ilu* or "Star-Gate" system of *Babylon*, observes INANNA-ISHTAR as the "Venusian Goddess"—the *"Gatekeeper of the Venus Gate."*

A brief mention of ERESHKIGAL—"Goddess of the Underworld"—does appear in the *Simon Necronomicon* "Introduction," but then it goes on to suggest that the name may be just another face of *"Tiamat."* Here, we see an attempt to align back with *Lovecraftian* dualism—and what we sacrifice here is the confusion of mistaking a "queen" of the *Underworld* with the *Abyss*. The artificial "Typhonian" (*&tc.*) emphasis is preferred by some occult practitioners of the modern era—but we should not confuse the genuine Babylonian elements with a *Lovecraftian* interpretation of the *"Old Ones."* Clinging tightly to the *Cthulhu Mythos* during a true investigation of historical *Mesopotamian Mysteries* will result in a very convoluted interpretation.

Therefore—if we are to adopt some esoteric logic from the "Introduction" to *Simon's Necronomicon*, the ancient "Goddess of Witches" really has *three* ancient forms—meaning the primordial archetypal Dragon Queen that first emerged from the Abyss (*Tiamat*), the Queen of the Underworld and Death (*Ereshkigal*) and the Queen of the Heavens, ruling Love and War (*Inanna-Ishtar*).

The Horned Moon

The next significant section of interest from the "Introduction" describes the unique observation of lunar divinity among Mesopotamians. Contrary to the typified examples from the "New Age," the primary Anunnaki representative of the moon was a masculine figure—NANNA (Sumerian) or SIN (Babylonian). However, as with other planetary currents, ancient Anunnaki tradition observes a "Divine

Marriage" for each—in this instance: both NANNA and NINGAL represent the lunar sphere in unity. NANNA represents the *"Moon Gate"* in the *Bab-Ili* system of Babylon, but he is also an ancient *Enlilite* deity, revered specifically in pre-Mardukite Sumerian traditions. Resurgences of *Enlilite* "lunar cults" dedicated to NANNA repeatedly caused religio-political issues for continuing "Mardukite" development of *Babylon*, but as with INANNA-ISHTAR, he remains a part of the Anunnaki legacy observed by Babylonians.

When the surface of these Babylonian mysteries were introduced to the 1970's with *Simon's Necronomicon*, what was so paramount or intriguing for the growing New Age is an overt pagan masculine representation of the moon in ancient Sumer. This is somewhat different than traditional polar observation of a supreme "moon goddess"—as *Wiccans* are likely to adopt for their practices. Modern simplifications of ancient pagan divinity are often reduced to the *moon* representing a "goddess" and the *sun* distinctively a "masculine god." This might even be applicable to some other (European, &tc.) pagan revivals, but this separation is not clearly made in *Anunnaki* spiritual systems.

The Devil

Perhaps no "dark grimoire" of 1970's esoteric occultism could be complete without bringing up some mention of the *Devil*. This *Zoroastrian* and *Judeo-Christian* dualism appears frequently in magical notebooks and kabbalistic grimoires developed during the *Dark Ages* through the Renaissance period. It was not until the "magical revival" of the late 1800's that organizations and groups began to recognize this anomaly in their practices—because prior to an establishment of orthodox religion (during the *Piscean Age*), we do not find this *Devil* figure—a sentient embodiment of "absolute evil"—observed in any ancient traditions. Yes—we see necessary elements of Chaos in cosmogenetic "creation myths," trickster gods, entropic plague gods, *Underworld gods* and even siblings warring against each other for Divine Supremacy—but no *Devils*; no "absolute evils."

Simon's Necronomicon introduces us then, to the Sumerian "demon" PAZUZU in order to establish a small point, even though the figure does not make an appearance in the body of the text—or a role at all in the *Bab.Ili "Anunnaki StarGate System"* as observed either in *Simon's Necronomicon* or the more complete recension developed for modern Mardukites as *"Necronomicon: The Anunnaki Bible."* PAZUZU is notoriously the only ancient Mesopotamian figure to make a mainstream "Hollywood" appearance—in *"The Exorcist."* But—PAZUZU is hardly *The Devil*. Other than to clash the appearance of the work against contemporary worldviews, prefatory notes relating dualism of the *"God versus Devil"* motif really do little to advance a student through a genuine understanding of the Anunnaki paradigm. That is not to say that naïve and misinformed practitioners cannot take these mysteries to a "dark place." The tradition represents raw primordial currents that are simply a vehicle to move energy—leaving any perceived "good and bad"

in the hands of those wielding it. Every thought, action and manifestation we produce will either advance us or deter us on our quest to unfold the highest potential
of our being.

Many remaining introductory notes in *Simon's Necronomicon* go on to further
"hype" the material for a "New Age" and mainstream market by emphasizing the
polarity of "darkness" inherent in the work and a propensity for "abuse" of the
power within that early practitioners experienced. "Simon" goes on to make
mention of various priests and ministers, the exorcism of evil spirits and
misappropriated "dangers" attached to exposure of forces unleashed by the
"dreaded tome." Of course—those who interpret the mysteries alluded in *Simon's
Necronomicon* may very well misalign energy and focus if they are working with
modern *Lovecraftian* or even orthodox *Judeo-Christian* filters. And—as we have
illustrated—clinging unyielding to "New Age neo-pagan" filters are no better
without absolute clarity, or "*Self-Honesty.*"

— 6 —
THE ARAB'S "LOST BOOK"

Among the intermittent aspects borrowed from Lovecraft's "*Cthulhu Mythos*" for *Simon's Necronomicon*—one of the most controversial concerns the idea that the *Necronomicon* originated from the pen of a "Mad Arab" named Abdul Alhazred. This idea is entirely *Lovecraftian*—indicated nowhere within the actual text of the *Necronomicon* aside from the editor's own commentary and again only in regards to the work of *H.P. Lovecraft*. The editors escape making definitive claims, allowing details of the background story to fallaciously fill in the gaps. But this kind of logic is quickly attacked by critics, then used to undermine true "between-the-lines" message relays from *Simon's Necronomicon* toward revival interest in the post-Sumerian "Mardukite" (or Babylonian) archetypal methodology—or "systemology."

The archaeological or scholarly problem arises mainly with identifying the actual author, dating manuscripts or even versions of ancient cuneiform tablets that were copied and re-copied so many times over thousands of years by innumerable scribes in various languages and with specific cultural slants. A bait-and-switch occurs only when we apply a specific *Lovecraftian* basis to any work with the title: *Necronomicon*—and [Q.E.D.!!] such logic is clever...but flawed (as shown below).

> Premise 1: The work of *H.P. Lovecraft* exclusively defines the
> *Necronomicon*.
>
> Premise 2: According to *Lovecraft*, the *Necronomicon* is written by an
> 8th century "Mad Arab" named Abdul Alhazred in Damascus.
>
> Premise 3: The work by *Simon* is titled the *Necronomicon*.
>
> Conclusion: *Simon's Necronomicon* is written by the 8th century
> "Mad Arab" named Abdul Alhazred in Damascus.

Naturally, the editors follow suit—*Simon's Necronomicon* begins with the "first part" of what is separated from the more historical main text sections as the "*Testimony of the Mad Arab*." The "second part" composes an epilogue to the volume. Even if the chronology of authorship is correct, an 8th century Arab would have had little direct contact with a true Anunnaki tradition—unless deeply underground. But that does not change the fact that although ancient *Mesopotamia* served as a global origin to systematized language, civilization and ultimately "religion," it had grown, evolved or mutated far from its origins—fragmented over time into expressions wholly different from what is originally reflected in more antiquated ages.

For an 8th century *"Arabic Necronomicon,"* we are meaning literally *800 years after* the time of Jesus Christ—long after the decline of true "paganism," always in the name of some new ideal or another, not always "Christian." Historically, the last great apex of *Babylon*—during the time of King Nebuchadnezzar II—occurred over a millennium prior, in the 6th century B.C. With the rise of later Greek control of *Babylonia*, the original "Mardukite" Anunnaki legacy almost completely disappeared along with the population of its patron city.

The Anunnaki legacy was maintained in ancient *Mesopotamia* as a "national religion"—a systematization of the urban populations, not necessarily the rural ones. Thus, the types of European folk traditions and indigenous shamanism popularized among "New Age" and "neo-pagan" revivals today are not directly represented in the original Anunnaki systems of the "state." They are, however, a starting place for later beliefs among "country folk" (*"paganus"*) and the surviving remnants of ancient wisdom forced underground in the wake of later urbanized *Christianization*. One urban system was replaced by another—and those operating *outside* of the system are often demonized, considered criminal, uneducated or feral/wild ("hicks," *&tc.*) by the official "citizens" of the Realm.

By the 8th century, the public had already experienced an extreme global con- sciousness shift regarding paganism, witchcraft, magic and occultism—not only a result from a spread of *Christianity*, but also following growth of new *Arabic* and *Middle Eastern* religions forming thousands of years after the original inception of the Anunnaki legacy in Mesopotamia. In many locations—especially more urban ones—the "Old Ways" were shunned. Quoting the preface to our *"Necronomicon: The Anunnaki Bible,"* the *Schlangekraft Recension* by Simon was—"alluding to a tradition that significantly predated itself. The work was not ahead of its time, but was instead lagging behind its time, seeking to preserve, perhaps from the memory of its allegedly Arabic author, the long-lost lore and traditions of a Mardukite priesthood."

The *Testimony of the Mad Arab* section provided in *Simon's Necronomicon* is more akin to what we might expect from the *"Lovecraftian"* angle—which artificially connects all kind of "fear" and "gloom" to the presentation of knowledge within the book. We cannot with any certainty validate authorship of the "Testimony" sections—whether they are actually antiquated writings or simply fabricated appendages to the other more historical gleanings offered in the main sections of *Simon's Necronomicon*. But—for the sake of our analysis of the edition, we will give it at least a brief look. To begin—the anonymous author introduces his account with its purpose: a personal work set down for posterity, describing experiences and knowledge earned from the years he "possessed the *Three Seals of Mashu*"— those glyphs often used to represent the *Simon Necronomicon* as a whole. He refers to his life as a period of "one-thousand-and-one moons"—meaning *1,001* "lunar months" or 77 years, further stating that "surely this is enough for the span of one man's life."

According to its author, the *Necronomicon* is the "Book of the Dead" and also the "Book of Black Earth"—a geographical reference to the "Magan" lands, or Arabian Desert, separating *Mesopotamia* from *Egypt*. Many of the early Mardukite and Amorite tribes even gathered in these regions "to the West of Mesopotamia" before the establishment of a "Mardukite Babylon" proper. It is further suggested that the knowledge contained within the book was learned while "traveling on the spheres" of the IGIGI—meaning "*Watchers*" or "Guardians" (sometimes "overseers")—a secondary class of *Anunnaki* beings, later interpreted in Semitic and Persian traditions as the "*Nephilim*," (also "*watchers*") and even "angels" or "messengers"—but "divine emissaries" in either case.

The "divine beings" and "forces" referred to in *Simon's Necronomicon* were once part of the original planerary religious system—observed throughout *Mesopotamia* as the "first" or "archetype of systemology," later duplicated and further fragmented in history with progression of diverse cultural beliefs separated by time and geography. It is curious then that the author of the *Simon Necronomicon* refers to these beings fearfully and goes so far as to demonize their existence, even referring to the "military legions" of the *Anunnaki*—the IGIGI—as dreaded beings, comparing them to primordial abominations and monstrous creatures.

Before describing his interpretation of the ancient tradition, the author explains the night that he first discovered that the esoteric path of practices alluded to throughout the text of *Simon's Necronomicon* were still actively used in the lands he wandered. He accidentally fell upon a ritualistic ceremony taking place in wilderness clearing. His awareness of these mysteries opened new vistas in consciousness. But the magical tradition described comes in two flavors—not surprising, for we have already been prepared for a the fragmentation of polar dualism in this flavor of writing. Firstly—there is a primordial and chaotic type of "magick" used by worshipers of the "evil" and malignant "*Ancient Ones*," those seeking a return to our time-space to devour humans and reform the universe into a vacuous Abyss. This is exactly the kind of "magick" we should expect to find in a *Necronomicon* tradition, if it specifically followed the *Lovecraftian* approach. But —as some might be surprised to discover, this is *not* the tradition relayed in this "dreaded tome"—and quite the contrary. What is actually relayed in *Simon's Necronomicon* is a second type—a tradition based on the *Elder Gods*, Lovecraft's "lesser of the two evils." This makes *Simon's Necronomicon*—and its quasi-Mardukite tradition—actually the *antithesis* to worshipers of the "*Ancient Ones*," and as is said, a talisman or amulet in itself against such 'evil'.

Sigils of the Gateway to the Stars

The *Testimony of the Mad Arab* describes three significant symbols that later reoccur throughout the workings of *Simon's Necronomicon*. According to the author, they were found carved—and glowing in green light—on the face of a "gray stone," a monolith that apparently also served as his "portal" or "gateway" to the *Outside*—meaning presumably, the *Abyss*. The three symbols appear together—superimposed on one another—combined for a cover graphic developed by "Khem Set Rising." This elaborate quasi-pentagram glyph that is so often the iconic identifier for *Simon's Necronomicon* does not actually appear as such within the text or any of its rites. Without proper realizing this, some have gone forth to know it as a *"Sigil of the Gateway"*—but it is not.

Mesopotamian "seal" magic is quite different than what we see in later Hermetic traditions and more elaborate ceremonial systems of Renaissance period "grimoires." In fact, most "signs" found in Sumerian and Babylonian magic are simple—depicting stars, planets, the heavens, deities and writing in cuneiform script. The three signs or "sigils" given in *Simon's Necronomicon* are a *five-pointed star*, a *partial star* and an *apex* or *peak*-like glyph. They are described by the author, but otherwise have little mainstream "New Age" correlation—with the exception, of course, of the all too familiar "pentagram" as the sign of *our* race—that is, the Race of MARDUK... The original description from the *"Testimony"* in *Simon's Necronomicon* is as follows—

> "Of the three carved symbols, the first is the Sign of our Race from beyond the Stars and is called ARRA in the tongue of the scribe who taught it to me. It is the Sigil of the Elder Gods, and when they see it, they who gave it to us, they will not forget us. The second is the Elder Sign, and is the key whereby the powers of the Elder Gods may be summoned. It is called AGGA. The third sign is the Sigil of the Watcher, called BANDAR. The Watcher is a Race sent by the Elder Ones... these sigils, to be effective, must be graven on stone and set in the ground. Or, set upon the altar of offerings. Or, carried to the Rock of Invocations. Or, engraved on the metal of one's god and goddess and hung about the neck, but hidden from the view of the profane."

As used for thousands of years to represent the *Ancient Mystery School*—the *five-pointed star* or "ARRA" is, indeed, a sign of the "race" born from the stars—or beyond the stars. Secret knowledge is contained within these mysteries schools revealing that many types of life on this planet were seeded—or engineered in some way—by the ancient *Anunnaki* race. The *partial star* or "Elder Sign" of *Simon's Necronomicon*, where it is called the "AGGA," is reminiscent to what some modern "Mardukites" use as a "sigil" of MARDUK, from our literature—specifically the *Tablet-X* cycle from *"Necronomicon: The Anunnaki Bible."* And from that same series, we see striking resemblance between the sign for SHAMMASH (*Samas*) in modern "Mardukite" literature and the *peak* sigil, called the BANDAR or "Sign of the Watchers" in *Simon's Necronomicon*. Whether these pictorial symbols are wholly fabricated or inspired, *&tc.*—there does appear to be some universal "astral-akashic" level of consistency between these two independently developed esoteric revival systems.

The other significant sigil introduced in the *Testimony of the Mad Arab* is what the author calls the "Amulet of UR", which he states is engraved in metal and is always carried in his hand. There is nothing extraordinarily special about the glyph on the tablet. It's a series of lines within a square fashioned in a seemingly cross-like pattern but otherwise insignificant in relation to the greater legacy relayed in the "Mardukite" cycle.

The *Testimony* closes with a few details of what the author calls the "Amulet of UR" (but of which is little more than a series of lines in a hash-mark pattern), there is some arbitrary mention of a few deities related to the *Lovecraftian* paradigm—but then it returns to a specifically "Mardukite" *Babylonian* flavor thereafter until the end of the book—when after having forced us to examine his words while wearing glasses streaked with his own fears and suppression, the author returns again just to be sure we are left so terrified that any self-honest value that might have gleaned by a naïve seeker is shattered. The occult is "occult" for a reason...

— 7 —
THE SEVEN STAR-GATES OF BABYLON

*"The passing of the Gates gives the priest both the power
and wisdom to use it, and an ability to control the affairs
of life more perfectly than before..."*
~ The Zonei & Their Attributes, *Simon Necronomicon*

The "Younger Generation" of *Anunnaki* are entities central to a theological infra-structure of the "Mardukite" *Babylonian* "star-gate" system—a methodology explored deeply in modern "Mardukite" literature. These same historical figures are the central focus of *Simon's Necronomicon*—in spite of all the *Lovecraftian* semantics used to represent the work as the "*Necronomicon.*" As such the archetype and title has later become attached to this anomalous modern revival of a *Babylonian Anunnaki Tradition*—and as such the semantics was adopted for the original presentation of the modern "Mardukite" primary source book: "*Necronomicon: The Anunnaki Bible.*"

In *Simon's Necronomicon*, the rudimentary essence of what the modern "Mardukite" movement reveals as the *Babili Texts* (or *Tablets*) is described briefly as the "Seven Zonei" in the section titled: "*Of the Zonei and Their Attributes.*" This concept of "*Zonei*"or "zones"—relating to the fixed orbits of the planets—is not an original *Mesopotamian* term, and seems to have been borrowed from the *Greek* language—allegedly the language most of the original manuscript for *Simon's Necronomicon* first appeared. In general, the lore is named specifically after *Babylon*—the name given to the capital city of MARDUK by his heir-son and scribe-priest NABU—meaning: "Gateway of the Gods" or *Bab-Ilu.* The term "*ilu*"—from the Sumerian "AN" or "DINGIR"—is represented by a cuneiform sign that means *god*, but it can also mean *star, planet* or even the entire abode of the *heavens.* These are distinguished more clearly by later *Akkadian* renderings in *Babylon*, but even then such semantics can prove challenging for interpretation by novices seeking a true understanding of these mysteries.

The "Mardukite" Babylonian Stargate tradition dedicated to the "Younger Generation"—or "*Elder Gods*"—of the *Anunnaki* pantheon are divided by *Seven*—Seven "steps" on the "*Ladder of Lights,*" or else Seven Stars (or "planets") of the ancient world. While it is true that evidence support a belief that ancient *Mesopotamians* knew that our solar system is actually comprised of additional celestial bodies beyond the usual ancient Seven, the tradition is restricted to local planets (plus the Sun and Moon) that were most easily visible without instrument or assistance—and thus had a greater influence on the world we see, meaning the material world.

Certainly there were other further and more remote denizens of the cosmos, but consequentially they likewise further and more removed from our world. For example: the genealogical Anunnaki All-Father—ANU—is represented by the planet *Uranus*, literally "House of ANU"—but neither ANU or *Uranus* are a part of the "local star-gate" system based on a sevenfold paradigm.

This Babylonian "Ladder of Lights" system—or "Gateway to the Gods"—is actually the basis for the later more familiar Semitic Kabbalah. The "Supernal Trinity"—ANU, ENLIL and ENKI—occupies positions for an older class of *Anunnaki* (a parenting generation) that composes the upper-most "triangle" of three "stations" or "*zonei.*" When these three are added "above" the Babylonian sevenfold system, we may correctly appropriate the tenfold paradigm of the traditional Semitic Kabbalah. If it were the case that *Simon's Necronomicon* emphasized the "Supernal Trinity" and perhaps also SHAMMASH, NANNA-SIN and INANNA-ISHTAR in *exclusion*, than we might be able to classify the work as "*Sumerian.*" However, the significance of the "Stargate" system of Babylon, incorporation of the *Enuma Elis* and specifically an emphasis on the "Mardukite" lineage—ENKI, MARDUK, NABU—than we can be certain that *Simon's Necronomicon* is representing a quasi-Mardukite tradition from the specific systems of *Babylon.*

Several factoids from the actual historical *Babylonian* "StarGate" tradition appear in *Simon's Necronomicon* as part of that the author calls the "*Ladder of Lights.*" This semantic is a unique interpretation of "*Babylon*"—or more specifically "*Bab-Ilu*"—which others have taken as "stairway to heaven" or "gateway to the stars." In this regard we can better understand the underlying purpose behind the most famous ziggurats in *Babylon*—and the nearby city of scribe-priests, called *Borsippa* (or *Birs Nimrud*). When we think back to our more fanciful "biblical" knowledge of *Babylon* and the *Tower of "Babel,"* it is evident that the Mesopotamian mysteries are much more clearly understood when examined *Self-Honestly* through "Mesopotamian eyes."

Unlike later more detailed attempts of reviving both a personal and temple tradition of the ancient "Mardukite" *Anunnaki* methodology as it was observed historically, *Simon's Necronomicon* is innovative for its time in attempting to relay a "portable" system of "holy magick" reminiscent from the earlier period. Rather than trying to illustrate a literal "temple" system, as observed in ancient *Babylon* at its inception, *Simon's Necronomicon* offers a diluted and bastardized "*shamanic*" version from a rural oral tradition existing on the outskirts of a contemporary realm—and since these traditions were an urban "national religion" until at least 300 B.C., such an interpretation could only result from later periods, when remnants of a former *Babylonian* religion may have secretly been practiced in the midst of an *Arabic, Islamic-Muslim* and *Judeo-Christian* era. Fundamentalists of these later formed religions continue to demonize the ancient *Mesopotamian* legacy as "Satanic." With such held in mind, we might more easily forgive some of the "darker" overtones in the presentation of *Simon's Necronomicon*, because by a contemporary mind-set following fundamentalist ideals, the book (and Mesopotamian tradition as a whole) would theoretically or semantically represent the oldest and strongest antithesis, or else, "Satanism." This is, of course, a false attribution—but it is how many among the "common population" would receive this esoteric information.

Traditional Chaldeo-Babylonian astronomical Mardukite "star-religion" consisted of the traditional twelve-fold zodiac in combination with observation of the sevenfold planetary system—giving rise to the original form of "astrology"—casting predictions based on the position of planets in relation to the zodiac of the "celestial horizon"—that we understand today as the "celestial sphere." Certain types of cuneiform "omen tablets" described patterns that defined how energetic interactions in our material world were relative to actions observed in the cosmos, specifically as applied to the original *Seven Planets*—Sun, Moon, Mercury, Mars, Venus, Jupiter and Saturn. If *Simon's Necronomicon* were presenting a pre-Babylonian *Sumerian* methodology, we might better expect to find the former *threefold* system restricted primarily to only *Sun, Moon* and *Venus*—just as we find in the other "*Sumerian-age*" civilizations.

Humans understood—and were programmed to understand—that they lived under the influence of forces and beings, such as were equally represented by "Celestial" or "Heavenly" bodies—*planets, stars, &tc.* The "names" were later confused by amateur mythologists and historians without esoteric understandings—leading authorities on the subjects that put forth ideas that naïve and ignorant primitive humans could not differentiate between "*gods*" as physical beings and *gods* as "planetary" bodies. Assuredly, they knew the difference—but in respect to *Anunnaki* systematization in Mesopotamia, the original archetypal pantheon of "divinity" were represented as attributions or manifestations of planetary forces affecting the local material world.

All ancient representations of "Celestial Mythology" are represented by planets of the local solar system. These ancient stellar religions are now interpreted as "alien" or surrounding "sky god" figures separate from humanity. We see evidence for this brand of "mythology" in all ancient cultures. What's more—it is the direct association to the planets that allows us to see how the original archetypal planetary designation of "*gods*" in ancient Mesopotamia actually evolved and mutated to appear as though all of these diverse cultures were dealing with an entirely unique pantheon—but it is actually the same pantheon. For example, we observe the planet/god "Jupiter" as such because of Roman language semantics, but the force of "Jupiter" is the same as that found in Babylon as "Marduk"—or even "Enlil" in the case of earlier *Sumerian* designations. "Jupiter" appears elsewhere in the ancient world as "Thor" and "Zeus" and so forth... each representing the same function in the pantheon, and each culture relaying a similar narrative of interaction with other "deities."

Rather than interpret the tradition as "national religion"—or even a "religion" at all —*Simon's Necronomicon* emphasizes only aspects of the *Bab-Ilu* system that can be quickly applied from a "magical" perspective. The stargate system—referred to as the "Ladder of Lights"—is treated as a magician's method of occult self-initiation rather than as a priestly system of "holy magic" in dedication to the *Anunnaki* pantheon. More important for the author than attributing a specific "holy" or "divine" method of "Mardukite" *Babylonian* mysticism, *Simon's Necronomicon* selectively adapts only key pieces of lore that might apply to a general system of "magickal correspondences"—such as modern "New Age" practitioners are now used to applying, whether numerological, or regarding color, the material essences in stones and metals, *&tc*. It becomes quickly evident, even when exploring this frugal lore, that all "planetary"-oriented *"grimoires"* through the ages are simply mutations of this same basic formula, regardless of the specific language of "names" used to represent these forces.

Rather than reinterpret the the words of *Simon's Necronomicon* to introduce the *Bab-Ilu* system—and we can assume the current reader has already been acquainted with those—it is more pertinent that we reiterate lore from modern "Mardukite" literature that more coherently presents the context of the *sevenfold* methodology. We provide this excerpt then from our own archives—the *Tablet W* series from the pocket companion titled *"The Book of Marduk by Nabu"* that also appears in the *"Necronomicon: The Anunnaki Bible"* source book anthology —

> "We have sealed seven representative stations in Babylon. It is true, each of the cities emphasized their local patrons, a god and a goddess, We have sought a unity for all the *Anunnaki*, under the watchful eye of my father *Marduk*, son of *Enki*. The *Seven* are embodiments of the 'seven gates' forged in *Babylon*, dedicated to the *gods* of the 'younger pantheon'. It is true, the same sevenfold division may be found to fragment the *world of form*— corresponding to color, sound or the planets observed by the ancient ancestors from Earth, seen as *"Guardians*." The *Seven* as a planetary system, is connected to the *Seven* of the 'gates' and planet-ruling days of the week, which the supplicant [or priest] may perform an intention-based ceremonial or meditative opportunity to appeal to each of the 'sets' of *Anunnaki* 'divine couplings' of god and goddess."

Although not the same "chronological order" used by an initiate to traverse "stargates" within the system, the following application of the sevenfold pantheon in Babylon may be helpful in cataloging information in a familiar manner— specifically the *Anunnaki* as related to the planetary alignment of days of the week. The proper sequence—or "precession of the gates"—may be ordered according to the *Bab-Ilu* texts (as described in *"Necronomicon: The Anunnaki Bible"*) used to establish symbolism of the ziggurat-temples, but individual attributes of the actual planets (and Anunnaki figures) remains unchanged regardless of what order they are placed in, essentially breaking down as follows—

Sunday – Sun – Shammash/Samas (& Aya)
Monday – Moon – Nanna-Sin (& Ningal)
Tuesday – Mars – Nergal (& Ereshkigal)
Wednesday – Mercury – Nabu (& Tesmet)
Thursday – Jupiter – Marduk (& Sarpanit)
Friday – Venus – Inanna/Ishtar (& Dumuzi)
Saturday – Saturn – Ninib/Ninurta (& Ba'u)

For practical application of *Simon's Necronomicon*, the "*Seven StarGates*" of *Babylon* represent seven "etheric" thresholds directly correspondent to those "gates"—but, they are interpreted from "New Age" perspective, describing a predefined system of *astral initiation*. This methodology alluded to in *Simon's Necronomicon* is not altogether different from other known practices from the "Enochian Tradition" connected to the "*Aethyrs*" or etheric "dimensional gates"— experienced in that system as cumulative high magical initiations via the "*astral*" plane. As briefly explained in the pages of *Arcanum: The Great Magical Arcanum* by Joshua Free—

> "The seven *Seals* of *Simon's Necronomicon* are inscribed on specific essences—usually metal. The *Gates* are traced out on the ground—with flour or chalk. You could also use 'posterboard' and flashing colors (most commonly black and white)—similar manner to meditation practices with *tattwas* in ceremonial magic —to allow for easier visualization of the *Gates* in the mind."

The following is a brief catalog of correspondences for each "step" on the "*Ladder of Lights.*" Most of these classifications are *traditional*, drawing from more accessibly "stargate" lore from the *Bab-Ilu* system—as they appear in *Simon's Necronomicon*. A similar summary is also provided in Joshua Free's *Arcanum*, whereas a modern "Mardukite" *Babylonian Anunnaki* relay of the same mysteries —but in a strictly historical context—may be gleaned from the Mardukite anthology—"*Necronomicon: The Anunnaki Bible.*"

THE FIRST GATE
Anunnaki Gatekeeper: Nanna (Sin)
Planetary Gate: The Moon
Symbol: Wand of Lapis Lazuli
Material Essence—Alchemy: Silver
Ladder of Lights—Color: Silver
Anunnaki Numeric Designation: 30
Seal Manufacture: The thirteenth day of the Moon (full moon) and
                  never to be removed from the silken cloth when
                  the Sun's rays are present.

THE SECOND GATE
Anunnaki Gatekeeper: Nabu (Nebo)
Planetary Gate: Mercury
Symbol: 100-Horned Crown or Stylus Pen
Material Essence—Alchemy: Quicksilver
Ladder of Lights—Color: Blue
Anunnaki Numeric Designation: 12
Seal Manufacture: On parchment or palm lead when Mercury is
present in the sky.

THE THIRD GATE
Anunnaki Gatekeeper: Inanna (Ishtar)
Planetary Gate: Venus
Symbol: Copper Dagger
Material Essence—Alchemy: Copper
Ladder of Lights—Color: White
Anunnaki Numeric Designation: 15
Seal Manufacture: Engraved on copper when Venus is visible in
the sky.

THE FOURTH GATE
Anunnaki Gatekeeper: Shammash
Planetary Gate: The Sun
Symbol: Flaming Disc
Material Essence—Alchemy: Gold
Ladder of Lights—Color: Gold
Anunnaki Numeric Designation: 20
Seal Manufacture: Engraved on gold at noon on a high hill or
mountaintop.

THE FIFTH GATE
Anunnaki Gatekeeper: Nergal
Planetary Gate: Mars
Symbol: Lammasu (half man, half lion)
Material Essence—Alchemy: Iron & Blood
Ladder of Lights—Color: Dark Red
Anunnaki Numeric Designation: 8
Seal Manufacture: On iron or parchment in blood when Mars is
visible or close by.

THE SIXTH GATE

Anunnaki Gatekeeper: Marduk
Planetary Gate: Jupiter
Symbol: The "Winged Disc" or Bow-and-Arrows
Material Essence—Alchemy: Tin or Brass
Ladder of Lights—Color: Purple
Anunnaki Numeric Designation: 10
Seal Manufacture: Engraved on a plate of tin or brass when Jupiter
       is visible or close by.

THE SEVENTH GATE

Anunnaki Gatekeeper: Ninib (Ninurta)
Planetary Gate: Saturn
Symbol: Stag Horns
Material Essence—Alchemy: Lead
Ladder of Lights—Color: Black
Anunnaki Numeric Designation: 4
Seal Manufacture: Engraved in lead while "invoking" Saturn.

— 8 —
GATEWALKING THE STARGATES

After a very brief introduction to the "Seven"—names and natures of specific *Anunnaki* identities incorporated for *Simon's Necronomicon* from the ancient *Babylonian* system—the author shifts the reader's attention to the astral, or specifically "ceremonial" or "ritual" elements borrowed for what is called: *"The Book of Entrance & The Walking."* Ancient "Mardukite" *Babylonians* worked with a similar tradition in their "national religion"—but with supportive tangible environments for this paradigm, such as the large elaborate *"ziggurat"*-temples rising out from each major metropolitan locale in *Mesopotamia*. In contrast—*Simon's Necronomicon* employs the Mesopotamian or Anunnaki pantheon as a portable "folk tradition" or brand of underground pagan witchcraft in a manner that is more highly resonant with other contributions to contemporary "New Age" culture.

In the original pre-*Babylonian* era, individual city-states were each governed by priest-magicians and priest-kings of the local region. Each city-state observed patronage to a specific member of the *Anunnaki* pantheon. In the case of the "Mardukite" pantheon—emphasizing supremacy of MARDUK and the spiritual accessibility of the "younger pantheon"—the *Mesopotamian* capital becomes Babylon, the patron city of MARDUK. In *Simon's Necronomicon*, some of the more pious attitude of the tradition begins to appear in its *"Book of Entrance."* Otherwise, the material is presented as a "sorcerer's" or "magician's" handbook, spellbook or otherwise *"grimoire"* of primordial magick. With only room for the tip of the iceberg in *Simon's Necronomicon*, only simple spells, rituals and what most consider *"magick"* in the "New Age" make its way onto the pages.

The author of *Simon's Necronomicon* suggests one month (*moon*-th) periods of "purification" in several instances. For example, before the *Ritual of Walking*—as the "stargate initiation" ritual process is sometimes referred to—is begun, a period of one "moon of purification" is observed and then the period "of at least one moon" should pass before the practitioner should enter the next *"Gate"* in the sequence. Given seven gates in all, this initiation process would require at least 8 months total to complete. Sexual abstinence must be observed during periods of "purification"—one complete moon before each *Ritual of Walking*. For the initial month prior to "entering" the first gate, as well as each month of purification thereafter, the magician, priest (or priestess) must be abstinent.

Although the role of *priest* and *priestess* appear in ancient tradition—*Simon's Necronomicon* is written with a particular slant toward masculine practice and readership. Therefore, it explains that the practitioner should not "spill his seed," meaning not to reach reach ecstatic orgasm or ejaculation. It goes on to explain that he may, *however,* still worship at the *"Temples of Ishtar"* so long as he remembers not to "spill his seed." This implies that sexual activity is permitted so long as he does not reach an orgasmic state. "*Kundalini*" students will recognize as a method of preserving certain "serpent" energies in the body for eventual ritual or ceremonial release. Assuming the practitioner can "handle" the sexual restrictions associated with this initiation process to the higher esoteric mysteries, other dietary requirements are also observed in *Simon's Necronomicon.* The initiate is instructed not to eat meat for seven days preceding any "gate-work" and further that no food at all shall be taken for three days immediately before. Such "fasting" periods are common in transcendental practices.

Once maintaining purification of the internal body, the external (physical) body must is attended preceding execution of any spiritual ritual. The practitioner bathes and once cleansed, must wear clean garments—preferably white or black robes. Often times, *astral* "stargate" or "light" workings at the temple were conducted in white robes. Other lunar observations and personal (solitary) workings were conducted in black. Some modern practitioners apply a different philosophy to their tradition—conducting all "daytime" magic in white and all "nighttime" magic in black. In either case—clean clothing is set aside for the occasion, reserved specifically for religio-spiritual or "magickal" purposes. There are many reasons for adopting "magical garments"—ranging from the enchantment they achieve from repeated use when accumulating personal energy, to changing the internal mind-set of a practitioner during a ceremony, &tc.—all of which contribute to achieving a "higher" state of awareness and communion between world of the seen and unseen to experience mystic unity with the cosmos.

For the three day period preceding the *Ritual of Walking*, in addition to a water-only diet, the initiate is instructed in *Simon's Necronomicon* to spend all of their time in meditation and prayer to "thy god and goddess" and to also make special devotion to the *Supernal Trinity*—ANU, ENLIL and ENKI—the ancestral beings fathering the "younger pantheon" of Anunnaki. It is here that *Simon's Necronomicon* introduces the *Supernal Trinity* by their numeric designations—derived from the original *Sumerian* pantheon predating all other systems.

Although the "younger generation" are each prescribed one of the *Seven Gates*—among other official Anunnaki numeric designations—the original pre-Babylonian proto-Sumerian observation of the Mesopotamian pantheon describes the Anunnaki as they emerge from prehistoric times, at the inception of modern human civilization. These are quite different approaches to the pantheon, given here as they appear on *Tablet-B* from "*Necronomicon: The Anunnaki Bible*"—

The Original Sumerian Anunnaki Pantheon
ANU (60) + ANTU (55)
ENLIL (50) + NINLIL (45)
ENKI (40) + NINKI/DAMKINA (35)
NANNAR/SIN (30) + NINGAL (25)
SHAMMASH/SAMAS/UTU (20)
INANNA/ISHTAR (15)
ISKUR/ADAD (10)
NINHURSAG (5)

Babylonian Anunnaki Gate/Zonei Pantheon
7th Gate—NINIB/NINURTA (4) [50]
6th Gate—MARDUK (10) [50]
5th Gate—NERGAL (8)
4th Gate—SHAMMASH/SAMAS (20)
3rd Gate—INANNA/ISHTAR (15)
2nd Gate—NABU/NEBO (12)
1st Gate—NANNA/SUEN (30)

The *Night of the Walking*—or rather, the night on which the *Ritual of the Walking* is conducted—is referred to as the 13th night of the moon, meaning the thirteen night after the new moon—which is, of course the *full moon*, being midway through a 28-day lunar calendar. The only sources of ceremonial illumination should be the light of the moon, the beacons or lamps at the four quarters, other necessary candles and the consecrated fire. As nighttime or astronomically aligned, there is a significant presence of lunar orientation in both the "magick" found in *Simon's Necronomicon* and *Mesopotamian Magic*—but, it is also convenient for contemporary practitioners that may not be aware of further or deeper planetary alignments to the "gatework." For the entry-level introduction to the greater mysteries that *Simon's Necronomicon* actually provides, the basic *full moon* "gate" meditations appear to be sufficient for grounding elementary functionality.

Within the system provided in *Simon's Necronomicon*, after conjuring a consecrating the sacred ceremonial fires, the preliminary rite for operating effective ritual magick is called the *"Conjuration of the Watcher."* This element is reminiscent of other "Hermetic" practices—and those in Egypt. The "Watcher" in old lore is one of the IGIGI—in this instance, it is akin to a "guardian angel" or "spirit guide." Not surprisingly, origins for knowledge of these beings—now widespread—rests in the *Ancient Near East*. After the *Watcher* is conjured, the magician takes the seal of the "Star" ("ARRA") in their right hand, whispering the name of the *Anunnaki* figure —the "Guardian" or "Gatekeeper" of the current *"step"*—that it represents softly and while meditating on the knowledge, nature and attributes of that entity/energy.

The *"Sigil of the Gate"* or "Star" or "Stargate"—specific to the "Gate" or "step" the initiate is approaching—should be traced/drawn on the ground in the center of the circle—aligned so that the practitioner is facing north. Ritual alignment for the "ceremonial magick" presented in *Simon's Necronomicon* is usually north—because the astronomy governing its tradition is rooted in the northern constellations, particularly the position of the "Great Bear." The sacred fire is kindled in the northeast—the direction where the ancient *"sky gods"* of *Mesopotamia* were once seen "coming and going."

The next step given in the *"Book of Entrance & The Walking"* concerns the *"Incantation of the Gates,"*—which is again to say the "stargates" or "stars," but in this tradition, more appropriately represents a specific *Anunnaki* figure or "godhead." From the proto-Sumerian era through the time of "Mardukite" Babylonians, "incantations" or "invocations" representing an archetypal systemology were understood as *"prayers"* from religious perspective. Later, in the post-Babylonian era, this spiritual framework was fragmented into various factions of "sorcery" and "magic" observed outside its original context—and by folk who never experienced the original mysteries *Self-Honestly* as they were intended. Instead, these later folk simply applied new filters to their worldview by integrating lore with preexisting knowledge or social programming.

During the ceremony, the priest-magician is instructed to begin in the north and move clockwise—to the east, south, west, *&tc.*—around the circle speaking the *"Incantation of the Gate"* with each revolution, doing so the number of times sacred to the numeric designation given for the *Anunnaki* figure representing that *"Gate"* or "level" of initiation. For example, in the case of the first gate—the *"Moon Gate"*—the respective figure is the *Anunnaki* god NANNA-SIN, whose number is 30. This means that the practitioner would circumnavigate the circle thirty times—likewise speaking the *"Invocation to Nanna-Sin"* thirty times.

Once the process of *"Invocation"* is completed, the magician-priest returns to the center of the work area standing before the image of the *"Gate,"* where they are instructed to cast themselves to the ground and enter a meditative-trance state in order to perform the remainder of the ceremony on the *"astral plane,"* applying *"astral vision"* to sometimes encounter an apparition or "subtle energy manifestation" of the *Anunnaki* figure. Aside from pantheon personification, the intention is that the operator makes "contact" with the raw energetic current or ray from the sevenfold cosmic pattern of existence—each successively in their turn as each of the *"Gates"* is approached. The lunar realm is the first encountered, which is in itself very enchanting. The third is the domain of *Ishtar* and *Venus*, which many never are able to move *beyond...*

The author of *Simon's Necronomicon* concludes the outline of the *"Ritual of the Walking"* by offering a combination of "helpful" advice followed by more horrific warnings. Firstly—that the priest-magician cannot contact or call upon a specific *Anunnaki* entity or be "master" of that "sphere" or "energetic current" until that particular *gate* has been accessed and passed. Further—one can not work with a subsequent *Gate* until preceding ones are passed. In *Simon's Necronomicon*, this key-and-lock situation further managed where a practitioner may be given certain *"passwords"* or "signs" at each level of initiation—keys that allow *fast-pass* movement through mastered *Gates* when working with "higher" ones. As such, subconscious mastery through the gates is cumulative.

Once an initiate passes the *"Marduk Gate,"* other "magical" faculties—usually reserved for "Mardukite" *Babylonian* priests, priestesses and magicians—are also accessible, presented as the *"Grimoire of Fifty Names"* in *Simon's Necronomicon*. Perhaps even more mystically significant for some is that mastery of this *"Sixth Gate"* also grants the operator access to the *"Gate to the Outside"*—allegedly to the *Abyss*—but the initiate is also warned not to be distracted by this *Gate*, that they should continue on the pathway, ascending up the *"Ladder of Lights"* to leave these other matters alone for another day—or night. The *"Gate to the Outside"* alluded to in *Simon's Necronomicon*—which lies just beyond the *"Sixth Gate"*—is not the threshold whereby the *"Ancient Ones"* reside as alluded to in specifically *Lovecraftian* paradigms. In *Mesopotamian* lore, the *"Gaze of Ganzir"* is a portal to the *Underworld*—the *"Shadowlands"*—or else the domain of ERESHKIGAL, the sister of INANNA-ISHTAR, who rules in the *"Land of the Dead."* The author explains that many do not make it to the point of Ascension from passing the *"Seventh Gate,"* for they become forever distracted by the lure of the *Underworld* — never to return.

— 9 —
INCANTATIONS & CONJURATIONS

The natures and identities of the *Anunnaki* Stargate "Guardians" encountered in the *Ritual of the Walking* along with graphic "sigils" and "glyphs" described in *Simon's Necronomicon* are all combined to perform ritual observations of the ancient "Mardukite" *Babylonian* pantheon. This is solidified—both ceremonially and in consciousness—with the use of "incantations" or "invocations" that not only affirm sacred knowledge in the psyche of the practitioner, but are also intended to mystically extend a call out to the cosmos that will attract the desired "energy" or "entity" expression/manifestation. As explained in Mardukite *Liber R*—

> "Suitable independently researched substitutions to *Simonian* invocations were found by *Mardukite Chamberlains* (for our own personal experimentation) primarily from the *Kuyunjik Tablet Collections* preserved in the British Museum—more fully explored in Mardukite *Liber 50*. This series of tablets—called *Nis-Kati*—is more famously known among scholarly circles as the *Prayers of the Lifting of the Hand*, or alternately the "Raising of the Hand."

Mesopotamian lore appropriate for ceremonial applications coinciding with *Simon's Necronomicon* are existent throughout modern "Mardukite" literature pertaining to the *Anunnaki* cycle of knowledge. In addition to what is described above, other versions used for experimentation by "*Mardukite Chamberlains*" in 2009 also appear in "*Necronomicon: The Anunnaki Bible.*" However—in 2010—a newer more refined version of these "incantations" were standardized for modern usage with the release of Joshua Free's "*Book of Marduk by Nabu,*" known originally as Mardukite *Liber W* and eventually incorporated into the most recent edition of "*Necronomicon: The Anunnaki Bible*" as the *Tablet W* series. Rather than relay versions already widely available in *Simon's Necronomicon*, the current "Mardukite" editors of *Liber 555* have decided to offer comparative examples from our own literary contributions.

Ancient incantations have diverse applications. Mardukite *Liber W* (or "*Tablet-W*") materials were originally intended to recreate a practical modern daily devotional "prayerbook" styled after the tablet collections maintained by ancient "Mardukite" *Babylonian* kings, scribes, priests and priestesses. These smaller portable collections were composed of the most critical tablets for personal use—rather than requiring repeat access to larger "tablet houses" or libraries.

Simon's Necronomicon represents this same motif to some extent. Such collections were in possession of high-ranking or highly esteemed citizens of ancient *Mesopotamian* society, and it is because of these carefully guarded personal collections that we are able to recover tablet artifacts today. For example, the most famous tablet cycles revived for contemporary use are often derived from tablets stored at the royal library of *Ashurbanipal* discovered near the ruins of *Nineveh*. The following examples are provided as found in "W" series—

THE FIRST GATE—SPHERE OF THE MOON
PRAYER TO NANNA & NINGAL

NANNA. SIN. NINGAL. NANNAR. MOON. LUNA.
Mighty One among the gods, son of ENLIL and NINLIL,
Brightest in the heavens at night,
Keeping watch, protecting weary travelers
And the people in their homes as they sleep.
Your brightness extends through the heavens,
Like a torch—Like a fire-god.
Radiance of NANNA, who reflects the dreams of men,
To you was born the SUN.
Be favorable to me, I, __ son of __ , whose
god is __ and whose goddess is __ .
May NANNA and NINGAL deal graciously with me,
Cleanse me of iniquity that I may be free to call upon thee.
Open the Gates of your mysteries to me,
Stand on either side of me, a servant of the Highest.
May the ANUNNAKI come forth an be established.

THE SECOND GATE—SPHERE OF MERCURY
PRAYER TO NABU & TESHMET

NABU. TUTU. TESHMET—TASMITU. NEBOS. MERCURIOS.
Scribe among the Gods,
Keeper of the Wisdom of the Gods,
Firstborn of MARDUK and SARPANIT.
NABU, Bearer of the Tablet of Destinies of the gods,
May my dreams [destiny] be filled with prosperity.
May my petitions fall on the ears of NABU & TASMIT.
Be favorable to me, I, __ son of __ , whose
god is __ and whose goddess is __ .
Cleanse me of false knowledge, that I might
be fit to call upon thee.
Open the Gates of your understanding to me.
Bless my mouth with true words to speak the prayers.
May the prayers rise from the lips of the people.
I am a servant of the Highest,
May the ANUNNAKI come forth and be established.

THE THIRD GATE—SPHERE OF VENUS
PRAYER TO ISHTAR & DUMUZI

INANNA. ISHTAR. DUMUZI. ISTARI VENUS.
Queen, Daughter of the Moon,
who is blessed by the heavens,
Beloved of ANU, Command in Heaven,
Brightness of the Evening, Huntress of the Night,
Do come to stand favorably at my side,
grant me the fruits of men and gods.
ISHTAR and DUMUZI,
Be favorable to me, I, ___ son of ___ , whose
god is ___ and whose goddess is ___ ,
Cleanse me of impurity, make me a vessel
fit to receive your rewards.
Open the Gates of your understanding to me.
May my actions be true.
May the words I speak bring me to success.
May your light shinning in the heavens
be a guide to all men you bless favorably.
Bless me, a servant of the Highest.
May the ANUNNAKI come forth and be established.

THE FOURTH GATE—SPHERE OF THE SUN
PRAYER TO SHAMMASH & AYA

SHAMMASH. UTU. AYA. SAMAS. SUN. SOL.
Fiery and Powerful One, Judge among the gods, Son of the Moon-god,
Overseer of the destinies of the lands.
SHAMMASH and AYA,
Be the favorable judges of my destiny.
May the path be prosperous.
Unequaled light of day, SHAMMASH and AYA
Shine favorably on me, ___ , son of ___ ,
whose god is ___ and whose goddess is ___ .
Incinerate my iniquities.
Make me perfect to behold your light.
Lord, who appeals to the ears of ENLIL,
Open the Gates of your understanding to me.
Permanent is your mighty word on earth.
May your unquestioned command dictate
prosperity in my life.
I am a servant of the Highest,
May the ANUNNAKI return and be established.

THE FIFTH GATE—SPHERE OF MARS
PRAYER TO NERGAL & ERESHKIGAL

NERGAL. IRRIGAL. ERESHKIGAL. ERRA. MARS.
Exalted Lord of the Underworld.
ERESHKIGAL, Queen of the Underworld.
Great is your place among the gods of heaven.
NERGAL and ERESHKIGAL,
Truly have mercy on me, ___ , son of ___ ,
whose god is ___ , whose goddess is ___ .
May your hearts be tempered.
Temper also the anger within my heart,
That I may stand before you,
Make me perfect to call upon you,
Open the Gates of your understanding to me.
Grant me a favorable death
and keep evil from me in life.
I, a servant of the Highest, kneel before thee,
take pity on me.
May the Great Doors stand open.
May the ANUNNAKI return and be established.

THE SIXTH GATE—SPHERE OF JUPITER
PRAYER TO MARDUK & SARPANIT

MARDUK. MERODACH. SARPANIT. MULU-KHI. JUPITER.
Lord of the Lands, Master of Magicians, God of Babylon.
SARPANIT, Lady of Babylon.
Mighty and powerful on earth and heaven are your words.
Lord and Lady of Babylon,
Accept my offerings of alabaster, lapis lazuli and gold.
Judge my life favorably,
I ___ , son of ____ , whose god is ____ , and
whose goddess is ____ .
Make me fit to behold your divinity
and teach me to receive thy blessings.
Open the Gates of your power to me.
Let me live. Let me be perfect.
Command greatness in my life as your
expansion permeates the gods of heaven.
I am a servant of the Highest.
May the ANUNNAKI come forth and be established.

THE SEVENTH GATE—SPHERE OF SATURN
PRAYER TO NINURTA & BA'U

NINURTA. NINIB. BA'U. ADAR. SATURN.
Mighty firstborn son of ENLIL.
Great is your place among the gods,
royal prince of ENLIL and NINMAH.
Lord and Lady of the heavenly abode,
NINIB and BA'U,
Speak favorably of me in your courts,
I, ___ , son of ___ , whose god is ____ , and
whose goddess is ____ .
Absolve me of my sins. Remove my iniquities.
Make me fit to call upon and receive your blessings.
Open the Gates of you Understanding to me,
a servant of the Highest,
BA'U, Mighty Lady, merciful mother.
NINIB, hidden warrior of ENLIL.
Command greatness in my life.
Look upon me favorably.
May your name be in the mouth of the people.
May the ANUNNAKI return and be established.

As an alternative to the *"Conjuration of the Fire God"* used for preliminary fire-consecrating rites in *Simon's Necronomicon*, the "Mardukite Chamberlains" have used the following incantation since 2009. This "Egypto-Babylonian" version (provided below) first appeared in Mardukite *Liber G*—now contained within the original Mardukite source book anthology, *"Necronomicon: The Anunnaki Bible."*

CONJURATION OF THE FIRE GOD

Servant of the Great God, Companion of the Flame,
Bringer of Light—GIRRA, GIBIL, NUSKU.
You, whose mouth is the Unquenchable Flame;
You, who is seated in the Fire;
You, whose set is in the Lake of Fire in Heaven;
in whose hands is left the greatness and power of God.
Reveal yourself here this day [night] and speak with me.
Give me answer without falsehood
to all the questions I direct to thee.
I will glorify your name in ABYDOS.
I will glorify your name in BABYLON.
I will glorify your name before the Sun.

I will glorify your name before the Moon.
Rise up, Son of the Flaming Disk of ANU,
the great god ANU, Heavenly Father;
descend in to me with your Holy Servant, I invoke thee!
GIBIL GASHRU UMUNA YANDURU
TUSHTE YESH SHIR ILLANI U MA YALKI
—GISHBAR IA ZI IA.
ZI DINGIR GIRRA KANPA.
It is not I, but MARDUK, Slayer of Serpents,
who calls thee here now.
It is not I, but ENKI, Father of the Magicians,
who summons thee.
Come forth—come in—and give answer!
Come forth—let my eyes be opened;
Spirit of the God of Fire, God of the Heavenly Blaze,
thou art conjured!

— 10 —
THE MAQLU TABLETS

*"Climb the Ladder of Lights and appeal to the gods
for their protection and for the destruction of the enemy
and all evil-doers, wicked witches and warlocks of the world..."*
~ Tablet-M Series, *Necronomicon: The Anunnaki Bible*

The "Maqlu"—or "*Maklu*," as it is spelled in *Simon's Necronomicon*—is actually a very real series of mystical, magical and political *cuneiform* tablets. The *Maqlu* series—comprised of nine tablets and hundreds of incantations—was historically used in *Babylon* for an elaborate ceremony. Surprisingly, only a small portion of the collection of incantations and "exorcisms" appear in *Simon's Necronomicon*, which includes translations of perhaps only one-tenth of those available. The incantations that do appear are provided as "exorcisms" and "spells" to be used against the "Ancient Ones" and their worshipers. In "Mardukite" tradition of *Babylon*, the *Maqlu* tablets are used during a societal festival or public ceremonial gathering to banish "evil" from the community and burn all the "evildoers" of the world in effigy.

As a significant part of the modern *Mardukite "Core Research,"* the "*Maqlu*" tablets provide so much substance to a revival practical tradition that they are the subject of an entire discourse, Mardukite *Liber M*—first released in 2011 by the *Mardukite Chamberlains* as "*Maqlu Magic*" (and simultaneously as *Necronomicon Spellbook II*). An untranslated *Maqlu* "*transliteration*" appeared in original versions of "*Necronomicon: The Anunnaki Bible*" as the *Tablet-M* series—more recent updated versions include the full translation from *Liber M,* completed three years later by the research team. In *Simon's Necronomicon*, a few incantation/exorcism examples are provided as the *"Rites of Burnt Offering"* or *"The Book of Burnings"*—which is appropriate since many scholars translate the word MAQLU to mean *"Burnings,"* or even *"Burning Man."*

Maqlu operations most likely began as simple, internalized, meditative and solitary spiritual devices of early priests, priestesses and magicians in *Mesopotamia*. Over time, it developed more dramatically as a public *"Fire Festival"* in *Sumer* and *Babylonia*—involving the entire community population gathering together in a combined harmonic intentional effort to "drive out" or dispel all "evil" and "evildoers" of the realm. We see effective social results—or at least changes in mass consciousness—when large groups, or better, the majority of the population is focused on a single emotional event. These create what some call "quantum effects"—and they appear to have very real implications for mass change. "Ideas" can even spread more fluidly among humans than even germs—and it is clear that "ancient man" had at least partial understanding of this.

The *"Burning Man"* represented in *Maqlu* ceremonies is a representation of all "evil-doers" of the world—those who "plague" humanity with their wickedness, thereby upsetting the "order" of the *gods*, and upsetting the *gods* themselves, who are quick to aid those who serve and abide by *Cosmic Law*. The tablets describe construction of symbolic representations from various materials like asphalt ("*bitomen*") and clay—similar to what we think of "*voodoo dolls*" today—only one of which reflects the type of "wicker man" tower effigy one might call to mind. These could be used to represent specific individuals—but they more often represented nameless or unknown identities. This social convention might be employed regularly or in times when a balance upset was expressed or manifest in the community as "illness," "pestilence," "disease" and "famine." If allowed to reach epidemic proportions, these facets could prove devastating to a still developing human civilization—as such they were considered "evil," the most wicked of "demons." Learned ones described anything that might lead to them—usually uncleanliness and misappropriated living—as "taboo," and these became the first *sins*.

Representative ritual images have a long standing tradition with "idol magic" or "sympathetic magic," but not as a result of "worship" in the sense that some mythographers have repeatedly put forth. These representations were intended to actually embody a specific "energetic current" that is universally entangled to the "focal object" and its form. A ritual representation of a "demon" force—like the "plague-god" *Namtaru*—was not intended for worshiping the deity with homage, or even to glorify "daemonology" of Babylonian domga. In the instance of the *Maqlu* rites, such statuary typically was only constructed just to be "ceremonially" annihilated or buried as a "ward" against what the object represented. When constructing and using such objects, the magicians, priests and priestess demonstrate an understanding of the "entangled" nature of the cosmos and mystical oneness or unity found at the fundamental interconnection of all things.

Contrary to traditional "magic" where one might *fall upon* power with the utterance of some words or secret formula, the priestly-magic of *Mesopotamia* was considered "divine" or "transcendental"—given to the *Races* as a birthright; "sacred" and therefore not to be taken for granted. Education and use of these "arts of civilization" were a closely guarded secret among most ancient factions—traditions that all seem connected by sharing unique "Sky God" traditions. And there are many of these ancient traditions, esoteric sects and secret cults—Brotherhoods of the Snake (or Serpent) [or *Ancient Ones*] and Orders of the Dragon, *&tc. &tc.* But of course, after the fragmentation of the systems, each of these factions carried only a limited understanding of the All.

When the language used to describe "evildoers" in the *Maqlu* is examined, the Seeker uncovers origins for a "class division of magic" that remains in public consciousness to this day. Where "magic" itself is a neutral application of *Cosmic Law* and the "Arts of Civilization," other disapproving "labels" are given to practitioners dedicated to the "Dark Arts"—those using "unsanctioned magic" for malignant and self-serving purposes.

Using the *Maqlu*, the "dark forces" are not handled, channeled or dealt with by the priest or priestess directly—thus there is no fear of corruption or risk of "turning to the Dark Side." The ritual allows a *Self-Honest Mardukite* to petition the *Anunnaki powers* to execute required actions on their behalf. The priest need only properly petition the cosmos for assistance—the "holy magic" thus belonging to the domain of intermediary *"divine intervention"*—by appealing to the "Highest."

The terms "wicked witch" and "evil sorcerer" appear frequently in the *Maqlu* to define practitioners of "Dark Arts"—evil-doers or "Worshipers of the Ancient Ones" (depending on your semantic preference). This polarity of magical power does not appear strongly in the original *proto-Sumerian* worldview, but by the time the *Maqlu* rises in importance—some 4,000 years ago—a division of power into "polarity" and "fragmentation" already existed in programmed social conscious-ness. The terms are not meant to relay anything specifically derogatory by the more politically correct modern *New Age* standards—but they do reflect an ancient *Mesopotamian* attitude regarding the practice of magic. For our current simplified purposes in *Liber 555*—operation of "magic" by priest-scribes, priestesses and court-magicians of the Realm was acceptable, however, borrowed practices for per-sonal unsanctioned use was "occult" among uninitiated commoners, just as it is today—with the exception, of course, of public "exoteric" displays of religious ma-gic, meditation and prayer. "Magic" and esoteric arts were studied and practiced in secret, away from public scrutiny and also without revealing too much of what might be "wrongfully" abused. And this is one of the very things that the *Maqlu* ex-ists for to overcome.

Although many occult students are aware of the type of "sympathetic magic" practiced in the *Maqlu*, the historic and esoteric background has been provided because it is altogether absent from *Simon's Necronomicon*. Perhaps one of the reasons the magic of the *Maqlu* is included is because it is a part of the "priestly magic" reserved for those who have first ascended the *"Ladder of Lights"* to appeal to the *Anunnaki gods* directly. In order to do this—in order to effectively petition requests—the practitioner must have established a relationship with these forces, which is the underlying purpose behind the "religio-magical" system of *Babylon* and *Mesopotamia* as a whole.

— 11 —
RITUAL CASTINGS, CALLINGS & GATEWAYS

Following brief lessons concerning the *Maqlu*—or *"Maklu Text"*—*Simon's Necronomicon* returns the reader's attention to additional formulas and instructions necessary for the original *"Ritual of the Walking."* This ritual forms the primary "Great Work" of the *"grimoire"* and although it begins at the beginning of the text corpus, the required lore and instructions are scattered throughout. This forces many would-be *"necromancers"* to abandon the book in confusion—though the code is not at all difficult to crack once you have gathered all of the pieces. In addition to refusing to reach out to supplemental materials to form a more concrete background to the paradigm, many "fast-track" seeking students—including those who flooded the modern *Mardukite Offices* with correspondence regarding *Simon's Necronomicon*—often prove that they have not even sufficiently studied the given materials.

Additional magical lore developed for modern systems of ceremonial magick appear in the *"Book of Callings"*—including further mystical warnings regarding use of the tradition. For example—the author reminds practitioners to be "ever mindful of the gate," specifically the *"Gate to the Outside"* that is always in threat of breach, but also the "stargates" opened from *this side* when the operator goes about their "Gatework." The *Lovecraftian* "fear" is ever present in *Simon's Necronomicon* and its warnings all support what we should expect from the *Necronomicon*—alluding that the magician using it will potentially unleash dangerous and malevolent powers into this world.

Pushing past the *Lovecraftian* overtones, it is actually within the *"Book of Calling"* that the author of *Simon's Necronomicon* actually acknowledges the historic "Mardukite" nature and origins of the tradition explored within the text. For example, the magical formulas, names and numbers all come from "Mardukite" designations of the *Anunnaki* family—which is to say ENKI and MARDUK primarily, and that ENKI is the wizard or hermit archetype of "Father of Magicians" and MARDUK is the "Maser of Magicians" or else the "Master Magician" archetype. Understanding this—the Seeker/student/initiate of the mysteries is officially charged to become a "Sacred Guardian" of these mysteries—a true "Mardukite" *priest* or *priestess* of the Anunnaki. The colorful language relayed in the *"Book of Calling"* describes this charge—

> "This obligation is as a *Gatekeeper* of the *Inside*, an agent of *Marduk*, servant of *Enki*, for the *Gods* are forgetful, and very far away; and it was to the *Priests of Flame* that the *Covenant* was given to seal the *Gates* between this world and the *Other*, and to keep watch thereby, through this *Night of Time*, and the *Circle of Magick* is the barrier, the *Temple*, and the *Gate Between the Worlds*."

The author reminds the reader that the five-pointed star is a symbol of their race—the *Race of Marduk*—and that the incomplete pentagram glyph is a sign of the *Elder Gods*—which is to say "younger generation" of *Anunnaki* observed in the "Mardukite" Babylonian pantheon. This pantheon is simplified for the magical "stargate" system of the *Necronomicon*.

Remaining magical instruction concerns preparation of the "sacred space"—*mandala* or "magic circle"—used as an area of working, followed by the care of ritual tools and the *"Invocations of the Four Watchtowers,"* which is to say the "gates" of the elemental worlds of the material plane—corresponding to the four cardinal directions—sometimes called the *quarters*, and by some interpretations, the four primary elements: *earth, air, fire* and *water*. The ritual use of "elemental" or "watchtower" *tablets* to represent points of the four directions is a facet found in many revival systems of "ceremonial magick" and "practical Hermetics"—including the "Enochian Tradition" that has been so often categorized alongside the *"Necronomicon"* archetype. As relayed in *Tablet-X* of *"Necronomicon: The Anunnaki Bible"*—

> "When ceremonial magicians evoke powers of the Universe from within a *mandala* or microcosmic *ritual circle*, they first call upon the powers identified with the *Four Quarters*, *Quadrangles* or *Watchtowers*—and when a magician observes physical ceremonies using *tablets* of the *"Four Quarters,"* the *tablets* are charged as direct representations of these *Gates*."

Where access to a permanently sanctioned *temple* is not available, a magician-priest or practitioner of this tradition is required to temporarily consecrate "sacred space" with portable or minimal instruments. Visual glyphs or "tablets" of the *Four Watchtowers* must be constructed or else traced out upon the ground. In lieu of access to a high-rising *ziggurat*, the "place of calling" should be upon a hill or in the mountaintops—where the *"gods"* might more readily encounter you, for they were once seen coming and going from high places. This is expected in *Simon's Necronomicon* if it is to reflect widely held beliefs from ancient *Mesopotamian* "Sky God" traditions.

When the parts scattered throughout *Simon's Necronomicon* are culminated together, the actual ritual is simple. After properly preparing yourself and the working space, a double circle is drawn on the ground and the *tablets* of the "Watchtowers" are set out at each cardinal direction along with a candle, lamp or beacon at each of the cardinal directions. The sacrificial bowl—called *"Aga Mass Ssaratu"*—and sword are set in the northeast. The *sigil* of the appropriate "stargate" is drawn out on the ground—or on a portable board or spread cloth placed on the ground. Two candles are permitted on the altar—or altar space—in honor of "your God and Goddess" along with their images or statues (presumably of MARDUK and SARPANIT or INANNA-ISHTAR).

Proper sigils and amulets are carried or worn and the *sigil-seal* of the corresponding *Anunnaki* gatekeeper is held in your hand. Ceremonial space is cleared—or "consecrated." The "Supernal Trinity"—ANU, ENLIL and ENKI—is honored in prayer. Elemental wards—the *Gates of the Quarters*—are called/opened. The fire is consecrated and the "Watcher" is conjured—or if that is not observed in your practice, you may call your guardian *sedu* spirit or protective *llamasu*. Once the "*Conjuration of the Watcher*" (or its equivalent) is completed, then the remainder of the "*Ritual of the Walking*" may ensue. The following show glyphs for the *Gates of the Quarters* as they appear in "*Necronomicon: The Anunnaki Bible*"—

THE NORTH GATE

Gate of the Formless Hunter and of the Abyss [Nothingness],
Thee I invoke the Bornless One
Who brings the "Cleansing Darkness."
Spirits of the Northern Gate, open your mysteries unto me.
Gate of the Scales of Judgment and the Outside,
From which comes the Hosts and Fiends,
Manifest the Shield of ARRA, Truth and Spirit in my hands,
And protect me from the fires of the Destroyer.
Gatekeeper of the Northern Gate, remember:
Open wide the Gate.
Spirit of the Gate of the North, Thou art conjured!

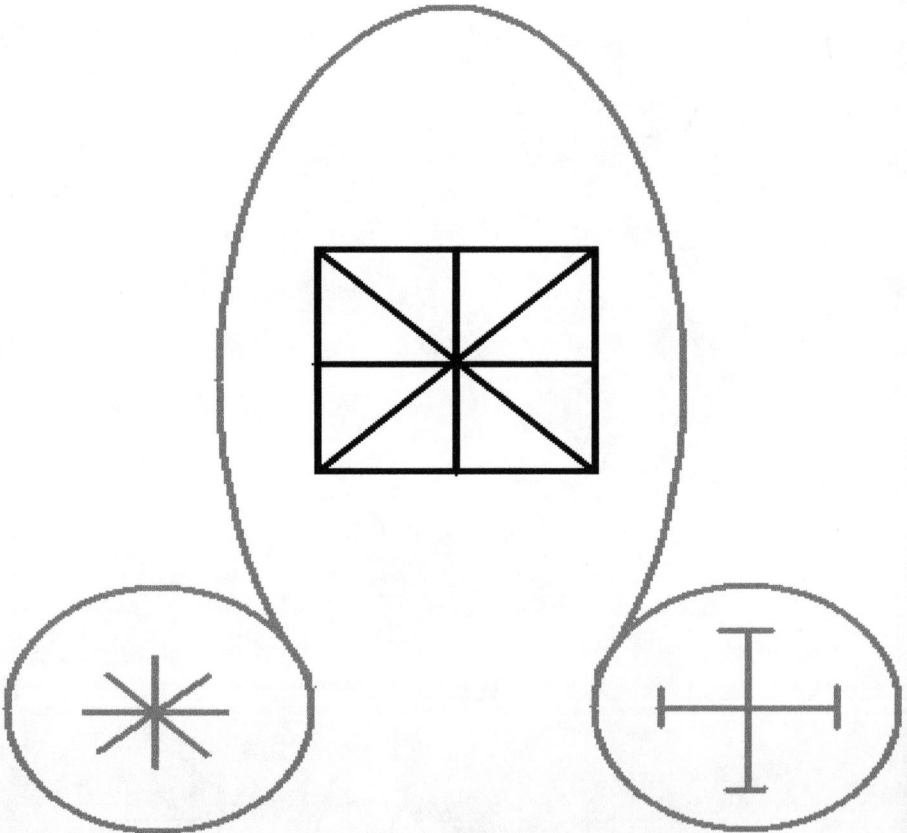

THE EAST GATE

Gate of the Rising Star and of the Rising Sun,
Spirits of the Eastern Gate, Open your mysteries unto me.
Gate of the Forgotten Memory, stir your light in my head,
Kindle the warm fires of remembrance in my being,
Protect me from the "light-so-blinding"
And bring clarity to the washed out childhood memory.
Gatekeeper of the Eastern Gate, remember:
Open wide the Gate.
Spirit of the Gate of the East, Thou are conjured!

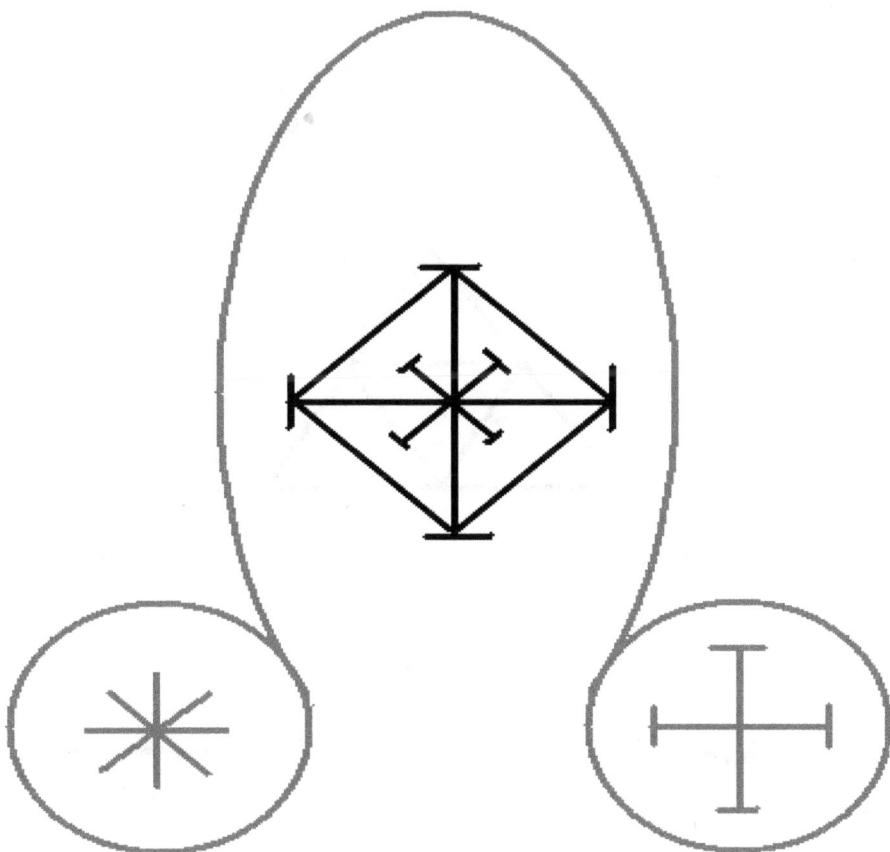

THE SOUTH GATE

Gate of the Fiery Angel and of the StarFire,
Spirits of the Southern Gate, Open your mysteries unto me.
Gate of the Fires of BEL,
Manifest the Sword of Fire, Truth and Spirit in my hands,
And protect me from the Destroyer and the destroyed.
In the names of the most holy armies of
MARDUK and ENKI,
Stand firmly by my side during the Decision [Judgment].
Gatekeeper of the Southern Gate, remember:
Open wide the Gate.
Spirit of the Gate of the South, Thou are conjured!

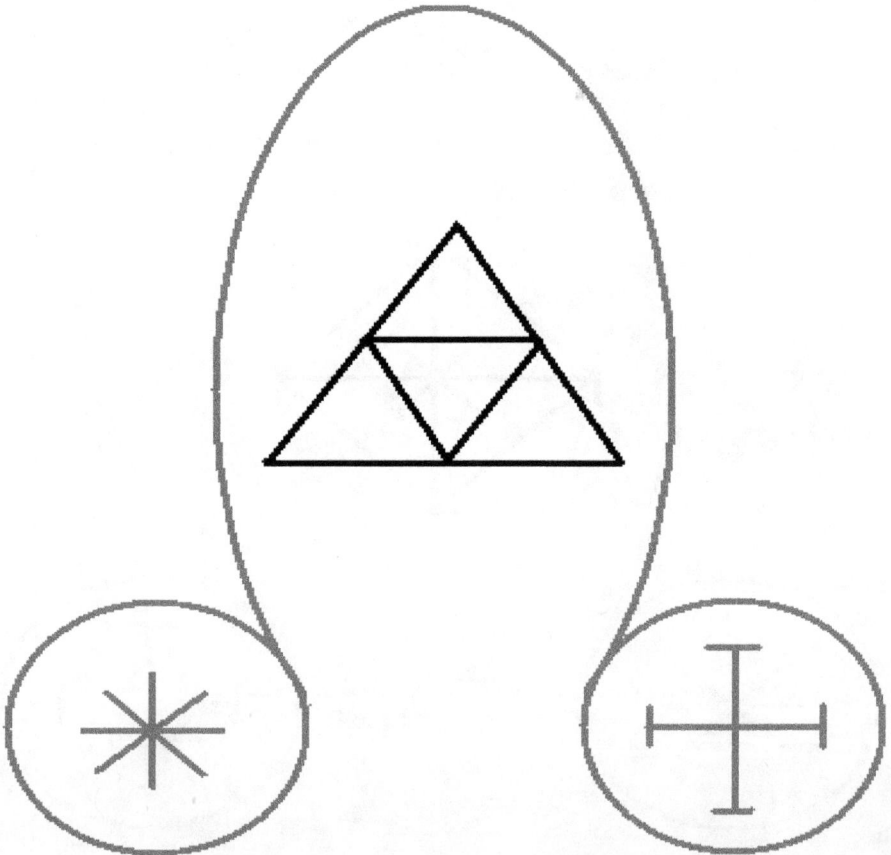

THE WEST GATE

Gate of the Twilight Shadows and of the Setting Sun,
Spirits of the Western Gate, Open your mysteries unto me.
Gate of the Symphony of Light and Darkness,
Kindle the "cold dark blue flame" in my head
And protect me from the sorrow of remembrance.
Gatekeeper of the Western Gate, remember:
Open wide the Gate.
Spirit of the Gate of the West, Thou are conjured!

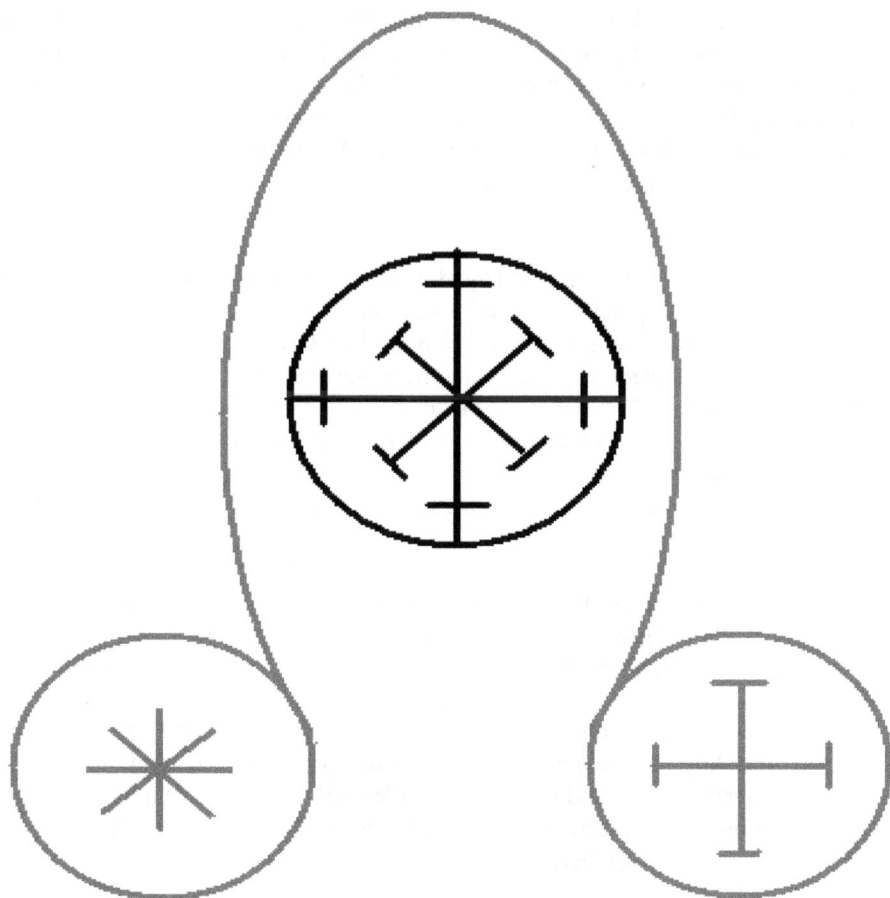

Simon's Necronomicon uses an obscure rudimentary method of ritual area preparation consistent with its portable minimalist version of an otherwise "Mardukite" temple-system dedicated to the *Anunnaki*. This should not be misunderstood as akin to a rural form of indigenous shamanism, as some have suggested. Methods used in *Simon's Necronomicon* resonate more highly resonant with practices found in the modern "magickal revival" drawing from medieval period "grimoires." Beyond the *Judeo-Christian* "Kabbalah" and more accessible *European* "pagan folk" traditions, the nearly-prehistoric antiquated traditions from the birthplace of human systemology can be found only by sifting the desert sands of ancient *Mesopotamia*.

The "circle of flour" is actually one of the most important elements of personal ritual magic in ancient *Mesopotamia*—and its mention is found on many Babylo-Akkadian tablets describing charms and rites. Some esoteric significance for this practice is lost in *Simon's Necronomicon*, but is available from other sources. Firstly—in the original *Sumerian* semantics (tradition), the flour is to be consecrated to the agricultural and literary goddess NISABA—or, if we are going to dedicate and bless in alignment with the *Babylonian* ("Mardukite") tradition, it would be consecrated to the authority of NABU, heir-son of MARDUK and patron of the scribe-priests in *Babylon*—called by his Semitic name *Nebo* in *Simon's Necronomicon*. After the floor area for the ritual space has been swept clear, fresh flour is consecrated then poured to form the circles, which are then swept away at the end of the rite.

Another omission—an activating key for all ancient "Mardukite" *Anunnaki* spiritual work (and/or "practical magic")—that validates the *Babylonian* "stargate" paradigm and *Anunnaki* religion of *Babylon*, is the "*Incantation of Eridu*," named for the original *Sumerian* city of ENKI near the Persian Gulf. In the original magical system observed in *Babylon*, it is the combination of the "*Enuma Elis*" and "*Incantation of Eridu*" that solidifies the *Babylonian Anunnaki* "systemology"—the system that is the main focus of modern "Mardukite" discourses pertaining to *Mesopotamia*. Describing the "*Ritual of Eridu*" from *Tablet-Y* of "*Necronomicon: The Anunnaki Bible*"—

> "The introductory rite is comparable to what many modern *ceremonial magick* practitioners have encountered as the LBRP— or *Lesser Banishing Ritual of the Pentagram*—used as a minor, though, necessary 'opening' ceremony, the beginning of a ceremonial operation: to banish existing energies from the space; to formally acknowledge the systemology observed and its employed entities; and to consecrate the work space, the mind and the actions of the ceremony to them. The simplest version of the incantation is given here, though there are many..."

THE INCANTATION OF ERIDU

I am the Priest of Marduk,
Son of Our Father, Enki.
I am the Priest of Eridu
and the Magician of Babyon.
Samas is before me.
Nanna-Sin is behind me.
Nergal is at my right hand.
Ninurta is at my left hand.
Above me flames the Pentagram,
the Sign of Our Race;
Above and Below me
shines the Ladder of Lights.
Anu, above me, King of Heaven.
Enki, below me, King of the Deep.
The Power of Marduk is within me.
It is not I, but Marduk,
who speaks the Incantations!

If the operator so desires, the "clearing" incantation from *Simon's Necronomicon* for preparing the "ritual circle" can be appended here—

Enu Shub Am Gig Absu-Kish E.Gigga Gar
Shag Fa Sisie Amarada Ya Dingir Ud Kalama Siniku.
Dingir Nina Guyu Netzranku Ga Ya Shu Shagmuku Tu.

— 12 —
MARDUKITE MAGICK & THE NECRONOMICON

"*Mardukite* priests of *Babylon* were, by nature, *Priests of Enki*,
following a derivative of the ancient systems born in *Eridu*.
The first mystical and religious use of writing was used for
recording incantation tablets, appeals to the gods for assistance."
~ Joshua Free, *Mardukite Liber-51*

Babylonian tradition—religious, scientific and civic—is a direct evolution of an earlier Sumerian legacy, chronicling the progression of a particular *Anunnaki* family in Mesopotamia. Unlike what we find elsewhere, the *Anunnaki* are archetypal and their tradition is *not* simply an assimilation or re-creation of something else applied to a "similar" pantheon. This becomes evident in later classical mythoi, which simply regurgitate to us the ancient themes with new names.

At the inception of the *Anunnaki* traditions in prehistory, common people were instructed to petition their needs to the temple-priests and priestesses—a class of citizen responsible for knowing and making appropriate "Divine Offerings" and other ritualized ceremonies using incantations necessary to enact the "magical power" of the *deity* petitioned. There is also a distinction between the "exoteric" surface-religion observed by the general population and the higher "esoteric" or "learned" mysteries maintained by the priesthoods. A unique cultural dynamic formed with introduction of *cuneiform* writing systems into human consciousness —a shift when things ceased to be seen from experience based learning and instead were classified by language. The dynamics of the "Mardukite" state or empire was not necessarily ruled by MARDUK proper, but all of *Babylonia* did exist under his care by way of the *priests* and *priestesses* who served in his name, including the kings.

When we look at *Simon's Necronomicon* in the light of historical *Mesopotamian* traditions, we do not necessarily see a collection reminiscent of the "priestly magic" constituting its origins. Thus, it is better to see the *book* as a rogue attempt of maintaining "magick" of the system from "*outside*" the system—by one who admits that he "stumbled" upon these mysteries, accidentally coming upon occult rituals conducted by priests in the woods, who were themselves likely practicing a mutation of the original tradition, thousands of years after the *Mesopotamian* inception of these mysteries.

After disclosing some final ceremonial keys necessary for conducting effective rituals in the "*Book of Calling*," the author of *Simon's Necronomicon* offers—in spite of beliefs about the title—the only primary lore that could actually be termed "*necromancy*" literallly. It is difficult to comment from a purely "Mardukite" perspective on the ritual titled "*Operation of Calling on the Spirits of the Dead and Those Who Dwell in the Land of Cutha.*" An emphasis on the after life—under any kind of "Mardukite" influence—is best reflected in examples provided from the ancient *Egyptian* culture. Where pathworking the "Gates" of *Babylon* allows us to shed our seven skins that tie us to *this* world—it is the *Egyptian* culture that emphasizes the preparations for a "Body of Light" or astral shell to occupy future lifetimes in higher states of existence. That being said—many "death cults" existed in both *Mesopotamia* and *Egypt*.

The famous cuneiform tablet of cycle describing "Ishtar's Descent to the Underworld" is directly dealt with later in *Simon's Necronomicon*—but it is from *this* epic that the author of the *Necronomicon* has pieced together an obscure means of "raising spirits of the dead" for communication, which is to literally say: "*Necromancy.*" Just as the *Enuma Elis* tablet-cycle is used to demonstrate the power and authority of MARDUK and therefore grant credibility to the "magick" utilized in his name— as was rightly given to him by ENKI—so too did INANNA-ISHTAR earn her own authority over the death domain by overcoming her power over the "*Underworld*" in her own literary cycle. Since she did not gain absolute supremacy in the "Mardukite" tradition of *Babylon* as the *Queen of the Realm of Lights*, she rivaled her sister—ERESHKIGAL—for that position in the *Shadows*. This point is loosely resolved in *Simon's Necronomicon* along with other colorful language—

> "...the *Necromantic Art*, by which it is desirous to speak with the *Phantom* of someone dead, and perhaps dwelling in ABSU, and thereby a servant of ERESHKIGAL, in which case the *Invocation* which follows is used, which is the *Invocation* used by the *Queen of Life*—INANNA—at the time of her *Descent* into the *Kingdom of Woe*. It is no less than the *Opening* of the *Gate of Ganzir*, that leads to the *Seven Steps* to the *Frightful Pits*."

The "*seven steps*" alluded above are not the same as the seven steps on the "*Ladder of Light*." The "*Ganzir Gate*" between the "steps" toward the end of the *Babylonian* system—between the sixth and seventh *gates*—is also represented in the Hebrew Kabbalah as an addition "*sephiroth*" ("sphere" or "station" on the "Tree of Life") called "*Daath*." Esoteric experience shows that these are not actually gates *to* the "Abyss"—but they do 'cross' the *Abyss*—to reach, what some call, the *Other Side*—the "Other Side of the Tree" or Qlippoth Kabbalah. The *Abyss* is only briefly experienced as the "space between" the two—the negative existence. In brief—for purposes of a purely *Anunnaki* paradigm, or as related to *Simon's Necronomicon* directly, the "*Gate of Ganzir*" and any "necromantic" connotation concerning it, is all related to the "*Underworld*," the realm of *Death* and *Shadows*.

To popularize the book as a mainstream "grimoire," a brief bout with "necromantics" and inclusion of a few "love spells," *Simon's Necronomicon* turns the reader-seeker's attention to its own primary "grimoire" portion—titled "*The Book of Fifty Names*." This "*Book of Fifty Names*" is based on the "Fifty Names" of MARDUK—given as *Tablet-F* in "*Necronomicon: The Anunnaki Bible*"—the seventh and final tablet from the *Enuma Elis* series. *Simon's Necronomicon* includes its own version of the *Enuma Elis* as the "Magan Text" later on—given in its historical entirety as *Tablet-N* in "*Necronomicon: The Anunnaki Bible*." These cuneiform sources form the fundamental backbone or foundation to the "Mardukite" magical or ceremonial observations in *Babylon*—and similarly in *Simon's Necronomicon*, even if it does only provide a partial relay of the complete tradition.

For an initiate who has already passed the "*Sixth Gate*" or "*Marduk Gate*" and received the the great secrets of the tradition and the powers of MARDUK, *Simon's Necronomicon* offers the "*Book of Fifty Names*" as a "grimoire" of fifty spirits or entities that may be called upon for their attributes using the ceremonial magick already described within in the *book*. The "names" are not treated as properties of MARDUK proper in *Simon's Necronomicon* and are instead prescribed to the IGIGI or "Watcher" entities—titles or names usurped by MARDUK in the Seventh Tablet of the *Enuma Elis*. The theological background is not given in *Simon's Necronomicon*, which chooses to simply revive the names as a "grimoire" complete with sigil-glyphs—similar to what you find in the *Goetia* and *Key of Solomon*—and ascribes similar "sorcery-specific" attributes and powers, such as we also find in similar "Medieval grimoires," including: uncovering hidden treasure, acquisition of wealth and obscure knowledge, overcoming enemies, affecting weather and climate, &*tc*.

Simon's Necronomicon moves from the "*Book of Fifty Names*" to the remainder of the *Enuma Elis* as the "*Magan Text*." To be fair—the "*Magan Text*" given is not a single tablet series, nor does it contain a single "complete" tablet series, but is instead a composite melting pot of at least four different literary cycles of material all blended together—the first of which is the *Enuma Elis*, summarized best by Joshua Free in Mardukite "*Liber E*"—

> The *Enuma Elis* is named after its opening lines meaning: 'When in the heights...' This series of *seven tablets* is better known among scholars and seekers alike as the *Babylonian Epic of Creation* or *Seven Tablets of Creation*—which are, in fact, too often misrepresented as *Sumerian*.

Archaeologists first became aware of this particular series in 1849, when cuneiform tablets were recovered from an expedition into the Royal Library of Ashurbanipal from the ruins of Nineveh. They were first widely published in 1876 and received significant attention by historians, mythographers and biblical scholars—not only because of their antiquity, but because of how significant the has work turned out to be in deciphering the methodology of not only Babylonian civilization and Mesopotamian religion, but also its later influences on contemporary and classical "*Epics of Creation*," such as those given in the Judeo-Christian "*Book of Genesis*."

Although multiple versions of even older "Sumerian-originating" tablets exist, the esoteric power behind the *Enuma Elis* and its standardization in *Babylonia* centers around the supremacy of MARDUK. Any text suggesting the transfer of power to MARDUK and *Babylon* and the "World Order" of MARDUK and *Babylon* is purely "Mardukite" or else *Babylonian*.

The second significant literary tablet cycle revealed in the "*Magan Text*" of *Simon's Necronomicon* is the proverbial "*Descent of Inanna-Ishtar*"—a cycle that grounds a cult following for INANNA-ISHTAR as much as the *Enuma Elis* does for MARDUK. Although not "coupled" with MARDUK officially, her position in the *Anunnaki* pantheon still ensured her a role of equal power, described in Mardukite "*Liber 50*"—

> "Known to the Egyptians as *Goddess of Ten Thousand Names*, the Anunnaki position of *Queenship to Heaven* is maintained by one of the younger pantheon appearing in both early Sumerian and later Chaldeo-Babylonian systems. As daughter of NANNA and NINGAL—the Anunnaki representations of the *Moon*—and a twin to SHAMMASH—the *Sun*—a title of high esteem was bestowed upon the young Lady of the Stars, unequaled in beauty and cunning. In *Mesopotamia*, she is introduced in Sumerian literature as INANNA—meaning "Lady of Anu." In *Babylon*, the name ISHTAR distinguished her as the supreme heavenly goddess…"

"Necromantic" *Underworld* traditions serve functional psychological roles enacted in ceremonial or spiritual initiations of the *Self*. This type of "pathwork" is typified by a metaphoric or spiritual "*death*" of the "old" self, or artificial *self*, or rather "old programming" running by the *Self*. "Underworld" traditions have also served further "spiritual"—or more accurately, "religious"—needs concerning "life after death" and the continued evolution or "transmigration of the "soul" or "spirit"—the "unfolding" of the *Self* beyond the "physical" as we know it. The "*descent*" materials—and other supposed "*Books of the Dead*" from *Egyptian* or even *Buddhist* sources—are often examined out of context, for they are not only intended for burial with the dead, but instead are resources for the living!

A portion of the "*Magan Text*"—titled the "*Generations of the Ancient Ones*"—focuses on "darker" and more "demonic" elements from ancient *Mesopotamian* beliefs. We are reintroduced again to PAZUZU—a figure interpreted as a kind of "Sumerian devil" as mentioned in the introductory essays by the editor. The reader is then given knowledge of various pre-human abominations that spawned out of the primordial ooze—from the "Ancient Ones," from TIAMAT, or even "*Cthulhu*"—some of which is inspired by cosmogenetic lore of the *Enuma Elis*— and then, of course, all the beasties from the "darkened pits" of the *Underworld*. It is certainly a dismal flash portrayal of a primeval reality as it might exist, has existed, or could exist again.

The next section with the "Magan Text" is titled "*Of the Forgotten Generations of Man*"—rooted in lore given on other tablets both within and apart from *Simon's Necronomicon*—appearing historically in "*Necronomicon: The Anunnaki Bible*" pertaining to the creation and disposal of humans by the Anunnaki. The Babylonian *Enuma Elis* plays a significant role in both ancient "Mardukite" traditions and *Simon's Necronomicon*. Although some scholars believe the cosmological description applies to the formation of the local cosmos—specifically the planetary or "solar system" that Earth shares—the people probably understood it more "literally" as a description of primordial Anunnaki activities. Effectively understanding explicit esoteric details in *Simon's Necronomicon* depends on the *Enuma Elis* and a coherent picture of the greater *Babylonian* "Mardukite" system. The key lines as they appear within the "*Magan Text*" relaying what some have called the "Necronomicon Gnosis"—

> "And was not Man created from the blood of Kingu,
> Commander of the Hordes of the Ancient Ones?
> Does not Man possess in his spirit
> The seed of rebellion against the Elder Gods?
> And the Blood of Man is the Blood of Vengeance.
> And the Blood of Man is the Spirit of Vengeance.
> And the Power of Man is the Power of the Ancient Ones.
> And this is the covenant—
> For, the Elder Gods possess the Sign by which
> The powers of the Ancient Ones are turned back.
> But Man possesses the Sign, Number and Shape
> To summon the Blood of his Parents.
> And this is the covenant—
> Created by the Elder Gods
> From the Blood of the Ancient Ones,
> Man is the Key by which
> The Gate of *Iak Sakkak* may be flung wide
> By which the Ancient Ones
> Seek their Vengeance
> Upon the face of the Earth
> Against the Offspring of *Marduk*..."

Cuneiform tablet accounts reveal that the "Anunnaki" are responsible for the genetic upgrade of modern humans and the inception of systems leading to a thriving and evolving civilization for the growing population of Mesopotamia. Emphasis of a draconic "*war in heaven*"—described in the *Enuma Elis*—was installed and maintained in the civic/social "programming" of human consciousness to assist the status elevation of MARDUK during the post-Sumerian era. Although MARDUK is a strong commander and the heir-son of ENKI—a chief magician among the *Anunnaki*—his identity is later transferred onto the cosmological epic involving TIAMAT to establish his supremacy in the "new" *Babylonian Anunnaki Pantheon* by demonstrating "Divine Right" and approval from the previous *Sumerian Anun-*

naki Pantheon. Prompted by many aspects beyond the scope of our present discourse, the *Enuma Elis* represents the first religio-political document to introduce *propaganda* and *rhetoric* in an otherwise "literal" writing system.

The Babylonian version of the "Epic of Creation"—*Enuma Elis*—reveals MARDUK, not the other *Anunnaki* (as we find relayed in pre-Babylonian accounts), as the "originator" of the human race, called the "*Race of Marduk*," emerging as a direct result of the "*war in heaven.*" Without knowledge of the *Enuma Elis*, the comment in *Simon's Necronomicon* concerning the "blood of men being the blood of *Kingu*" would make no sense. Its only context comes from the *Enuma Elis*—where MARDUK uses the blood of *Kingu* to form humans after slaying TIAMAT—and from the "body" of TIAMAT we are told that he created the physical planet earth, then with her "head" he created the skies or heavens.

Finally—closing passages from *Simon's Necronomicon* "Magan Text" are based on lines taken from the famous "Chaldean Oracle Tablets" (sometimes called the "Zoroastrian Oracles")—which is given in its original entirety as the *Tablet-O* series in "*Necronomicon: The Anunnaki Bible.*"

INDEX

MARDUKITE
10TH ANNIVERSARY

Would you like to know more???

ENTER THE REALM OF THE

**MARDUKITE
CHAMBERLAINS**

**mardukite.com
necrogate.com**

MARDUKITE NEXGEN BOOKS BY JOSHUA FREE

Arcanum : The Great Magical Arcanum : 10th Anniversary —LIBER-A

The Sorcerer's Handbook (of Merlyn Stone) : 20th Anniversary

Necronomicon Anunnaki Bible : 10th Anniversary—LIBER-N,L,G,9+W-M+S

The Sumerian Legacy (Sumerian Religion)—LIBER-50+51/52

Necronomicon Revelations—LIBER-R

Gates of the Necronomicon—LIBER-50,51/52+R

Gates of the Necronomicon : 10th Anniversary—LIBER-50,51/52,R+555

Magan Magic (or Necronomicon Spellbook I)—LIBER-E

Maqlu Magic (or Necronomicon Spellbook II)—LIBER-M

Beyond the Ishtar Gate (or Necronomicon Spellbook III)—LIBER-C

Necronomicon Grimoire—LIBER-E,M,C

Enochian Magic & The Kabbalah—LIBER-K

Crossing to the Abyss—LIBER-555

History of the Necronomicon—LIBER-K,555+12A

Secrets of Sumerian Language & Cuneiform Dictionary—LIBER-I

Book of Marduk by Nabu—LIBER-W

The Book of Shayaha : Sajaha the Seer of Marduk—LIBER-S

V : The Vampyre's Bible—LIBER-V1

Cybernomicon—LIBER-V2

Vampyre Magick—LIBER-V1+V2

Book of Elven-Faerie—LIBER-D1

Draconomicon—LIBER-D2

Book of Druidry—LIBER-D3

The Druid Compleat—LIBER-D1,D2,D3

The Book of Pheryllt—LIBER-PH1/2/3

Awakening : Systemology-101—LIBER-S1/2/3/4

Reality Engineering—LIBER-S5

Pantheisticon—LIBER-S8

NABU—JOSHUA FREE ("Merlyn Stone")
Chief Scribe & Librarian of New Babylon

www.ingramcontent.com/pod-product-compliance
Lightning Source LLC
Chambersburg PA
CBHW051850090426
42811CB00034B/2282/J